Small Town Talk

BARNEY HOSKYNS

SMALL TOWN TALK

Bob Dylan
The Band
Van Morrison
Janis Joplin
Jimi Hendrix
& Friends
in the Wild Years of
Woodstock

FABER & FABER

First published in 2016
by Faber & Faber Ltd
Bloomsbury House
74–77 Great Russell Street
London WC1B 3DA

Typeset by Ian Bahrami
Printed in the UK by CPI Group (UK) Ltd, Croydon CR0 4YY

A CIP record for this book
is available from the British Library

ISBN 978–0–571–30975–7

FSC
www.fsc.org
MIX
Paper from
responsible sources
FSC® C101712

2 4 6 8 10 9 7 5 3 1

In memory of my father

CONTENTS

Part Three: Dangerous Fun

ILLUSTRATIONS

PLATES

PROLOGUE: INTO THE MYSTIC

Listen, oh don't it get you,
Get you in your throat . . .
  VAN MORRISON, "Old Old Woodstock"
  (1971)

If you listen, it all comes back. It comes full circle here on a rain-spotted night in the heart of the old Byrdcliffe art colony in New York's Catskill mountains, in a small theatre built of dark cedar a hundred years ago. A son of Old Old Woodstock takes the stage with a micro-ensemble of guitarist, cellist and fiddler and says: "We're so happy you've joined us in this historic place in the woods. This is a significant mystical zone that we inhabit."

1

Simone Felice knows we are sat in the foothills of Overlook
Mountain, a place sacred to Native Algonquin Indians centuries
before it became a destination and settlement for artists and craftsmen and bohemians of the early twentieth century. He is also a
child of Woodstock's musical history, the thirty-seven-year-old son
of a carpenter who came to the Catskills for the 1969 Woodstock
Music and Art Fair and never left.

In 2005 Felice and his brothers Ian and James formed a group in
the mode of Bob Dylan and The Band, drawing on the woodsy influence of the "basement tapes" recorded by Dylan and his Canadian
friends in a pink house due east of here in West Saugerties. Now
putting the finishing touches to his second solo album, Felice – like
Dylan in 1967 – has turned his back on modern technology and
urban overstimulation. He's a country boy whose primarily acoustic music grows out of the land and the trees in nearby Palenville,
where he and his brothers were raised. "You and I belong to the
woods!" he exhorts in a song for his baby daughter Pearl.

As he switches from strummed acoustic to a very unfancy drum
kit, the handsome man with the Terence Stamp eyes morphs for a
minute into The Band's late drummer Levon Helm, with the same
sparse beard and curling hair, the same shapes thrown on the drum
stool. "This is a song," he announces, "about falling madly in love
with a hooker on heroin." And thus, in an instant, do we get the
dark flipside to Woodstock's bucolic rock idyll. For as Felice also
knows, this small town, housing as it did so many maverick talents,
fostered a scene of damage and dysfunction that endures to this
day. It pulled in all manner of wannabes and hangers-on, alcoholic
philanderers, dealers in heroin and cocaine, and left at least one
generation of messed-up children with no direction home.

Just a few hundred yards away from the theatre is Hi Lo Ha, the
house that Bob Dylan bought in the summer of 1965, and where he
lived for a few apparently happy years as a self-reinvented pater-
familias in spectacles and seersucker jackets. Yet Dylan himself got

out while he could, removing his young family for a while to a more remote property on Ohayo Mountain Road before abandoning altogether the town that had given him succour and sanctuary.

Van Morrison was another who came for the clear mountain air and the stunning views from atop that same Ohayo Mountain. Morrison, however, recoiled at the cultural after-effects of the Woodstock Festival and went on his curmudgeonly way to northern California. Others stayed and came to sticky ends as they sank into the hedonistic mire of Woodstock's bars and clubs. The Band returned from a glitzy sojourn in Malibu and remained forever linked to Woodstock and its satellite hamlet Bearsville. A year after the group's most soulful singer, Richard Manuel, hanged himself in 1986, transplanted Chicago harp master Paul Butterfield died of peritonitis in Los Angeles. Other Woodstock denizens perished of similarly premature causes: Tim Hardin, Karen Dalton, Jackson C. Frank, Wells Kelly and more. The Band's Rick Danko suffered a fatal, drug-induced heart attack in 1999. Folk legend John Herald killed himself in 2005.

Then there were the survivors. After decades of scuffling and financial disaster, Levon Helm rallied for a last wind of Woodstock life with the beloved "Rambles" shows staged in his wooden barn off Plochmann Lane. And perhaps it is more than cosmic coincidence that, as I sit tonight in Byrdcliffe and think of Helm reborn as Simone Felice, I'm unable to expunge from my mind an email I've just received from Sally Grossman – widow of The Band's and Dylan's old manager Albert Grossman – accusing me of taking Helm's side in his long and fruitless war against her late husband and Band guitarist Robbie Robertson. I should be basking in the peace of Felice's "mystical zone", yet I sit here and feel the sting of Sally's attack. A few days later I receive a second email from her, demanding I leave town and vowing to sue if I quote from the email.

"There's a veil of secrecy round all this stuff," the folk singer Artie Traum told me when I first visited Woodstock in the summer of

1991. "And for no particular reason, because there's really nothing to hide. I don't think there are any skeletons that aren't already public. But one of the whole things that Dylan started was '*Don't talk to anybody.*'"

A few days after Felice's Byrdcliffe show I'm motoring slowly up a driveway that Dylan would once have known like the back of his hand. In the passenger seat is David Boyle, a cantankerous carpenter who, fifty years ago, was obliged to vacate a cottage on this very property to make way for Dylan. Having been fired by Sally Grossman some years ago, Boyle is urging me on towards the big Bearsville house that her late husband bought in 1964, dismissing my fears that she will see us and call the police. "*If you haven't telephoned you are trespassing,*" declared a sign that Boyle once put up for the Grossmans at the entrance. We haven't telephoned.

"Sally has her Queen of Sheba thing," Boyle mutters at my side. "Best just to creep along." Creep along is what I accordingly do, though I find it hard to see how it will make us any less visible to Mrs Grossman, whose lights are clearly on in the late-afternoon twilight. As I steel myself, gripping the wheel with clammy hands, Boyle points out various landmarks of interest, including the cottage he had to give up for Dylan. Finally I exhale a giant sigh of relief as we head back down the driveway and exit the property.

Small Town Talk is the story of what happened after Albert and Sally Grossman first came to Woodstock and then, on the advice of their friends Milton and Shirley Glaser, bought an estate that had belonged to illustrator John Striebel. It is simultaneously the story of what happened after Grossman's biggest client, Bob Dylan, came to Woodstock that same year to stay in a steel-house cabin belonging to the mother of folk-music star Peter Yarrow.

From the roots put down in Woodstock by Grossman and Dylan, an extraordinary scene emerged and evolved over the subsequent years. It gave rise to the notion of "Woodstock" as countercultural touchstone, a hippie state of mind that went so far beyond the town itself that when Michael Lang had to move his 1969 festival sixty miles away, he did not for a moment consider dropping the name. And, to this day, summer tourists in their thousands pour into Woodstock to visit the site of the famous festival that never happened there.

Now I'm driving up to Palenville to visit Simone Felice in his very own Big Pink, a mountain-top barn with huge windows that open onto the woods below. The unfancy drum kit is set up in the corner, and I sit on a sofa and ask Felice about the mystical spirit of Woodstock – or, more accurately, ask him if said spirit is anything more than a pathetic fallacy.

"I got to grow up here before I had a GPS in my pocket," he replies. "I was born in 1976 in a dilapidated house on the creek. My father got out of Queens and went to Woodstock in '69. My folks were more just country-folk hippies, as opposed to the kind trying to change the world. From the earliest time, I was always hearing Dylan, Hendrix, The Band, Van Morrison. You can feel it: there's a mystical quality to these hills. People still come up here for the same reasons – for the quiet, for the nature, as well as the proximity to New York City and the belly of the beast. You can go out into the woods here and feel the pre-Columbian vibrations. Once you tap into it, it's amazing. I still get teary-eyed coming home. I have friends who don't even know where home *is* – spiritually *or* metaphorically."

As sentimental as these words might sound, I know what Felice is talking about. I too found something in Woodstock that one might call spiritual. You could say that I bought into the received mythology of the place, based heavily on the music I associated with it before I ever set foot there: *The Basement Tapes*, *Music from Big Pink*, *Moondance*, *Hermit of Mink Hollow*. You might

protest that I found only what I was already looking for: a refuge
from the congestion of cities and the amplification of the modern
world. Yet the day before meeting Felice I had for the thousandth
time driven north along Route 375 – rechristened Levon Helm
Boulevard earlier that year – and felt the old heart-surging bliss
as Overlook Mountain reared up to meet me, the smoky evening
smells of autumn seeping through the car windows. As I always do,
I felt like I was coming home.

"Once you get Woodstock in your blood, the temptation is to
come back once in a while to check things out," says Ed Sanders,
the former Fug and Beat poet who has called the town home since
1973. "Dylan still owns property on top of Ohayo Mountain, and he
stops in now and then to say hello."

"Every summer I get this longing in my bones to be back in
Woodstock, and I've managed to do it for three or four summers in
a row," says the folk-blues singer Maria Muldaur, who lived in the
town in the early seventies. "It's so green and so beautiful, a sort of
juicy, lush green that doesn't exist in California."

Back in the nineties, I myself lived in Woodstock for four years,
putting down roots in the town that have never quite been torn out.
"Woodstock is like a Venus flytrap," says Elliott Landy, the photographer whose images of Dylan, The Band and Van Morrison have
done much to fix Woodstock in the popular imagination. "Whether
you get stuck to it or not depends on whether your vibration is in
harmony with it. It's like they say there are vortices in Sedona or
Nepal, certain spiritual places, and I would say Woodstock is certainly that."

For all my misgivings about its New Age shops and its crystals and
tie-dye T-shirts, I got stuck to Woodstock. And something tugged me
back there again and again. Was I feeling pre-Columbian vibrations?
Probably not. And yet I believe in the spirit of a place, a psycho-
geography that may be little more than a kind of romanticism but
that enshrines something good about the people who've lived there.

I won't ever forget the first pilgrimage I made to Big Pink, the unprepossessing and, in fact, rather small house occupied in the summer of 1967 by Dylan and The Band. I remember standing in the neighbouring fields as a bootleg of their basement tapes played in my ears on a Sony Walkman. I longed to go back in time and peep through Big Pink's windows, to watch Dylan singing "Lo and Behold" and "Million Dollar Bash" as Rick Danko and Richard Manuel yelped behind him. For me this was the perfect tableau of musical brotherhood, of songs made organically by men who'd pulled back from the insanity of fame. The ripples of those primitive recordings changed music for ever.

"Woodstock has a way of downshifting you from high gears into neutral," says Mercury Rev's Jonathan Donahue, that shamanic dandy of Hudson Valley rock. "It's not a coincidence that it is a strange attractor for the Tibetans and the Zen people. The Buddhists would have a word for 'neutral' – the void. All of that is there, from ages earlier than Dylan. I don't want to get too mystical about it, but there's more to Woodstock than it being a cute little town in the mountains where Bob had a place and some funny things happened to The Band on the way to the Forum. It is that place, at least to me – the creeks and the winding roads and the pitch-black nights – but all of that is on the inside. It's the mountains of the mind."

While one can't imagine The Band talking about Woodstock in such poetic terms, this book is absolutely about "the mountains of the mind": the ease and peace, the beauty and wonder that Woodstock offered to musicians, and offers still. From Dylan to David Bowie, no less – via folk singers and swamp-rockers, country pickers and free-jazz composers – musicians of all kinds have called Woodstock home, a creative oasis that's just close enough to New York City and just far enough away. "We don't feel up here like we are just out in the woods," says Karl Berger, founder of Woodstock's esteemed Creative Music Studio, a hub for jazz improvisation in the seventies and eighties. "My personal viewpoint is that New York is an industrial suburb of Woodstock."

While Woodstock is hardly unique as a mystical locus of art and creativity, nor is it exactly like the other picturesque spots to which artists and seekers have gravitated. "Places like Key West, Taos and Sedona, they're unique because of where they're situated," says Brian Hollander, a well-liked musician who was the first Democrat to be elected Woodstock's Town Supervisor (and who is the current editor of the town's weekly newspaper). "With Woodstock it's partly about what people have to do to survive here. It's not a lot, but you do have to survive the winters, and sometimes it gets way down below zero. I've felt all along that it's an extraordinary place, even in the anti-Woodstock years when the cultural world laughed at the hippies."

Hollander says he recently asked the famous TV interviewer Dick Cavett if he'd ever been to Woodstock. "He said, 'No, but I know a couple of people who went to it,'" he says with a chuckle. "But in a way it's right that you come to Woodstock the town to find what it was that caused Michael Lang to give his festival that name – the essence of the place and the consciousness it created."

This is what I have attempted to do in *Small Town Talk*. I have come back to the garden of Woodstock to understand and chronicle the remarkable music made there between the early sixties and the mid-eighties; to tell a story whose cast includes not only Dylan and The Band and Morrison, but Janis Joplin, Jimi Hendrix, Karen Dalton; Bobby Charles and Paul Butterfield; Tim Hardin and Todd Rundgren; Holy Moses and Hungry Chuck; and Happy and Artie Traum and Geoff and Maria Muldaur. Most of them lived here and played and drank in such fabled establishments as the Café Espresso, the Sled Hill Café, the Village Jug, the Elephant, the Watering Troff [*sic*] and the legendary Joyous Lake, and ate at Deanie's, the Squash Blossom, Rosa's Cantina, the Bear Café and the Little Bear.

Above all, this is a story that revolves around the larger-than-life figure of Albert Bernard Grossman, the manager, studio builder, property developer and gourmet dubbed "the Baron of Bearsville" by those who loved him and those who feared him. It is Grossman's reign, from his first visit to Woodstock in 1963 to his sudden and unexpected death in 1986, that offers the best framework for what is really a biography of Woodstock itself during its musical glory years.

For Grossman, as for Dylan and everyone else who ventured up there in his wake, Woodstock was the place that Bobby Charles – on the run from a drugs charge in Nashville – was searching for when he first showed up there in the late summer of 1971: "*A place I'd feel loose / a place I could lose / these Tennessee blues . . .*"

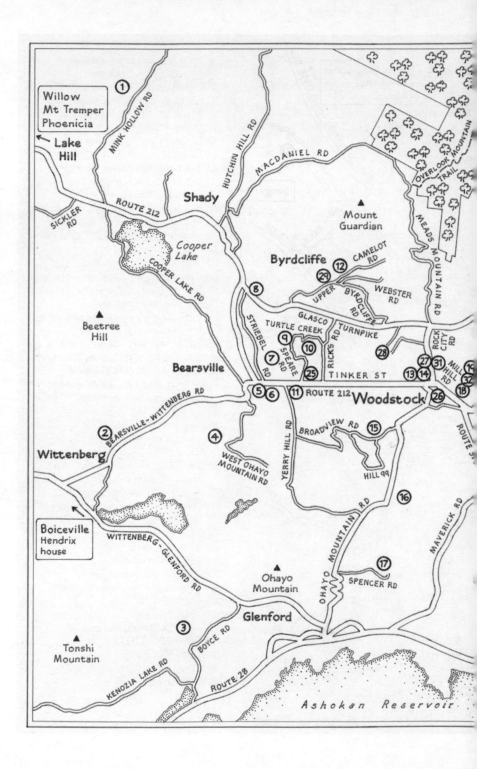

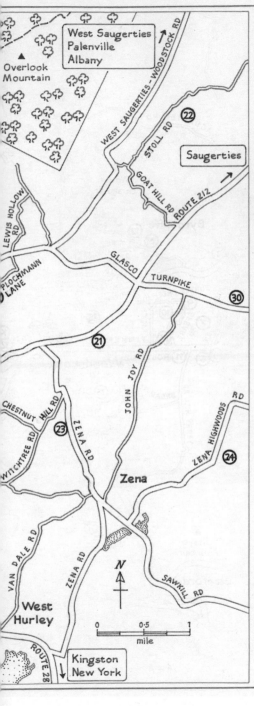

1. Todd Rundgren's house and Utopia Sound studio
2. Paul Butterfield's house (1970s)
3. Garth Hudson's and Geoff and Maria Muldaur's houses (early 1970s)
4. Levon Helm's (and briefly Rick Danko's) house (late 60s/early 70s)
5. The Bear, the Little Bear and the Bearsville Theatre
6. Utopia video studio
7. Albert and Sally Grossman's house
8. Approximate site of Bob Dylan's motorcycle accident
9. Bearsville studios
10. Turtle Creek Barn studio
11. The Watering Troff
12. Bob and Sara Dylan's first house
13. Squash Blossom Café
14. Café Espresso (and Dylan's 'White Room')
15. Peter Yarrow's cabin
16. Bob and Sara Dylan's second house
17. Garth Hudson and Richard Manuel's house (late 60s), later Van and Janet Morrison's 1969/70 home
18. Deanie's
19. The Joyous Lake
20. Levon Helm's 'Barn', home of the Ramble
21. Jim Colegrove and N. D. Smart's house/Nevessa studio
22. Big Pink, home and recording space for Dylan and the Hawks (1967/8)
23. Rick and Grace Danko's house (late 60s/early 70s)
24. Tim Hardin's house
25. Robbie and Dominique Robertson's house (late 60s)
26. Sled Hill Café
27. The Elephant
28. Mike Jeffery's house
29. Byrdcliffe Theatre
30. Peter Pan Farm
31. Colony Arts Center/Café
32. Woodstock Playhouse

Overlook Mountain from West Saugerties (Art Sperl)

PART ONE

A PLACE I'D FEEL LOOSE

Take advantage of the opportunity to spend time in the country away from distractions caused by diverse needs. Use the time to create a new mythology, to recreate a panorama of vision, enlarging, specifying, painting, pointing out a larger vision than what you lost. Make it work for yourself. Grab your possibilities and make them realities.

KAREN DALTON, notebook entry, date unknown

1

THE UNEASY ALLIANCE

When one considers that the two men who did more than anybody to make Woodstock one of America's great music towns were both Jewish, it is a curious irony that the man who founded the town's first arts colony over half a century earlier was – like so many otherwise civilised people of his generation – a virulent anti-Semite.

What Albert Grossman and Bob Dylan (né Zimmerman) thought of Ralph Radcliffe Whitehead has not been recorded, but Dylan bought his Woodstock house on Camelot Road from Whitehead's son Peter and probably did not confront him about his late father's distaste for Jews. By the same token, Whitehead Jr had probably evolved far enough beyond his father's ingrained prejudice against "Hebrews" not to stall the sale of Hi Lo Ha. The anti-Semitism that had been rife throughout New York state had in any case ebbed by 1965, when Dylan bought the house as a domestic base for his wife-to-be, her four-year-old daughter and the baby boy they were expecting. There were no longer any hotels in the area that catered – as Woodstock's Irvington Arms had done as late as the thirties – to "Gentiles Only". And in the second decade of the twenty-first century, when numerous Jewish Americans make their first or second homes in or around Woodstock, it's hard to conceive of a time when this was an issue at all.

His anti-Semitism aside, what Ralph Whitehead found in the verdant foothills of Woodstock's Overlook Mountain was what Bob Dylan found there sixty-odd years later: a place of refuge, a bolt-hole of wooded bliss where a man could breathe deeply and create in peace. The same went for Dylan's manager in Bearsville, a mile or so south-west. "I once asked Albert why he'd moved up here," says Woodstock singer-songwriter Robbie Dupree. "He said, 'Clean air and clean water.'"*

Whitehead had been casting about for a pastoral paradise for some time when his friend Bolton Coit Brown happened upon Woodstock in the spring of 1902. The wealthy son of a Yorkshire felt-mill owner, Whitehead had fallen under the spell of writer-artists John Ruskin and William Morris, who lamented the effects of the Industrial Revolution on the human soul and the artistic spirit. In this he was in accord with the New England transcendentalists Ralph Waldo Emerson and Henry David Thoreau, who both prose-lytised for retreats into the bosom of nature.

What Bolton Brown saw in 1902 was a more or less unspoiled landscape that for five thousand years had been home to Native American Indians: indigenous peoples who had lived in rock shel-ters on Overlook and hunted in the surrounding forests before their lives were traumatically interrupted by immigrant invaders from Germany and the Netherlands. After the Esopus Wars of 1659–60 and 1663, when Dutch soldiers brought gifts of destruction and dis-ease, the Indians were driven back from their historical habitat and ever higher into the mountains. Forty years later, a group of Esopus Indians sold off Woodstock's best land to Hendrick Beekman, whose name still lends itself to the self-styled "Oldest Inn in America" across the Hudson River in Rhinebeck. By the time Beekman died in 1716, many of Woodstock's Native Americans were gone.

The Indian spirit of the place lived on, however. "There was this thing about it having been a burial ground," says Procol Harum lyr-icist Keith Reid, a regular visitor to Woodstock in the late sixties. "It was considered that there was some real bad karma and people shouldn't be living there. Our band were doing some Ouija board

---

* At the turn of the century Woodstock enjoyed a reputation – possibly self-cultivated – as the healthiest town in New York state. "Woodstock, Where People Seldom Die," ran a 1907 headline in one local newspaper.

stuff and thought they'd summoned up this Indian chief who was telling them to leave." Sixties hippies weren't the only people to speak of the power of Overlook and its ancient burial sites. To this day it is almost a local assumption that the mountain exercises a mystical influence over Woodstock. The fact that one of America's largest Buddhist monasteries stands on Meads Mountain Road, halfway up Overlook, lends weight to this conviction. "The Tibetans say Woodstock is on a major ley line," says Elliott Landy. "There's a certain energy right in this area. It doesn't exist in Saugerties and it doesn't exist down in Hurley. When you come up Route 375 and you see those mountains, something changes in you."

"It always was a Mecca, a power spot," says Maria Muldaur, who first visited the town as a Greenwich Village bohemian in the late fifties. "There are other perfectly cute towns in the Catskills, but there's some mojo there, some spirit that Whitehead found."

By the start of the American Revolution in 1776, farmers – mainly Dutch tenants of landowner Robert Livingston – were living in and around Woodstock in forest clearings. There were sawmills on the Sawkill River that runs through the town, one of them owned by Livingston, who gave the settlement its new name after people had referred to the area for years by the Algonquian word *"Waghkonk"* ("at or near a mountain"). With its allusion to the small English town of the same name in Oxfordshire, "Woodstock" derives from the Saxon *"wudestoc"* (which can mean both a clearing in a wood or a tree stump).

It took time for Woodstock to recover from the Revolution, when its inhabitants were under constant threat from British raiders and their Indian allies. The settlement was all but deserted at the Revolution's end in 1783, yet six years later it received township status, covering a vast and unwieldy area of over 450 square miles. Early Woodstockers survived through a combination of farming, hunting and lumbering, but there were also apple orchards and cider mills, together with a very smelly tannery in the heart of the village.

In the early years of the new century there were even glass-making factories in the Sawkill valley. Working at one of them were a father and son, Lewis Edson Sr and Jr, who have a claim to being Woodstock's first musicians of any note: in 1800 Edson Jr even published a collection of hymns and songs entitled *The Social Harmonist*. Glassmaking brought money to Woodstock, increasing its population and bringing the first bank and post office to the area. Another source of employment came from the quarrying of bluestone, much of which found its way down the Hudson to New York City.

Through the tumultuous nineteenth century of the Anti-Rent wars – and of the Civil War itself – Woodstock slowly emerged from ancient country customs that included a pervasive belief in witch-craft. Churches and schools were built in the town. Tourists began visiting, seduced by descriptions of the Hudson Valley in best-selling novels by Washington Irving and James Fennimore Cooper. In August 1846 Thomas Cole, founder of the Hudson Valley school of painters, climbed Woodstock's most famous mountain and coined the phrase "the Overlook" after seeing its south peak.

Such was Overlook's appeal to romantic travellers that plans for a hotel at its summit were made within two years of Cole's climb. The Overlook Mountain House opened its doors in June 1871 and – in late 1873 – was visited by President Ulysses S. Grant. Artists and consumptives followed, though rarely in numbers sufficient to make the place financially viable. The Mountain House – and similar trav-ellers' hostelries, such as George Mead's boarding house – helped turn Woodstock into a semi-fashionable summer resort.

It was the view from the Mountain House that convinced Bolton Brown he had found what Ralph Whitehead and his American wife Jane Byrd McCall were looking for. "Like Balboa, from his 'peak in Darien'," Brown recalled of that May day, "I first saw my South Sea. South indeed it was and wide and almost as blue as the sea, that extraordinarily beautiful view, amazing in extent."

Brown also did his homework on the issue of Hebrews. Having ascertained that Woodstock had resisted the tide of New York City Jews that engulfed the Catskills every sultry summer, he urged the Whiteheads to join him in the town as soon as possible. By the late summer, the prospect of a harsh winter notwithstanding, clearing and construction had begun on 1,500 acres of Mount Guardian, acquired somewhat ruthlessly half a mile north-west of Woodstock's centre.

A rural arts colony was hardly a new phenomenon in America. Inspired by Monet and his fellow French impressionists at Giverny, artists and students of the late nineteenth century had established such retreats all over the US. One of the earliest was the Palenville colony established by Asher B. Durand, a friend of Thomas Cole's who specialised in views of local beauty spots like Kaaterskill Clove. Byrdcliffe – the name an amalgam of the middle names of Whitehead and his wife – was new only in its greater emphasis on the Arts and Crafts Movement inspired by Ruskin and Morris.

So deeply was Whitehead influenced by Ruskin, whose lectures he'd heard as a student at Oxford, that he walked away from his family's business and spent a decade travelling and immersing himself in the works of Dante Alighieri. In 1890 he journeyed to America and met McCall, marrying her in New Hampshire two years later. After establishing the small Arcady colony near Santa Barbara – and following an affair with an opium-smoking heiress in that Californian coastal town – Whitehead met with two of his followers, Brown and Hervey White, and resolved to scout locations for a new colony on the East Coast.

It took the better part of a decade to complete the construction of Byrdcliffe's many buildings. In June 1903, when the colony began life, Whitehead published "A Plea for Manual Work", a manifesto in which he argued that "living in peaceful country places" while working at handicrafts and enjoying the arts would bring "repose" to Americans stressed by life in cities. Joining the Whiteheads in

the utopian experiment were Brown, White and others. For the
entrenched Woodstock population of old Dutch and German farming families, the newcomers were a sight to behold. They might
have read about "bohemians" in Paris or even Greenwich Village,
but they hadn't bargained on them showing up on their doorstep.

Few of the Byrdcliffe bohemians were more startling to the eye
than Hervey White, hailed by some as Woodstock's first hippie.
Bearing a distinct resemblance to Levon Helm, he was a proud
socialist – and closet homosexual – who wore his hair long and dis-
pensed with hats and conventional trousers. Indeed, so much his
own man was this Midwesterner that it took only two years for him
to fall out with the controlling Whitehead. While the Byrdcliffe programmes of furniture-making, metalworking, weaving and print-
making continued, White set up camp south of Woodstock in the
Hurley Patentee Woods, eventually founding the rival Maverick
colony at the onset of the First World War.

Woodstock's locals braced themselves for another shock when
New York's Art Students' League – inspired by Byrdcliffe – chose
to base its summer school in a former livery stable in the middle
of town. In the summer months Woodstock was soon overrun by
free-spirited students, establishing a kind of double life that persists
in the town to this day. For while Woodstock was for decades a pro-
foundly conservative place, its natives soon adapted to the influx of
outsiders, if only because the arts (and the crafts) brought money
into local shops and businesses. Natives even turned blind eyes to
the nude female models who posed al fresco in Woodstock's woods
and streams. Boarding-house owners overcame moral scruples and
profited from the patronage of aspiring young painters and poets,
some of whom even stayed on through the tough months of winter.

In November 1923 the Woodstock Artists Association was
formed, exhibiting as a group in New York and giving rise to a
"Woodstock School" of artists whose work broadly combined
earthy immersion in Catskills landscapes with influences from

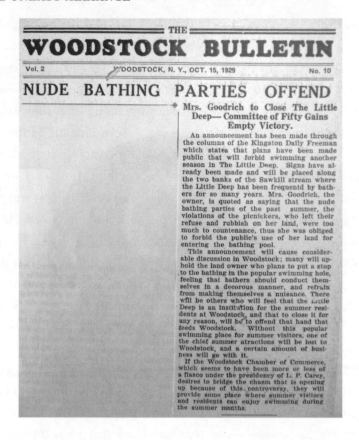

THE WOODSTOCK BULLETIN

Vol. 2   WOODSTOCK, N. Y., OCT. 15, 1929   No. 10

NUDE BATHING PARTIES OFFEND

Mrs. Goodrich to Close The Little Deep— Committee of Fifty Gains Empty Victory.

An announcement has been made through the columns of the Kingston Daily Freeman which states that plans have been made public that will forbid swimming another season in The Little Deep. Signs have already been made and will be placed along the two banks of the Sawkill stream where the Little Deep has been frequentd by bathers for so many years. Mrs. Goodrich, the owner, is quoted as saying that the nude bathing parties of the past summer, the violations of the picnickers, who left their refuse and rubbish on her land, were too much to countenance, thus she was obliged to forbid the public's use of her land for entering the bathing pool.

This announcement will cause considerable discussion in Woodstock; many will uphold the land owner who plans to put a stop to the bathing in the popular swimming hole, feeling that bathers should conduct themselves in a decorous manner, and refrain from making themselves a nuisance. There will be others who will feel that the Little Deep is an institution for the summer residents at Woodstock, and that to close it for any reason, will be to offend that hand that feeds Woodstock. Without this popular swimming place for summer visitors, one of the chief summer atractions will be lost to Woodstock, and a certain amount of business will go with it.

If the Woodstock Chamber of Commerce, which seems to have been more or less of a fiasco under the presidency of L. P. Carey, desires to bridge the chasm that is opening up because of this controversy, they will provide some place where summer visitors and residents can enjoy swimming during the summer months.

European Post-Impressionism and Cubism. Early members of the Association included George Bellows, Konrad Cramer and Lucile Blanch. By the end of the decade, several other renowned painters and sculptors – from Yasuo Kuniyoshi to John Flannagan – were living at least part-time in Woodstock.

Music assumed a more central role at the Maverick. When in 1915 a well was urgently needed to supply water to Hervey White's colony, the Maverick Festival was born as a way to raise funds for it. This annual event soon attracted flocks of unconventional Greenwich Villagers to the colony, most attired in playfully outlandish costumes and enjoying entertainment that included modernist classical music, while also extending to more spontaneous expressions of dancing, juggling and even sack-racing. By 1916, the Maverick had its own theatre, carved from a nearby bluestone quarry.

The festivals upped the ante in the uneasy relations between bohemians and townspeople. Writing in 1916 in *The Wild Hawk* – the Maverick's own monthly publication – White confidently stated that "there are motives that bring opposites together". He subsequently offered to decorate Woodstock's public buildings, though the offer was refused and many Woodstockers continued to view the Maverick festivals with suspicion – even after the opening of a new wooden theatre in July 1924 brought to the colony such stars of the stage as Helen Hayes and Edward G. Robinson.°

And yet, as each year went by, increasing numbers of Woodstock natives felt curious enough about the neo-pagan (some said orgiastic) revelries at the Maverick to join in, donning their own eccentric attire. At least part of the reason for this was their appreciation of the dollars flowing into Woodstock via bohemian tourism. As Alf Evers noted in his epic *Woodstock: History of an American Town* (1987), "an uneasy alliance between art and business had been formed". It would be ever thus in this most singular of Catskills towns.

"If you come into Woodstock for the first time on a Saturday morning and land in the center of the village," the *New York Herald-Tribune* reported in a piece from the twenties, "you rub your eyes, blink, and wonder whether you have suddenly been magically transported to some carnival in southern Europe." When future *Woodstock Times* publisher Geddy Sveikauskas first arrived in town in the late sixties, he was accosted by a female senior citizen who told him, "You people think you've invented it all, don't you. Well, if you had lived here thirty years ago you'd have seen what an arts town really was like."

° By the end of the decade, White's theatre had a rival in the Woodstock Playhouse. Rebuilt in 1938 after an earlier fire, the theatre would play a major role in the town's cultural life for decades. In 1970 The Band would record their aptly named *Stage Fright* there.

The last Maverick festival took place in 1931, after a boom decade in which Woodstock's annual summer population swelled to
over eight thousand and – to the distaste of most Byrdcliffe veterans – a new Chamber of Commerce was created. Underpinning the
resentment was the anti-Semitism that made strange bedfellows of
the Whiteheads and the older Woodstock families. When Jewish
developer Gabriel Newgold began work on the Colony Hotel on
Rock City Road, local newspapers referred to it as "the brick syna-
gogue". Yet increasing numbers of Jewish artists were moving into
the area, assimilating as the colony craftsmen themselves had done.
Alarm at the prospect of Woodstock's ruin by business was, in any
case, rendered irrelevant by the financial crash of 1929 and the dev-
astating Depression that followed.

1929 was also the year Ralph Whitehead died, though his widow
kept Byrdcliffe going until her own death in 1955. If the thirties were
as tough economically on Woodstock as on the rest of the country,
there was the unexpected upside of Roosevelt's Public Works of Art
Project, which brought funding to nearly fifty of the town's resident artists. This angered the townspeople, who resented their taxes
going to support feckless creatives, and thus did the decades-old
tension between artists and natives rumble on. "The town's government was very right-wing, all the way back to the Roosevelt era,"
says Ed Sanders.

By the time America entered the Second World War, Woodstock's
year-round population had reached two thousand. It was hailed by
Charles E. Gradwell, editor of the *Overlook* newspaper, as "the
most cosmopolitan village in the world", a place that included "men
with beards, ballet dancers, farmers, flute players, business men,
actors, poets, restaurateurs, potters, writers, weavers, painters,
press agents, politicians, lawyers, historians, illustrators, cartoon-
ists, philosophers, remittance men, educators, theatrical producers,
wine merchants . . ."

By 1960, Woodstock's year-round population had all but doubled again, bringing in a wave of post-war artists that included Fletcher Martin, Manuel Bromberg, Ed Chavez, Doris Lee and Wendell Jones. After Philip Guston won a Guggenheim Fellowship in 1947, he moved first to Byrdcliffe and subsequently to the Maverick, where – as his daughter Musa wrote in her 1991 memoir *Night Studio* – "you stoked your own wood stove, pumped your own water, padded to the outhouse in the moonlight".

"Woodstock was pretty quiet," says the artist Bruce Dorfman, who first visited the town with the Art Students' League in 1951. "But there were a lot of heavy hitters in the artistic community who lived there in the summers or year round. Guston was probably the greatest of the painters here. Another Woodstock artist whose star has risen again is Kuniyoshi."

"The town was small and safe and you knew everybody," says Norma Cross, who spent summers in a cabin off the Maverick belonging to Russian-born artist Nahum Tschacbasov. "But it was pretty wild too. My parents were in their thirties and were partying and being outrageous." Along with the artists came musicians such as composer Henry Cowell, who lived in the hamlet of Shady with his folk-song-collecting wife Sidney; writers such as *Casablanca* screenwriter Howard Koch and CBS sports commentator Heywood Hale Broun; and actors such as John Garfield, who taught Norma Cross how to swim, and Lee Marvin, who was a plumber before a lucky break gave him a part in a 1947 summer-stock production at the rebuilt Playhouse.

Marvin was one of the many hard-drinking patrons of Woodstock's most colourful bar. Four years after the end of Prohibition, Dick Stilwell had bought a disused stable on Rock City Road and turned it into the nautically themed S.S. Sea Horse, complete with port-holes for windows and paintings by local artists on the walls. Macho sculptors bumped elbows with gin-swilling former madam Louise Hellstrom and Martini-sipping German plumber Adolf Heckeroth, to whom Marvin was apprenticed. Extramarital affairs began at the

Sea Horse and fights broke out as a result, though not as many as erupted up the road at the Brass Rail. When Stilwell collapsed and died at the Sea Horse, instead of summoning an ambulance the patrons simply laid his corpse out on a ping-pong table and helped themselves to free drinks.

"I don't know that my mother was one of those Sea Horse bohemians, but she knew that element," says Jonathan Donahue. "She came up with her father in the Jewish exodus of the early forties. She'd seen Charlie Parker and Dizzy Gillespie on 52nd Street, so she brought that beatnik sensibility up with her. But it was different up here. There wasn't an influx of people coming up from the city saying, 'Where are the Beats?'"

The Sea Horse was one of several places in Woodstock where artists and natives mingled. "I remember my mom telling me how she would go to the Sea Horse and hang out with her cigarette holder and play pool," says the dobro player Cindy Cashdollar, whose family owned one of Woodstock's dairy farms. Though for many years the town remained Republican, farmers' kids like Cashdollar – who was born there in 1955 – were schooled alongside the children of painters, slurping the same ice creams at Charlie's Ice Cream Parlor. Potters from the Maverick shopped at the same hardware store as natives whose old way of life was now disappearing from the fields around Woodstock.

By the early sixties, Woodstock had properly joined the twentieth century. The New York Thruway now made it possible to reach Manhattan by car in two hours, while a bridge linked Kingston to Rhinebeck across the Hudson. Route 28, the highway from Woodstock to Kingston, was widened and resurfaced. A supermarket and a branch of the Bank of Orange County appeared in town. The fifties had brought IBM and electric-fan manufacturers Rotron to the area, both building housing developments for their employees off Route 375. "There was a whole section of town where the IBMers lived and commuted to Kingston," says Brian Hollander. "It made for a pretty interesting mix of people, since everybody had to go to the same places for their entertainment."

Among the "entertainment" on offer in Woodstock was the folk music that was now taking middle-class American youth by storm.

2

FOLK SONGS OF THE CATSKILLS

Inside the Colony Café's old Mission-style interior, with its wrap-around balcony and its original sign stating rates of "$1.50 and up, all with private baths", a thin straggle of local groovers has drifted in from Woodstock's Sunday-night drizzle. Two youngish men are tuning a banjo and a dobro, one a scrawny fellow in denim with short hair and a long beard. "We're staying for as long as my daughter can stay awake," a young mother says at an adjacent table.

Thanks to strictly enforced drink-driving laws in New York state, it's all a long way from Woodstock's glory years, when clubs along Tinker Street – and Mill Hill and Rock City Roads – heaved with roots-rocking revellers. "Woodstock in those days was comprised of freak musicians, local craftsmen and a few artists," says artist manager Mark McKenna. "It was low-key and everybody kept their mouth shut. The cops were tolerant and there was a friendly atmosphere. Now there are more cops in that town than in just about any other small town I've ever seen."

"I used to go from the old Deanie's to the Brass Rail to the Elephant to the Espresso to the Joyous Lake and then over to the Bear," says Richard Heppner of the Woodstock Historical Society. "You could see three bands in a night if you wanted. But since DUI the town's gotten more touristy and more policed. There *is* no real nightlife."

The Colony's main attraction tonight isn't the two faux-Appalachians but a kind of all-star Woodstock troupe fronted by Simi Stone, the female fiddle player I saw only two nights ago with Simone Felice (and who played with him in Bearsville side project the Duke and the King). Behind a Hammond keyboard sits the genial David Baron, whose father Aaron owned the mobile truck used to record The Band's *Stage Fright* at the Woodstock Playhouse. Stone's rhythm section consists of former Gang of Four bassist Sara Lee and drummer Zachary Alford, beat-keeper on the recent come-back album by Catskills resident David Bowie.

The music is very different from Felice's – soulful, Motownish pop with blasting horns and Stone's Little-Eva-meets-Amy-Winehouse vocals. When at the night's end they encore with a cover of "Everyday People", it's impossible not to link this infectiously funky ensemble to their unisex mixed-race forebears Sly and the Family Stone, who lit up the Woodstock Festival with a storming wee-small-hours set that had the stardust hippies bumping and grinding on Max Yasgur's hillside.

Fifty-five years ago Gabriel Newgold's old hotel resonated to very different sounds. The Colony Arts Center, as it was known in 1959, was the venue booked by Alf Evers for the First Annual Catskill Mountain Folk Festival, which brought together Woodstock's premier exponents of folk song and mountain music, from seventy-five-year-old Mary Avery to twenty-nine-year-old Billy Faier.

Other performers included veterans "Squire" Elwyn Davis and "Bearded Bill" Spanhake, a fiddler and folklore humorist who regularly played at a sportsmen's club out in nearby Wittenberg. "They had square dances there," says Dean Schambach, who moved to Woodstock from New York City in 1963. "Old Bill played the fiddle so that everybody just vibrated. These were great characters that people still revere, people you could trust and love."

Also performing at Evers's festival were fifty-one-year-old Sam Eskin, a Jewish folk-song collector who'd moved to Woodstock in 1948, and his French protégée Sonia Malkine, who'd come to America with her surrealist painter husband Georges. It was just a year earlier, at a party of Eskin's on Chimney Road, that Malkine's

Poster for the 1st Annual Catskill Mountain Folk Music Festival, summer
1959 (courtesy of Fern Malkine)

voice had first been heard in public. Asked by painter Ed Chavez
if she sang – he himself performed Mexican folk songs – she broke
into an a cappella version of the exquisite thirteenth-century ballad "Robin", silencing the entire party with the beauty of her voice.
Within a week, Eskin had arranged the recording of an album for
Moe Asch's New York label Folkways, with Malkine accompanying
herself on a lute.

    Country and barn dances had been staples of the town's enter-
tainment ever since Irish immigrants brought jigs and reels into
the area in the previous century. By the fifties, farmers and artists
alike gathered to enjoy the indigenous music of the Catskills. On

Saturday nights there were square dances at the Irvington Arms, where a trio known as the Catskill Mountaineers performed for a well-lubricated mix of painters and natives. "That's where I first became acquainted with the artistic people," says Billy Faier, whose stepfather ran the town's gas station. "It was all one big crowd: all the cultural people, the artists and the musicians. They all loved each other. I was a fifteen-year-old kid and I met all these incredible people. It changed my life."

Among the "artistic people" were the Ballantines, a well-heeled but politically enlightened family with a house in Woodstock. David Ballantine and his sister-in-law Betty were entrenched in Woodstock's folk circle, David as an avid collector of 78s, Betty as a singer and guitarist who often played duets at the Irvington with the besotted Faier. It was through a friendship with the Ballantines that Sonia and Georges Malkine moved to the Maverick colony in 1951 and then, two years later, bought a place of their own in nearby Shady.*

Many Woodstock artists and intellectuals – particularly those of a left-wing persuasion – had shown interest in folk music since the thirties. In June 1937 the blues singer Leadbelly, freed from prison after his discovery by the folklorist John Lomax, performed at the Zena home of John Varney for an audience that included Hervey White, fellow Maverick colonist Marion Bullard and *Overlook* magazine editor Charles Gradwell. Later, as anti-communist hysteria grew in America, connections formed between Woodstock and summer camps such as Camp Woodland, near Phoenicia, where Pete Seeger was welcomed in the wake of the House Un-American Activities Committee blacklist. Run by two veteran Greenwich Village radicals – one of whom, Herb Haufrecht, had helped assemble the

---

* David Ballantine, a friend of Lee Marvin's, was the son of Maverick-actor-turned-sculptor E. J. Ballantine and his wife Stella, niece of radical anarchist Emma Goldman. David's brother Ian helped bring Penguin Books to the US in 1939, before becoming the first president of Bantam in 1945 and later founding Ballantine Books.

print collection *Folk Songs of the Catskills* – Camp Woodland was
where Seeger first heard not only those Catskills songs but the revolutionary Cuban anthem "Guantanamera". It was also where he
himself was first heard by Billy Faier, Alf Evers and John Herald,
who claimed that witnessing Seeger at Camp Woodland in 1954
was what inspired him to become a singer. It was in Woodstock,
meanwhile, that Seeger met his wife Toshi Ohta, whose father had
designed theatre sets at the Maverick.

Despite all this, folk music remained low-key in Woodstock.
Too small to compete with Greenwich Village or with the nascent
Club 47 scene in Cambridge, Massachusetts, the small Catskills
town was barely on the radar of the urban folk revival. "There was
always, within the community, an interest in folk music," says Bruce
Dorfman. "People listened to Woody Guthrie and Josh White, but
it was very laid-back. Apart from some peripheral vision that somebody like Moe Asch had about the potential of a Billy Faier, the
folkies in Woodstock were left alone. The impression I had was that
they were sort of wistful about not being paid more attention but
didn't quite know what to do about it."

In August 1962 Pete Seeger appeared at the Woodstock Playhouse – where, a year earlier, its new owner Edgar Rosenblum had
started a Monday-night folk series – to raise funds for Sam Eskin's
Ulster County Folklore Society. This newly formed body in turn
sponsored the First Annual Woodstock Folk Festival, held on the
weekend of September 14–16. Once again Eskin and Malkine were
among the main attractions, together with Seeger himself, dulcimer player Mona Fletcher and her bagpipe-playing spouse Frank,
Greenwich Village singers Peter La Farge and Ramblin' Jack
Elliott, and Barbara Moncure, who the following year would record
the Folkways album *Folksongs of the Catskills* with singer-historian
Harry Siemsen. "I must have been in Woodstock about twenty years
before Albert or Bob," Jack Elliott said with some exaggeration in
2007. "Then I found out about Sam Eskin . . . a nice man and . . .

one of the earlier Woodstock musicians. So there was that type of
person up there then . . . but no famous ones as there were later on."

The Woodstock Folk Festival was a perfectly timed celebration
of the fever that had seized the imagination of middle-class America
since the first gatherings of folk singers in Washington Square in
the late forties. "There were a lot of people from middle-class backgrounds who were looking for some cultural expression that they
were lacking in the area where they were growing up," says Happy
Traum, a folk singer who has lived in Woodstock since the sixties.
"We looked into blues and mountain music and cowboy songs and
all the rest of it, and found in that a way of expressing ourselves."

By 1962, Billy Faier, another star of the Folk Festival, had been
playing banjo for well over a decade. His hobo-esque career had
taken him all over the States, including California – in the company of Woody Guthrie and Jack Elliott – but he was now back in
his beloved Woodstock, where he'd built himself a cabin in Lake
Hill. Faier was also an habitué of the Café Espresso, Woodstock's
version of a Left Bank bistro, complete with red-and-white-check
tablecloths and a jukebox that only played classical music. The café
had started commercial life in 1921 as an ice-cream and sandwich
parlour known as the Nook, celebrated in a song of Faier's ("The
Unpleasantness at the Nook") that described a drunken fistfight
between co-owners Jim Hamilton and Franklin "Bud" Drake.
Hamilton and Drake had made up for long enough to transform the
Nook into the Espresso Café in 1959, and then to sell it to Bernard
and Mary Lou Paturel, who a year later changed the name again to
the Café Espresso. Unimpressed by the entertainment that French-
born Bernard brought up from the city – "one was a German folk-
singer, and there were some belly dancers and flamenco guitarists"
– Faier suggested he hire a few up-and-coming folk singers instead.

Securing a regular slot for his own banjo instrumentals, Faier
began booking acts for the Frenchman. "It was a weekend place,"

BILLY FAIER

will be at the

CAFE EXPRESSO

Memorial Day Weekend
FRIDAY, MAY 31 — SATURDAY, JUNE 1

*An exceptional menu will be offered
from our fine French kitchen including*

Coquilles de Bourgogne

Coq au Jin

Brochette d'Oigneau

Prime Beef

Cigob au Flageolets

Fine Wines, Cocktails, Liqueures

Superlative French Pastries

OR 9-9478   WOODSTOCK, N. Y.

Billy Faier at the Café Expresso [*sic*], May–June 1963
(courtesy of Fern Malkine)

he says. "Friday and Saturday nights and Sunday afternoon. You got
fifty bucks, all the food you could eat and a place to stay upstairs.
Dave Van Ronk and Tom Paxton came up; so did Patrick Sky, Billy
Batson, Jerry Moore and Major Wiley." Between 1962 and 1965,
the Espresso also hosted appearances by Phil Ochs, Jack Elliott,
Joan Baez, Tim Hardin, John Hammond Jr, the Rev. Gary Davis,
Mississippi John Hurt and other stars of the urban folk and country-
blues revival. Sonia Malkine, who'd waited tables at the Nook, also

performed at the Espresso, as did Sam Eskin, Dan and the Deacon, and other locals.

One cold day in the late winter of 1963, Happy Traum took a long bus trip from the city to play at the café. He had spent a summer in Woodstock with the Art Students' League and even performed at a folk-music night at the Woodstock Playhouse, but nothing quite prepared him for Tinker Street at the tail end of winter. "I remember getting off the bus," he says, "and it seemed like the end of the world." What made things worse was that Traum's friend Bob Dylan was, that very night, due to play at New York's Town Hall.* And yet being in Woodstock out of season gave Traum a window into what made the place so special: "There were a lot of town characters, and I got to meet some of those people around the big pot-bellied stove in the middle of the Espresso. It was a very bohemian atmosphere, very much like the Village, except very rural."

Among the "town characters" were Faier, who Traum had seen perform in the Village, and Sam Eskin and Sonia Malkine. Also present was Greenbriar Boys singer John Herald, who was spending time in the town to which his Armenian poet father had first brought him as a boy. "Johnnie had this soulful, plaintive voice, and I had the biggest crush on him," says Maria Muldaur, who gave Herald rides to and from Woodstock with her banjo-playing boyfriend Walter Grundy. "He showed us where all the sacred swimming holes were in Woodstock." Herald would later take Traum and his wife Jane to Big Deep, a swimming hole in the Sawkill where art students had swum since the twenties. "It was the most idyllic place you could imagine, with the rope swing and the stream," Traum says. "It all seemed so pristine and beautiful, and it gave me a sense that I wanted to be here."

Another presence on the Village scene often came to the Espresso.

---

* In September that year the Folkways album *Broadside Ballads, Vol. 1* would feature Traum singing the first recorded version of Dylan's "Blowin' in the Wind", as a member of Gil Turner's New World Singers.

Peter Yarrow had been a fellow pupil of Traum's at New York's High School of Music and Art, but the two had only been on nodding terms. Yarrow had been visiting Woodstock since 1945, when he was seven years old: he was there the day the Second World War ended.* The Yarrow family owned two cabins on Broadview Road, which ran parallel to the Sawkill south of Tinker Street, and Peter spent most of his summers there with his divorced mother Vera. "Woodstock was completely warm and friendly," he says. "It had no sense of its importance on the map in the world of tastemakers or money-makers. It was not high-velocity, and everything was handmade."

Milton Glaser, who designed album covers for the folk trio that Yarrow had joined in 1961, agrees: "In those days the artist colony was a glamorous thing, but only at a distance. As you got up close it was just like any other poor town in the Catskills. We started going there in the mid- to late fifties because it was a cheap place to go, but it hadn't coalesced into anything discernible."

Something discernible, however, was just around the corner. Within five years of Happy Traum's Espresso gig in April 1963, Woodstock had changed from a place famous for its painters into a magnet for the popular music that shook sixties America to its core.

"For us it was an artists' community," said Jean Young, who moved to Woodstock with husband Jim in 1963 and two years later opened the Juggler emporium on Tinker Street. "But once we got here, we realised that the musicians who came here were more advanced in what they were doing. So it shifted, for us, to things more concentrated on music . . ."

---

* An even earlier arrival was that of Allen Ginsberg, who spent at least one summer in Woodstock in the thirties with his parents Louis and Naomi.

3

INSIDE ALBERT GROSSMAN

It's as if a bunch of midnight cowboys – or "citybillies", as they were once called – has just stumbled into New York's Town Hall from nearby Times Square. There are ten-gallon hats everywhere, and endless banjos and mandolins. On the stage, raw young men and women lean into vintage microphones, awaiting cues and signals. Pre-empting the release of the bleak but deadpan-funny *Inside Llewyn Davis* – Joel and Ethan Coen's film about the New York folk scene in 1961 – this gathering of the music's Great and Good is a one-night-only Village Preservation Society.

American folk music may now be quaintly fossilised – just as *Inside Llewyn Davis* may itself be a semi-jokey segue from the Coens' earlier *O Brother, Where Art Thou?* to Christopher Guest's spoof *A Mighty Wind* – but the evening is a well-paced delight, less because of star turns by the likes of Joan Baez and Jack White than because of its sheer abundance of lovely songs: Tom Paxton's "Last Thing on My Mind", Ian Tyson's "Four Strong Winds", Hedy West's "500 Miles", Jackson C. Frank's "Blues Run the Game" and the oft-covered traditional "Green, Green Rocky Road". Bob Dylan's "Tomorrow Is a Long Time" is exquisitely rendered by Keb' Mo', Utah Phillips's "Rock Salt and Nails" endearingly croaked by Dylan's legendary sixties henchman Bob Neuwirth. Dylan himself is absent, but the show – like the film – fittingly closes with his song "Farewell".

There is such pleasure in these songs of loss and longing, of distance and resistance; enough, at least, to remind us that for a long moment "folk" music did its bit – in the mighty line from Patti

Smith's closing anthem "People Have the Power" – to "wrestle power from fools". It may be hard in late 2013 to hear this music as it was originally sung, but the concert says so much about how our culture clings to an organic Eden of acoustic roots in the digitised world of virtual connection. That it's staged in a venue where Dylan played one of his breakthrough concerts – and where the ghosts of Guthrie, Leadbelly and Van Ronk still lurk – gives it extra lift and poignancy.

One of the key sequences in *Inside Llewyn Davis* involves Davis (Oscar Isaac) hitching a ride to wintry Chicago in the company of a disdainful hophead of a jazz musician (John Goodman). Davis only just makes it to the icy Windy City but manages to bag an audition for Bud Grossman, manager of the Gate of Horn nightclub. Played by F. Murray Abraham as a sterner version of Columbia Records' goatee-bearded A&R chief Mitch Miller, Grossman listens to Davis and responds with the terse feedback that "I don't see a lot of money here". Quick to blow a golden opportunity, Davis shuffles back into the deep snow of the Chicago streets – just as Dave Van Ronk had done. "I got to Chicago," Van Ronk said in 1966, "and he said, 'I've got Muddy Waters and Memphis Slim here. What do I need with *you?*' [. . .] And I stormed out."

"I don't see a lot of money here": the harsh words are certainly of a piece with what the real-life owner of the Gate of Horn might have said to an aspiring troubadour. "The guy was a real asshole," says Billy Faier, who played the Gate not long after it opened in 1955. "He was rude, he was arrogant. After I played he comes up to me, towering over me, and starts chewing me out in a loud voice about what a terrible performer I was."

Albert Grossman, who was thirty-five in 1961 but always looked fifty, was a new type of impresario on the folk scene: saturnine, intimidating, greedy, the opposite of everything the folk revival was supposed to be about. He had opened the Gate of Horn after graduating

from Roosevelt University with a degree in economics and working
as an administrator for Chicago's public-housing authority – a job
from which he was fired for "gross irregularities". "He couldn't get
a job very easily after that," said Les Brown, his original partner in
the club. "He seemed very depressed, he had a lot of problems with
women, and so we decided to set up a nightclub."

The Gate of Horn was a hundred-seat room in the basement of
the Rice Hotel on the city's North Side, and everybody who was anybody in folk or country-blues played there. The club made stars of
the bellowing African American singer Odetta and of Bob Gibson,
a charismatic and influential Chicago native who headlined at the
club within a year of first appearing there. "Albert had the first and
only club in Chicago that reflected what was going on in terms of
contemporary music," says Paul Fishkin, who later ran Grossman's
record label Bearsville. "He integrated Lenny Bruce with Odetta.
He was truly of that generation."

"Albert was a real hipster," says blues keyboard player Barry
Goldberg, who met him in the early sixties. "He set a precedent for
management, for not being just a shyster but someone with a brain
who was astute. He was on his way to becoming a major player. The
way he looked at you, there was an immediate intimidation. You
knew he could make it happen."

Grossman even played his part in the rise of folk's new princess.
"He was a very generous man," said Joan Baez, who was yet to break
out of Boston and Cambridge. "Though he never managed me, his
cajoling me to perform at the Gate of Horn when I was 18 marked
the beginning of my career." Unlike Odetta or Gibson – whose
recommendation of her for the 1959 Newport Folk Festival broke
her even bigger – Baez resisted Grossman's managerial overtures.
Bristling at his aggressive ambition, she not only turned him down
but signed with the small Vanguard label rather than the corporate behemoth that was Columbia. Nor was she the only person to
turn away from Grossman's ruthlessness. Les Brown loathed him so

much that, after his death, he made a special trip to urinate on his grave.

One thing nobody doubted about Grossman was his commitment to folk music as an art form: like all the best music entrepreneurs he was in awe of true talent. "If the audience wasn't attentive, if they really didn't *listen* to the act, then they were asked to leave," remembered Bob Gibson, who shared a North Side apartment with Grossman. "This was unheard of at the time."

It was through his representation of Gibson and Odetta that Grossman first intersected with the record business in New York. It didn't take long for him to figure out that if he was going to be a genuine force in music, he needed to be in Greenwich Village. Having helped to plan the first Newport Folk Festival with its founder George Wein, Grossman sold his interest in the Gate of Horn, moved into Wein's apartment on Central Park West and began the hunt for folk talent. "He told me that when he first came to New York, it was like a movie unfolding in front of his eyes," says Michael Friedman, who began working for Grossman in 1968. "And then gradually he got pushed into the movie, having to deal with all the noise and the people."

Making the move east with Grossman was his partner John Court, who some said was the good cop to Grossman's bad. The two men set up a temporary perch in the offices of Bert Block, who'd managed such jazz legends as Billie Holiday and Thelonious Monk. "Bert told me that he met them when they first arrived here," says Friedman. "They were, like, sitting on a milk crate with a phone."

Grossman had a concept for a musical *ménage à trois* that he pitched to Dave Van Ronk and others.* When he heard a singer named Hamilton Camp in the Village, he packed him off to Chicago

* Grossman also wanted to turn Van Ronk into a novelty act, Olaf the Blues Singer, in order to prove that he was corruptible. "Integrity bothered Albert," Van Ronk reflected years later; "he used to say there was no such thing as an honest man."

to join forces with Bob Gibson, hoping to complete the trio with a girl singer. But neither Camp nor Gibson was interested. Instead they formed a duo in 1961 and cut the best-selling album *Gibson and Camp at the Gate of Horn*. In the autumn of 1959, however, Grossman was sitting in the Café Wha? on MacDougal Street and half listening to a short set by Peter Yarrow. "He saw me perform and walked out in the middle of my show," Yarrow says. "Later, after I was on *Folk Sound USA*, the first folk 'spectacular' on TV, he saw me rehearsing and said he'd like to talk to me. I went to the office on Central Park West and our relationship started."

"Albert had a real nose for talent," says Jim Rooney, who booked acts at Cambridge's new Club 47. "He didn't have any money, he was sleeping on George Wein's couch, he had Peter as a client and that was *it*. So he was putting in his own money, and no, he wasn't paying huge advances to these people. But no one else was paying them either."

Though for a brief period he managed Yarrow as a solo act, Grossman saw the Cornell graduate as one third of his dream trio. The leading candidate for the female place was a blonde named Mary Travers, then stepping out with David Boyle. "She was young and beautiful in her own horsey way," Boyle says. "She said, 'Do you think I should do it?' I told her to get into it, and they clicked." Boyle was doing carpentry work for the third and final piece of Grossman's puzzle. The only problem with Noel Stookey was his name. A comedic singer who regularly gigged at the Wha? and the Gaslight, Stookey swallowed his pride – or at least his name – and became the "Paul" of Peter, Paul and Mary. In a managerial master-stroke that would forever make record executives wary of him, Grossman courted Atlantic Records, who were primed to sign the trio, and then landed them an unprecedented five-year deal with Warner Brothers. "Albert allowed us to be what we were," says Yarrow. "He made sure that we could evolve, and he had certain concepts about the sound. For instance, our voices were spread in a way that had not been done before, and the intimacy of that was totally different. When he thought the work was not good he would literally say it was 'bullshit' – at a time when not too many people used a term like that."

Grossman soon had a reputation for insisting on the best. For Peter, Paul and Mary's debut album, released in May 1962, he hired top arranger Milt Okun to be their "musical director" and brought in Milton Glaser of Push Pin Studios to design the album's cover. "He had this incredible vision," says Jane Traum, wife of Happy. "It was a very conventional era, and who would have thought these off-centre people would become such superstars?"

Peter, Paul and Mary's first album (1962)

In 1962, when the trio's rousing version of Pete Seeger's anthem "If I Had a Hammer" hit No. 10 on the singles chart, Jim Rooney caught them on Cape Cod. "It was an extremely professional and polished act that they had right from the start," he says. "And that was all Albert's doing. He had Chip Monck doing lighting when Chip was just starting out in that business. Everything was already first-class."

While Peter, Paul and Mary earned Grossman his first big money, his private life remained altogether murkier. Few on the Village scene knew, for instance, that he was married to a bisexual junkie prostitute. "David Boyle can confirm this," says Dean Schambach, who was busy making countertops for the new GrossCourt Management offices at 75 East 55th Street. "There were three girls – Betty, Sheila and Jackie – who came to Albert's office and solicited him. And I couldn't believe I was seeing him come in the rear door of the Fat Black Pussycat with Betty Spencer, with snow on the shoulders of his cashmere coat. Because she was a hopeless junkie. But she was also beautiful and brilliant, and he thought that with instruction and guidance she might materialise into something wonderful. And that was Albert's doom. It got grisly."

"Albert was walking on the wild side," says Peter Yarrow. "He had many friends who were on the edge of discovering new dimensions. It was Albert who introduced me to marijuana. I had never smoked a joint. There were many aspects to him that were adventurous, peripheral and even dangerous."

Doomed though his marriage may have been – the couple divorced after nine months – Grossman was now a player, a Village potentate. "He referred to his clients as 'artists', and it was put that way in the contracts," says John Byrne Cooke, who later road-managed acts for Grossman. "He imposed – on people who were not necessarily prone to adopt this position – greater respect for the musicians."

Stories began to filter through about Grossman's negotiation techniques, which relied heavily on the weapon of silence. "He would simply stare at you and say nothing," recalled Charlie Rothschild, poached by Grossman from the Village club Gerde's Folk City. "He wouldn't volunteer any information, and that would drive people crazy. They would keep talking to fill the void, and say anything." When Grossman *did* speak, people listened. "He had this compelling authority in his voice, which was very rich and deep," says Dean Schambach. "He could sometimes get arrogant and splash you around. He would force you to go in his direction, but you couldn't resist it. He knew how to play the Big Daddy role, because a lot of us were like orphans."

As time went on, Grossman created a persona that distinguished him from the other managers in the business. "He came from Chicago in a suit and short hair, and he wound up looking like Ben Franklin," says Paul Fishkin. "He was so hip-looking and such a part of the artists' world that it was very hard for the other business guys to get a read on him and negotiate with him. Because he was nothing like *them*."

"He was extremely eccentric and intimidating," says Michael Friedman. "He used to keep his office so dark, and you'd sit so low in this chair in front of his desk that you couldn't even really see him. There would just be this booming voice from the other side of the desk, and it scared the crap out of everybody."

"Albert was a curious mixture of aggression and shyness," says Milton Glaser. "In some cases he was so withdrawn, and in other cases he would just bully people into submission." Glaser wondered if Grossman's persona was simply a compensation for his outsider status: "Sometimes when people come from Chicago they feel very intimidated by New York, and with him there was certainly a kind of estrangement." Peter Yarrow saw it differently: "I wouldn't say Albert was shy so much as deliberately closed to certain people. With those he didn't know, he could be immediately very combative if he felt they were pulling some kind of interpersonal quick-draw stuff – like, 'Who's got the dominant moment in this room right now?' But there was a warmth and a delight and a joy and a sense of humour that he shared with *all* his artists."

"Albert was a most interesting man," said Edgar Cowan, who accompanied Canadian husband-and-wife duo Ian and Sylvia Tyson to New York in search of a manager. "A lot of people didn't like him, but I liked him an awful lot. [. . .] I found him to be a fascinating guy; a very intellectual guy." The Tysons, though, were under no illusion that Grossman was taking them on for their songs. "He signed us as much for our looks as the music," Ian claimed. "He definitely saw us as a big commercial folk act. He saw in us our clean-cut Canadian naivety."

And then there was the callow, tousle-headed boy who'd just blown into town from small-town Minnesota with a guitar and a headful of Woody Guthrie songs. Bobby Zimmerman looked about fifteen years old but affected the singing voice of a man of fifty. His day-to-day life was based on his Guthrie infatuation and the hipster-dropout persona he'd cobbled together from *On the Road*, *The Catcher in the Rye* and *Rebel Without a Cause*. He called himself Bob Dylan – probably after the Welsh poet who'd drunk himself to death in the Village in 1953 – and fabricated a past that read like a Beat novel. After he surfaced in the Village in January 1961, men were intrigued and women wanted to mother him – even the ones who thought him a phoney. He was naïve, intense, charming and narcissistic in about equal measures. "At the beginning he wasn't that big of a deal," says Norma Cross, who waited on him at the Fat Black Pussycat. "At least *I* didn't think of it that way. But it was always fun to see him and always interesting, because he was different from regular guys."

That summer, Grossman heard Dylan for the first time. He also picked up on the buzz about the kid whose vibe was so different to the wholesomeness of Peter, Paul and Mary. To "Bobby", meanwhile, Grossman resembled Sydney Greenstreet in *The Maltese*

Falcon: "Not your usual shopkeeper," he would note dryly in his *Chronicles*. In the eyes of *New York Times* critic Robert Shelton, whose review of Dylan's set at Gerde's Folk City on 26 September thrust him into the spotlight, the enigmatic manager was "a Cheshire cat in untouched acres of field mice".

According to John Herald, whose Greenbriar Boys were head-lining that night at Gerde's, Dylan was in a state of high excitement before the show. "This was a real big deal, and he knew it," Herald told author David Hajdu. "He was excited. He dressed in a certain way. He asked everybody what he should wear that night, what he should sing . . ." By the time Shelton's review ran, Grossman had homed in on Dylan, convinced he could either make him a star or make lots of money through his songs – preferably both. "Albert was sort of pursuing Bob," says Dean Schambach, who observed Dylan up close as he was soundchecking one afternoon. "Bob was hard to get to know, because he was aloof and remote. But his driving inner force was so powerful, it forced you to love him. It electrified the audience's awe and wonder, and Albert knew this."

"Bobby was hot off the presses and sounding like a copy of Woody in his delivery and his point of view," says Peter Yarrow. "Nobody initially thought of him as somebody who would transform music, but Albert came to me and asked me, 'What do you think about my taking him on?' And he was asking me for two reasons. One was, 'Would you be averse to this for any reason?' And two was, 'Do you think it's a good idea?' And I said, 'I love Bobby and I think he's amazing.' Albert said, 'He's too good not to happen.'"

If dollar signs were flashing before Grossman's eyes, he was pres-cient all the same. None of the other folk managers was convinced by the kid from Minnesota – or even too sure what he was all about. "Albert was the second choice for Bob at that point," says Arline Cunningham, who worked for Woody Guthrie's manager Harold Leventhal. "Bob had done a little audition for us, but people in the office were like, 'We've got Woody, what do we need with this kid?'"

As it turned out, Dylan already *had* a manager named Roy Silver, an archetypal New York hustler who also looked after comedian Bill Cosby. (He had also been helped by Dave Van Ronk's wife Terri Thal.) Legend has it that Grossman flipped a coin with him to see who would get the white folk singer and who the black comedian. "Albert won the toss," says Michael Friedman.

In June 1962 Grossman paid $10,000 to prise Dylan free of Silver. He was taking a chance on an artist who was hardly to everyone's tastes, who sang in an astringent voice, strummed his guitar in the most rudimentary manner, punctuated his Guthrie-esque phrasing with wheezy harmonica phrases and could not have been described as good-looking. "I thought he was a terrible singer and a complete fake," admitted guitarist Bruce Langhorne, who played on a Columbia session for Carolyn Hester that provided Dylan with his first New York studio experience. But Grossman heard what his fellow kingmakers could not: original language, a genuinely nonconformist stance, the authentic voice of post-war youth.

What began as a consequence was a father–son relationship that was mostly about protection – keeping Dylan from the imperatives of commercial crassness – but also about money. "Albert wanted to get into music publishing, which is where all the money is in the music business," said Charlie Rothschild. "He started looking to sign folk singers who could write, and he started calling them poets."

For Joan Baez, there was a "general strangeness and mystique" about Dylan. He was, she said, "already a legend by the time he got his foot into Gerde's". Grossman was simply hip enough to see the edge of intelligence and irreverence and, yes, weirdness that others could not. As a result he became almost as much of a legend as Dylan himself. "We heard about Albert before we ever met him," says John Byrne Cooke, the urbane son of British broadcaster Alistair and a member of Club 47 regulars the Charles River Boys. "We heard that from the moment he signed Dylan he said, 'Bob Dylan does not play coffee houses, he plays concerts.'"*

Dylan knew enough about folk morality to know that, for many on the scene, Grossman was The Enemy: a capitalist pig, or at least a capitalist bear. "He was kind of like a Colonel Tom Parker figure," Dylan said in the 2005 documentary *No Direction Home*. "He was all immaculately dressed every time you'd see him. You could smell him coming." Yet Dylan knew he needed Grossman to make his dreams come true. "A lot of Albert did in fact turn up in Bob," noted Al Aronowitz, the *New York Post* journalist who became one of Dylan's most ardent champions. "If I never got a straight answer out of Bob, I never got one of Albert either. [They] weren't cut from the same cloth but from the same stone wall."

By July 1962, in a contract that would give Grossman 20 per cent of his overall earnings and 25 per cent of his gross recording income, Dylan had signed to Grossman for seven years. He was already contracted to Columbia, whose blue-blood A&R man John Hammond distrusted almost everything about Grossman and would soon be butting heads with him over Dylan.† "The mere mention of Grossman's name just about gave [Hammond] apoplexy," Dylan would write in *Chronicles*.

Twelve months later, with Dylan feted by the folk establishment at that year's Newport festival, money and radical politics converged in Peter, Paul and Mary's version of his song "Blowin' in the Wind". "It was an act of pure premeditated genius," says Peter Walker, who ran the Folklore Center in Boston. "The idea of taking Dylan, who had no commercial appeal, and connecting him to Peter, Paul and Mary was a one–two punch – the Dylan songs and the Peter, Paul and Mary act, which brought those political camps together. So everybody stepped back and let this thing happen."

Yarrow told Dylan he might make as much as $5,000 from "Blowin'

---

* This wasn't strictly true: Dylan was still playing coffee houses in October 1962.
† After the pronounced failure of his Columbia debut album, Dylan was famously referred to in the company as "Hammond's Folly".

in the Wind". Unbeknownst to Dylan, who didn't read his contracts very closely, Grossman would be making the same amount. In fact, Grossman was already wealthy enough that year to buy himself a Rolls-Royce. To anyone who flinched at the commissions that he took from his clients – 10 per cent more than the industry standard – Grossman would respond that "every time you talk to me you're 10 per cent smarter than you were before". And he was probably right: 75 per cent of what Grossman made for you was usually more than 85 per cent of what most other managers would have brought in. "I thought he was incredible," says Grossman's friend Ronnie Lyons. "I was used to seeing groups getting offered 3 per cent royalties and never getting paid. Albert was scoring 18 per cent, 21 per cent royalty deals for his artists *and* getting tour support. He had a master's degree in theoretical economics and he used it well."

"In those days contracts were essentially indentured servitude for five or seven years with a fixed royalty rate," says Jonathan Taplin, who later road-managed The Band for Grossman. "Albert introduced the idea that you could renegotiate a record deal in the middle of the contract. As soon as one of his artists began to get successful, Albert would say, 'We're gonna go on strike.' He threatened that with Dylan at Columbia and he did it with Peter, Paul and Mary too. People like Clive Davis and Mo Ostin loved Albert on one level and feared him on another." (One of Grossman's favourite threats to record labels was: "If the bird's not happy, the bird don't sing.")

"What you see today in the music business is the result of Albert," said record executive Bob Krasnow. "He changed the whole idea of what a negotiation was all about."

4

"THE GREATEST PLACE"

By the time Bob Dylan's "Blowin' in the Wind" was turbo-charging the folk-protest movement in the summer of 1963, Albert Grossman had become a wealthy man. His financial advisors suggested it was time to invest some of his money.

Milton and Shirley Glaser had owned a second home on Woodstock's Lewis Hollow Road for almost a decade. When a check-out girl at the town's Grand Union supermarket mentioned that a large stone house had come on the market in nearby Bearsville, Shirley took down the details. Fairfields had been home to the late John Striebel, who illustrated the popular *Dixie Dugan* cartoon strip written by J. P. McEvoy. (Woodstock occasionally appeared in the cartoon as "Stoodwock".) Following his death in May 1962, Striebel's widow Fritzi decided to sell up and downsize.

"It was always a party house," says Richard Heppner. "Striebel was a good musician himself and often played with fellow Woodstock artists." (Other regulars at Fairfields were Sam Eskin and pianist/accordionist Clemmie Nessel, a much-loved Woodstock music teacher.) The asking price for the house, set in almost sixty acres of land, was an eye-watering $50,000. "We didn't know a single person that had $50,000 except Albert," says Milton Glaser. "He had no direct reason why he would be interested in Bearsville, outside of the fact that people often called him bear-like." (As it happened, the hamlet of Bearsville had nothing to do with the local bears: the name came from German immigrant Christian Baehr, who'd established a post office there in the mid-nineteenth century.)

When he came up to visit the Glasers, Grossman looked over the

Striebel property and instantly fell in love with it.* "You know what
he paid for that house?" says Ronnie Lyons. "$7,500 down and $150
a month in repayments. He used to brag about that all the time."
While some of his peers in the business expressed surprise at his
choice of second home, those closer to Grossman understood precisely why he'd bought it. "The folk-music community would never
have gone out to the Hamptons," says Jonathan Taplin. "If you were
going to have a place outside of New York City, the idea of going to
what had been an art colony was probably a smart move. It was in
keeping with the folk aesthetic, which was very much rooted in this
don't-show-off kind of thing."

It didn't hurt that Peter Yarrow had spent much of his life in
Woodstock. And when he invited Bob Dylan up to stay at his moth-
er's cabin, the area made even more sense to Grossman. "Albert
had great taste and he fell in love with the place," says Arline
Cunningham. "I suspect that he wanted a place to hide out with
Bob."

Dylan himself first came to Woodstock with his girlfriend Suze
Rotolo, whom he had met in late July 1961. She was the politi-
cised daughter of socialist parents, a "red-diaper baby" raised on
Guthrie and Seeger songs and by now working for the Congress of
Racial Equality. Dylan was besotted with her and inspired by her
to write several of his most powerful love songs. She reciprocated,
though she took his exotic version of his past with a pinch of salt.
The pair were inseparable, snuggling up against the winter cold in
his West 4th Street apartment or hanging out with Yarrow, Dave
Van Ronk and others.

Though Rotolo remembered staying at his mother's cabin in late

* In *Chronicles*, Bob Dylan claimed it was *he* who had told his manager
about Woodstock, and had swung by the town with him after a gig at Syracuse
University's Regent Theatre on 3 November 1963. According to Dylan, Grossman
"spied a house he liked and bought it there and then". Then again, you can't
believe everything you read in *Chronicles*.

May of 1963, Peter Yarrow dates it slightly later: "It was the summer of the March on Washington, and I called Bobby and said, 'Come on up, it's sweltering in the city.'" Rotolo had been to Woodstock with the Art Students' League in the fifties – and met Yarrow there – but this was Dylan's first trip to the Catskills. "It was a very innocent and joyous time," Yarrow says. "Bobby fell in love with the place." While Yarrow and Rotolo took off to go sketching with the League, Dylan remained behind in the cabin, recalled by guitarist Mike Bloomfield as "a little two-room hut [. . .] isolated out in the woods". "We would come back with a picture," Yarrow says, "and Bobby would have written 'Only a Pawn in Their Game'. Out of him would spout these extraordinary, earth-shaking songs, but in personal terms he was laughing all the time. 'Bob Dylan's Dream' feels like the spirit we shared in Woodstock at that time."

After Dylan appeared at that summer's Newport Folk Festival – with Yarrow hailing him as "the most important folk artist in America today" – the attention on the young prodigy grew almost exponentially. Where the folk revival had been about just that – reviving – *The Freewheelin' Bob Dylan* (1963) transformed folk music into a potent mouthpiece for politicised poetry. Excessive weight was placed on Dylan's scrawny shoulders. Angry young men and women wanted answers, even if they were blowing in the wind.

Dylan both loved and feared the attention; his new fame was doing strange things to his head. "Even though he intentionally sought success, I don't think he thought about the side effects," says Norma Cross. "I don't think he knew that he wouldn't be able to walk down the street." Both in New York and on tour, he was constantly hailed and hassled as a savant and a seer. The more glaring the spotlight, the more of a bolt-hole Woodstock became. "The kids all wanted to crowd around," says John Byrne Cooke. "There comes a point where if you're Bob you think, 'I want to get out of here.'" Dylan told Robert Shelton that Woodstock was a place where "we stop the clouds, turn time back and inside out, make the sun turn on and off". He said it was "the greatest, man, the greatest place".

"Woodstock was a place where you could kind of go and get your thoughts together," Dylan reflected in 2014. "There were plenty of painters who lived in that area, but very few musicians. We certainly didn't know anybody up there playing any music. Later there was, but when we were up there [in the] middle Sixties, we were pretty much by ourselves." As intoxicating as New York had been for him, Dylan was a small-town boy at heart and worked better with peace and quiet around him. It helped that Woodstockers didn't bother him the way people did on the sidewalks of Greenwich Village. Many of the locals didn't even know who he was, figuring he was just a freaky beatnik from the Art Students' League.[*]

It didn't take long for Albert Grossman to invite his hottest young artist to stay in Bearsville, less than a mile from the Yarrows' cabin. Soon Dylan would have his own room in the house, and then the use of one of the property's cottages. Grossman was busy turning the Striebel house into a shrine to his own taste, complete with the finest furnishings and appurtenances. "He was the first yuppie, really," says Paul Fishkin. "He was always diddling around in his kitchen with condiments from India that nobody else had. There was the best dried salami hung up, and he was always slicing shit up and offering it to you."

Helping Grossman spend his *nouveau* riches was a pretty Hunter College literature dropout, thirteen years his junior. Sally Buhler had seen him around the Village as she waited tables at the Café Wha? and the Bitter End. "I had real upward mobility as a waitress,"

---

[*] Even so, compared to the surrounding Catskills towns Woodstock was the quintessence of hip. "I don't know if we were [hip] or not, but we felt that way," recalls Jeremy Wilber, who grew up in the town in the fifties and early sixties. "While we were watching *The Seventh Seal*, all the other kids in school were watching *Under the Yum Yum Tree* with Jack Lemmon." Wilber and his hip Woodstock pals would joke that people in Shandaken "still ate out of wooden bowls and skinned dogs, and at that time I don't think it was very far from being true".

she joked later, adding that "back then Albert never even said hello to me". No less ambitious than Grossman, Sally quickly hitched her wagon to his star. They made quite a power couple, both in Manhattan and in Bearsville. "Our life was incredibly intense," she remembered. "Every night about thirty of us would meet at Albert's office to go out. The office was constantly packed with people – Peter, Paul and Mary, of course, but also Ian and Sylvia, Richie Havens, Gordon Lightfoot, other musicians, artists, poets . . ."

Some even thought Buhler was calling the shots behind the scenes. "The way it was told to me," says her friend Peter Walker, "*she* was the brains behind the throne, the motivator. She was young, she was brilliant, she was beautiful. And the plan started to unfold. It really was a tremendously successful enterprise."

In the summer of 1963 Dylan's relationship with Suze Rotolo started to unravel. Discovering he had kept his real name a secret was troubling enough to her; realising that he was secretive about much else besides was too much – especially after she got pregnant by him. "I believe in his genius," she wrote in a notebook the following year; "he is an extraordinary writer but I don't think of him as an honorable person . . ." She compared him to Picasso in the way he "took no responsibility" in his relationships. Peter Yarrow, who had grown fond of her, began to see Dylan as he really was: "I looked upon him, as I do on most of us, as someone with severe faults and feet of clay."

Others thought Dylan distraught after Rotolo moved out of 161 West 4th Street. They noticed how Grossman and Buhler tended to him in Bearsville, feeding him in their well-stocked kitchen. "Bob hadn't sunk his own roots yet, so being up there was a protection," says Daniel Kramer, who photographed him in Woodstock and the city in 1964. "It made perfect sense to go and hide out with Albert in the country, because these were the people he could trust." Still others thought Grossman was feeding Dylan's incipient paranoia. "Before Albert, he was accessible," said blues singer-guitarist John

Hammond Jr, son of the Columbia executive who'd fallen out with Grossman. Hammond felt that Grossman was deliberately creating "a mystique of exclusiveness" around Dylan, "secluding him away up in Woodstock".

When Mason Hoffenberg, co-author of the scandalous soft-porn novel *Candy*, visited the Bearsville house he was disappointed to find it so quiet. "I thought I was going to have a ball, because Dylan was real famous then, with girls climbing all over him," said the man who first met Dylan in Berlin. "But instead of fun, it was grim, like a museum. Dylan was very uptight . . . because he's not really into balling groupies. Millions of girls were going berserk to get to him and he was doing things like hiding in the closet whenever the door opened."

"Just as he'd protected Peter, Paul and Mary, Albert protected Bobby," says Peter Yarrow. "And in terms of Woodstock, that's where the darker side of his genius enters. Because for all his bravado, Bobby was a very sensitive and delicate entity and needed to be protected. People wanted to get high with him and get busted with him or get into bed with him. Being the object of that kind of fame and pursuit was not a comfortable thing. In Woodstock, Albert partially created this division between the people that were in and the people that were out."

As his relationship with Rotolo went through its death throes, Dylan set his sights on a new consort. "Somebody got him over to a party in Cambridge where he met Joan Baez," says John Byrne Cooke (though the two singers had met before that April 1963 encounter). "There was a natural connection between Cambridge and Greenwich Village. Dylan and Albert got to know people in our scene, and we got to know people in *theirs*." Baez instinctively knew that Dylan's songs would transform folk music. Meanwhile he was in awe of her "heart-stopping soprano voice" and intricate guitar-picking.

In the late summer of 1963, before they sang together at the

March on Washington on 28 August, Dylan and Baez spent time
together in Bearsville. They swam in Grossman's pool, watched
movies and rode Dylan's new Triumph motorcycle through the surrounding hills. Though he was a terrible motorcyclist – and an even
worse driver of automobiles – he loved to bomb around Woodstock's
back roads. "I have rode alone tho thru the hills on backroads", he
wrote to Rotolo, "an have discovered all kinds of magic places an
great sweepin views . . ."

Dylan took to riding the Triumph east along Tinker Street to the
Café Espresso – "the Depresso", as local wits referred to it. "He
was so relaxed then," remembered Mary Lou Paturel, who was
introduced to Dylan in the café by Tom Paxton. "[He was] smiling,
very shy, witty, Chaplinesque. He wasn't Bob Dylan, he was Bobby
Zimmerman." Fern Malkine, daughter of singer Sonia, remembers
Dylan hanging out at the café after his Carnegie Hall concert on

The Café Espresso, summer 1962 (courtesy of the Paturel family)

26 October 1963. "He was just a little scruffy guy sitting at a table,"
she says. "He was always very nice to me. He'd come in with his
dark sunglasses, smoking a lot, and say, 'Hey girl, heeey . . .' And my
mother would say, 'Bob, she's only fifteen!'" When he came in with
Baez, says Malkine, "she seemed very nervous about the relationship, but I didn't know what was going on or care a lot". A decade
later, Baez's sweetly pained "Diamonds and Rust" included a lyrical
snapshot of Dylan in Woodstock, "standing with brown leaves falling all around and the snow in your hair".

According to producer Paul Rothchild, it was in Woodstock in
April 1964 that Dylan – in the company of his bodyguard Victor
Maymudes and of Rothchild himself – first took LSD. "We drove
straight back [from New England] to Albert Grossman's new house
. . . where Dylan had a room at the end of the hall," Rothchild told
Bob Spitz. "When we got there, we discovered that Albert was
out of town. Bob started smoking grass, everyone else was higher
than a kite and hungry. We all had a serious case of the munchies.
Sometime after midnight, Victor was dispatched to the refrigerator,
where he found a couple of tabs of acid wrapped in aluminium foil
[. . .] So we dropped acid on Bob." For Rothchild, "that was the
beginning of the mystical Sixties right there".

Bernard and Mary Lou Paturel's bistro slowly became Dylan's
home away from home – especially after a stinging *Newsweek* profile in November 1963 that exposed many of his autobiographical
claims as fictions. "As soon as he began to get famous in late '63,
there were a lot of obsessive fans who would come up to him on the
street in an almost aggressive way," says Jonathan Taplin. "Whereas
he could hang out at the Espresso and not be bothered. And then,
of course, in Albert's house he could be *incredibly* private. Albert
had a long driveway and a bunch of 'No Trespassing' signs."

Soon Dylan was spending so much time at the Espresso – drinking
coffee, playing chess, reading the *New York Times* – that the Paturels
asked if he wanted to work in the room above it. Painted white with

a beamed ceiling, the room measured thirty feet by twenty and had windows that overlooked Tinker Street. It also had a couch and a small desk at which Dylan could write. He gratefully accepted the offer and moved a guitar and a typewriter into the room. "It was supposed to be a secret," says Billy Faier. "But of course everyone knew it." Sometimes Dylan even stayed there overnight: Mary Lou Paturel would hear him tapping at the typewriter at three in the morning. "He kind of moved in with us and held a symbolic key to the room," Bernard Paturel told Robert Shelton. "No rent involved, just a mutual understanding that he could stay there whenever he wanted." Dylan had found another set of surrogate parents.

It was in the "White Room" that Dylan began to veer away from the topical songs inspired by Rotolo. After *The Times They Are a-Changin'*, with its anthemic hymn of a title track, he wearied of the role he'd been given by folk's old guard. New songs like "It Ain't Me, Babe" and "My Back Pages" rejected those who'd loved and supported but also, he felt, restricted him. When these and other inward-looking songs saw the light of day in August 1964, it was on a long-player entitled *Another Side of Bob Dylan*, recorded in a single Beaujolais-fuelled night in June. For Suze Rotolo, the album made for tough listening. "Bob sure knew how to maul me," she wrote. "I felt laid bare and sorry for it."

Dylan may never have been happier than he was during the summer of 1964. Much of that had to do with feeling ensconced in the bosom of the Paturel family. When *Look* photographer Douglas Gilbert came to Woodstock in June, he took shots of a smiling Dylan with Bernard, Mary Lou and their children. He also photographed him at work in the "White Room", realising later that the singer had been typing out liner notes for his new album. John Sebastian, a jug-band singer who'd become a friend of Dylan's in the Village, visited and ended up in several of Gilbert's shots.

At a point in Dylan's career when he was already writing the acerbic songs on *Bringing It All Back Home*, these endearing images – unseen for forty years – give us a preview of the contented family man to come: still young and boyish, still capable of carefree-ness before the whirlwind of notoriety struck. Gilbert's pictures of Dylan in Grossman's kitchen with a visiting Allen Ginsberg – one of Dylan's heroes and now a friend and mentor – tell a similar story. Sitting in on the shots are Sally Buhler, along with Al Aronowitz and his young son Myles. "We all thought he was God," Aronowitz later said of Dylan, though he also compared him to Billy the Kid.

Dylan by now had his own guest cottage on Grossman's estate: he could come and go regardless of whether his manager was at home or in New York attending to his other artists. He also had a minder and driver in the form of Maymudes, a sometime actor, poet and occasional singer who was six years Dylan's senior. "Victor was a very complex guy and a very talented musician," says Billy Faier, who had known him on the West Coast. "He played the guitar and wrote some very beautiful songs, but he hid his light under a bushel." Suze Rotolo found Maymudes "silent and creepy", and others thought him intimidating; Faier maintains that he was actually very gentle.

David Boyle, who vacated the largest of Grossman's three cot-tages for Dylan, had moved up from the city in April 1963 to help Grossman with building and planning permissions. Among the pleasant surprises on offer in his employer's home were the atten-tions of the young women there: not only Buhler, but a former room-mate of hers from the city. Born Shirley Noznisky in Wilmington, Delaware, Sara Lownds was the twenty-four-year-old daughter of a Belarusian-Jewish scrap-metal dealer. As a seventeen-year-old she had traumatically found her father's body after he was shot dead in a hold-up. Later she moved to New York, modelling for *Harper's Bazaar* and working as a Playboy Bunny ("Vicky"), before marrying photographer Hans Lownds and changing her name to the more poetic Sara. In October 1961 she gave birth to a daughter, Maria, but became estranged from Lownds, preferring the company of hipper people her own age in Greenwich Village. "Sara was, of course, beautiful," says Norma Cross, who knew her when she was separating from Lownds. "She had a great style about her, but there was a sadness too."

With little Maria in tow, Sara moved into Sally Buhler's West 8th Street apartment in 1962. "I thought Sally was maybe more interested in women," says Donn Pennebaker, director of the Dylan documentary *Dont Look Back*. "She kind of hit it off with Nico, but then she started hanging out with Albert. All the young women were interested in being Playboy Bunnies, because there was a lot of action there. People were trying to get Sally to do it, but she seemed kind of vulnerable. I suspected that Albert was going to be her protector."

In late 1963 Buhler invited Lownds up to Bearsville. "She was a very beautiful girl," says Billy Faier, whom Norma Cross introduced to her in Woodstock. "We sat around in Norma's kitchen for a couple of hours while they did the *I Ching*, and finally I found myself alone with Sara in her bedroom. We did not get it on, but I spent some nice time with her and she told me a lot about her marriage to Hans." Exactly when Bob Dylan first met Sara Lownds isn't clear; her stepson Peter thought they'd crossed paths as early as 1962, and that Dylan was the reason her marriage had ended.* But Dylan was still seeing – and regularly performing with – Joan Baez in the summer of 1964. Indeed, the two folk stars spent much of that August together at Bearsville while the Grossmans were on honeymoon in Mexico. Joining them were Baez's beautiful sister Mimi and Mimi's writer husband Richard Fariña, who were about to record their first album together as a duo. The four of them drove down to the city for Baez's 8 August concert at Forest Hills tennis stadium – where a soused Dylan sang with her during the

---

* To the *Daily Mirror*'s Don Short, in 1969, Dylan mischievously claimed that he and Sara "grew up together as kids in Minnesota", then "met again in a New York restaurant where [she] was working as a waitress".

second half of the show – but otherwise remained in Bearsville.*

Dick Fariña was working on the novel that became *Been Down So Long It Looks Like Up to Me*, creating a competitive tension with Dylan, who struggled with his own book while also working on songs. If Dylan was the star, the Harvard-educated Fariña had the greater literary cachet. Fariña was meanwhile envious enough of Dylan's fame to suggest to Mimi they ask Grossman to manage them. Remembering her sister's rejection of Grossman's overtures five years earlier, Mimi told Dick she was "not going to sign with that fat pig". Without even telling her, the ambitious Fariña signed them to Grossman anyway.

In the afternoons, once he'd got enough work done, Dylan took Baez on more motorcycle trips around town and up into the mountains. He was now riding a cherry-red Triumph 350 acquired from Barry Feinstein, a photographer he'd met through Grossman. (Feinstein, the husband of Mary Travers, had shot the portrait of a contemptuous-looking Dylan on the cover of *The Times They Are a-Changin'*.) As they had the previous year, Dylan and Baez often wound up at the Espresso, where the greatest discretion was observed by the Paturels. One night they were at the café with the Fariñas and Peter Yarrow when a behind-closed-doors jam session broke out after dinner. "I played the spoons," says Daniel Kramer, who had just arrived in town to photograph the Fariñas. "I was so thrilled. It was one of the great nights of my life."

But all was not entirely well within the Dylan–Baez relationship, and the presence of Sara Lownds in town wasn't helping matters.

---

* Another house Dylan and Baez stayed in, according to Bruce Dorfman, was the home of painter Arnold Blanch, halfway between the Playhouse and the Art Students' League. Dylan was also a regular visitor to the Plochmann Lane home of artist-singer Ed Chavez.

5

BOY IN THE BUBBLE

If Bob Dylan had always been capable of cruelty, he now surrounded himself with a coterie of cronies who actively encouraged
his mean streak. They included Eric Andersen, Jack Elliott, David
Cohen (aka David Blue) and others. But foremost among them was
the charismatic Bobby Neuwirth, a Boston-based painter who sang
and played banjo and hung around Club 47.

"Bobby didn't play a lot but he was painting and he'd been to the
Boston Museum School," says John Byrne Cooke, who'd roomed
with Neuwirth in Cambridge. "You could say there was a certain
similarity of style between him and Dylan. It was a synergistic relationship. Dylan was not exactly a chameleon, but there were a number of people that he drew from." Dylan himself would compare
Neuwirth to Neal Cassady, the inspiration for Dean Moriarty in
Kerouac's *On the Road*, writing in *Chronicles* that "you had to brace
yourself when you talked to him" and that he "ripped and slashed
and could make anybody uneasy".

Neuwirth had first met Dylan in 1961 but was now firmly at the
heart of his inner circle, to the point where some onlookers thought
he had the singer under a spell. "I could never figure out whether
it was Dylan who'd copped Neuwirth's style or vice versa," wrote Al
Aronowitz, one of their many victims. But Al Kooper, who got to
know the duo the following year, was convinced that "Neuwirth was
actually the personality: he was the creator of the image and Dylan
just jumped on it".

If the Dylan-and-Neuwirth combo was at its most vicious holding
court in the Village at the Kettle of Fish – where rivals like Phil Ochs

were routinely humiliated – it was no less lethal up in Woodstock. "What they used to do, they called a 'truth attack'," says Billy Faier. "Upstairs at the Espresso, I'm talking to the Paturels about running for office in Woodstock. Dylan starts a truth attack: do I really think I could do any good, even if I won, which I undoubtedly wouldn't. All this really negative stuff. He would interrupt me whenever he wanted, and then Neuwirth would interrupt in specific places where he was supposed to. You could see the pattern."

Faier also observed the cruelty later meted out to Victor Maymudes. "Victor was no longer Dylan's sidekick, but we're in Woodstock and he says, 'Hey, I'm going up to visit Albert, you wanna come?'" Faier recalls. "So we go to Albert's and he's sitting at a big table outside with everybody, and Sally is waiting on them, and we're both just sitting there with our thumbs up our asses. You could see that Victor was miserable, but he couldn't tear himself away. So I said, 'Come on, these people are not your friends.' And we left." Maymudes later described Grossman as "an asshole who bent over for quarters when thousands were flying by".

Others were more forgiving of the "mind guard" that Neuwirth provided for Dylan. "Neuwirth was kind of a guide dog, and Bob needed that," says Donn Pennebaker. "Bob felt very vulnerable to certain attitudes and tried to avoid them whenever he could. And Neuwirth helped to keep him out of this morass. Bob expressed it sometimes as throwing pearls to swine: the idea of trying to explain what he was doing, to people who didn't understand. Neuwirth protected him from that role."

Among those who now felt the sting of Dylan's and Neuwirth's sadism was Joan Baez, whose treatment went far beyond affectionate teasing. Deciding that she was the epitome of all that was uncool – the embodiment of unctuous folk goodness, in fact – they undermined and belittled her at every turn. Like a neglected puppy following its abusive master, she strung along on Dylan's English tour in the spring of 1965, Pennebaker filming her humiliation for all to see. By her own admission she couldn't tear herself away.

Just as he had two-timed Suze Rotolo with Joan Baez, so now Dylan two-timed Baez with Sara Lownds. "Don't worry," Mimi Fariña overheard him say on the phone after her sister had gone. "She just left." Lownds was a kind of Jewish Madonna: there was something mysterious and melancholy about her that made her an irresistible muse. "It was almost like she was surrounded by mist," says Norma Cross. "She was very involved in mystical or spiritual things. We were all throwing the *I Ching* in those days, but Sara went beyond that." A decade later, on *Desire*'s "Sara", Dylan called her his "radiant jewel, mystical wife", a "glamorous nymph with an arrow and bow". At least a part of the attraction for him was that she wasn't overawed by him.

"She was just gorgeous-looking," says Donn Pennebaker. "If we accept the Schopenhauer idea that you recognise in somebody the children you want to have, maybe something like that took place for Bob." In New York he moved into the Chelsea Hotel to be near Lownds and her daughter. In Woodstock, meanwhile, he installed them in Vera Yarrow's cabin. "We made a picture in the backyard," says Daniel Kramer of a March 1965 photo session there. "We emptied out the shed and Sara posed for me. We called it 'The Shack'." Sara had already appeared in photographs taken by Douglas Gilbert at the Espresso, where – with short, boyish hair and wearing a Breton shirt – she was the object of besotted glances from not just Dylan but John Sebastian, Victor Maymudes and Mason Hoffenberg. "He obviously fell for her," Sally Grossman told David Hajdu, adding that Dylan wanted the relationship to be kept quiet. "That was one of our jobs, to help give him that privacy." Over a decade later, Lownds and Baez would reminisce about the months when Dylan was seeing them both; they even appeared together in his 1978 film *Renaldo & Clara*. Off-camera, Baez alluded to a "lovely blue nightgown" that Dylan had once given her. "Oh, *that's* where it went," Sara said with a laugh.

As hard as it was for Baez to view Dylan dispassionately, she was genuinely concerned as she watched him being enveloped by what she described as "a huge transparent bubble of ego". Irwin Silber said much the same thing in his famous "Open Letter to Bob Dylan", published in the November 1964 edition of *Sing Out!*: "You travel with an entourage now – with good buddies who are going to laugh when you need laughing and drink wine with you and ensure your privacy – and never challenge you to face everyone else's reality again."

Even before her humiliation in England, Baez was alarmed by the changes in Dylan – changes that had at least something to do with a trip he made into New York in late August of 1964. It was Al Aronowitz who'd suggested that Maymudes drive Dylan down from Bearsville to meet the Beatles at the Delmonico Hotel. Aronowitz had reported on the group's tumultuous arrival in America that February, and now he had a green light from John Lennon to extend an invitation to one of their only real peers. "I want to meet him," Lennon told Aronowitz, "but on my own terms." Aronowitz recalled the meeting as initially "very awkward, very demure . . . nobody wanted to step on anybody's ego". The encounter has gone down in pop history as the day Dylan turned the Beatles on to marijuana, but equally important was the effect the meeting had on Dylan, who – at the time he saw their show at the Paramount Theatre on 20 September – was becoming a bona fide pop star. And when the Fab Four's fellow British invaders the Animals hit No. 1 that month with their version of "The House of the Rising Sun" – a song he had himself sung – Dylan was knocked out by its bluesy electric arrangement.

"When I first met him, Bob was a folk-music protest singer and he pooh-poohed rock music," Al Aronowitz told me. "My position was that today's hits are tomorrow's folk music. Later he wrote me a letter from England telling me that I was right. My wife even drove him to Rondout Music in Kingston to buy an electric guitar." Dylan was hardly a stranger to rock 'n' roll: he'd played in amplified bands back in Minnesota; his first Columbia single used electric backing. But he knew full well how the *Sing Out!* crowd would respond to any "Beatle-isation" of his music. Over Christmas and New Year 1964/5, with band arrangements in his head, he spent two weeks in wintry Woodstock finishing up the songs for his fifth album in the "White Room". "My songs're written with the kettledrum in mind," he stated in the liner notes to *Bringing It All Back Home*, adding that his poems were "written in a rhythm of unpoetic distortion/divided by pierced ears".

When that album was released in late March 1965, it was split between electric and acoustic sides. Producer Tom Wilson, heard howling with laughter at the false start of "Bob Dylan's 115th Dream", brought in a trusted crew of New York session men that included guitarists Bruce Langhorne and Al Gorgoni, pianist Paul Griffin, drummer Bobby Gregg and film director Spike Lee's father Bill on bass. As Daniel Kramer's shots from the session show, spirits were infectiously high: the album was the sound of Dylan breaking free of folk constrictions while still delivering acoustic classics in the bracingly nihilistic "It's Alright Ma" and the closing kiss-off of "It's All Over Now, Baby Blue". "Obviously Bob liked Elvis Presley and all that," Sally Grossman said in 2014. "You know, rock and roll was going to be more fun. Plus he was pretty smart, Bob, and how far could he go with that folk music thing?"

As striking as Dylan's new electric sound was the cover shot for *Bringing It All Back Home*. The portrait – taken by Daniel Kramer in the sitting room of Grossman's Bearsville house and featuring a languorous Sally draped across a chaise longue in a red dress bought from a boutique on St Mark's Place – made Dylan's intentions plain. He was no longer the baby-faced faux-hobo who worshipped Woody Guthrie; he was a svelte, almost hostile-looking star cradling a grey cat like some James Bond villain.

"Cool" was now vital to Dylan as he geared up to promote his new

record. Cool meant not showing your feelings and it meant medi-
cating them with drugs, foremost among them amphetamine. Cool
was how Dylan and his inner circle played most of their social inter-
actions, and how Grossman played them too. Some even perceived a
kind of three-way dynamic between Grossman, Dylan and Neuwirth.

"[They] were a very special trio," wrote Suze Rotolo. "They were
very different people and they weren't really a trio – more like two
duos with Dylan in common." Rotolo witnessed their cruelty when
she stayed in Bearsville with Grossman and his wife in the summer
of 1965. Dylan was "thin and tight and hostile" and had "succumbed
to demons". It was depressing, she said, to watch the fawning
hangers-on "bow and scrape to the reigning king and his jester",
and she saw afresh what a "lying shit of a guy" he was with women.
"I think the whole Albert thing was so destructive for him," Joan
Baez told Anthony Scaduto in 1971, "and it's so sad because Albert
used to think he was doing right by people, money and fame . . ."
When Scaduto asked if Grossman was "screwing up [Dylan's] mind"
by enabling or even encouraging his truth attacks, Baez replied that
"*everyone* was, around Bobby, because he's so powerful".

It was Sara Lownds, officially the new woman in Dylan's life, who
arranged for him to see Donn Pennebaker's 1953 film *Daybreak
Express*. From the screening came the notion of shooting a *cinéma-
vérité* documentary about Dylan's upcoming tour of England.
"I don't think I was Bob's choice but Albert's," says Pennebaker.
"Albert was looking for somebody who had done some film-making
but who could get into that world. I was going to shoot some stuff,
and Dylan would get used to being shot in that style." Pennebaker
warmed to Grossman, who became the same kind of father figure
for him that he was for Dylan. "I liked him and I liked the role he
played with Dylan. He went along, he was interested in what happened. He didn't just sit at a desk and type."

Pennebaker is all too aware that the resulting film, which became
a cult classic after its 1967 release, fixed Grossman in the pop-culture

imagination as unsympathetic and charmless – not least when, with
Dylan looking on admiringly, he informs the manager of Sheffield's
Grand Hotel that he is "one of the dumbest assholes and most stupid persons I've ever spoken to in my life," adding that "if it was
some place else, I'd punch you in your goddamn nose".

"Albert could be very aggressive to people who blocked his
way," says Pennebaker, "but he never was with me." Interestingly,
Grossman didn't mind how he came across in *Dont Look Back*; if
anything, he was proud of it. "Once we went down to the Kettle of
Fish," says Pennebaker, "and a woman came up and berated him
for a scene in the film. She really was giving it to him, and I was
sitting there amazed. Finally she went away, and I said, 'Albert, I
didn't realise I was messing up your life with that film.' He said,

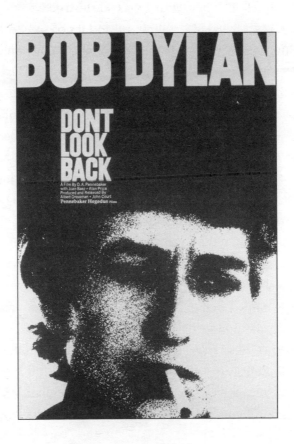

'Don't worry, it's never going to be a problem.' He loved the way we didn't compromise the film." For Pennebaker, Grossman's paternal protectiveness towards Dylan was crucial. "I don't think people saw Albert as an ogre in the film," he says. "They just saw him as the way Dylan had to meet the world. Albert kept him from doing things he might have been ready to do."

In *Eat the Document*, the disjointed and little-seen film Dylan pieced together about his 1966 European tour, an English journalist asks Grossman if he knows whether his client is enjoying the tour. "We don't talk to each other like that," Grossman unsmilingly replies. Profiling Dylan for the *Saturday Evening Post* that year, Jules Siegel described how, around Grossman, the singer would go "into a kind of piping whine, the voice of a little boy complaining to his father". In *Dont Look Back*, Dylan rarely addresses Grossman, who hovers in the shadows of hotel suites and dressing rooms, only occasionally grunting in a dreary baritone reminiscent of Henry Kissinger. "I came up with a nickname for Albert that stuck," said Nick Gravenites of the Grossman-managed Electric Flag. "*Cumulus Nimbus*. We called him the Cloud. You could see it – it's huge, grey and august – but when you went up to touch it, it wasn't there."

For anyone who did business with Grossman, *Dont Look Back* made for some calling card. "It was a groundbreaking, momentous film because of the magic of what was going on with Dylan," says Paul Fishkin. "You were watching Dylan transitioning into this rock guy, and at the same time you gained a little insight into the business side with Albert. You could see a contemporary manager who understood the artist so well while dealing for the most part with people who didn't. I think Dylan loved that Albert was this killer guy who loved to torture business people."

Watching the film today, it is clear that Dylan is not only operating within a "huge transparent bubble of ego" – abetted by Grossman and the goading Neuwirth – but is deeply bored by the act that's served him so well for four years. The performances of songs such as

"The Times They Are a-Changin'" are perfunctory and almost con-temptuous. Having reinvented himself on record as an electric per-former, he now acts and dresses like the foppish English pop groups making such waves in America. In London he buys polka-dot shirts and Anello & Davide boots. He lets his hair grow into a tousled nest and constantly masks his eyes with sunglasses. Amphetamines make him aggressive, and he has tantrums unbecoming in a four-year-old. When his advances towards Marianne Faithfull are rebuffed, he yells at her to leave his hotel room.

In a pained letter to her sister in early May, Joan Baez noted that even Bobby Neuwirth was "going mad with it all". But it was Neuwirth who delivered the knockout punch when – with Dylan sniggering behind her – he cast aspersions on the size of Baez's breasts. Deeply hurt, she left for Paris the next day. When she returned two weeks later, she learned of Dylan's dirty little secret. After he was admitted to St Mary's Hospital in Paddington – he'd been dosed with acid, claims Clinton Heylin – Baez's knock at the door of his room was answered by none other than Sara Lownds.

"I was just trying to deal with the madness that had become my career," Dylan explained disingenuously in 2009. "[And] unfortu-nately [Joan] got swept along and I felt very bad about it. I was sorry to see our relationship end." Perhaps he should just have sung her the song he'd performed with her so many times: *I'm not the one you want, babe / I'm not the one you need . . .*"

6

SOMETHING IS HAPPENING

"It Ain't Me, Babe" was directed as much at the many fans who'd deified Dylan as a prophet with a "message" as it was at Joan Baez, Suze Rotolo or any of the other women in his life. So empty did he find the adulation on his seven-date English tour that when he and Sara returned to Woodstock in early June 1965, he thought about quitting music altogether.

Instead he sat in the Yarrows' cabin on Broadview Road and, in his own words, "vomited out" the six pages of rage and revenge that became "Like a Rolling Stone".* "We had come up from New York," he said, "and I had about three days off up there to get some stuff together." Boosting his confidence was the No. 1 hit that the Byrds had just had with their chiming electric version of "Mr Tambourine Man" – a defining moment in the new folk rock and a welcome source of royalties for the Dylan/Grossman coffers.

Assisting with the arrangement of the ascending chord sequence in "Like a Rolling Stone" was a nice Jewish boy who showed up in Woodstock on 12 June, carrying a white Fender Stratocaster without a case. Dylan had met and jammed with Mike Bloomfield in Chicago in 1963, but the trust-funded guitar whiz was now a member of the powerful, multiracial Paul Butterfield Blues Band. As Sara prepared a curious salad of tuna fish and toasted peanuts in the Yarrows' cabin, Dylan played the song's chords on an upright piano and Bloomfield filled in the available spaces with vicious blues licks.

---

* Ian Bell has rather dispelled the notion of "Rolling Stone" being "vomited out", pointing out that the lyric drew on passages from his novel-in-progress *Tarantula*.

Three days later, the two of them were at the Columbia studios in
New York with Tom Wilson and some of the crew who'd played on
Bringing It All Back Home. And, by the end of Wednesday, "Like a
Rolling Stone" had been recorded, with a crucial organ part added
by another nice Jewish boy.

"There was a little magic thing going on," says Al Kooper, the
boy in question. "Dylan, Bloomfield and I were Jewish and approx-
imately the same age, which was unusual for the New York session
scene. Most of the other session guys were older and Italian." The
date marked the end of Wilson's relationship with Dylan. "Tom and
Albert didn't get along at all," says Kooper. "That was why he got
the boot as Dylan's producer. When I was invited back for the next
session, Tom was gone and there was Bob Johnston."

When Dylan received an acetate of "Like a Rolling Stone", he
was ecstatic. "He was so excited he wanted everyone to hear it,"
remembered John Herald. "Anybody he knew who passed by the
Café Espresso, Dylan would run out and say, 'I've got this great new
song, it's going to be really big, you've got to hear it.' Then he would
take them inside and play it for them." By August, the single – all six
uncompromising minutes of it – was at No. 2. Bob Dylan was now,
officially, a pop star.

Dylan spent the rest of June and most of July in Woodstock, writing and recording material for his next record and house-hunting
around town. Having visited John Lennon's impressive new home
in the Surrey "green belt" south-west of London, he wondered how
it would feel to possess so many material things. Just as she had
alerted Grossman to the Striebel house, Shirley Glaser learned on
the grapevine that Ralph Whitehead's son was selling a property
in Byrdcliffe's East Riding that had previously been inhabited by
German artist Lotte Stoehr. "Shirley heard about the house on
Camelot Road," says her husband Milton, "so you might say she's
responsible for everything that happened to Woodstock." The rambling eleven-bedroom property, known as Hi Lo Ha, was acquired

for $12,000 through Davasee Enterprises, a business set up by Grossman. Surrounded by rhododendrons and boasting its own swimming hole, it was the first home Dylan owned.

As Sara – pregnant by now with Jesse Dylan – busied herself with furniture and decorations, Dylan knuckled down and wrote half a dozen more of his greatest songs, proving just how much of a break-through "Like a Rolling Stone" had been. If that song was unprec-edentedly confrontational, "Ballad of a Thin Man" and "Positively Fourth Street" were more savage still: "truth attacks" set to rolling, roiling electric music and sung in what Philip Larkin described as a "cawing, derisive voice".

It was the same voice people heard when Dylan took the stage at that summer's Newport Folk Festival with a hastily flung-together band that included both Kooper and Bloomfield. On a whim of sorts – and resplendent in Ray-Bans and one of his new polka-dot shirts – he commandeered three-fifths of the Butterfield Blues Band, added Kooper and Barry Goldberg to the mix, and strode defiantly onto a stage that for six years had been a hallowed platform for folk elders and Delta bluesmen. Even Albert Grossman couldn't have prepared himself for the furore that Sunday evening.

In truth it sounded horrible. By Newport standards the amplifi-cation was deafening and distorted. Dylan had barely ever played electric guitar before. Worse, the Chicago rhythm section couldn't acclimatise to the songs Dylan had taught them, since the music had nothing to do with the twelve-bar grooves they'd played with Butterfield or Howlin' Wolf. Yet Al Kooper disputes the claim that the audience booed because the music was amplified; he says they were upset because Dylan only played three songs. Barry Goldberg agrees: "There were more people there that really dug it and reacted favourably than hardcore folkies that felt betrayed. We thought we did a good job, and we thought we were part of something impor-tant. It signalled the end of that folk era."

Peter Yarrow, who was on the Newport board, begged Dylan to

go back on and throw the faithful a bone. Johnny Cash, who had met folk's rising star at the previous year's festival, made similarly encouraging noises. Shocked by the booing – an onstage photograph shows a tear running down Dylan's left cheek – he borrowed Yarrow's guitar and went back on stage to sing "It's All Over Now, Baby Blue". "He went out," Kooper says, "and it was one of the most amazing things I've ever seen in my life when he played that song – the irony of it, and the fact that he was using a borrowed guitar."

It *was* all over now, and folk's old guard knew it. "They had gotten to the point of having all their dreams come true two years before," reflected Joe Boyd, a stalwart of the Cambridge scene who was present that night. "And suddenly they could see it all slipping away in a haze of marijuana smoke and self-indulgence. As far as they were concerned, Grossman was the money-changer at the gates of the temple." As Pete Seeger marched indignantly back to the festival's car park, his wife burst into tears. "This was the Birth of Rock," Boyd wrote in his memoir *White Bicycles*, adding that "anyone wishing to portray the history of the Sixties as a journey from idealism to hedonism could place the hinge at around 9.30 pm on the night of 25 July, 1965".

Four days after his folk apostasy at Newport, Dylan returned to the studio in New York to record more songs. Among them was "Positively Fourth Street", possibly addressed to one of his many envious Village judges but more likely laying waste to the whole lot of them. This time there was another young gun on the session, a bass-playing pal of Al Kooper's who was as struck by the glowering presence of Albert Grossman as he was by Dylan. "I'd been playing small dates in the city, so I didn't know who Bob was," says Harvey Brooks. "Then when I saw this old guy with long grey hair sitting there, I thought, 'Who *is* this man?' Albert had a style unto himself that emerged even in that moment."

On the weekend of 31 July/1 August, Dylan invited Kooper

up to Bearsville to write chord charts for the remaining songs on
Highway 61 Revisited. Dancing attendance was the inevitable
Neuwirth. "Dylan had ways of imposing distance when he wanted
to, but mostly he was very loose with us," Kooper says. "When I
first started spending time with him, I didn't say anything. I was
learning – or, as Neuwirth said, 'getting my hip card punched'. It
took me a while to assimilate." On one of the evenings, stoned out of
their minds, they ran a reel of *Rebel Without a Cause* on Grossman's
projector, thereby revisiting Dylan's teenage infatuation with James
Dean. "We watched it in slow motion and then we watched it backwards," says Kooper. "There was very little of Albert involved when
I was there. Neuwirth was the ersatz Albert: he was doing Albert's
job so that Albert could get some time off."

The following week, Dylan's sixth Columbia album was completed. Released in late August with a Daniel Kramer cover shot of
Dylan in a Triumph T-shirt on the steps of Grossman's Gramercy
Park building – and Neuwirth standing behind him – *Highway 61*
was unapologetically electric, with only the apocalyptic "Desolation
Row" offering any sort of sop to Dylan's older fans.° The gloves
were off, and he was determined to push things to the limit with a
full electric tour. Disappointed when Mike Bloomfield left – saying
he was committed to the Butterfield band – Dylan put out word
that he wanted a new guitarist and drummer to augment Kooper
and Brooks for shows at the Forest Hills tennis stadium and the
Hollywood Bowl.

Dylan had already met red-hot R&B band Levon and the Hawks
when Levon Helm, Garth Hudson and Robbie Robertson backed
John Hammond Jr on his 1964 album *So Many Roads*, but he
was unaware they were holding down a summer residency on the

° *Highway 61 Revisited* was the last album cover that Daniel Kramer shot for
Dylan. In December 1966 Albert Grossman placed an injunction on Citadel Press
in an attempt to prevent the publication of Kramer's book of Dylan photographs.
The injunction was rejected and the book appeared in March 1967.

Jersey shore that very month. Mary Martin, a Canadian working for Grossman and later described by Dylan as "a rather persevering soul", made the reintroductions. The Hawks were from a very different music world, honing their chops in rough nightclubs and oblivious to the new pop order of "Like a Rolling Stone" and the Byrds' "Mr Tambourine Man". Though Arkansas-born Levon Helm was sceptical of the benefits of playing behind this tousled poet, Toronto native Jaime "Robbie" Robertson was more forward-thinking. The two men bade a temporary farewell to their bandmates and drove up to New York to rehearse with Dylan, Kooper and Brooks.

Somehow it all gelled in time for the 28 August show at Forest Hills, where the anti-electric protestors were out en masse. "They came like lemmings," says Kooper. "They sang along to 'Like a Rolling Stone' and then *booed*. It was farcical. Bob had taken 'Ballad of a Thin Man' from Ray Charles's 'I Believe to My Soul', so we played the intro to that. And then he sang the line 'Something is happening and you don't know what it is . . .' It was like 'Baby Blue' at Newport – fabulous theatre." At an after-show party at Grossman's apartment, Dylan was all but levitating, delighted to have stoked the controversy still further. At the Hollywood Bowl, six days later, the reaction was significantly hipper: the city of the Byrds and the Mamas and the Papas was altogether more embracing of Electric Bob. Rock was completing its violent birth as a fusion of poetry and amplification.

The shows set the tone for the next nine months. When Kooper and Brooks bowed out, Helm told Dylan he had to take all of the Hawks or none. In mid-September Dylan flew up to Toronto to rehearse with the group. Suddenly the small-town boys from Arkansas and Ontario found themselves on the world stage with the most charismatic song-poet of the times – a mod band in dark suits desecrating his revolutionary folk anthems.

Starting in Austin, the tour was booed from the get-go. It was as if Jesus had gone over to the dark side and hired Lucifer to play lead guitar. The sound was intense, irreverent and often deafening.

Dylan was sticking it to the people and upping his speed intake in the process. Watching in the wings was Grossman, whose willingness to empower Dylan was being tested to the limit. "Albert was back in the blues and folk mentality for his whole career," says Michael Friedman. "He was trying to get Bob to get rid of The Band. He told me, 'Every time I went to him to tell him to get rid of them, Bob would tell me to give them an extra hundred dollars a week.' So he stopped asking."

Dylan's seismic changes may have made him uneasy, but Grossman knew better than to second-guess him. Instead he attempted to keep pace with him, altering his appearance to match Dylan's and switching his image from tweedy left-wing professor to shaggy-haired nonconformist. "I used to remember Albert as a nice-looking businessman, the kind of middle-aged man you would meet in a decent restaurant in the Garment District," said Gloria Stavers, editor of *16* magazine. "Then, a while after he signed Dylan, I met him again. I just couldn't believe what had happened. 'Albert!' I screamed when I finally recognised him. 'What has Bobby *done* to you?'"

The basic script for Dylan's 1965/6 shows was invariably the same: a solo acoustic set, performed fairly indifferently but greeted ecstatically, followed by an electric set played with gusto and greeted with outraged howls. As Robertson spat out angry Telecaster riffs at Dylan's side, Garth Hudson filled every available space with inspired noodling. Dylan's jaded, sneering voice was proto-punk a decade ahead of its time. The fuss about guitars and amplifiers obscured the real point, which was that he'd sabotaged his own boy-hero-in-overalls image and become a narcissistic icon. When Phil Ochs wrote that there was "something very dangerous, something very frightening" about him, it made clear what a threat Dylan posed to the bastions of *Broadside* and *Sing Out!*. °

° Ochs was himself briefly managed by Albert Grossman, until he grew weary of being overlooked in favour of GrossCourt's bigger acts and fobbed off with Grossman's loftiest cop-out – "It's not your time yet, Phil." Richie Havens

Dylan had invented Attitude, the mode of cooler-than-thou remoteness that's driven pop ever since. It was undiluted ego on skinny legs, James Dean via Elvis and Rimbaud – in the words of Don DeLillo from his Dylan-inspired novel *Great Jones Street*, "the circumstance of one man imparting an erotic terror to the dreams of the republic".*

On 22 November, at the end of an East Coast tour, Dylan married Sara Lownds in a ceremony in Mineola, Long Island, so low-key that almost nobody – Grossman aside – even knew about it. The knot was tied so hurriedly because an old-fashioned part of Dylan wanted the heavily pregnant Sara to be married before having their baby. As much as he'd earlier tried to pretend they didn't exist, he had his parents' feelings to consider (though they weren't invited). He also knew that being married didn't quite sync with the image he was projecting into the world.

The old-fashioned Dylan also materialised in a New Year encounter with the decadent entourage surrounding Andy Warhol. Though he was intrigued by the silver-haired pop artist, Dylan was repelled by what he saw at Warhol's Factory studio. "Dylan represented a certain milieu that was almost the antithesis of Andy's milieu," said Factory artist and dancer Gerard Malanga. "[. . .] you had the heterosexual grouping and you had the so-called homosexual grouping . . ." Attempting to break the ice was the boyishly beautiful Edie Sedgwick, then sleeping with Bobby Neuwirth and being courted as a possible client by Albert Grossman (until he realised she couldn't sing). It didn't work: Dylan sat sullenly in a corner and only agreed to sit for one of Warhol's "screen tests" on the condition that he

---

regularly heard the same words from Grossman, before John Court took over and produced his 1967 debut, *Mixed Bag*.

* The story of reclusive and enigmatic star Bucky Wunderlick, *Great Jones Street* (1973) involves the theft of his unreleased *Mountain Tapes* and features a guitarist (Azarian) said to be modelled on Robbie Robertson and a manager (Globke) partly based on Grossman.

help himself to a diptych of the gun-toting Elvis Presley in Don Siegel's 1960 western *Flaming Star*. When Warhol obliged, Dylan and Neuwirth strapped the painting to the top of Dylan's station wagon like a dead deer and drove it up to Woodstock. "Bob wanted not to care about the painting," says Bruce Dorfman, Dylan's new Byrdcliffe neighbour. "I think he *did* care, because it fascinated him, but he wanted *not* to. Because there was a very strong middle-class or lower-middle-class ethic lurking with him all the time. You could really see it when he was around his mother or when he talked about his brother."

Compounding the contemptuous transportation of Warhol's *Double Elvis* were the stories its creator later heard about its mis-treatment. "I got paranoid when I heard rumours that [Dylan] had used [it] as a dartboard up in the country," Warhol reminisced in 1980. "When I'd ask, 'Why would he do that?' I'd invariably get hearsay answers like, 'I hear he feels you destroyed Edie' or 'Listen to "Like a Rolling Stone"' . . ." Over a decade passed before Warhol found out what had really happened to his *Double Elvis*: Dylan had traded it for a leather couch imported from Scandinavia by his man-ager. "The story I heard was that Bob had spent a year living on this funky old couch," says Michael Friedman. "Albert had got it in a tag sale for, like, ten bucks. So he said he'd trade it for the Warhol. Bob said, 'Seems like a fair trade.'"*

The sybaritic demi-monde of Andy Warhol and his Factory workers permeated *Blonde on Blonde*, a double album recorded in Nashville with Bob Johnston in February and March 1966. Some even thought the withering ballad "Just Like a Woman" – like the unreleased "She's Your Lover Now" – was at least partly about the doomed Sedgwick, while "Leopard-Skin Pill-Box Hat" was a song about fashion-victimhood that would have been inconceivable in

---

* According to Ronnie Lyons, Dylan admitted later that it was "the dumbest thing he ever did in his whole life". Sally Grossman later sold the Warhol for $750,000; today its value would be closer to $40 million.

Dylan's repertoire two years earlier. *Blonde on Blonde* was rock's first double album, with a blurred Dylan running horizontally across the sleeve and Nashville session men riffing behind the bird's-nest-headed speed freak. It was *Highway 61* times two, with raw blues routines giving way to flowing ruminations such as "Visions of Johanna", "One of Us Must Know" and "Sad-Eyed Lady of the Lowlands", an epic song inspired by Sara.

"Albert didn't know if it was a good idea or not to record in Nashville," says Al Kooper, who flew there with Grossman and Robbie Robertson. "He was watching this thing that he didn't con-done. Some press guy got into the studio one day and said, 'My God, what is that guy *on*?' Albert said, 'Columbia Records and Tapes.' Then he threw him out."

The electric tour continued, but without the Hawks' drummer. Levon Helm had jumped ship in late November, weary of being jeered for music he didn't even like. "That was a dose of medicine," he told me. "I took about one tour of it, and when they got ready to go to Europe and Australia, that's when I passed. They were on us hot and heavy, boy. Them beatniks was tough!" Heading south from Washington DC, Helm got himself a job with the Aquatic Engineering and Construction Company in Louisiana. "He ended up on some kind of oil rig," remembered Rick Danko. "He said, 'You'd go out for four or five days and they'd pay you a lot of money.' He had his mandolin and his harmonica with him, and they'd play music more than they'd scrape paint off rusty boats or whatever it was." Robbie Robertson was hit hard by the loss of his musical brother. "It broke my heart when Levon left," he said. "I remember, I walked him down to the corner and said goodbye as he got a taxi."

What Robertson didn't twig was how turned off Helm was by the guitarist's obsequiousness towards Dylan: it just didn't sit right with the dirt farmer's son who'd been raised to be true to his authentic musical self. And yet Robertson was correct in his belief that the hook-up with Dylan – even a reviled Dylan – would take the Hawks to a level of fame they would never otherwise have known. Thus the band continued with session man Bobby Gregg on drums, playing for almost three weeks in California. Another drummer, Sandy Konikoff, took over when the tour resumed in February. But it was the pounding Mickey Jones who played on the most infamous leg of the gruelling tour, beginning in Stockholm on 29 April. Along for the ride on this stretch were Donn Pennebaker and his assistants Howard and Jones Alk. "I may have made a movie about drugs without realising it," Pennebaker says of the footage shot during the European tour. He remembers Dylan "scratching himself a lot" and being told this was a sign of amphetamine abuse. It may also have been a symptom of opiate use, since Dylan confessed his use of heroin to Robert Shelton.* For the most part, Grossman looked the other way – and perhaps even encouraged the drug use. "It was a source of his power," an anonymous client of Grossman's told David Hajdu. "He was bacterious [*sic*]. He made sure his clients had anything and everything they wanted, which made them all the more dependent on him." Ed Sanders, then of the Fugs, agrees: "Our managers worked out of the Grossman office, so I had a lot of inside information. I'm not that much of a fan of Albert, because too many of his artists were junkies, and I think it's possible he used their addiction as a way of controlling them."

Though the Hawks were used to amphetamine – they'd popped what Helm called "fat girls' pills" throughout their years on the road – being part of the retinue of a sadistic rooster on dope was uncharted territory for them. Rick Danko and piano player Richard Manuel stuck to their roles as bemused country boys; organist Garth

---

* The confession only became public knowledge when Shelton's Dylan biography *No Direction Home* was revised and updated in 2011, sixteen years after the author's death. However, like so many of Dylan's boasts, it has to be taken with a pinch of salt. "When I first met Bob he claimed that he had been a junkie," Al Aronowitz told me. "I believed him then, but in retrospect I didn't." To Bob Spitz, Dave Van Ronk said he "knew [Dylan] was playing with heroin", though he added that he was "flirting with it and wanted us to know – as if it would shock us".

Hudson was in another world anyway. Only Robertson seemed at ease with Dylan's behaviour: so tightly did he stick to his new boss that Mickey Jones referred to him behind his back as "Barnacle Man". The humiliation of journalists and hangers-on had continued on the Australian leg of the world tour. Now even old friends of the Hawks felt excommunicated. "Albert didn't like me at all," John Hammond Jr told me. "As soon as Robbie and the others got with Dylan, I fell out of touch with them. They had been the coolest guys – wide-open, full-throttle – but all of a sudden I was just a complete idiot to them."

Once Dylan was being filmed, the tour became a twenty-four-hour-a-day performance. "Filming on the 1966 tour turned out to be hard," says Donn Pennebaker. "Dylan was supposed to be in charge, but he was as wild as I'd ever seen him: all-night sagas of traipsing around shooting this and that, and none of it made sense. He was in over his head and he was vamping, and I didn't know what to tell him." But Pennebaker did capture the legendary moment at Manchester's Free Trade Hall when young John Cordwell shouted "Judas!" as a protest against Dylan's apparent disdain for songs that had meant so much to people. "That onstage posturing and rock-star arrogance was new in Manchester in 1966," Cordwell said thirty-three years later. "Even super-egos like Jagger, Lennon *et al.* had yet to treat live audiences with the sort of contempt that Dylan seemed to show that night."

Dylan was about to crash into the wall of his own drug-crazed megalomania. Footage that Pennebaker shot of him being chauffeured around London with John Lennon showed just how far he had gone. "I wanna go home to baseball and TV," Dylan whined pathetically as the limo glided through Hyde Park at dawn. He was ready to be an ordinary American again.

Woodstock Week, 10 May 1966

PART TWO

GOING UP THE COUNTRY

Gonna leave the city, gonna catch the Hudson Line,
You know I love the city, but I haven't got the time.
MERCURY REV

1

HUNDRED-AND-FORTY-DOLLAR BASH

In January 1996, on a blindingly bright day after a snowfall so heavy I could barely beat a path to its front door, I drove with a letting agent to view a large reddish-brown house on Zena Road, a mile east of Woodstock's village green. Set back from a hairpin bend that hugged the Sawkill River, the house – formerly home to surrealist painter Dimitri Petrov – was a sprawling barn of a place with giant windows and a vast backyard. Since I urgently needed to find a home for my young family, I said I would take it.

Only when I had been living in the house for some months did I learn – from former Band producer John Simon – that a similarly reddish-brown property sitting immediately below us was the house Rick Danko had once lived in with his first wife Grace, and where Elliott Landy had shot dozens of photographs of The Band. I'd pored over those pictures on the inside sleeve of the group's second album, and now every morning I was looking down at the very rooms where they'd been taken.*

And then, in *Fodor's Rock & Roll Traveler USA* – published the very year of my move to Woodstock – I read that "the most commonly quoted crash site is on a very sharp bend about a mile up Zena Road near an old barn". Had I unwittingly picked the very spot where Bob Dylan was thrown off his motorcycle?

By the time he was home in June 1966, the strain on Dylan had become too much. Exhausted by four months of almost non-stop

---

* Though it appears to sit on Zena Road, the address of Danko's old house is actually 373 Chestnut Hill Road.

touring, he returned to Byrdcliffe to recuperate, only to find new pressures building up: Albert Grossman had scheduled another run of North American concerts for the autumn; ABC television had bought rights to a film from Pennebaker's footage of the European tour; and Macmillan was gearing up to publish Dylan's "novel" *Tarantula*.

Photographs of the ghostly-pale singer in the woods in July make clear just how wrecked he was. "[This] was the time that he was most caressed and possessed by the various drugs that he was taking," said Carly Simon, then briefly being managed by Grossman. "The effects on him were that he was pretty displaced." Simon had seen Dylan just a week before his accident, when "he seemed like he was very high on speed: very, very wasted and talking incoherently, saying a lot about God and Jesus . . ." When painter Brice Marden came to a party at Dylan's Chelsea Hotel suite, the singer was lying "comatose" in the middle of the sitting room, and was still unconscious when Mick Jagger arrived.

Back in Woodstock one night, Dylan looked up at the moon shining over the mountains and a voice spoke in his head. "Something's gotta change," it said. Suddenly Columbia, ABC and Macmillan were just "leeches" trying to bleed him dry. Meanwhile he had a loving wife who only wanted him home.

For the better part of two months, Dylan did his best just to function. He pieced together fragments of Donn Pennebaker's footage with the help of Bobby Neuwirth and Howard Alk, who'd once worked for Grossman in Chicago. After Grossman berated him for "not helping Bob enough", Pennebaker himself came up to Bearsville. "Sally would make lunch for us," he says. "There was a lot of angst about the film. Bob was much less comfortable with me than he'd been on *Dont Look Back*. He asked Neuwirth and me to put something together so we had something to show ABC."*

---

* This was the amazing forty-five-minute reel known as *Something Is Happening*, which I was lucky enough to see when I first visited Pennebaker in his Upper West Side office in 1991.

If Dylan was attempting to moderate his intake of drugs, Alk was hardly the most sensible person to be working with. "He was a very political guy but a completely drugged degenerate," says Peter Coyote. "It was a very crazy scene: a lot of drugs and a lot of madness." On the other hand, Alk was not a hanger-on, which was refreshing to anyone turned off by the Grossmans' airs. "There was a culture around them that sort of rewarded pretentiousness, but Howard was not like that at all," says Danny Goldberg, who worked for Grossman at the end of the decade. "He was just a teddy bear of a guy without a scintilla of arrogance or snobbery." Pennebaker saw Alk as "a kind of lifeguard" for Dylan, who was drowning under the demands of ABC, Macmillan and Grossman himself.

Dylan told Al Aronowitz that he'd been up for three days straight on speed when, early on Friday 29 July, he set off from the Grossmans' home on his Triumph 500, Sara following close behind in their Ford station wagon. From Dylan's description of what happened, he must have ridden the bike north up Striebel Road and then turned right on Glasco Turnpike. (He almost certainly didn't get as far as Zena Road, whatever *Fodor's Rock & Roll Traveler USA* surmised.) The fullest account of the accident comes from a one-act "play" that Sam Shepard based on a 1987 conversation with Dylan. "I was driving right into the sun," Dylan said – or so we must assume – "and I looked up into it, even though I remember someone telling me a long time ago when I was a kid never to look straight at the sun 'cause you'll get blinded [. . .] and, sure enough, I went blind for a second and I kind of panicked or something. I stomped down on the brake and the rear wheel locked up on me and I went flyin' . . ."

Sally Grossman was on the phone to her husband when the Dylans set off. She was still talking to Albert when the station wagon reappeared in the driveway. She saw Dylan almost fall out of the passenger seat and collapse onto the porch, clearly in pain, though not injured enough for anyone to call an ambulance. Sally returned to the phone to tell Albert what had happened. Sara then drove

Dylan down to Middletown, an hour south-east of Woodstock, and left him in the care of Dr Ed Thaler. "It was away from his ordinary life," said Thaler's wife Selma, "and I think that provided some peace of mind." Another of Grossman's clients, Odetta, came to see the doctor and was astonished to find Dylan occupying almost the entire third floor of the house.

The fact that Dylan stayed with the Thalers for at least ten days hints at what many suspect: that either he needed to detox from whatever drugs he'd been taking or he was suffering a total breakdown. (Or both.) Either way, it gave him a perfect get-out. The upcoming tour, a week away, was cancelled. The film and novel were put on hold. For a few days Dylan lay in bed and stared out of the window, feeling relief that he could simply stop. "I just remember how bad I wanted to see my kids," he said in Sam Shepard's dialogue. "I started thinkin' about the short life of trouble. How short life is. I'd just lay there listenin' to birds chirping. Kids playing in the neighbour's yard or rain falling by the window. I realised how much I'd missed. Then I'd hear the fire engine roar, and I could feel the steady thrust of death that had been constantly looking over its shoulder at me."

Dylan was back at Hi Lo Ha by mid-August, when Allen Ginsberg visited with a bootload of books for the younger man to read as he recovered. "This accident may have been a good thing," the poet told the *World Journal Tribune* in October. "It's forced him to slow down." Other visitors reported that Dylan was in a neck brace but seemed mobile. Rick Danko told me the accident was "serious enough that it took him a year or so to get himself back together",* but Al Aronowitz thought the brace looked like "a prop", and Al Kooper says that "if he'd had a serious accident, I would have known more at the time". In Grossman's office, Myra Friedman

---

* Danko later claimed that Dylan had actually been pushed over by a young woman who was fed up with him revving the Triumph's engine at a stop sign outside her house.

issued a press release that failed to quell rumours that Dylan had been maimed or disfigured. His own parents couldn't get any definitive word on what had happened.

For Dylan himself, the only thing that mattered was that he'd bought some time to step back from the madness of his career. "He was trying very hard to escape that really crazy thing you see in *Dont Look Back*," says Happy Traum, who spent that summer in Woodstock and, in his own words, "became kind of injected into the cauldron of people" around Dylan and Grossman. "It was getting out of control, and this was his way of reining everything in and just saying, 'I've got to get a normal life here and the only way I can do that is to shut everybody else out.'"

For the remainder of the year Dylan did very little, even as he worked at Bearsville on the film for ABC. "He didn't know anything more about directing than I did, so the two of us were just sort of mucking around with this material," says Donn Pennebaker. Dylan may not have written a single song before the turn of the year. He told *Newsweek* that he'd "stared at the ceiling for a few months", adding that he was "a country boy myself, and you have to be let alone to really accomplish anything".

Most mornings Jesse woke his parents, who fed him as they got his half-sister ready for school. Dylan would walk Maria down to the bus stop on Upper Byrdcliffe Road, chatting on the way to fellow father Bruce Dorfman, who lived next door and worked in a grey cube of a studio on Webster Road, just below Hi Lo Ha. "It was after the accident, and he was getting ultrasound treatments for that," Dorfman says. "He was walking with a cane." Dylan dug the fact that Dorfman – a respected artist in his own right – wasn't starstruck and didn't particularly care that he was Bob Dylan. (Slightly more star-struck was Woodstock musician and fellow parent Billy Batson, a recent arrival in town. "We were all trying to live a 'normal life' and take care of our women and our kids and somehow do the music at the same time," Batson said in 2010.)

Dylan didn't even look like "Bob Dylan" any more: he'd cut his hair and grown a sparse beard; the polka-dot shirts were stowed and old denim ones retrieved from the closet. He seemed to be walking away from the mind-expanding world of pop culture. "My sense was that he was trying to reclaim some way of incorporating his sense of family into his life," Dorfman says. "He had an idea about some kind of middle-class life, and the closeness and comfort of family. He just doted on the kids. His relationship with Sara seemed to be a very, very husband-and-wife arrangement."

When Dylan made moves to adopt Maria Lownds as his daughter, he asked Dorfman for a character reference. He also asked if he would teach him to paint, and so began making regular visits to the grey cube with either his giant poodle Hamlet or the even larger Buster, a St Bernard that sometimes attacked Dorfman. "The paintings were terrible, but he *did* them and that was valuable," Dorman says. "I remember him sitting in the studio and dwelling on his notoriety and the inner tension that came from it. He'd sit there and say, 'I can't understand it – all I am is an entertainer.' I think he really believed that somehow, and it comforted him in some ways."

The impact of Dylan's accident was felt keenly by the Hawks, who'd been expecting to tour with him and were now cooling their heels in the summer heat of Manhattan. "From 1960 to 1965 we'd played every night in clubs," Rick Danko said. "We didn't really know any better." In limbo, the group killed time in the Village, where Robbie Robertson moved into a small apartment with his new French Canadian girlfriend Dominique Bourgeois, and where the other three roomed together near Grossman's home in Gramercy Park. (A regular hangout was Mickey Ruskin's Max's Kansas City on Park Avenue South, where Dylan had held court.) Thanks to Grossman, the group recorded demos at Barry Feinstein's photography studio on East 73rd Street. "I suppose they were close enough for Albert to keep his eye on them from his office," Feinstein remembered, though he never heard anything from the sessions till Robbie Robertson included Richard Manuel's "Beautiful Thing" on the 2005 Band box set *A Musical History*.

"My wife and I gave Robbie and Dominique our old dishes and other household stuff," Al Aronowitz said. "Robbie was very straight and charming and quite naïve." Aronowitz even dragged Robertson to see his friends the Velvet Underground play as part of Warhol's Exploding Plastic Inevitable: "He stayed for about five minutes and then split. He couldn't stand it." To spare them from going back on the road, Dylan asked Grossman to put the Hawks on retainer. "It allowed us some freedom to figure out what an artist really is," said Danko. "It got us out of that rut every night."

Dylan went one better and invited the group up to Woodstock. "Robbie called me up one day and said, 'What's happenin'?'" he recalled. "And I said, 'Nothin'.' He said he was in the mood for some nothin' too." Danko and Manuel were the first to arrive and quickly found themselves pressed into service in new scenes that Dylan and Alk were shooting for *Eat the Document*. The town was deep in snow but felt like a home from home to the two Ontarians. "We stayed at the Woodstock Motel for a couple of weeks," Danko told me. "And then, country boy that I am, I just realised that ever since I had left Ontario I'd been living in cities. And I realised I didn't have to *be* in cities any more." Through the motel's owner Bill Militello, he learned of a house for rent in nearby West Saugerties. "It was $125 a month," he said. "It sat in the middle of a hundred acres and had a pond and mountains and a lot of privacy. So Garth, Richard and myself ended up renting the house." Robertson and Bourgeois followed shortly afterwards, fleeing the urban sleaze of the Velvet Underground for the clean air of the Catskills. Later that year they were married.

Robertson was already enjoying preferential treatment from Grossman, who'd earmarked him as the one member of the Hawks with an interest in bettering himself. He was knocked out by the

Big Pink, summer 1991 (Art Sperl)

Striebel house, with its big kitchen and imported antiques. "The kitchen had a long counter with stools at it," says Jonathan Taplin. "You'd go up there in the morning and have coffee with him and Robbie. Albert liked to kind of potter around, and he was a decent cook." The guitarist was also keen to establish himself as Dylan's new right-hand man, Bob Neuwirth having temporarily departed the scene to live in a commune. Intrigued by avant-garde cinema, Robertson volunteered his services to help with the completion of the film. He also mastered the art of the Dylan/Grossman freeze-out. "There was a whole thing with Bob and Robbie and Albert," said Artie Traum, who stayed in Woodstock with his brother Happy that summer. "They had a way of coming into a room and really chilling it, just by being there and not saying anything. You'd say to yourself, 'What's going on here? Am I doing something wrong?'"

As the three less aspirational Hawks settled into the modestly sized home they nicknamed Big Pink, tucked at the end of a long dirt driveway, Dylan began seeing the value of having the group close by.* After a few get-togethers at Hi Lo Ha, he took to driving a baby-blue Mustang over to the pink house.† Robertson would make his own way over from a small cottage Grossman had provided, and the five men would jam together in what Dylan remembered as "a typical basement, with pipes and a concrete floor, a washer-dryer". "Before I realised it, Bob had been coming every day for six, seven days a week," Danko told me. "It was part of his rehabilitation. He was getting stronger and feeling better."

Happy Traum, who'd made a permanent move to Woodstock that summer, knew about the house but did not hear it referred to as "Big Pink" for some time. Says Jonathan Taplin, "Nobody knew what was going on there or even really where it was." Exceptions were made for pot dealers and pretty girls. "We were dealing with men in their early twenties," Robbie Robertson recalled. "Not so much for me or Bob, but the other guys would go into town and pick up chicks and come back and party all night long."‡ Woodstock's Town Supervisor Jeremy Wilber – a former bartender whose unpublished 2013 novel *Miles from Woodstock* is an amusing snapshot of the town in the late sixties and seventies – remembers that the local girls had been surprisingly prudish. "When I left town in 1966, they were all virgins,"

---

* Big Pink's original address was 2188 Stoll Road. The house is now on Parnassus Road.
† Before the basement tapes there were sessions with the Hawks in the so-called "Red Room" at Hi Lo Ha. Recently discovered photographs from March 1967 – of Dylan in a fur hat and white dungarees, Danko with a Fender Telecaster and Manuel with Tiny Tim – may have been taken at Hi Lo Ha.
‡ Other visitors included the Bauls of Bengal, a group discovered in Calcutta by Sally Grossman. Around the time that two of their number appeared on the cover of Dylan's *John Wesley Harding* – along with local carpenter/stonemason Charlie Joy – the Bauls were recorded by Garth Hudson in Big Pink's basement, the result being the 1968 Buddah album *The Bengali Bauls at Big Pink*. "They had brought herbs from India and a chillum pipe," says John Simon. "That was a new way of smoking for us." In 1971 Sally hired Howard Alk to direct *Luxman Baul's Movie*, a fifty-two-minute film about the group shot in West Bengal.

he says. "By the time I came back in '68, the whole meadow was mowed."

"My girlfriend was really sociable, so we'd go to Big Pink a lot," says Graham "Monk" Blackburn, an English horn player who'd moved upstate after a period in New York. "We just used to hang out, and as they gradually accumulated women we became friends with all of them. Rick [Danko] had inherited Hamlet, and the dog used to sleep in this big old Hudson he'd bought."

"Hamlet and Bob weren't getting along too well," Danko remembered. "I pulled up one day and it looked like Hamlet was trying to bite Bob on the ankle and Bob was trying to kick him in the ass." Al Kooper remembers being woken at Hi Lo Ha by Dylan yelling, "No, Hamlet, no!" "He didn't lead a very good Bob life," Kooper adds. "He led a better Danko life." Though Dylan had fallen out with Hamlet, he didn't object to the poodle's presence at Big Pink. "They were a kick to do," he said of the basement sessions. "Fact, I'd do it all again. You know, that's really the way to do a recording – in a peaceful, relaxed setting – in somebody's basement. With the windows open . . . and a dog lying on the floor."

Danko recalled Dylan showing up at noon most days and then splitting before six o'clock to be home for dinner. "If we were sleeping he'd get us up," he said. "He'd make some noise or bang on the typewriter on the coffee table." In Danko's recollection, as many as "a hundred and fifty songs" – an exaggeration, though not far off – were taped in the basement of Big Pink between June and October. More than a few were cover versions of folk staples Dylan had known since his early Village days – Pete Seeger's "Bells of Rhymney" and Brendan Behan's "The Auld Triangle", along with such traditionals as "Po' Lazarus" and "Bonnie Ship the Diamond" – together with country songs by Hank Williams ("You Win Again") and Johnny Cash ("Big River", "Folsom Prison Blues").

Though Dylan later said he didn't know what people meant by the term, the ragged songbook that he and the Hawks assembled that summer was really the inception of the hybrid genre we now refer to as "Americana". "Regardless of whatever's been written about Bob and his creative genius, he's basically a lover of American music," says Larry Campbell, who played guitar and other string instruments in Dylan's touring band between 1997 and 2004. "What The Band did behind him and what the band that I was in did behind him gave me an angle to look at folk music and how ubiquitous and how malleable it can be."

"It was the kind of music that made you feel like you were part of something very, very special and nobody else was a part of it," Dylan said of the songs. "And back then, it was hard to get *to*." The basement tapes turned their back on the sixties and towards the kind of old-timey ballads on Harry Smith's hugely influential *Anthology of American Folk Music* (1952). Inspired by those songs, Dylan began writing new ones of his own. "Bob would sit at the window, and it was this perfect writing situation," said Garth Hudson. "A couch, coffee table, a typewriter, two yellow legal pads with pencils, and he'd look out the window, and way off in the distance there were mountains. And he'd write."

"I'd pick up a piece of paper on the kitchen table", Rick Danko told me, "and I'd read, '*My comic book and me, just us, we caught the bus / The poor old chauffeur was back in bed with a nose full of pus / Yea heavy and a bottle of bread . . .*' And I'd think, 'Wow!' We'd just go downstairs and play some chords, figure out some phrasing. Then Bob would come down and we'd take it from there." Though the basement was hardly conducive to good acoustics, recording went ahead on a reel-to-reel recorder that Richard Manuel had bought for $140. "Garth ran it," Danko said, "and we had a little mixing board with maybe five inputs going into the two-track machine."

As the five men played – and drank and smoked and howled with helpless laughter – the tumultuous events of the day unfolded in the background. "They seemed to be a million miles away," Dylan said in 2014. "We weren't really participating in any of that stuff where it was 'the summer of love' . . . we weren't there, so we did our thing. We wrote 'Million Dollar Bash' to go along with the summer of love." Yet signs of the times were there nonetheless: as they had always done for Dylan, stories plucked from newspapers or television sparked ideas for songs. "You kind of look for ideas, and the TV would be on," he said. "*As the World Turns, Dark Shadows* or something . . . just any old thing would create a beginning to a song, names out of phonebooks and things. When China first exploded that hydrogen bomb, that just kind of flashed across the headlines and newspapers . . . so we'd just go in and write 'Tears of Rage'. They were rioting in Rochester, New York, and that wasn't that far away, so we wrote 'Too Much of Nothing'."

By turns lustily comic and hauntingly sad, Dylan's new songs were funny and friendly after the frenzy of the 1965/6 tours. Even the throwaway pieces were infectiously pleasurable. If "I'm Your Teenage Prayer" and "See Ya Later, Allen Ginsberg" were stoned goofs accompanied by uncontrollable giggles, Ian Tyson's "Four Strong Winds"* and the traditional "Young but Daily Growing" were clearly songs whose lyrics and melodies moved Dylan. And when he experimented with the "automatic singing" of "I'm Not There" or "Sign on the Cross" – a semi-tongue-in-cheek slice of country gospel – the results were extraordinary.

For Dylan this music afforded a liberation, a diminution of ego through immersion in folk myth. "I didn't have nothing to say about myself," he said in 2014. "I didn't figure anybody else would be interested anyway." On bluesier numbers like "What's It Gonna Be When It Comes Up" and "Dress It Up, Better Have It All" he sounded like he'd wandered into a half-empty blues lounge in 1964 to find the Hawks jamming there. "He was bringing it all back home, trying to get back to what it was that initially made him do

---

* Later covered by Neil Young, "Four Strong Winds" had been written by Tyson in the late summer of 1963, in a Lower East Side apartment that belonged to Albert Grossman.

music in the first place," says Simone Felice. "Before anything else was hanging in the balance, like money and prestige and fame, all that horseshit."

When the wider world finally heard the basement tapes, in the form of a 1975 double album released by Columbia, it was clear just how counter-revolutionary Dylan and the band had been. The man who'd inspired the hippie generation had become the ultimate anti-hippie. "Bob and the guys were like, 'We don't really wanna go to the Fillmore East every night,'" says Jonathan Taplin. "And I mean, Bob had three kids in four years."

"When we began writing at Big Pink, we weren't aware really of what was going on," says Garth Hudson. "I remember hearing the Jefferson Airplane and the Grateful Dead on recordings, but we were over in the hills." Worse than the psychedelic bands was the deafening sound of "heavy" groups like Cream. "While people were stacking up Marshall amps and blowing out their eardrums, we were down in the basement trying to get a balance," said Rick Danko. "It wasn't about one person trying to blow the others away, it was about trying to play together and find an economical common ground."

One wonders what Albert Grossman made of the recordings from Big Pink. He must have thought his cash cow had deserted him, which was very possibly what Dylan intended. But by September it was evident that Dylan had actually written some of the catchiest songs of his career – songs with busy, chattering verses and gloriously open, almost hymnal choruses: "Million Dollar Bash", "Lo and Behold!", "You Ain't Goin' Nowhere", "Open the Door, Homer" and "Nothing Was Delivered". With Manuel he'd written the strange, tender "Tears of Rage"; with Danko the broodingly apocalyptic "This Wheel's on Fire". The six men even returned to songs such as "One Too Many Mornings" and "It Ain't Me, Babe", which suggests they were contemplating going back out on the road.

When Hudson was asked to copy ten of the best basement songs onto a seven-inch mono reel, Grossman copyrighted them in

October. (Hudson added five more songs in December, Grossman copyrighting them in January 1968 and then distributing a Dwarf Music acetate of the tracks to various acts he managed – and several he didn't.) Peter, Paul and Mary recorded a cover of "Too Much of Nothing" that Peter Yarrow was ashamed of, but the Byrds cut wonderful versions of "Nothing Was Delivered" and "You Ain't Goin' Nowhere" on their country-rock album *Sweetheart of the Rodeo*. Julie Driscoll scored a UK hit with a powerful reading of "This Wheel's on Fire" that brought Danko the first of what he called "cheques from God". Manfred Mann cut "Quinn the Eskimo" as "The Mighty Quinn", and the Box Tops did "I Shall Be Released"; Fairport Convention and Jonathan King (of all people) had stabs at "Million Dollar Bash". McGuinness Flint included no less than seven basement songs on their 1972 album *Lo and Behold*. "It's always interesting when somebody takes a song of yours and re-records it," Dylan later reflected, "but these songs weren't tailor-made for anybody. I just wrote when I felt like writing."[*]

While the basement sessions continued and work slowed on *Eat the Document*, another "underground" was hatching within the Grossman camp, though without his direct involvement. In the spring of 1967 the Hawks found themselves sucked into *You Are What You Eat*, a pointlessly non-linear "documentary" co-produced by Peter Yarrow and directed by Barry Feinstein.

Sprinkled with scenes of hippie kids cavorting at San Francisco's Human Be-In, the film also featured Super Spade, a racially offensive cartoon dealer, and Clarence Schmidt, a real-life Woodstock eccentric who for twenty years had been creating extraordinary sculptural works that sprawled across a slope of Ohayo Mountain.

---

[*] For the convoluted history of the basement tapes through their years of bootlegs, see Clinton Heylin, "What's Reel & What Is Not: Some Historical Notes on Those 'Basement Tape' Tapes", in *The Basement Tapes Complete* (Columbia, 2014).

(Unfounded rumour had it that some of the zanier basement tapes – "Apple Suckling Tree", "Even If It's a Pig, Part Two" – were recorded chez Schmidt.) Even crazier than Schmidt was singer/ukulelist Herbert "Tiny Tim" Khaury, who'd been invited up to Woodstock by a fascinated Bob Dylan and who – backed by the Hawks – performed the Ronettes' "Be My Baby" and Sonny and Cher's "I Got You, Babe" in the film.

"It was going to be a documentary about the Hells Angels," says John Simon, producer of the film's soundtrack, which included songs by John Herald, Paul Butterfield and Yarrow himself. "But then the Summer of Love happened and they started filming people taking drugs. It's brutal to watch." Simon first came up to Woodstock that summer and met Howard Alk, who'd been hired to edit the film. "They put me in this house in Bearsville", Simon says, "and told us to make a movie." On Alk's birthday they were at work on the film when a discordant noise came seeping through the windows. It was the four Hawks playing various instruments they clearly had not mastered, performing a stoned serenade for Alk.

A bright Princeton graduate who'd produced the Cyrkle's 1966 smash hit "Red Rubber Ball", Simon quickly bonded with Robertson. "Howard said, 'These guys are right for each other,'" he says. "After I went back to the city, Robbie said, 'Come on up.' So we went over to Big Pink and they played me stuff live that they were working on." Simon's timing was perfect. In the autumn Levon Helm returned to the fold. The errant drummer had been in Texas with Kirby Pennick, whose Houston-based family made oil-pump liners and rods, and the two men strolled around Big Pink like they owned the place. "They were walking back out of the woods with big smiles on their faces," says Simon. "Levon said, 'Boy, ah like this place!'"

"I'd been lonesome for the band," Helm told me. "I guess I believed that at some point we would get back together. I didn't figure they would give up their dreams just to be Bob's back-up

band." In reality, he had been lured up to Woodstock by news that
Grossman was in the process of landing the Hawks their own record
deal. "I called Levon up and told him about the deal," said Danko.
"He said, 'Well, I think it stinks but I'm on my way!' I said, 'You need
a ticket?' and he said, 'No, just pick me up at the airport!' He came
up to Woodstock and I took him to Big Pink. I had a king-size bed
and he just walked in and moved into my bedroom." Helm had been
sorely missed. That southern ingredient, welding blues and country
together in one irresistibly swinging package, was the vital germ the
Hawks needed if they were ever going to move beyond being supporting players for other people's songs. "At Big Pink there were
lots of late-night parties," said Al Aronowitz. "They'd pass the guitar
around and Levon was always the star of the evening. He'd play the
mandolin and sing great old songs like 'Caldonia'."

Helm's presence at Big Pink signalled the end of the long summer idyll. Dylan knew that all good things must pass. As summer
turned to autumn he was already moving into his next phase.

2

FRANKIE AND JUDAS

The music world remained in the dark about Bob Dylan's accident. Rumours continued to circulate that his long silence was the result of serious injury or even disfigurement. Never had such a prominent musician simply disappeared in such a Garbo-esque manner. He wanted to be alone, or at least out of sight. When the *New York Post*'s Barry Cunningham came to Hi Lo Ha in January 1967, Sara Dylan threatened to call the police.

The first journalist to "penetrate the veil" – in Jonathan Taplin's phrase – was *New York Daily News* reporter Michael Iachetta, whose persistent calls to the East 55th Street office were eventually met by Albert Grossman's terse statement that Dylan was recovering from a broken neck and "is not seeing anybody" . . . followed by the sound of the dial tone. Iachetta, who'd interviewed Dylan in October 1963, drove up to Woodstock in early May 1967 and, after forty-eight hours of "vague answers" from protective locals, found his way to the "mahogany-stained estate" that was Hi Lo Ha. Fortunately for him, Dylan was in a good mood and remembered their earlier encounter. He invited Iachetta in and talked openly. He spoke of the accident and of money. He spoke of "mystery, magic, truth and the Bible in great folk music". He was, wrote Iachetta, "a gypsy-like figure in faded dungarees, lavender shirt with collar turned up to cover his neck and a purple-and-blue striped blazer".

One remark stuck out among the otherwise affable statements that appeared in Iachetta's story. Dylan said that songs were "in my head like they always are" but were "not goin' to get written down until some things are evened up. Not until some people come forth

and make up for some of the things that have happened." What was
he talking about? Who *were* these people? Iachetta chose not to
probe, and the comment was left to the conjecture of those insiders
who could read between the cryptic lines. One of them was Victor
Maymudes, who a year earlier had tipped Dylan off to the fact that
Albert Grossman was making a lot more money out of his biggest
star than anyone (including Dylan) realised. "Bob did not know that
he was giving away the rights to his songs when he handed them
over to Albert to publish," Maymudes said later. "Bob was receiving
all of the money from writing the songs but was splitting fifty–fifty
the proceeds from the publishing of the songs, which is where the
real money was."[*]

For informing on Grossman, Maymudes was rewarded with
excommunication, Dylan apparently refusing to believe Grossman
could do him any wrong. On checking his contracts, however, the
truth was revealed. Naomi Saltzman, one of Grossman's bookkeep-
ers, confirmed that her boss owned half of the Dwarf Music company set up to administrate Dylan's publishing royalties – which
meant that he was making the same amount from Dylan's songs as
their author was. Dylan was shocked, as much by his own naïvety as
by Grossman's greed. Like many entertainers he had simply trusted
in his protector and skipped the small print. His sense of betrayal
was bitter. It was as if his own father had been stealing from him. He
called a meeting with Saltzman, inviting Grossman's lawyer David
Braun and his accountant Marshall Gelfand to join them. "The tension, I believe, came from Naomi," says Jonathan Taplin. "And then
unfortunately Braun made it worse. They essentially got Bob to feel
that Albert was taking way too much of the music-publishing rev-
enue. Once Bob began to believe that Albert was screwing him, it
was all downhill from there."

[*] In point of fact, Dylan was receiving "all of the money" from *recording* the
songs, not from writing them – as the second half of Maymudes's sentence makes
clear.

"The only thing remiss in Naomi's mind", suggests Ian Kimmet, who worked for Dylan's sub-publishers B. Feldman in London, "was that it was a ten-year contract, which was not appropriate for a management contract. It was in the small print, and she told Bob not to sign. So that's where it all started breaking down." It wasn't long before Saltzman left Grossman's office and began working exclusively for Dylan out of her high-rise apartment on Bleecker Street at LaGuardia Place. Simultaneously, Braun ceased working for Grossman and then, in the autumn of 1968, helped Saltzman set up Dylan's new publishing arm, Big Sky Music. Grossman continued to receive a share of Dylan's royalties but agreed to a lower percentage rate. He was keen to keep things out of the press. "I finally had to sue him," Dylan later said. "Because Albert wanted it quiet, he settled out of court . . . He had me signed up for ten years . . . for part of my records, for part of my everything."

Not everyone saw the situation in black and white. "There are two sides to the coin," says Linda Wortman, a copyright administrator who worked for Grossman. "Most musicians of that period didn't read anything, and Dylan wasn't any different. All managers take percentages. Albert was no different, he was just smarter." Others agree. "There are those who say Albert took advantage of people," says Peter Yarrow, who saw Dylan's breakaway as little more than adolescent rebellion. "I see that as absolutely unfair and inappropriate. I never felt that Albert's contracts with Peter, Paul and Mary were in any way excessive or unfair. I also have very serious questions as to whether Bobby would have emerged as an artist *without* Albert."[*]

Dylan's fury at Grossman's perceived malfeasance came out obliquely in songs he was writing – possibly without the Hawks even being aware of them – as the Big Pink sessions wound down.

---

[*] "Did Grossman rip off Dylan?" industry commentator Bob Lefsetz wrote in 2014. "I'll let you decide. But without him there'd be little to steal."

"There is the music from Bob's house, and there is the music from our house," Robbie Robertson told Al Aronowitz. "*John Wesley Harding* comes from Bob's house. The two houses sure are different."

John Wesley Harding certainly *was* different – in mood, texture, arrangement – from the rollicking songs on the Big Pink tapes. Despite being recorded once again in Nashville with two of the key players on his previous album, Charlie McCoy and Kenny Buttrey, it was also radically different from *Blonde on Blonde*: austere and haunting, with harmonica once again in the foreground and Dylan sounding like a travelling soothsayer. In a 1969 interview with *Rolling Stone's* Jann Wenner, Dylan mentioned "the sound that Gordon Lightfoot was getting" with McCoy and Buttrey on the stripped-down, John Court-produced *The Way I Feel* (1966), claiming that *John Wesley Harding* was an (unsuccessful) attempt to "get it". Strewn with biblical references – the result of his daily poring over a large Bible set up on a *shtender* at Hi Lo Ha – the *Harding* songs were parables, allegories shot through with portent and foreboding. "The biblical resource is not an unusual one, but it certainly was special to *him*," says Bruce Dorfman. "My assumption always was that he was treating it as literature, in much the same way as he might have treated Melville as something he could draw on."

John Wesley Harding also hinted at Dylan's grief over the recent death of Woody Guthrie, whose spirit could be felt on songs such as "Drifter's Escape" and "I Am a Lonesome Hobo". Written for the most part as poems before music was added to them, they were, Dylan later said, "dealing with the devil in a fearful way, almost". Given the recent merriment at Big Pink, which devil was he talking about? Was it Grossman? At least three of the songs on *John Wesley Harding* appeared to express feelings towards his manager. Most transparent was the slow, loping "Dear Landlord", with its imprecation not to "put a price on my soul" and its sneering observation

that "anyone can fill his life up with things / he can see but he just
cannot touch".*

Equally loaded with possible allusions were the song of pity for
"the poor immigrant" who "falls in love with wealth itself / and turns
his back on me" and the implacable "The Ballad of Frankie Lee and
Judas Priest", with its description of the almost Faustian pact Dylan
had signed with Grossman in 1962 and reference to a "big house as
bright as any sun / with four and twenty windows / and a woman's
face in every one".† Even "All Along the Watchtower", the most
famous song on *John Wesley Harding*, appeared to speak of Dylan's
breakdown at the time of his accident, with businessmen drinking
his wine but not knowing "what any of it is worth". Was the joker
in that song Dylan and the thief Grossman? And was there indeed
any "way out of here"? Nowhere on the album did Dylan sound
more devil-haunted than in that song's final image of the two riders
approaching as "the wind began to howl".‡

If these extraordinary songs *were* at least partly about Grossman,
they may have been the only way Dylan could express his anger
towards him. "Albert was having a terrible battle with Bob, but I
stayed close to him," says Donn Pennebaker. "And that was a problem for me, because I was kind of in the middle of it." For the
moment, manager and artist were still yoked together by the contracts Dylan had signed in 1962. Indeed, after months of trying
to prise Dylan free of Columbia and score a huge advance out of

* In a 1971 phone conversation with self-appointed "Dylanologist" A. J. Weberman, Dylan claimed that "Dear Landlord" "wasn't all the way for Al Grossman",
adding that "only later, when people pointed it out to me that the song might
have been written for Al Grossman, I thought, well, maybe it could've been". He
specifically asked Weberman not to report that the song was about Grossman.
† At Big Pink, Dylan had cut a version of a big Porter Wagoner country hit that
warned "it's so hard to find / one rich man in ten with a satisfied mind". One could
also suggest that basement originals such as "Too Much of Nothing" ("can turn a
man into a liar") and "Nothing Was Delivered" ("some answers for what you sell
that has not been received") were veiled comments on Grossman.
‡ The *Village Voice*'s Richard Goldstein heard the line as "two *writers* were
approaching". He was informed that Dylan "got a good laugh out of that".

MGM Records' Mort Nasatir – who came to Woodstock to make sure the singer hadn't been too damaged by the motorcycle accident (and to hear tracks from the basement tapes) – Grossman had finally agreed to an improved offer from Columbia's Clive Davis, who was desperate not to lose one of the label's marquee names. But when *John Wesley Harding* was delivered as the first Dylan album under the new terms of a 10 per cent royalty rate, Davis was understandably baffled by it.

Many in Woodstock were unaware of the new *froideur* in Dylan's relations with Grossman. "My first hint of bad blood boiling between Albert and Bob came when Bob started sneering at the very mention of [his] name, muttering angry words about a mysterious incident concerning somebody's wife," Al Aronowitz wrote. "Whose wife? Albert's wife? Bob's wife? My wife? If the truth be known, all three wives were in love with Bob. Each loved Bob a little too much." Years later, Sally Grossman denied that either she or Albert thought "Dear Landlord" was about him. The general impression Dylan gave to those who socialised with him was of an almost blissfully happy family man. "He calmed down," said Eric Andersen, who'd known Dylan at his most merciless in the Village. "[He] got into his family, got into something more real and more tangible, and he was really grooving on it for a while." When Macmillan's Bob Markel visited in February 1968 to discuss *Tarantula*, he found Dylan "far more friendly, far less distracted . . . more grown-up and professional, easy to be with". Aronowitz described Dylan and his wife as "the ideal loving couple [who] flirted with each other constantly" and "put on an impressive show for me, a drama full of romance and wisecracks and everyday common sense".

  "That was the time we knew Bob best," says Happy Traum. "It was very family-oriented – dinners together, hanging out and playing a lot of music. He would come down to our house and say, 'Hey, you wanna hear this new song I wrote?' What were we gonna say, 'No'?

I remember some of the songs from *John Wesley Harding*. Very few
people were let into that world – a couple of artists and a couple of
stonemasons – so we were very careful not to abuse the privilege."
Indeed, when he agreed in the summer of 1968 to do three interviews with Traum and John Cohen for *Sing Out!* – which Traum
was then editing – Dylan preferred to talk about stonemasons than
about Vietnam. To Bruce Dorfman he even expressed support for
George Wallace, the pro-segregation governor of Alabama who ran
for president that year. "He was a small-town kid, and a lot of his
thinking politically was quite conservative," says Dorfman. "What
I was getting from him was, 'At least you know what you're getting
with Wallace, so you can deal with it.'"*

Affectation or not, Dylan took his country-boy act to such an
extreme that when he needed a new suit he asked Dorfman to
accompany him to Sears, Roebuck in Kingston. "He had this big
truck and he put Buster in the back," Dorfman recalls. "At Sears
he found a horrendous green suit with saddle-stitched collars and
pockets. He thought it was terrific, and I don't think he was making
it up. Innocence gets shattered at some point, but then it comes
right back again." When Dylan showed the suit to Sara – who in her
hippie-maternal way was quite chic – she smiled. "She said, 'That's
a lovely suit, Bob,'" says Dorfman. "She just tolerated this stuff in a
bemused way."

Dorfman saw something troubled in Dylan's "sad-eyed lady". She
had problems squaring her Playboy Bunny past with her new role as
muse and fertile momma. (The couple's third child, who was given
the very Hebraic names Samuel Abraham, was born in July 1968,
a little over a year after the birth of his sister Anna.) "There were

* Dylan said the same thing when Elliott Landy photographed him at Hi Lo Ha.
After leaving the house, Landy ran into Richard Manuel and told him what Dylan
had said. "I don't know," Manuel said with a chuckle. "You can never tell with Bob
if he is serious or not . . ." In *Chronicles* Dylan admitted that he had "a primitive
way of looking at things and I liked Country Fair politics".

times in her life when she was very unkind to herself and became very involved with the possibility of doing herself in," Dorfman says. "There was a self-destructive dimension to her, emotionally and psychologically, that she was very actively trying to somehow hold off to the side."

It was Sara who made Dorfman and his wife aware of the war that had broken out between her husband and Grossman. "Over the course of maybe a year", Dorfman recalls, "what I got from her was that Bob was going through a very bad thing with Grossman and was thinking of changing managers. The idea was that he shouldn't have had to read the contract, which I think a lot of artists would say. They should be able to trust people."

By early 1968, the falling-out between the two men had become obvious to those around them. When Dylan appeared onstage with the Hawks during two Carnegie Hall memorial concerts for Woody Guthrie – "so changed, serene, smiling, oddly respectable in his grey suit and open-checked blue shirt," Lillian Roxon wrote – Levon Helm noticed that he did not speak a single word to his manager the entire evening.

3

SOMETHING TO FEEL

Levon Helm and his fellow Hawks had not performed together as a unit since the autumn of 1965. Backing Dylan at Carnegie Hall on Guthrie songs that dipped back into the camaraderie of Big Pink – while also bringing Bob back into the bosom of folk's older guard – they were taking a night off from the recording sessions for their debut album at nearby A&R Studios. In his 1993 autobiography, Helm noted that "just as Bob was leaving Albert's stable, we were arriving".

With a new name for the group still undecided, Grossman had struck a deal with Alan Livingston at Capitol Records, the Los Angeles label whose acts included the Beatles and the Beach Boys. Encouraged by Dylan, the group were breaking away and – as song-writers – learning to stand on their own feet. "I was there when Robbie realised he could write," said Sally Grossman. "I'm sure Bob was an inspiration. Robbie thought, 'Wait a minute, let me try.' And he started writing those Americana songs." Among the tracks released that summer as *Music from Big Pink* were two of the basement songs co-written by Dylan. Featuring a mournful Richard Manuel melody – and a vocal worthy of his great influence Ray Charles – "Tears of Rage" unequivocally set out Dylan's counter-revolutionary position,* while a thrusting version of the Dylan/Danko song "This Wheel's on Fire" also made the cut. Arguably, though, the true flavour of

* In 1997's *American Pastoral*, which could almost be "Tears of Rage" in novel form, sometime Woodstocker Philip Roth wrote of his hero's terrorist daughter that she "transports him out of the longed-for American pastoral and into everything that is its antithesis and its enemy, into the fury, the violence, and the desperation of the counterpastoral – into the indigenous American berserk".

the reborn group came through in the songs inspired by the rural backgrounds of Danko and Helm – "The Weight", "We Can Talk" and "Caledonia Mission". "Levon and I have a powerful kinship," Danko told me in 1995. "I grew up in southern Ontario, he grew up in Arkansas. He grew up in a cotton belt and I grew up in a tobacco belt, and it was under similar situations – a farming community and those values. And we listened to similar blues and country music, so our influences were much the same."

On *Music from Big Pink* a unique white-gospel country-funk style was patented and never successfully copied. "To us", says Robbie Robertson, "southern music that was white or black all got swirled in the same gumbo." *Big Pink* was the sound of all the Hawks' R&B and country influences filtered through Dylan's poetics and expertly pieced together by John Simon. "John referred to it as 'Robbie's album' and invited me down to the sessions," says Al Kooper, who reviewed *Big Pink* for *Rolling Stone*. "I had no idea what was going to be on there, and then I heard it up at Albert's and went, 'Oh my God! Those guys did *this*?!' Something had happened that I'd missed, and I think it was all that Woodstock stuff."

From "Tears of Rage" to "I Shall Be Released" – another of Dylan's basement songs – *Music from Big Pink* was about empathy and chemistry: five instinctively soulful players working together, their voices blending, their parts locking in time: *"One voice for all, echoing around the hall,"* as they sang on "We Can Talk". Nothing smooth or slick: a gutty, gritty sound conjuring a funky backwater world. Sweet pining reverie and rollicking gospel from Richard Manuel, ribald Arkansas bravado from Levon Helm, feckless bemusement from Rick Danko; an afterthought, "The Weight", that became The Band's most famous song; one blasting, organ-churned rocker in "Chest Fever", but mostly a deep spirit of fraternity and small-town oddness.°

° The gospel influence on The Band was made even clearer by Garth Hudson's 2014 account – in the *Basement Tapes Complete* box set – of the group listening to a bunch of late-fifties Savoy and Vee Jay singles owned by the Hawks' road

"John Simon understood the recording console," Robertson recalled of the sessions. "He asked us how we wanted the record to sound, and we told him, 'Just like it did in the basement.'" Capitol were so delighted by what they heard that they flew the group out to LA, where six more tracks were taped at the label's eight-track studio in the basement of the Capitol tower in Hollywood. "All those tunes like 'In a Station' were so dreamy, instead of banging away like all the hard-rock stuff at the time," says guitarist Jim Weider. "It created a sound up here that really became the Woodstock sound."

Rumours unsurprisingly spread that Dylan was playing on *Music from Big Pink*. Aside from his three songwriting credits, however, all he contributed to the album was the faux-naïf painting on Milton Glaser's cover. More of a cultural signifier was Elliott Landy's group portrait of the five band members with their families at Rick Danko's brother's farm in Simcoe, Ontario. "The idea of the picture was totally unusual to me," Landy admits now. "Despite having a lot of relatives, my whole issue at the time was to *separate* from my family." At a time when Jim Morrison was threatening to kill his father on "The End", *Big Pink*'s sleeve honoured the bonds of kith and kin.

The first people to sit up and pay attention to *Big Pink* were other musicians. When Eric Clapton obtained an acetate of the album, it ruined any pleasure he got from playing with Cream. "[It] came as a bit of a shock in 1968," recalled Richard Thompson of Fairport Convention, who holed up in their own Hampshire version of Big Pink to work on 1969's *Liege and Lief*. "It seemed to vault over the zeitgeist, back to purer roots – kind of counter-counterculture. The psychedelic bands were playing bits of blues and country, but The Band seemed to have real authority [. . .] And they wore suits! And had short haircuts!" Three decades on, *Big Pink* still sounds wholly fresh and original. "Out of all the idle scheming," Richard

---

manager Bill Avis. "There was a Caravans song called 'To Whom Shall I Turn' that Richard listened to over and over," Hudson recalled. Equally influential on the group were the early recordings of the Staple Singers.

Manuel sang on his dreamy "In a Station", "can't we have something
to feel?"*

Albert Grossman's estimation of The Band suddenly skyrocketed.
"I ran into him one night at the Tin Angel above the Bitter End,"
said Artie Traum, himself now being managed by Grossman. "He
had the cover of *Big Pink* in his hands and he turned to me and –
with his very pretentious way of speaking – said, 'I've got the best
group that ever lived, and this is it.'" At least a part of the reason
for Grossman's embrace of the group was the loss of Dylan's trust
in him: he needed new stars. "He hadn't cared a thing about the
Hawks," says Michael Friedman. "When The Band became successful, all of a sudden he started looking at the balance sheet and
decided Robbie was the way to go. He was an opportunist."

Though Robertson was hardly the sole talent in The Band,
Grossman chose to focus on him – just as Robertson focused on
Grossman, frequently socialising with him in Bearsville. A street
urchin at heart, Robertson was busy reinventing himself as a debo-
nair man of the world and as Grossman's new favourite son. "Albert
could see that Robbie was probably the most driven and the least
fucked-up of them, so he named him as bandleader," says Barbara
O'Brien, who waitressed at Woodstock restaurant Deanie's and
later managed Levon Helm. "So he made a right move, looking at
it from the outside." The problem was, Grossman taking Robertson
under his wing sowed seeds of distrust and disharmony within the
group. "Nowadays I would so warn against that with a young band,"
O'Brien says. "I would say you should incorporate and make sure it's
a partnership where everything gets shared equally."

In contrast to Robertson, the other Band members hung loose
in Woodstock. Helm and Danko, who'd moved out of Big Pink

---

* One of the more unexpected tributes to *Music from Big Pink* was the
appearance of its sleeve in the video for ABBA's 1981 hit "One of Us", in which
Agnetha Fältskog was seen unpacking and filing her record collection in her new
post-break-up apartment.

into a house off the Wittenberg Road, held court at the Espresso, wolf-whistling the hippie girls who drifted along Tinker Street.* "Most of us were single at that time," said Rick Danko. "It was a promiscuous kind of moment. People couldn't get away with that these days, but it was a very good time to grow up in terms of history."

Neither Danko nor Helm was overly impressed by the Grossmans; if anything, they had more time for local craftsmen. "Levon had more respect for carpenters – for getting your hands dirty and really working," Barbara O'Brien says. "He was always uncomfortable with his celebrity status. He would say, 'I'm just a farmer who loves to play music.'"

As it turned out, The Band were unable to capitalise on the rave reviews for *Music from Big Pink*. Before the album had even come out, Rick Danko broke his neck in one of the many accidents that he and his bandmates suffered over their years in Woodstock. "It was in the winter," says Jonathan Taplin, then being lined up to road-manage the group's first tour. "Rick had a big 'Lincoln Confidential', as he called it, and he just ran it off the road. I'm sure he was drunk. He still had a very stiff neck in February of 1969." Grossman must have cursed his bad luck: once again a road accident was going to cost him money. "It was the first time I ever saw anybody with those rigs that put spikes into your head," says Happy Traum. "We saw a lot of Rick at that time, since he was courting Grace Seldner, who lived on the same street as we did."

Meanwhile, Garth Hudson and Richard Manuel were living on Spencer Road at the top of Ohayo Mountain. The rambling single-storey house, built into rocks and belonging to concert promoter Sid Bernstein, offered dizzying views of the Ashokan

---

* The Wittenberg Road house, outside which Elliott Landy took his famous Band shot for the inside sleeve of *Music from Big Pink*, is now – through a quirk of address-changing – on West Ohayo Mountain Road, a mere quarter mile south of the Grossman pile in Bearsville. For a wonderfully convoluted account of how the house came to be identified, see www.popspotsnyc.com/the_band.

Reservoir below. The large living room became a rehearsal space for The Band, while Hudson occupied one end of the house and Manuel inhabited the other with his girlfriend, Danish model Jane Kristiansen.

Just as Dylan's Woodstock hibernation had enhanced his mystique, so The Band's inability to tour enhanced theirs. When Al Aronowitz interviewed them during the hot and turbulent summer of '68, he emphasised the back-to-nature flavour of their music and their adopted home. "*Music From Big Pink* is the kind of album that will have to open its own door to a new category," he wrote, "and through that door it may very well be accompanied by all the reasons for the burgeoning rush toward country pop, by the exodus from the cities and the search for a calmer ethic, by the hunger for earth-grown wisdom and a redefined morality, by the thirst for simple touchstones and the natural law of trees."

As riots raged and body bags came back from Vietnam, Dylan chilled out. "I met him in the loving stage, when he was existing to love and be loved by his family," says Elliott Landy, who photographed the boyishly clean-shaven star for a *Saturday Evening Post* cover story by Aronowitz. "What he became afterwards I had no contact with, but when I saw him he was experiencing stillness and quiet and love – what Woodstock was about. He was just a nice guy, very friendly, laughing."

"Bob goes to bed every night by nine," Dylan's mother, Beattie Zimmerman, told writer Toby Thompson. "[He] gets up in the morning at six and reads until ten, while his mind is fresh. After that, the day varies; but *never* before. The kids are always around, climbing all over [his] shoulders and bouncing to the music . . . they love the music, sleep right through the piano . . . and Jesse has his own harmonica, follows Bob in the woods with a little pad and pencil, jots things down . . . these are the things Bob feels are important . . . and this is the way he's chosen to live his life."

Where at the start of the year he'd been phobic about being photographed, now Dylan permitted Landy to shoot him emptying the trash and sitting in his truck. Inside Hi Lo Ha he posed with Sara and their children, sitting at his piano in a seersucker jacket. It could almost have been the beautiful *New Morning* song "Sign on the Window" come to life: "Have a bunch of kids . . . that must be what it's all about." It's possible Dylan even believed these sentiments, or thought he'd found a way of assuaging his restlessness. "He'd like to be somewhere comfortable and I don't know if that's possible for someone with a mind like that," Joan Baez told Anthony Scaduto. "I think he's attempting that with his wife and children . . . [but] I can't imagine him saying, 'I've finally found peace.'" Asked in 2015 if it was painful to give up his art to protect his family, Dylan replied that it was "totally frustrating and painful" but that he "didn't have a choice". It was no coincidence that he was struggling to write songs, later referring to his painful creative block as an "amnesia" that hit him as he was out walking one winter's morning.

When George Harrison visited Woodstock with his wife Pattie Boyd in late November 1968, he was astonished to find Dylan barely able to communicate.* Compounding the withdrawnness was Dylan's grief at the sudden and unexpected death of his fifty-six-year-old father in June. It said much that Bernard Paturel could chauffeur Dylan all the way to Kennedy airport – to catch a flight back to the funeral in Minnesota – without even knowing that Abe Zimmerman had died.

Robbie Robertson had arranged for Harrison and Boyd to stay with the Grossmans, the Beatle's visit prompted as much by *Music from Big Pink* as by Bob Dylan. "It was strange, because at the time Bob and Grossman were going through this fight, this crisis about managing him," Harrison told Timothy White in 1987. "I would

* The late Bob Johnston had a similar experience when he came to Hi Lo Ha. "My old lady Joey and Sara talked for a couple of hours while Bob and I sat and watched the fire," Johnston said. "He never said a word, and neither did I."

George Harrison with David Boyle, chez Albert Grossman, November 1968
(courtesy of David Boyle)

spend the day with Bob and the night with Grossman, and hear
both sides of the battle."

Disillusioned by the friction back home with his bandmates,
Harrison heard in The Band's album what his friend Eric Clapton
did: a warmth, a spirit of brotherhood that offered freedom from
the pitfalls of stardom. "George came to visit at a time when there
were all these tensions with the Beatles in London," says Jonathan
Taplin. "I think he felt that the music being made in Woodstock was
getting back to the roots of what he and Lennon had grown up with.
And if you listen to *Let It Be . . . Naked*, it has the kind of simplicity
that The Band had."*

Harrison's encounter with Dylan was painfully awkward. Dylan

---

* In 1993, when Viking Press solicited an endorsement of my Band biography
Across the Great Divide, Harrison sent back this generous line: "They were the
best band in the history of the universe." Quite a statement for an ex-Beatle.

was on edge before Harrison and Boyd even arrived. "He came down to my studio and said they were coming," Bruce Dorfman remembers. "I didn't really care, but there was a whole thing about them coming to the house. From the grey box, you could sort of see some movement up on the road, and there clearly was a vehicle. Bob got himself all excited and said, 'That must be George, he's taken the wrong road.' He was absolutely awestruck."

"Bob was an odd person," Pattie Boyd recalled. "God, it was absolute agony. He just wouldn't talk. He certainly had no social graces whatsoever. I don't know whether it was because he was shy of George or what the story was, but it was agonisingly difficult. And Sara wasn't much help, she had the babies to look after." Ironically, one of the two songs Harrison and Dylan managed to write together – on the third agonising day at Hi Lo La – was a guileless plea for trust and intimacy called "I'd Have You Anytime".

Things were easier when Harrison and Boyd came for Thanksgiving dinner at Hi Lo Ha, where they were joined by the Dorfmans, the Traums, Mason Hoffenberg and others. Initially the atmosphere was stiff and formal, Dorfman becoming so irritated by the general sycophancy towards Dylan that he left. "Everybody was deferring to the master when they were out shooting hoops in the yard," he says. "I became very annoyed and just walked away from it." Later, says Happy Traum, "there was a knock at the door and in walked five guys looking like they had just stepped out of a nineteenth-century daguerreotype". It was the first time Traum had encountered The Band. "What totally broke the ice", he says, "was when Richard Manuel sat down at the piano and the other guys gathered around for an impromptu rendition of 'I Shall Be Released'." Any lingering stiffness was dispelled by Hoffenberg's suggestion of an orgy. "Let's get all the boys over on that side and all the girls over on *this* side," the co-author of *Candy* yelled. "First couple to get their clothes off and screw wins." History fails to record what happened next.

The host of the star-studded evening was slowly falling out of love with the Byrdcliffe house he'd bought three years before. Hippies were finding their way up to Hi Lo Ha, searching for the folk messiah who'd forsaken them. The Dylans often came home to find hippies in their swimming pool. Most were harmless, but some were scary. Fearing for the safety of his family, Dylan requested a personal hotline to Woodstock police chief Bill Waterous and even bought a Winchester rifle that he referred to as the Great Equaliser. "He had a very gutsy, confrontational side," says Bruce Dorfman. "One time he asked me to come up to the house because he'd heard some noises in there. So we went in and roused a couple out of his and Sara's bed. He went to get his gun, and it wasn't a conversation."

As he weathered the winter of 1968/9, Dylan thought hard about two things: an album of country-and-western songs – to be recorded once again in Nashville – and a move to somewhere less accessible than Hi Lo Ha.

4

PAINT MY MAILBOX BLUE

Bob Dylan wasn't the only artistic giant to seek sanctuary in the Catskill mountains in the sixties. Just as the singer had fled controversy and hysteria by hiding out in Woodstock, so novelist Philip Roth chose to escape the scandal of his best-seller *Portnoy's Complaint* by moving from Manhattan to Byrdcliffe, at the very time when Dylan was making plans to leave it.

"The visibility unnerved me," Roth said in 2014. "I liked it the old way. And so I moved out to the country." Woodstock, he recalled, provided "a combination of social seclusion and physical pleasure" as he wrote his novella *The Breast* and his young girlfriend worked on her dissertation in an adjacent cabin. He added that he'd "never felt more imaginatively polymorphous than when I would put two deck chairs on the lawn at the end of the day and we'd stretch out to enjoy the twilight view of the southern foothills of the Catskills". Among his closest friends in Woodstock was the painter Philip Guston, who'd made a permanent move to the town two years before. The two Phils took a shared delight in what Guston called "crapola" – in Roth's words, "billboards, garages, diners, burger joints, junk shops, all the roadside stuff that we occasionally set out to Kingston to enjoy . . ." Phil the Painter and Phil the Writer would, Roth said, "drive over to Kingston, have a walk around, take in whatever was hideous, [and] have lunch in my favourite diner The Aim to Please".

Few of the musicians who'd moved to Woodstock could have expressed themselves as eloquently as the creator of compulsive onanist Alexander Portnoy, yet most would have agreed with Roth about "the twilight view of the southern foothills of the Catskills". They had left the city in order to breathe clean air, gaze at the mountains and feel a little more creative than they did in cold-water walk-ups in lower Manhattan. "Things got so rough in the East Village, with motorcycle gangs and race wars on my block, it was very scary," said Artie Traum, who moved up to Woodstock in 1968 and became the caretaker at Hi Lo Ha. "So when Bob and Albert and everyone started moving up here, I just felt I had to follow."

Traum had a direct connection to Dylan and Grossman, but others followed in his tracks simply because they knew Dylan was there. "The image of Woodstock for me was defined primarily by him," says Danny Goldberg. "It was this sort of magical place in the country that the great genius of our culture had chosen to live in." Hot on the heels of that knowledge, Goldberg says, *Music from Big Pink* had "created a mythology of the place as somewhere where musical greatness was comfortable and alternative to the city".

What many of those now coming into town failed to notice was that the musicians who'd made Woodstock famous as a creative hub were the very ones who were trying to shake people off. "Most of them went there to disappear," says Milton Glaser, who continued to do design work for Albert Grossman. "Albert came up to disappear too. Every once in a while he used the house to entertain, but mostly he used it to isolate himself." Recluses such as Dylan liked the fact that, at heart, Woodstock was still a small blue-collar town in the mountains. And some of the older bohemians had been there for so long that they thought of themselves as natives anyway. "The Byrdcliffe people had faded away, but the artists were still here," says Graham Blackburn. "And because they'd been here for fifty years, Woodstock was one of those rare places in America where you could walk about with long hair and not get lynched."

As more musicians and their fans trickled into town, some of the natives grew restless. Cindy Cashdollar grew up in Woodstock with a dad who drove through town muttering curses on the "goddamn hippies" arriving by bus. For Jon Gershen, who moved to Woodstock with a band called the Montgomeries in the spring of 1969, "the people who really managed the town – the supervisor, the fire chief, the guy that had the plumbing business – had gotten used to the quirky element and figured out a way to deal with that. But as the rock folks started to come up here, it was a challenge for them."

Certain Woodstock landmarks remained impervious to the cultural upheaval. Deanie's was still the only proper restaurant in town, a place where – of necessity – natives and artists supped together. Deanie Elwyn had been serving unpretentious American food since 1936, opening his eponymous establishment at the corner of Mill Hill Road and Deming Street. When he reopened it in 1960, once again it became the centre of the town's low-key nightlife. "Deanie's was where Republican attorneys and insurance agents would go," says Graham Blackburn, "*and* all the nouveau riche rock 'n' rollers.

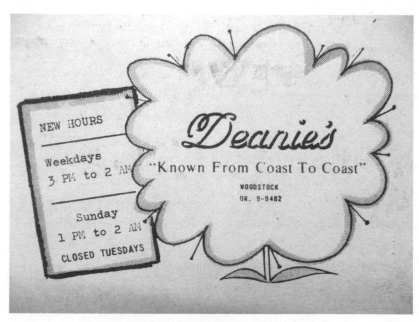

(Courtesy of the Woodstock Historical Society)

If those two groups had met anywhere else in America, it would have been instant antipathy." Regular patrons of Deanie's included Rick Danko and Richard Manuel, who often caroused with the very police officers who'd charged them with DUIs. When The Band brought George Harrison to the restaurant, the house pianist Flo Odell instantly switched to her arrangement of the Beatles' "Michelle". "Everyone ran over and told her to shut up," says Richard Heppner. "They said, 'You'll get him mad and he'll leave!'"

Woodstock had long been a sort of staging post between Greenwich Village and the Great American Wilderness. "Some people really took things seriously and went to communes in Vermont," says Robbie Dupree, who relocated from Brooklyn. "We urbanites weren't really up for that. We wanted to be some place where you could get a *New York Times* and a bagel." Yet Dupree acknowledges the impact that Stewart Brand's book *The Whole Earth Catalog* had in fostering a new back-to-the-land conscious-ness in Woodstock, whose very name seemed to encourage pastoral retreat. ("We like that name, it has a familiar ring to it," Dylan told Al Aronowitz. "That's one of the reasons we moved up here.") The *Catalog*, says Dupree, was "the bible of dropping out and getting out of the city . . . people who came to Woodstock started dressing down and putting their TVs in the closet".

Charles Reich's 1970 best-seller *The Greening of America* took things even further, blending sociology with celebrations of mari-juana and denim. *Village Voice* pop critic Richard Goldstein had a college friend who was "tilling the land in the Catskill Mountains" and for whom – in Goldstein's words – "leaving the city was the only way to maintain the hippie ideal against the urban corruptions of commerce and chic". Communes sprung up around Woodstock, one blessed with the name True Light Beavers, who in June 1969 bought a small property in Willow and expanded to include a number of families that grew their own food and even founded a free school. Another newcomer was Alan Gordon, who moved to

Woodstock from Haight-Ashbury and later founded the monthly *Woodstock Aquarian*. In its inaugural issue he described Woodstock as "a town but more a name that symbolises a state of consciousness . . . a Mecca for the culture of the new age".

"I can't say that Dylan was the *sole* attraction for me coming here," Gordon later told Elliott Landy, "but it was symbolic of what the place represented. I was very much into his poetry and so forth, and having had my own vision of whatever you want to call it – spirituality, God – I felt I was being swept along in something." Similarly swept along was Michael Lang, whom Gordon had known in Florida. "[Michael] had . . . a place there called the Head Shop," Gordon recalled. "I told him I was coming up here to live and he said he was coming here also. We agreed that we would meet up here . . . and we kind of hit it off fairly decently with each other."

Lang, who arrived in Woodstock in the early spring of 1968, recalls "a whole Coconut Grove contingent" that relocated there in the late sixties. Among them was folk singer Fred Neil, who'd been one of Dylan's first points of contact in Greenwich Village and whose velvety baritone had influenced singers from Tim Buckley to David Crosby. "Fred was someone who was talked about with great reverence," says Procol Harum's Keith Reid. "I don't know that I'd even heard his records, but people spoke about him all the time." Neil was a recluse who'd struggled with drugs before finding redemption in his passion for dolphins. There weren't many of those in Woodstock, but Neil found the town healthier than Manhattan after he moved into a cabin built for him by his manager Howard Solomon.

"The cabin was off Route 212 past Glasco Turnpike, near Big Pink," says Lang, who took over Neil's management from Solomon. "Freddie was in good shape, though he didn't want to work." Jeremy Wilber, who returned to his native Woodstock in the summer of 1968, says that "once in a while, after about his twelfth or fifteenth Irish coffee", Neil would "belt one out in the Sled Hill Café, but it

was very, very rare". He did, however, submit to the recording of the
first side of his 1971 album *The Other Side of This Life* at Woodstock's
Elephant club, with guitarist Monte Dunn backing him on loose,
convivial versions of "The Dolphins" and "Everybody's Talkin'" (the
song that took Harry Nilsson to No. 2 after John Schlesinger used it
in his 1969 hit film *Midnight Cowboy*).

Two other hard-drug users from the Village folk scene, Tim
Hardin and Karen Dalton, based themselves at least part-time in
Woodstock in an effort to steer clear of narcotic temptation. Peter
Walker even remembers them singing together in Fred Neil's
cabin. "Tim was trying to get past his habit so he could be the man
he wanted to be," says Harvey Brooks, who played on sessions by
the three singers. "I think they all found Woodstock to be a place
where they could stare up at the mountains contemplating how
things could be or should be." Not that it proved easy to avoid
heroin in Woodstock, since the drug had followed the music up
to the Catskills. "There was an *epidemic* of it here from 1967 till
about 1970," says Jeremy Wilber. "The town was just awash in it.
Some of my friends got caught up in it. Most of them, thankfully,
survived."

Hardin, who had moved into a house on Zena Highwoods Road, at
least moderated his drug use there. "The house is a beautiful country home, [with] real logs," he told *Hullabaloo* magazine, though he
added that he didn't "get along very good" with fellow Woodstock
import Bob Dylan.* "I don't think it would have been hard for Tim
to get drugs *anywhere*," says Michael Lang. "But moving up here
might have taken him out of that environment."

One of Hardin's local performances was at the first "Sound-Out", a
small music festival held near Fred Neil's cabin. Although it was in

---

* That didn't stop Dylan recording Hardin's best-known song, "If I Were a
Carpenter", with the Hawks. Though it may not have been taped at Big Pink, it
was included on *The Basement Tapes Complete*.

Saugerties, the festival was known from the start as the Woodstock Sound-Out – and retained that name till the following year, when it became simply the Woodstock Sound Festival. "Tim would regularly show up at these outdoor events," says Jeremy Wilber, "and he'd get up on the stage and keel over from too much heroin."

For most of the few hundred spectators, the first Sound-Out – held on Labor Day of 1967 – was not an especially druggy affair. Rather, it was an idyllic gathering of hippies who'd moved into the area, grooving to music by Richie Havens, Phil Ochs and Billy Batson. "Richie was the first major artist to play there," says Dean Schambach, who built a low stage for the concert. "On a beautiful starry night there were people with Volkswagen buses, and they built fires and cooked chicken. And Mike Lang saw this."

Lang himself confirms that "being out in nature, smoking a joint and not being hassled and listening to these wonderful artists was the blueprint for the elements that needed to come together". For him, the owner of the land where the Sound-Outs were staged was herself a force of nature. "She was a wily old girl," Fern Malkine says of Pansy Drake "Pan" Copeland. "She had things going on all over the place, including an art gallery in town." Though her day job was running Ann's Delicatessen on Tinker Street, the fifty-seven-year-old Copeland loved artists and musicians, providing them with cheap accommodation in a quasi-communal property known as the Peter Pan Farm. "What is now the Woodstock Day School was the Farm," says Lynne Naso, then the girlfriend of Paul Butterfield's drummer Philip Wilson. "Pan had three or four little houses, and lots of musicians lived there." Among them were the band Chango, members of Butterfield's group and singer-songwriter Tim Moore. "It was this farmstead kind of thing, and you can imagine what went on out there," says Robbie Dupree. "There was a sort of teepee sauna that was always filled with naked girls." Another of the Peter Pan musicians was Jim Weider. "It was a whole scene," he says. "The artist Peter Max was in the front room, and there was a place where you could practise and a few little apartments where Butterfield's guys lived."

Weider was well-placed, therefore, to catch the Sound-Outs, whose free-spirited promoter John "Jocko" Moffitt booked acts such as the Lower East Side band Cat Mother and the All Night News Boys, themselves residents of the Farm. Other groups included the Bronx-reared Blues Magoos, who'd had a Top 5 hit with "(We Ain't Got) Nothin' Yet"; the Boston-based Colwell-Winfield Blues Band; Jerry Moore's hippie-gospel troupe the Children of God; and powerful blues-rockers Fear Itself, fronted by southern singer Ellen McIlwaine. "Ellen had this voice that could bring down the house," says Fern Malkine. "And while she was singing, there was this strobe light. None of us had ever seen one before."

On the folkier side were Peter Walker, Happy and Artie Traum, Don McLean, Jerry Jeff Walker and a young James Taylor. Even England's Soft Machine and Incredible String Band played the festival. MC for the shows was usually Bob Fass, host of WBAI's Radio Unnameable in New York. Julius Bruggeman, who took over the booking of the Sound Festivals after Jocko Moffitt fell out with Pan Copeland, recalled Bob Dylan, Albert Grossman and Jimi Hendrix among the backstage visitors. And that's without even mentioning the mind-expanding goulash.

Thanks to the Sound-Outs, but mainly because of Dylan and *Music from Big Pink*, musicians were showing up in Woodstock in ever-greater numbers. In the groovy parlance of the times, they wanted to "get it together in the country". On the West Coast, Canned Heat were "Going Up the Country" in their big 1968 hit, while Taj Mahal was "Going Up to the Country, Paint My Mailbox Blue". The hippie exodus from cities was in full swing.

"We'd heard that Woodstock was a place where you could work on your material and find your voice," says Jon Gershen. "It was very cheap and there weren't a lot of distractions." With his fellow

Montgomeries – his brother David and bass player Tony Brown – Gershen found a bright-yellow house off Route 212 in Shady. Turning a parlour room into a rehearsal space, the band set about writing the songs they hoped would get them a record deal. Before long they'd bonded with other aspiring musicians who'd come to town. "There was this sense of Woodstock being a cloistered village with the mountains around you," Gershen says. "And because you felt kind of boxed in, you got to know other musicians. Someone would say, 'I'm a singer.' And you'd say, 'Well, come on over.'" Nearly all the musicians frequented a coin-operated laundromat in what was known as the Bearsville Flats. "It was run by 'Sam the Laundromat Man'," says Gershen. "He'd had a tracheotomy and had a hole in his throat that he smoked through. You'd run into Garth Hudson there. You'd run into *everyone* there, except Dylan."

Gershen noticed that most of the musicians came from urban backgrounds, which initially exacerbated the animosity of the locals. Yet as the newcomers settled into the small-town, backwoods lifestyle, slowly they were accepted. "You pretty quickly started to have a love affair with the place," Gershen says. "We would go and get our state fishing licences so that we could go down to the Ashokan Reservoir and fish. When people ponder how all of a sudden Dylan went from the wild maniac to the serene family man, you have to know that when you moved up to Woodstock, the place was a powerful force."

"It was a sort of back-to-the-farm thing that seemed attractive to people who wanted to get out of the rat-infested rehearsal rooms," says Mark McKenna, who came to Woodstock in 1968 to meet Fear Itself. "Chris Zaloom [Fear Itself's guitarist] was living in a cold-water flat on the Bowery – it was like Dresden! So it was a no-brainer for these guys to say, 'Let's get out of here and go where there's grass and trees and no rats or roaches!'" Another musician who wound up in town was a drummer with the splendidly hippiefied name Daoud Elias Shaar. "Every weekend half the people in the East Village would get on buses and go to Woodstock," says the man now known more economically as plain Daoud Shaw. "And they would sleep anywhere: in the woods, crashing at somebody's house." Shaw had joined a New York art-rock band called Chrysalis, who made an under-promoted album for MGM Records and then had the same bright idea that everyone was having. "It was, 'Let's get out of New York City,'" he says. "It was, 'We'll get a house together and we'll rehearse in the living room.' And that's exactly what we did." Featuring singer Nancy Nairn and guitarist/writer J. Spider Barbour, Chrysalis were one of the first amplified groups to play regularly at the Café Espresso, which the Paturels had sold. "It had a crummy PA system, but there was a drinking crowd that seemed to like good music," says Shaw. "And there were always people sitting in – sometimes people who *shouldn't* have been sitting in."

Tim Hardin was another regular at the Espresso, often wreaking minor havoc there. One night he was at the piano when David Boyle asked why he couldn't play "something nice like 'Misty Roses'". Fuming, Hardin reached to grab hold of a chainsaw that Boyle had with him. Boyle stood his ground. "You can ask my girlfriend if she wants to dance," he said, "but you can't touch my chainsaw." Another local legend has a smacked-out Hardin nodding off in his car in the depths of a Woodstock winter and being entombed by a heavy snowfall. To Jeremy Wilber, Hardin was "one of those people born with an overwhelming burden of unrelievable pain". When Wilber visited the singer's house with Sonia Malkine's guitarist son Gilles, it was "a very subdued scene".

The house in question provided the location for one of the stranger recordings of the late sixties. The mouthful of a title alone, *Suite for Susan Moore and Damion – We Are – One, One, All in One*, had the Columbia executives scratching their heads. But it was the experiment of the recording itself that made one wonder who could possibly have green-lit such a project. The house was literally wired for sound by engineer Don Puluse, with cables running through to a console and board in the nursery. Hardin had stipulated that tape should run 24/7 to capture every stray moment of inspiration. "This was the *mothership* of originality," says the album's producer Gary Klein. "Don couldn't believe it. He said, 'Gary, this is going to be some ride.' It was a project that was the first of its kind and maybe the *last* of its kind."

Holding the chaos together was Susan Moore herself – or, more accurately, Morss – the mother of Tim's son Damion. She made tea and baked cakes for Klein, Puluse and a smattering of musicians from Paul Butterfield's new band: guitarist Buzzy Feiten, trumpeter Keith Johnson, alto saxophonist David Sanborn and drummer Philip Wilson. Butterfield himself played harmonica on "Last Sweet Moments". "They were in a good place," Klein says of Hardin and Morss. "Tim was kissing Susan and grabbing her in front of everyone. He loved showing his affection. He loved playing with his kid when he wasn't recording." But things can't have been quite as happy as they seemed. A mere two weeks after tying the knot with Hardin in a small private ceremony, Morss – to whom the whole meandering opus had been an extended poetic hymn – took baby Damion and split.

"It's a very impressionistic recording," Klein says of *Suite for Susan Moore* . . . "It's just *out there*, and they paid a lot of money for it. I'm surprised they even released it, to tell you the truth." Even Hardin fan Will Sheff of Okkervil River struggled with the album, writing in 2005 that "its sadness comes not from contemplation or from clear-eyed and hard-won wisdom but from how empty Hardin's pronouncements on romantic commitment and fatherly love ring".

Another local musician who played on the album was keyboard player Warren Bernhardt, who'd gigged with Hardin in New York and followed him up to Woodstock in late 1968. "Tim called me the 'Minister of Joy'," he remembers. "When he was *on*, he was the best singer I ever heard in my life. But the *Suite* recording was pretty haphazard. There was a lot of sitting around and waiting. Tim had a

couple of gofers: Michael Lang was one of them. It was, 'Mike, go
get us some cheeseburgers and coffee . . .'" Bernhardt was playing
the Espresso on the night Hardin wandered off to find a fingerpick
and didn't return for three hours. "But everybody stayed," he says.
"And when he got back we did a long, long set till about five in the
morning. It was like going to see Charlie Parker: you just had to wait
till he showed up."

Hardin was also a regular at the Sled Hill Café, a funky dive at the
intersection of Deming Street and Sled Hill Road opened by Buddy
Sife in 1964.* A notorious local known as "Crazy" Wayne Ambrosio
was in his cups one night at the Sled Hill when Hardin sauntered
past to retrieve his guitar from the storeroom. "There goes Tim
Hard-On," Ambrosio muttered, to which Hardin responded by
returning with the guitar and lifting it high over the drunk man's

(Courtesy of the Woodstock Historical Society)

* Between 1967 and 1968, the Sled Hill had a brief makeover as macrobiotic
restaurant the Paradox.

head. "I happened to be standing behind Tim at that moment," says Jeremy Wilber, one of Sife's bartenders. "I grabbed the body of the guitar so that he couldn't kill Wayne. I'm pretty sure I kept him out of jail."

By early 1969, the Sled Hill was the main hangout for Woodstock's musical in-crowd, a former lumber shed where the more bibulous stars would show up in the small hours. "If you played a serious gig, that was at the Espresso," says Graham Blackburn, "but the Sled Hill was the main meeting place." Even Dylan came by. "He wouldn't come to play," says Jeremy Wilber, "but when the guitars were passed around after hours he'd say, 'Hey, I know a tune.' And Bobby Neuwirth would pick up a guitar and sing back, and then Levon would sing something else. That was not unusual."

Less of a hangout per se was the Elephant. Seizing on Woodstock's status as a bucolic outpost of Greenwich Village, Gaslight Café manager Sam Hood converted the former home of the S.S. Sea Horse into a properly functioning club where folk singers and bluesmen played over summer weekends. "A lot of live venues in Woodstock were kind of ad hoc affairs," says Jon Gershen. "Sam was the first guy who'd actually owned and managed a big-city club. He put a lot of money into the Elephant, and that made people take notice. He was able to bring in a lot of well-known performers. I remember a riveting show by Doc and Merle Watson. Everyone turned up for that one, including all five guys from The Band."

By the early summer of 1969, the Elephant and the Espresso were packed almost every weekend. Just a year earlier, Larry Packer of Cat Mother and the All Night News Boys had strolled down Rock City Road with a fellow musician. "The guy said to me, 'You watch, one day this town will be like Provincetown,'" Packer says. "I said, 'Come on, you're crazy.' But he was right."

5

EVERYBODY'S APPLE PIE

Such was Woodstock's almost mystical appeal that other British musicians followed in George Harrison's tracks, making pilgrimages to the town to see what the fuss was about. "We were getting input from people who came to visit us," says Happy Traum. "The Incredible String Band came and spent a bunch of time here because their manager Joe Boyd was friends with Jim Rooney and Geoff and Maria Muldaur from the Cambridge days."

Through Boyd came another folk act from across the water. John and Beverley Martyn had met just a few months before Boyd brought them to New York. Shortly after tying the knot in April 1969, the couple flew to America with Beverley's baby daughter to work on an album for Island Records. Escaping the infernal humidity of Manhattan, they took a bus up to Woodstock, where Boyd had rented them a house – recently vacated by the Traums – on Lower Byrdcliffe Road. To their surprise they learned that their friend Jackson C. Frank was living in town with model Elaine Sedgwick and their newborn son. It turned out Frank had spent time there the previous year; he'd even edited a newspaper called the *Woodstock Week* and helped Pan Copeland with the Woodstock Sound Festival. But it was clear that all was not well with the feted composer of "Blues Run the Game", who as a boy had survived the horrifying trauma of a school fire in his native Buffalo. "He wasn't right and he would do strange things," says Beverley. "He turned up one afternoon with an axe and confronted John saying, 'It should have been me.' There was a jealous thing going on, like *he* should have been making an album for Island."*

There were idyllic moments with Frank nonetheless. He drove the Martyns up to Palenville, where John floated down Kaaterskill Creek in a rubber tyre and Beverley fantasised about living the hippie life in the Catskills wilderness. John fell so in love with the area that he wrote a winsome song – called simply "Woodstock" – in the town's honour, complete with lyrics such as *"Butterflies flutter by, every-body's apple pie / Even the man next door can sing . . ."* "I thought it was rather naïve," confesses Beverley, "especially since right next door to us was a Mafia family that was straight out of *The Sopranos*." Another neighbour turned out be Pamela Feeley, childhood sweet-heart of Lee Marvin, who'd recently returned from Hollywood to marry her. "She took me to meet Lee," says Beverley. "She was a great woman. She wasn't all nail varnish and blow-dried hair."†

Though the album that Joe Boyd had brought the couple over to record was supposed to be a solo release by Beverley, her husband slowly took control of the project. To her alarm, the half-Scottish charmer with the face of a Renaissance angel was morphing into an insecure, controlling alcoholic. Not wanting to upset him, she

---

* The death of his son from cystic fibrosis would push Frank into a deep depression and eventually into severe mental illness. "He proceeded to fall apart before our very eyes," remembered singer Al Stewart, a friend from the London folk days. His decline inspired Sandy Denny's painfully beautiful song "Next Time Around". In Woodstock there were rumours about him screwing up an audition for Albert Grossman that might have turned his career around. In the late seventies he lived briefly in the Broadview Road cabin where Bob Dylan had first stayed in 1963. After a period spent homeless on the streets of New York, where he'd gone in search of help from his old friend Paul Simon, he lived his last years in sheltered accommodation in Woodstock. "The last time I saw him", said Tom Paxton, "[. . .] he was in terrible condition, drunk and minus an eye." Frank died in March 1999.

† Feeley's father was old-school Woodstock and no admirer of rock stars. When he heard a jam session taking place in a neighbouring house rented by songwriters John and JoHanna Hall, he came over and threatened to call the cops. "Clearly he thought there was an orgy going on," says JoHanna. "With people like that it was very much like, 'Go back to New York where you came from!'"

"STORMBRINGER!"

John and BEVERLEY MARTYN

played along. Rehearsals for the recording sessions took place in the Lower Byrdcliffe Road house, where they were joined by keyboard player Paul Harris, and by Harvey Brooks and Levon Helm, the rhythm section for Dylan's 1965 shows at Forest Hills and the Hollywood Bowl.° "Paul came up from the city with his wife," says Beverley. "They had a little log cabin there, like a lot of people did. Harvey also came up, bringing bagels and smoked salmon that he kept in our fridge." The album itself was recorded at New York's A&R Studios, with additional contributions from John Simon and

° Many years later, John Martyn was reunited with Helm on a duet version of "Rock Salt and Nails". According to Beverley, Helm told him, "I don't remember you too well, but your wife had a fine pair o' torpedoes on her!"

drummers Billy Mundi and Herbie Lovelle. John Martyn wound up
with six songwriting credits to his wife's four.

When the couple were invited by Happy Traum to perform at a
Fourth of July charity concert at the Woodstock Playhouse – ben-
efiting Pete Seeger's Clearwater Project to clean up the Hudson
River – John told Beverley it would be better if she didn't sing.
"He didn't want me to be seen because he thought I outshone him
onstage," she later wrote. "I said, 'Let me do one song,' which was
Lonnie Johnson's 'Jelly Roll Baker'. As I came on, there were wolf
whistles, which upset him. Then I started to sing, and you could
have cut the air with a knife. I was wailing away, and then I finished
the song and walked off to rapturous applause."

Afterwards, Beverley noticed Bob Dylan entering the Playhouse
foyer. "Tiny and gazelle-like he wore a black frock coat and a white
shirt," she later wrote. "He looked like a yeshiva boy in his gold
spectacles, a student of the Talmud." A Sephardic-Jewish beauty,
Beverley was just Dylan's type, so it was no surprise when he made
a beeline for her. Seeing them together, John crossed the room rapidly and pulled her away from him. "Don't hurt her, man," Dylan
remonstrated. "She's only saying hello." Back on Lower Byrdcliffe
Road, Beverley learned the terrifying truth about the abusive boy
who'd been abandoned by his mother and was unable to trust
women. "He started shouting and throwing things at me, including
a fork that hit me under the eye," she says. "I thought he had gone
mad. I had no idea he was capable of this sort of violence." Martyn
then burst into tears and threw himself at her feet, begging for-
giveness and beginning a cycle of marital abuse that would last for
another decade.*

*

* Though he never returned to Woodstock, it may have been more than
coincidence that – almost thirty years later – John Martyn recorded Bobby
Charles's Woodstock songs "Small Town Talk" and "He's Got All the Whiskey" on
his 1998 album *The Church with One Bell*.

Dylan himself was now living with Sara and their children in a large house on Ohayo Mountain Road. Once the home of Progressive Movement leader Walter Weyl (1873–1919), it sat at the end of a long driveway and had gates that deterred the sort of fan who – in Jeremy Wilber's words – got off the bus and said, "Where's Bob? I have to tell him something." Moreover, Dylan had recently released *Nashville Skyline*, an album of plangent country songs that wrong-footed fans and critics even more than *John Wesley Harding* had done. "The intelligentsia of the folk and rock world were very confused by it," says Michael Friedman, who had just begun working for Albert Grossman in New York. "But Dylan was always ready to surprise the world with every move he made. Albert didn't like that album either."

At least on the new album there weren't any veiled attacks on Grossman; instead Dylan presented a new musical persona – complete with an unrecognisably plummy voice – that was so completely at odds with the counterculture it felt like an attack on it. Either that or *Nashville Skyline* was exactly what it purported to be: a work of artless country comfort, picking up from where the last two *Harding* songs had left off. For its few lyrics of loss – the opening duet with Johnny Cash ("Girl from the North Country"), the green-eyed "Tell Me That It Isn't True", the resignedly lovely "I Threw It All Away" – there were many more of backwater bonhomie and desire. "In many ways [it] achieves the artistically impossible," Dylan's old Minnesota acquaintance Paul Nelson wrote; "a deep, humane and interesting statement about being happy."

Was Dylan happy? Or was *Nashville Skyline* a canny attempt to throw people off the scent, Dylan aligning himself with the music of conservative rednecks? Certainly his hatred of hippies had increased with each trespass on Hi Lo Ha. "I wanted to set fire to these people," he wrote nastily in *Chronicles*. But then he also had a pointed dig at Robbie Robertson for asking where he planned to "take" the music scene. His stance was this: people were welcome to their fantasies about him, but the only fantasy *he* had was of a normal life for his young family. And for a period the twelve-bedroom Weyl mansion, set in thirty-nine acres, offered something like the white-picket-fence existence he craved. It gave him a northerly view of Overlook Mountain and boasted huge rooms in which his children could run wild – along with the "big brass bed" of *Nashville Skyline*'s big hit "Lay Lady Lay".

"It was just very homey," says Maria Muldaur, who took her four-year-old daughter Jenni over for play dates. "Lots of rug rats crawling around on the floor playing with toys. The plates didn't match, and it was very much like I would have had it." In *Chronicles*, Dylan wrote that he "went into the bucolic and mundane as far as possible . . . the Little League games, birthday parties, taking my kids to school, camping trips, boating, rafting, canoeing, fishing". When in 1973 he came to record his rapturous hymn to his children, "Forever Young", Dylan told *Planet Waves* engineer Rob Fraboni that he'd been "carrying this song around in my head for five years".

When George Harrison came for another visit in the summer, Dylan was considerably more relaxed than he'd been on the Beatle's previous visit. "He and George and Artie and I spent about three hours just playing folk songs," says Happy Traum. "It didn't even *occur* to me to bring a camera. It was a passing thing, like a feather in the wind." At night, Dylan would make a call to Woodstock's Millstream Inn and ask owner Mitchell Rapaport to make him a pizza, which he would then eat in the inn's kitchen.* "There was a lot of time spent walking around the pool," Bruce Dorfman recalls of visits to the new house. "Bob used to clean it and clean it and clean it. I think the Ohayo Mountain Road experience was something other than Byrdcliffe had been for him. He was able to figure

* The following year Bernard Paturel, who had worked as Dylan's driver after selling the Espresso, opened a pizza place on Tinker Street, near Bearsville. He called it Country Pie after the song on *Nashville Skyline*. The Dylans occasionally ate there with their children.

out a way of delivering a persona that worked, and I don't entirely blame him for that."

"He was sort of remote," says Dean Schambach, who posed with Dylan and David Boyle for photographs that Elliott Landy took on the steps of the Woodstock Bakery on the village green.° "To a great extent there was a cold, defensive mechanism there: 'I'm insulating myself slightly. Please forgive me, but I need to do this.' And we understood that." Boyle, however, claims Dylan stole the sprinkles off the bakery's doughnuts when people weren't looking. "Bobby", he says, "was a rather dirty old dishrag who treated people like shit . . . he was never a happy family man."

While Dylan kept his adopted home town at arm's length, Woodstock's music scene flourished, not only in its clubs and bars but in the homes and cabins where musicians jammed and collaborated. "The whole thing was growing," says Happy Traum. "People would suddenly turn up in town. You could see *anybody* on the streets of Woodstock."

"It was a rarefied and fertile time for music," says Robbie Dupree. "There was an understanding and a tolerance for it all that you wouldn't have found twenty minutes away. We had interracial couples, which doesn't seem like anything today, but back then it was a big deal in rural America. So this was a refuge for people with different lifestyles." The town was, above all, *loose*. "It was an oasis, but it wasn't like people were screamingly freaked-out," says Graham Blackburn. "To us it was more normal than living in the city and wearing a hat and smoking a panatella and going to work in an ad agency."

For others, though, Woodstock's golden age was already over; the days when Dylan could sit undisturbed at the Espresso were

---

° The shots with Boyle and Schambach were Dylan's own original idea for the *Nashville Skyline* album cover. After he saw them he rejected them.

gone. "It seems to me it went fairly quickly from being the hippest place you could go to almost Touristville," says John Niven, whose 2005 novella *Music from Big Pink* is an uncanny portrait of late-sixties Woodstock. "It was already becoming a caricature of what it had been. A lot of the people were quite troubled, so there was this notion that 'If I put myself in some kind of bucolic surrounding, things will get better.' But changing your locale doesn't change what's going on inside you."

For those who went further back than Dylan, the dream of Woodstock as an artistic oasis had indubitably passed. "The town I knew, and that I'd grown up in, ceased to be," says Peter Yarrow. "There was a real shift. It became about celebrity as well as about the art. And unfortunately there were elements of this celebrity that created a very unsavoury hierarchy, whereby some people were 'in' and some were not. To my mind, that division was unhealthy and not loving. In retrospect, the simple goodness of Woodstock at that point was gone."

6

COMBINATION OF THE TWO

"You didn't talk about God, and you didn't talk about Albert," says Elliott Landy, who photographed many of Grossman's biggest clients. "Either you believed in him or you didn't."

It was difficult *not* to believe in Grossman, who had built his power base on the backs of his folk superstars but was now moving firmly into the sphere of electric rock. By 1967, he was as much of a legend in his own right as any manager had been. "Even more than Colonel Tom Parker, he was larger than life," says Danny Goldberg. "He had two reputations. One was that he knew what artists were worth and would fight for their right to be weird. The other was that he had personally made a lot of money and maybe was a little tricky in the way he made it. When I got to know him, he was clearly somebody who had a sense of his own mythology and milked it at all times."

It was as if Grossman had become the very person people thought he was. When they interpreted his long silences as power plays, he decided that that was what they would be. "Only a fool would not smile back at Albert Grossman," Warner Brothers executive Carl Scott said of him many years later. The Grossman that Dylan fans saw in *Dont Look Back* – gruff and bullying when he needed to be – was as useful a persona as any employed by Dylan himself. "He was one of the first managers to create his own brand," says Paula Batson, who worked for him in the early seventies. "You think of the long hair with the ponytail, his demeanour of being so cool and aloof. That was really something new, that a manager would attain that kind of power."

The hair and ponytail – held in place by a twist of wire – were key to Grossman's persona. As much as he liked to make money, he preferred looking hip to looking rich. One night in New York he was eating in an expensive restaurant with Robbie Robertson, John Simon and Jonathan Taplin when a middle-aged woman approached the table and began bawling "God Bless America" at the top of her lungs. "Those kinds of things would happen everywhere you went," says Michael Friedman. "Just walking down Park Avenue with Albert was a trip."

That the ponytail persona was deceptive was irrelevant to Grossman. He paid lip service to radical politics, but more important was not being mistaken for a typical businessman. "Albert would never venture a political opinion because (a) it might not be hip and (b) it might be proven wrong," says Peter Coyote, who came to Woodstock at Grossman's invitation with Emmett Grogan, co-founder with Coyote of radical San Francisco street troupe the Diggers. "Emmett and I frightened him and attracted him. He was an older guy dealing in a business populated by young kids who were changing the social structure incredibly rapidly. They knew they were making bargains with the devil, but this particular face of the devil had a ponytail and ate organic food."* For Grossman hipness was everything, though it often meant belittling lesser mortals. "He had that imposing countenance and all his little quirks," says Paul Fishkin. "But I also discovered that he was a very flawed character. He was not a nice person in a lot of ways, and a lot of people hated him because as his power grew, he abused it."

"I know people that were long-time friends of Albert's who said they wouldn't want to be on the other side of a negotiating table from him," says John Byrne Cooke, who became one of Grossman's stable of road managers. "Because when you walked out on the street you would realise you didn't have your pants on any more."

* To his credit, Grossman *did* bankroll Howard Alk's 1971 documentary about the police killing of Black Panther Fred Hampton. "That man's got to be heard," he told Alk.

Bob Dylan still had his pants on, but his rupture with Grossman was
now common knowledge. "Albert's basic thing was, 'If you're going
to sign a contract, maybe you should *read* it,'" says Jim Rooney. "He
taught a lot of his artists that this was a business and you'd better
look out for yourself. And I think Dylan came to that realisation."
If people knew about the Dylan rupture, Grossman kept schtum
about it, knowing it could only be bad PR. "Albert never even mentioned it to me," says Linda Wortman, who filed copyrights for him
at Fourth Floor Music. "It was just a fait accompli: Albert was mid-
town and Bob was downtown. It was two separate places, two separate things." Eventually Naomi Saltzman poached Wortman herself
from Grossman: "She set up Big Sky Music and hired me to run it
out of her apartment. There was an air of paranoia about it: nobody
should find out that I was working for Dylan."

Other things were changing in the Grossman office. By the end
of 1969, both John Court and Bert Block were gone. "Something
happened between John and Albert, and it must have been about
money," says Norma Cross. Having overseen albums by such artists as Gordon Lightfoot, Richie Havens, the Electric Flag and
the Paul Butterfield Blues Band, Court left to pursue his career
as a producer. "He was a great guy, very *simpatico*," says Warren
Bernhardt, who played in Court-produced jazz-blues band Jeremy
and the Satyrs. "He was always fun to work with, and he bought a
big house up near Palenville." Procol Harum's Keith Reid visited
Court's Palenville mansion with his then girlfriend Nico. "It was the
first time I'd ever seen a bucket of cocaine," he says. (Nico also took
Reid to meet Tim Hardin, who never even made it out of his bedroom to say hello.)

Bert Block's old-school sensibility, meanwhile, no longer chimed
with Grossman's hipness. "I liked him, but it was an odd mix for
him to be with Albert," says John Byrne Cooke. Michael Friedman,
who later worked with Block when he managed Kris Kristofferson,
recalls him as "a Friar's Club type who wasn't a clever eccentric guy

like Albert and didn't really care about the music that was coming out of the office". With Block gone, it was down to twenty-five-year-old Friedman to keep the show going. "I was in over my head," he says. "But because I was there, Albert felt he could spend more time in Bearsville, which was really where he wanted to be."

Into the breach stepped a new partner, Bennett Glotzer, who was younger and more ambitious and came into the company as part of a package with his brother-in-law Bobby Schuster. He also brought with him his own acts: Seatrain, Rhinoceros and Blood, Sweat and Tears. "Bennett didn't have the poetic hippie mystique that Albert had," says Danny Goldberg. Grossman's friend Ronnie Lyons recalls Glotzer as "a real douchebag" who was despised by The Band when he occasionally showed up at their concerts.

A key reason Grossman partnered with Glotzer was his legal background, which proved useful during the negotiations to sign Grossman's hottest new act to Columbia Records. That act was Big Brother and the Holding Company, a San Francisco band fronted by singer Janis Joplin. Grossman had seen them play in June 1967 at the Monterey Pop Festival, where Joplin's blood-curdling rasp of a voice so stunned the crowd that Big Brother were asked to perform a second set the following day. She was pockmarked and bacchanalian, a wild child who'd fled her native Texas to become a queen of the hippie scene in San Francisco. She was clever and funny but also deeply insecure, alcoholic and nymphomaniac, keen to live the white-negro blues life she sang about. The Big Brother musicians were stoned and clunky, but when Joplin let rip with the howling pain of Big Mama Thornton's "Ball and Chain", it didn't matter.

"This was pretty much the end of Peter, Paul and Mary and Odetta, all those early folk singers," says Michael Friedman. "And I think Albert found this a strange world. He wasn't really into rock 'n' roll at all." Yet Grossman was quietly mesmerised by Joplin, who seemed to hold the counterculture in the palm of her hand. At Monterey he was one of a cluster of powerful managers and record executives who understood that the festival was really a rock trade show masquerading as a hippie love-in. "We all thought it was great that the Grateful Dead got signed by Warner Brothers," says John Byrne Cooke. "But when you look at the effect of this over time, it was like [the record companies] co-opted the counterculture." The Dead's manager Rock Scully watched Grossman "trying to snag Janis and . . . doing it in the most ruthless, shabby way, dangling Bob Dylan, whom [she] adores, right in front of her eyes". At the back of Grossman's mind as he watched her was his need for a new solo star to replace Dylan, yet he also had to tread carefully and not show his hand too early (especially since Big Brother already *had* a manager). "The paranoia about being ripped off was universal in the San Francisco community," says Cooke. "Which was why everyone believed you shouldn't do business with 'those people in New York and LA'." As word filtered through to the group that Grossman was interested in them, Joplin felt the same ambivalence the Dead had felt: she wanted to be a star, but she also wanted to be true to the hippie cause.

In *Buried Alive*, her 1973 biography of Joplin, Grossman's in-house publicist Myra Friedman defended him even as she captured his mix of ruthless scheming and vulnerable shyness. "The most well-founded charge against [him]", she wrote, "is a tendency to become overly involved with the tomato patches in back of his Woodstock home." In the end, the overture came from Joplin to Grossman, who flew to San Francisco to meet Big Brother in November 1967. According to Friedman, Grossman told the band he could get them a generous deal and laid down only one condition: that they eschew the use of heroin. Joplin, who'd already dabbled in it, assumed her most innocent look and agreed wholeheartedly that smack was a very bad thing.

In February 1968 the group flew to New York to sign their contract with Grossman and perform at Bill Graham's Fillmore East. According to John Byrne Cooke, Grossman had already made a deal worth $250,000 with Columbia's Clive Davis, who had himself witnessed the Joplin phenomenon at Monterey. Grossman also hired John Simon, hot off *Music from Big Pink*, to produce their first album. "Albert had been working with John Court, but that was falling apart," Simon says. "I remember walking on the street in New York with him, and he said, 'I'll scratch your back and you'll scratch my back.' Which turned into, 'You'll scratch my back and *I'll* scratch my back.' But it was good for me to be affiliated with him."

As it turned out, Simon wasn't a good fit for Big Brother. Having worked with The Band, he was unimpressed by the sloppiness of Big

Janis Joplin with John Simon at Columbia's studios in New York, spring 1968 (Elliott Landy)

Brother's playing. Though Columbia had agreed that a live album would best represent the raw energy of the group's sound, Simon insisted on overdubs to make their performances sound more competent. "He didn't reach out to Big Brother in a way that made them feel appreciated," says Cooke, by now the band's road manager. "They never really established a lot of communication."* From the viewpoint of the group's lead guitarist Sam Andrew, Simon's secret dream was to be a member of The Band: "They were wonderful players, really tight. And then he comes into this insane group of Californians, who are playing these jangly, out-of-tune guitars."

"Janis and I were both young, and I was impatient with her," Simon admits. "Meanwhile, she saw me as Mr Smarty-Pants who didn't get what they were doing." He was especially turned off by what he heard as the studiedness of her shrieking. "She'd go, 'How about *this* scream?'" he says. "She'd say, 'Tina Turner does this' or 'Mama Thornton does it *this* way.' It was just too ersatz and calculated for me." *Cheap Thrills* was powerful nonetheless, a kind of acid-soul album that sounded like Etta James fronting the Jefferson Airplane. On "Ball and Chain" and Erma Franklin's "Piece of My Heart", Joplin was an R. Crumb hippie chick wracked by heartbreak. "I've come to appreciate her more than I did then," Simon says. "I mean, she was more important sociologically than she was musically, but her actual talent gets overshadowed."

Though Simon had witnessed how close Grossman was to Robbie Robertson, he realised the relationship with Joplin was closer still. If Dylan was the favourite son who'd rebelled and left home, Joplin was Grossman's new favourite daughter – especially after *Cheap Thrills* climbed to No. 1 on the album chart. "Janis *loved* Albert," says Simon. "I don't know what her situation was with her own father, but Albert was such a father figure to her."

* Something of Simon's exasperation can be detected in the Columbia studio footage shot by Donn Pennebaker and included in Howard Alk's 1975 documentary *Janis*.

While Joplin kept her home base in northern California, she often visited Grossman in Bearsville. So close did they become that some wondered if the relationship had gone beyond a surrogate father–daughter dynamic.

Grossman's close attention to Joplin had the knock-on effect of making his other acts jealous. "All good managers develop a wagon circle," says Ed Sanders, a friend of Joplin's. "When Janis calls in the middle of the night with a complaint, you pick up the phone. Somebody else calls, you don't answer." Peter, Paul and Mary, who'd made him his first million dollars, were unhappy enough with Grossman's neglect of them to leave his stable in 1970. "Peter Yarrow told me, 'Albert's wearing too many hats,'" says Ronnie Lyons. Odetta, who went even further back with him, felt so "betrayed" that "at one point in my life I could not hear [Grossman's] name without the hairs on my back standing up".

Another act hurt by the lack of attention was Ian and Sylvia. "Ian Tyson was a tough guy, but he felt that Albert had stopped caring," says Michael Friedman, who went on the road with the duo. "The people Albert was really concentrating on were The Band and Janis. The problem was that Albert had signed all these artists but didn't have enough staff to service them." About the only act that didn't scream and yell when he couldn't reach Grossman was Gordon Lightfoot. "Nobody put anything over on Gordon," says John Simon, who'd produced his 1967 album *Did She Mention My Name?*. "It wasn't like Albert was his Big Daddy like he was to Janis and other acts, because Gordon didn't need that." Two years later, Grossman negotiated a Warner-Reprise deal for Lightfoot worth over $1 million; by early 1971, the Canadian folk star was in the US Top 5 with "If You Could Read My Mind", the first of four Top 10 hits he chalked up in the seventies. "That put him in a whole other category," John Court recalled. "Gord hasn't been hungry since."

On the publishing side there was residual Dylan business, but most of the effort was now expended on songs by The Band, primarily those by Robbie Robertson. "That was the big thing," says Danny Goldberg, who worked for Sam Gordon, Grossman's head of publishing. "Otherwise it was just me trying unsuccessfully to get people to cover Ian Tyson songs." A month after starting at Fourth Floor Music, Goldberg was summoned to Grossman's office, where his new boss peered out from behind his vast desk and asked which songwriters he'd been focusing on. When Goldberg nervously mentioned the Australian writer Gary Shearston, Grossman groaned. "He looked at me with great disgust," Goldberg recalls. "He said, 'You know, I just can't care about an artist's career more than *they* do.' It had the effect of making me feel incredibly small. But that line? Forty years later I quote it all the time."

The line expressed the enervation Grossman was feeling after a decade of artist management. "John Court said to me, 'Albert is getting tired of doing this,'" says Dean Schambach. "'But he's so *good* at it.'" Years later, Sally Grossman said that her husband was "burned out" by this point and "couldn't wait to get out" of management. As the sixties neared their end, Grossman's tomato patches began to look more alluring than his demanding artists. Ian Kimmet, who chaperoned Janis Joplin around London in the spring of 1969, was once on a plane with Grossman when the *Cumulus Nimbus* turned to him and said, "Ian, I would never manage anybody again unless it was fifty–fifty. I was continually bringing things to Bob and I would set them up for him, and he would change his mind." Michael Friedman thinks Grossman had come to believe that he was responsible for his artists' success: "He thought that without him they would have had nothing. And maybe that's true. But then without them *he* would have had nothing."

One act that Grossman did *not* regret taking on was the Jim Kweskin Jug Band, whose progress he had followed from their early days on the Cambridge folk scene. He particularly enjoyed the company of Geoff and Maria Muldaur, who'd played in the group

together since marrying in late 1964. "They were very witty and sarcastic," says Jonathan Taplin, who'd roadied for the Kweskin band
at Newport in 1965. "They were steeped in the jazz and blues of the
twenties and thirties, and a lot of the music they played came out
of that world."

Geoff Muldaur had made two folk-blues albums with Paul Rothchild at Prestige, while Maria had sung with John Sebastian in the
Even Dozen Jug Band in Greenwich Village. In the Kweskin band
they were managed by folk doyen Manny Greenhill and signed to
Vanguard Records. One night at Dick Fariña's apartment, Geoff
spotted Grossman across the room and pushed Jim Kweskin towards
him. "I said, 'Go ask him to be our manager,'" Muldaur says. "He
said, 'He won't wanna be our manager!' I said, 'Go ask him!' So he
asked, and Albert said yeah. It did change the band a little bit. We
started dressing differently. But I resisted all that kind of showbiz
stuff, so I probably wasn't best equipped to 'jump on the escalator',
as Albert used to put it."

The first thing Grossman did was get the Kweskin band off
Vanguard and onto Reprise, the Warner Brothers label – founded
by Frank Sinatra – that was now home to all that was hip in Los
Angeles. "Frank's name was still in the parking lot on the kerb," says
Geoff, "but they were picking up all these young hip artists who
would talk about *other* young hip artists." The group's first Reprise
album was 1967's *Garden of Joy*, their line-up by now bolstered by
violin player Richard Greene and banjo maestro Bill Keith. "It was a
big change for them to become part of Albert's group of artists," says
Jim Rooney, who'd booked them at Club 47. "Before that, they were
a fairly raffish, ragtag group of people who liked to travel around in
a Volkswagen bus. People started to think, 'Gee, maybe we could do
a little bit better if we had someone like Albert managing us.'"

The Muldaurs were soon invited to stay in Bearsville, where –
like Robbie Robertson before them – they were swiftly initiated into
the finer things in life. "Albert had quite a bit of money by then,"

The Kweskin Jug Band make their Reprise debut in 1967

says Maria. "He and Sally would pore over hundreds of coloured sheets in order to find exactly which shade of pale cantaloupe they were going to paint the bedroom. These days you'd call Albert a foodie. He built a greenhouse because he wanted to grow organic vegetables. So this tough guy from the heart of Chicago turned into quite the country gentleman."

"You couldn't know Albert without knowing his house," says John Simon. "It was the nexus of the Woodstock scene, and you weren't really accepted until you were invited there. And within the house was a room that was *the centre of the centre*. That was the dope room, the drug room, which was where all the funny stories and the giggling went on."

By late 1969, the Kweskin Jug Band was no more, its titular leader having gone off to join the Fort Hill Community, founded by the group's former member Mel Lyman. "It was like a cult, like Charlie Manson," Al Aronowitz said of Lyman's "family". "Not that he did anything violent, but Mel certainly had his people brainwashed." Parting ways with Kweskin, the Muldaurs became a duo act with Grossman's help and started work on their own Reprise album, *Pottery Pie*. "By the time Albert had Janis, we saw the possibility of our music being accepted by much larger audiences," says Maria. "There was big commercial stuff starting to happen. But it was still very rootsy."

Validating the rootsiness of all Grossman's acts were The Band, who finally got to perform live after Rick Danko recovered from his broken neck in early 1969. "They'd been a backing group for so long," says John Simon. "All of a sudden they got the chance to be a band in the forefront. It happened really quickly, and there they were on the cover of *Time* magazine."

Promoter Bill Graham heard about the "mythical group of guys that lived up in the country and woodshedded", falling so heavily for what he called their "funky, groovy, swirly" sound that he made his own pilgrimage to Woodstock to plead with them to play live. By the time The Band made their nervous Winterland debut for him in April 1969, they had finished work on their second album. Recorded not on the East Coast but in a sound-baffled pool house in West Hollywood, *The Band* took the lo-fi elements of *Music from Big Pink* to a logical extreme: it sounded like rock 'n' roll made in the nineteenth century.

"Everything in rock was kind of going in that high-end direction," Robbie Robertson said. "We wanted something different, a kind of woody, thuddy sound." Much of the flavour came from the south, or rather from Robertson's filtering of Levon Helm's southern background. On "Rag Mama Rag" and "Up on Cripple Creek", Helm was bawdy and knowing; on the Civil War swansong "The Night They Drove Old Dixie Down", he was mournful and indignant. "It was like these guys had come from 1878 or something," says Robbie Dupree, for whom The Band were the main lure that took him upstate. "It was so different and so counter. Southern life was something that was not revered in America at all, because of all the associations that northern people had with the lynchings and the beatings. So to meet people who seemed like they *came* from there, there was nothing like it."

"To me they were the next most influential band after the Beatles," says Larry Campbell, Levon Helm's right-hand man in his last years in Woodstock. "They were taking everything that said 'America' musically and inventing this thing that hadn't existed before. There was so much talk about that record, and then the talk turned to this place in upstate New York where these guys were living and where this scene was going on." Indeed, *The Band* spoke not just of the south but of Woodstock itself. As the autumn leaves reddened on Overlook's maple trees, Robertson wrote the farmer's plaint "King Harvest (Will Surely Come)". "It was a time of year when Woodstock was very impressive," he recalled. "It just made you realise that this was the culmination of the year for so many people." Meanwhile, "Oley" in "When You Awake" was a guy who worked at the Houst general store in Woodstock, and "Unfaithful Servant" was inspired by a couple who'd worked for Albert Grossman and been sacked for stealing from him.

As much as the music itself – earthy, gritty, exultant, sorrowful – what The Band represented was a kind of benign gang. "It was a great bunch of brothers," says Garth Hudson, whose keyboard counter-melodies elevated The Band's sound to a higher musical plane. "The respect was always there. We tried to make the track fit the words and the voices. I never used a sound that was close in harmonic structure to someone's voice." For Al Kooper, "Garth was obviously so far ahead of all of us musically . . . the way Bob was Shakespeare compared to all the other songwriters, Garth was the Shakespeare of the organ."

"I started thinking that the music was finally taking shape with the second album," Levon Helm told me. "We had actually figured out some methods of how to really turn the heat up and get the music to cook; how to blend our voices three different ways, how to get the track together and not make it so complicated." It helped that The Band were all settling into more or less monogamous relationships in Woodstock: Rick Danko with Grace Seldner; Richard Manuel with Jane Kristiansen; Robbie and Dominique Robertson with their newborn daughter Alexandra. Even the introverted Hudson had hooked up with a dark-haired beauty named Suzette Green. "She was drop-dead gorgeous," says Geoff Muldaur. "Levon would tell her, 'Y'oughta come over to our place tonight, we're havin' a party.' But none of them got near her except Garth."

To John Simon, the Robertsons were one of the few couples in Woodstock who stayed faithful to each other. "I mean, everybody was fucking everybody else," he says. "You could tell who was fucking whom by what car was in what driveway. It was all pretty open, but Robbie and Dominique were a real solid *couple*. And then Rick married Gracie, and Richard married Jane." Rather fierier was the hook-up between Helm and Libby Titus, the Woodstock-born wife of Barry Titus, grandson of cosmetics magnate Helena Rubinstein. Libby was a well-read bohemian who'd dropped out of nearby Bard College in 1965 and moved to Greenwich Village, where she became pregnant with Barry's son Ezra. Under the aegis of Albert Grossman, she had also released a self-titled album of songs by writers such as Tim Hardin, the Beatles and the Lovin' Spoonful. "Libby was like a cross between Joan Didion and Fran Drescher," says Peter Coyote. "She was gorgeous, she was louche, she was languorous. I don't know how she got Levon, because there could not have been two more disparate souls on the planet."

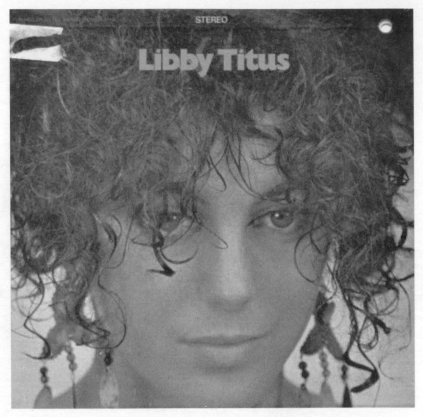

The 1968 debut album by Levon Helm's future common-law wife

According to the scurrilous Mason Hoffenberg, Titus "got" Helm in the spring of 1969 because she'd set her sights on The Band, whom she later described as "the most seductive young men I'd ever met". "One night," Hoffenberg recalled in 1972, "Rick and Levon are coming over to my house to get her at about a hundred miles an hour, and Rick had his big accident, broke his neck. So Levon got her." After she and Ezra moved into the Wittenberg Road house in early 1970 – Danko having moved east to Zena Road – Titus became "obsessed" with Helm and "very isolated", thanks to the jealousy that made him reluctant to show her off in front of other men.

"They were oil and water," says Jonathan Taplin, who by now was

road-managing The Band. "But there was obviously a sexual attraction there and they were very funny together. Libby and Maria
Muldaur both had the same sarcastic sense of humour and could
drop the bon mot that would just devastate you." The Dorothy
Parker of Tinker Street, Titus decided to make the best of it in the
Helm shack. "It could have been in Arkansas," says Taplin. "There
were dogs out on the porch, a couple of cars that didn't work any
more, a huge fireplace that he kept going all winter long. Libby
found it rather amusing and refused to dress like a country girl. She
wore her silk dresses and high-heeled boots. She wasn't going to go
downmarket and wear a pair of Levi's."

The dogs were named Light and Brown – possibly drug references – and were the joys of Helm's life. "They'd follow when [he]
took me for rides through the woods," Ezra Titus later wrote of
his life in the Helm homestead. "We'd go far enough away from
the house so that my mom couldn't hear and he'd break out some
firecrackers. We'd shoot a few bottle rockets and blow up tin cans.
When my mom went out, Levon would let me bring the dogs inside
which, to me, was like a party." In December 1970 five-year-old
Ezra found himself with a new half-sister, Amy. "Levon was just salt-
of-the-earth, right from the soil of Arkansas," says Maria Muldaur.
"While people like Libby were floating around putting on airs, he'd
bring Ezra and Amy over to play with Jenni."*

If there was a blot on The Band's landscape at this time, it was the
niggling anxiety over Richard Manuel's drinking. "He was the most
deeply sensitive of the lot of them," says Jeremy Wilber, who witnessed Manuel's alcohol consumption almost nightly from behind
the bar of the Sled Hill Café. "I think he would have had so much

---

* In July 2009, after writing several short pieces about dysfunctional teenage
life in the Woodstock of the seventies and eighties, forty-three-year-old Ezra
Titus took his own life in Florida. "Though his relationship with Libby was
tumultuous," wrote her husband Donald Fagen, "Ezra and his mother were so
close that it seemed at times as if they shared a single soul."

happier a life if he'd been the piano player in a whorehouse. He could drink and drink and drink and drink, and it never changed his personality." Manuel's favourite tipple was a cocktail that he and Rick Danko called "the Go Faster": two hits of vodka, one hit of cherry brandy, topped off by 7 Up.

As their profile rose, so The Band's relationship with Grossman changed. Given their long association with Dylan, it was a delicate transition to navigate. "Some of the other guys in the Band didn't appreciate Albert as much as I did," Robertson recalled. "But I thought he was a great teacher of things . . . he kind of took me under his wing and I became pretty close to him in those days." For his part, Danko "always got along with Albert . . . if it hadn't been for him I might have had to get a serious job".

"Rick kind of admired Albert," Jonathan Taplin confirms. "Levon was very on and off with him: sometimes he hated him, sometimes he liked him. Garth was distant, as Garth was to a lot of people. The closeness was with Robbie, who lived next door to Albert and shared intellectual interests. But there wasn't closeness with the rest of the band, because they were really kind of country guys."

If Grossman shared "intellectual interests" with Robertson – as he did with Janis Joplin and others – ironically with each passing year he was becoming more of a "country guy" himself. Increasingly Bearsville provided an escape from the frenzied pressures of the industry. Even Joplin found it hard to track him down there sometimes. "Everybody was looking for attention, and nobody was getting it," says Michael Friedman.

For Ronnie Lyons, a frequent guest of the Grossmans, there was a feature of the Bearsville estate that summed up his old friend's attitude to the music industry. "It was a building that looked like a garage, but it was not a garage," Lyons remembers. "It was called the Car Wash. And if anybody came up that Albert didn't want to see, he'd go into the Car Wash, open the electric door and drive straight out the other side."

7

BRAND NEW DAYS

"I got to Woodstock by accident," Van Morrison tells me on a muggy summer afternoon in London's Portobello Hotel. The Belfast-born singer dabs at his brow with a handkerchief and casts his mind back to 1969, when he performed at the Woodstock Sound Festival on a bill that included Tim Hardin, Paul Butterfield, Fear Itself and Happy and Artie Traum. "I got up to do a couple of songs, and there was just a piano player and a bass player and a drummer," Morrison says. "They were really good – unbelievable, actually."

"Van had an acoustic guitar with a pick-up, plugged into an amp, and that's really all that mattered," remembers Jon Gershen, who was also playing the festival with the Montgomeries. "That was the main force, Van standing there with his guitar, just on fire and totally free. He was at the peak of his powers." Actually, Morrison was recovering from two years of trauma as an artist signed to Bang Records. He had been brought to New York by the maverick, mob-connected Bert Berns, Bang's boss and the (co-)writer–producer of such melodramatic soul hits as Solomon Burke's "Cry to Me" (1962) and Garnet Mimms and the Enchanters' "Cry Baby" (1963). Berns had produced Morrison's punkish R&B band Them in London, taking them to No. 2 in the UK with his song "Here Comes the Night", and knew a great voice when he heard one. Convinced he could make a solo star of the squat, flame-haired Ulsterman, he signed him to a heinous contract and got him into the US Top 10 with the maddeningly catchy "Brown-Eyed Girl".

Baulking at Berns's huckster tactics and old-school approach to production, Morrison rebelled and made enemies of both Berns

and his wise-guy cronies.* Stuck in a fleabag Manhattan hotel with
his Californian girlfriend Janet "Planet" Rigsbee and her young son
Peter, he was in deep trouble. And then, just as he was about to
meet Berns to smooth the way to a resolution, the producer died of
a heart attack.

Matters deteriorated still further in the New Year of 1968, when
one of Berns's heavies, Carmine "Wassel" DeNoia, threatened
Morrison's life and broke an acoustic guitar over his head at the
King Edward Hotel. Penniless and terrified, the singer left with
Janet for Boston, where they briefly slept on WBCN disc jockey
Peter "Woofa Goofa" Wolf's couch. The future J. Geils Band singer
was not the only person shocked that Morrison was scrounging bar
gigs less than a year after scoring a Top 10 hit. Fortunately a white
knight was waiting in the wings. Andy Wickham was an Englishman
who'd landed a plum A&R gig at Warner-Reprise in Los Angeles.
Like Berns, he knew how special Morrison was and urged Warner
Brothers Records boss Joe Smith to extricate the Irishman from
Bang. "We were used to artists like Van," says Ted Templeman, who
subsequently produced Morrison's Warners albums *Tupelo Honey*
and *Saint Dominic's Preview*. "We understood people like Van Dyke
Parks and Randy Newman. Van was in the right place at the right
time, but compared to those artists he was like Dylan Thomas. You
just never knew what was going to happen next."

After Joe Smith personally handed $20,000 over to a represent-
ative of Bert Berns's widow Ilene, Morrison found himself a free
man. Disenchanted with the commercial mainstream after his experience with Berns, he began exploring alternatives to conventional
pop and rock, developing his more experimental, Dylan-influenced
songs – long pieces like "T.B. Sheets" and "Madame George" –
with the help of jazz bass player Tom Kielbania and drummer Joey
Bebo. Playing bars around Boston and Cambridge, they stripped

---

* He later sang about them in the bitter 1991 song "Big Time Operators".

everything back to the bare essentials and opened up space for vocal improvisations that Morrison had never attempted before. (Peter Wolf recorded early live versions of Morrison's new songs at the subterranean Catacombs club.) Adding flautist John Payne, Morrison sang for small handfuls of New York admirers – Jimi Hendrix among them – at the Café au Go Go and Steve Paul's The Scene. "One thing I learned from this is how far and how quickly you can fall in this business," says Payne, who dropped out of Harvard to play with Morrison. "Here was a guy who'd had a Top 10 hit, and a year later he was thankful to play for free at 1 a.m. at the Scene."

Frustrated and broke, Morrison wasn't the easiest person in the world to work for. Joe Smith, who hailed from Boston and managed to catch one of the singer's Catacombs sets, remembered him years later as "a hateful little guy". John Payne was constantly amazed at how much the sunny-natured Janet – by now Morrison's wife – tolerated from her sullen partner. "She was doing all kinds of stuff for him," Payne says. "She kept his lyrics in a big book, and she was unbelievably supportive and working on his career."

In Boston that summer Morrison heard The Band's "I Shall Be Released" on the radio. He was instantly smitten and bought a copy of *Music from Big Pink* to hear more. "It just seemed really different from what they were playing on FM radio," he says. "It wasn't like rock, it seemed more like a country thing that I can't really describe. I thought, 'Wow, these guys are really onto something that comes through.'" Though Morrison was already a certified Dylan fan, having covered "It's All Over Now, Baby Blue" on 1966's *Them Again*, *Big Pink* connected with him at an even deeper level. "I Shall Be Released" inspired *Moondance*'s "Brand New Day", a song of hope that all the "dark clouds" of his Bang period would "roll away", while the laid-back groove of "The Weight" was clearly the template for that album's "And It Stoned Me". Yet Morrison's first Warners release bore little relation to *Music from Big Pink*. Put together by Inherit Productions, a partnership consisting of manager Bob

Schwaid and producer Lewis Merenstein, *Astral Weeks* was a jazz-folk detour off the singer's R&B highway, a troubadour tour de force that made him an icon of musical mysticism. More than anything it was about the sheer power of Morrison's voice, pleading and howling over a bed of acoustic bass, brushed drums, vibraphone and overdubbed strings and horns. "I'd never had that feeling from a singer before," says John Payne, who played flute on the album's bleak finale "Slim Slow Slider". "Here was a guy whose sense of rhythm and phrasing went very, very deep."

Though Morrison barely acknowledged the peerless jazz players booked for the session by Merenstein, the accompaniment of bassist Richard Davis, drummer Connie Kay, guitarist Jay Berliner and vibraphonist Warren Smith Jr – which recalled the musical palette Tim Hardin had used on his sublime Verve-Forecast albums – was magically intuitive. In later years, as was his wont, Morrison played down the wonder of *Astral Weeks*, claiming it failed to capture what he heard in his head. The album also stiffed, selling barely 15,000 copies in the first year of its life – and those 15,000 generally bought by the kind of stoned hippies he despised. "He was . . . suspicious of us and everybody around him," Joe Smith recalled. "[He] faced this situation where everybody told him what an enormously powerful album he had written, and we weren't selling any."

Still broke – and now tied to a contract with Schwaid and Merenstein that he was already regretting – Morrison was back in New York at another low ebb when singer Garland Jeffreys alerted him to the Woodstock Sound Festival.

After his set at Pan Copeland's farm, Morrison and Janet Planet went for dinner in Byrdcliffe with Happy, Jane and Artie Traum. He was all too aware that the Traums' friend Bob Dylan lived near by, and that The Band were also in Woodstock. "He really wanted to get in with them," says Keith Reid, who'd recently met him in New York. "He wanted to be in their sphere." When someone mentioned

From the Sound-Outs to the Woodstock–Saugerties Festival(s), summer 1969 (courtesy of the Woodstock Historical Society)

that Richard Manuel and Garth Hudson were about to vacate a house at the top of the very road Dylan lived on, it felt like serendipity. "They said, 'Do you want to get out of New York?'" Morrison remembers. "And I said, 'I wouldn't mind getting out of the city.'"

Though it was Bob Schwaid who drove the Morrisons up to Woodstock, he found it all but impossible to bond with Van. "He was never open with anybody," Schwaid says. "It was like somebody watching you with a third eye all the time." Tom Kielbania

– "Ringworm", Morrison called him – had also moved to town and was soon introducing him to other Woodstock musicians. Too nervous to pay a visit to Dylan, Morrison would often pass his driveway, staring wistfully out of the passenger seat as Janet drove down Ohayo Mountain Road. "I'd ask Van, 'Have you seen Dylan?'" says John Platania, a local guitarist recommended by Morrison's new Yorkshire-born road manager Thomas Reynolds. "He'd say, 'I haven't met him yet.' On the one occasion the two men did meet in Woodstock, Morrison didn't even realise he was talking to Dylan. "I only knew him from the pictures and he didn't look anything like he was supposed to look," Morrison says. "He just looked like a normal Jewish guy. Somebody said to me afterwards, 'That was Bob.' I said, 'You're kiddin' me.'"

With Morrison apparently unable to so much as change a light bulb, Janet Planet was by turns his nursemaid and his social secretary, despite having a child of her own to raise. "She was obviously really good for him," says Graham Blackburn, John Payne's replacement as Morrison's flautist and sax player. "For all his determination to do what he wanted to do, he wasn't very confident. What occasioned that extreme lack of self-confidence, I don't know. I put it down to (a) being Northern Irish and (b) becoming involved in rock 'n' roll when really he was an artist. He was a hundred per cent sincere about whatever he was trying to get out. That was what gave it the intensity it had, and the moment it gelled with anything halfway sympathetic it blossomed."

Working through the summer of 1969 with Blackburn, Kielbania, Platania and new drummer Bob Mason, Morrison felt under pressure to deliver a second album that stood a chance of receiving the radio play he'd had with "Brown-Eyed Girl". "It wasn't Joe Smith telling me, it was just the order of the day," he says. "It was basic survival, because I hadn't got any money from 'Brown-Eyed Girl'." For at least two months Blackburn and the others made almost daily trips to Spencer Road. There in the living room, with views that made them feel they were floating over the Mid-Hudson Valley, they rehearsed the same songs – "Moondance", "Domino", "I've Been Working" – over and over again. "Van could not have articulated what it was he was aiming for," says Blackburn. "But whatever it *was* about Woodstock, he really hit it at the right time, and all sorts of odd songs came together to make that happen."

At least once a week Morrison and the band hit the road to New York, where they recorded endless versions of "Moondance" and other songs: as he sang on "I've Been Working", *"Been up the thruway, down the thruway / Up the thruway, down the thruway / Up, down, back and up again . . ."* Though the swinging jazz of "Moondance" had been written in London as a sax instrumental, the song's lyric spoke of a place very like Woodstock, with October leaves falling "to the sound of the breezes that blow". "Domino" lifted lyrics from another Morrison song called "Down in the Maverick", a reference to Hervey White's old colony, which was barely a quarter of a mile through the woods from Spencer Road. Though "And It Stoned Me" was rooted in memories of his Ulster childhood, its essential flavour was the pastoral bliss of Woodstock. It was as if Morrison had found in the Catskills the very landscapes he'd written about on *Astral Weeks*. "Van was obviously not going to do *Music from Big Pink*," says Jon Gershen, who, with his brother David, introduced himself to the Irishman at the Café Espresso. "But at the same time you couldn't live in Woodstock without it having an effect on you. He knew he was going to incorporate some of this feeling into his music."

Sessions for the album began at the end of July 1969, with some of the *Astral Weeks* players again recruited by Lewis Merenstein. It didn't take Morrison long to decide he wanted to start afresh. He had already parted ways with Blackburn and Kielbania, playing the Newport Folk Festival on 20 July with only John Platania accompanying him on an Ovation guitar. "We drove there – myself, Van and Janet, who was pregnant," Platania says. "Van was real nervous."

Now the singer pieced together various alumni of Boston's Berklee School of Music: pianist Jef Labes, drummer Chuck Purro, and saxophonists Jack Schroer and Collin Tilton from the defunct Colwell-Winfield Blues Band. With Platania on guitar and John Klingberg on bass – and Gary Mallaber replacing Purro on drums – this was the group Morrison rehearsed on Spencer Road through August and took to New York's A&R Studios for sessions that continued intermittently till December. "It was an incredible band, a synergistic thing," Platania says. "*Moondance* was such an antithesis to *Astral Weeks*, and I think calculatedly so for Van. It was a joyous thing for him."

Morrison confirms that he was "very pleased" with *Moondance*. "I thought it worked out great," he says. "There was a lot of working stuff out with the band. But I didn't think it was commercial at the time." As indeed it wasn't, although the album scraped into the Top 30, with "Come Running" – possibly its weakest track – reaching the Top 40 as a single. However, *Moondance* does boast one of the most perfect sequences in all of rock 'n' roll – or "gypsy soul", as Morrison would have put it – on its first vinyl side, starting with "And It Stoned Me", finishing with the magical "Into the Mystic", and incorporating the gossamer soul of "Crazy Love" and the exuberant anthemics of "Caravan". Side Two, meanwhile, included the ecstatic rock gospel of "Brand New Day", which cathartically worked through the abuse and humiliation of Morrison's Bang period to the point where his heart was "still" and he didn't really "feel so mean" any more.

The *Moondance* songs expressed a longing for the love that Morrison couldn't quite allow himself to receive in his life. "He was uncomfortable in his own costume," says Elliott Landy, who shot the sulky-faced singer for *Moondance*'s cover – though he also captured the leafy serenity of life on Ohayo Mountain in pictures of Morrison with Janet Planet and her son. At this time the singer was drinking heavily, often stopping in at the Sled Hill to nurse his grievances. "Van would come in either to buy cigarettes or to order a Haig &

Haig Pinch on the rocks," says Jeremy Wilber. "I told him many times that we didn't have Haig & Haig Pinch, only Johnnie Walker Black. So he would give me a very sour look and then condescend to drink the Johnnie Walker Black. He was the most unpleasant man, but I will say this: the up-and-coming musicians in town loved and respected him. With the songs he produced in that time, there had to be something soft and tender in him."

"Almost any night at the Sled Hill you could see Van dropping in," Artie Traum told me in 1991. "Van was one of the funniest people that ever lived, just totally strange. He would call us up to come to the house for a jam session, but by the time you got there he had forgotten that he'd called and would summarily send you home." John Platania says that "if you get Van at the right moment, he's gregarious and great fun", and Jon Gershen speaks of many happy hours spent in Morrison's company. "He was not some sort of misanthrope," Gershen says. "He was just incredibly shy and ill-prepared for social interaction of any kind. He didn't know how to fit in."

Morrison himself would probably concur with this. When I remarked on the warmth of *Moondance* – and of *Tupelo Honey*'s encomium "Old Old Woodstock" – he pointed out that he was simultaneously writing songs such as "Really Don't Know", with its confession that *"I really don't know what's wrong / Feel like I don't belong"*, and "Wonderful Remark", a song Robbie Robertson revisited years later for the soundtrack to Martin Scorsese's *The King of Comedy*. "'Wonderful Remark' was the only song that was really what Woodstock was about," Morrison says. "'Brand New Day' was kind of what it had *been* about, but it wasn't a brand-new day any more."

One wonders if the withering "Wonderful Remark" – originally recorded at the *Moondance* sessions in 1969 – had anything to do with a visit Morrison made to Albert Grossman in Bearsville. Having befriended The Band while they were making their second album in LA, he took up with them again in Woodstock and was introduced to their manager. "It was kind of put forth that Albert might manage me, so I went up to see him," Morrison says. "He was in his garden and he said, 'Come over for dinner sometime.'" Two weeks later, Robbie Robertson told Morrison he was going to the Grossmans for dinner and invited him to tag along. Morrison felt uneasy the minute he walked into the kitchen. "It was one of those weird scenes," he says. "I think they were all stoned. I had a reel-to-reel and I had some stuff that I was demoing, just me and a guitar. Albert listened to it and Robbie said, 'Whaddya think, Albert?' And Albert said, 'Burn it.' I didn't know what that meant, but to me it was some kind of mind-bending. And given the situation I'd been in with Bert Berns, I thought, 'I don't need any more mind-bending.' So I just kind of backed off."

Woodstock, Morrison says, was "a very closed world" that seemed to revolve around Grossman. "He seemed to be the guru or something," he recalls. "It was like, 'Don't worry, Albert'll fix it,' like he was the big daddy."

"*How can your empty laughter / Fill a room like ours with joy*," he sang on "Wonderful Remark", "*when you're only playing with us / Like a child does with a toy?*" Was this, then, a song about the "real" Woodstock that Morrison had discovered behind the seductive mythology of Dylan and Big Pink?

8

SOME WAY OUT OF HERE

The two men couldn't be more different. One is a psychedelic dandy in Swinging London, blasting rock into the future with his frenzied guitar solos; the other is singing country songs and sea shanties in a pink house in West Saugerties. Yet Jimi Hendrix is another Bob Dylan disciple who will eventually follow the master upstate in search of whatever he has found in the Catskill mountains.

For Hendrix, Dylan is the man who's proved it is possible to be an artist – and a poet – within the circus of popular music. "Dylan really turned me on," he says in March 1968. "Not the words or his guitar, but as a way to get myself together." Without Dylan, indeed, he suspects he might never have grown beyond his talent as a guitar phenomenon. "Bob and I once went to see Otis Redding at the Whisky a Go Go in LA," says Donn Pennebaker. "Otis wanted to get Dylan, and Jimi was the same way. Dylan was the magic thing, and anything that connected with Dylan they would have done at the drop of a hat."*

Though Hendrix has only met Dylan once – a fleeting encounter at the Kettle of Fish in the Village – he is obsessed by (and indeed covers) songs such as "Like a Rolling Stone". He even styles his hair to make it look like Dylan's wild bird's nest of 1966. When publicist Michael Goldstein gives him the Grossman-authorised demos from Dylan's basement sessions, Hendrix records at least one of the songs, "Tears of Rage", during an early London session for *Electric*

---

* The Redding show that Dylan saw was on 8 April 1966, with some of the performances included on the 1968 Stax album *In Person at the Whisky a Go Go*.

Ladyland. "He came in with these Dylan tapes," said the late Andy
Johns, an engineer at Olympic Studios. "We all heard them for the
first time in the studio."

   Hendrix has also just obtained a copy of the newly released *John
Wesley Harding* and decides to cover its "All Along the Watchtower".
From its beginnings at Olympic, the track undergoes a series of
transformations at New York's Record Plant, Hendrix overdubbing
layer upon layer of guitar through the summer. Dylan later claims
to have felt so "overwhelmed" by the finished product that he all
but regards it as Hendrix's song. It takes the low-key original – as
bleak and sparse as anything on *John Wesley Harding* – and turns it
into something both kaleidoscopic and apocalyptic. "[Hendrix] took
some small songs of mine that nobody paid any attention to," Dylan
said in his MusiCares "Person of the Year" speech in February 2015,
"and pumped them up into the outer limits of the stratosphere . . ."

The troubling quality of Hendrix's "All Along the Watchtower" perhaps reflected the fact that he, like Dylan, was in a deeply unhappy
relationship with his supposed protector. If Hendrix was the joker
here, the thief was manager Mike Jeffery, then wresting control
away from the guitarist's original mentor–producer Chas Chandler.
Jeffery was part *Get Carter* gangster, part Age of Aquarius bullshit-
ter. Born in south London, he told tales of working for MI5 and
resembled a low-ranking Long Island mafioso. He wore double-
breasted suits with fat paisley ties, his eyes masked by aviator shades
and his lank black hair falling over his shirt collar. There is no evi-
dence that he worked for MI5, but he certainly worked in espionage
before muscling in on the nightclub scene in north-east England.
He may even have played a part in getting the notorious François
"Papa Doc" Duvalier elected to the presidency of Haiti in 1957. And
working with him there was the equally shady Jerry Morrison, a former song plugger (born Gerald Herbert Breitman) who'd worked
for Louis Armstrong and other jazz stars – and for Papa Doc.

Jeffery and Morrison renewed their acquaintance in New York in 1968, by which time Jeffery – in emulation of Albert Grossman – had bought a large Woodstock home on the south-east corner of Lower Byrdcliffe Road. Hendrix began making visits to 1 Wiley Lane that year and was given the use of a small apartment over its garage. (Like Van Morrison, he was all too aware that his idol Bob Dylan lived barely a quarter of a mile away.) Perhaps he even believed that Jeffery was sincere in his stated desire to enter into the spirit of the place. There were parties at the house, their host sometimes dropping LSD with his guests. "Mike was taking a bunch of acid with Jimi," Hendrix's studio manager Jim Marron claimed. "He was getting very spiritual."

On the other hand, Jeffery may simply have seen Woodstock as a useful hunting ground for new bands. "Mike was kind of aloof," says Christopher Parker, drummer in the Jeffery-managed band Holy Moses. "He had Hendrix, and that was his big guy, though kind of unmanageable, but he was looking to spread out into something more current – the country-rock Band thing, the Woodstock thing."

Hendrix was staying in the Wiley Lane apartment when he drove down Rock City Road one afternoon and heard an old New York acquaintance jamming on the village green. Juma Sultan had been commuting between Woodstock and the city since 1966, when he became involved with the Saugerties-based arts collective Group 212. He and percussionist Ali Abuwi had formed a loose Afrocentric entity known as the Aboriginal Music Society, playing around Woodstock and bringing together jazz and R&B musicians united by a commitment to black consciousness. "Their scene was 24/7 and they had connections in New York with great players who came up," says Daoud Shaw. "But I never saw a real master plan."

When Sultan told Hendrix what he was up to, the guitarist invited him back to Wiley Lane for a jam. "He was telling me about how he wanted to start a new band," Sultan remembered. "He . . . was thinking about getting a house in the area, and that's when his quest for a house started, looking for a place that could become a band house up in Woodstock."

Though Hendrix kept a low profile in town – since it was rather harder for him to blend in than it was for, say, Rick Danko – he was occasionally seen bombing along Tinker Street in a red Corvette. "Nobody in Woodstock had a red Corvette," remembered Leslie Aday, who worked for Albert Grossman and befriended Hendrix that summer. "They were all into organic vegetables and making their own clothes . . ." On at least one occasion, Hendrix went to the Elephant to see a gig. "The vibe was that he wanted to hang and connect the dots and not be Jimi Hendrix," says Jon Gershen, who observed him at the club. "He was really hungry to understand how Dylan had undergone his transformation. He was feeling the Woodstock thing and wanting to make it work for him, even though it was too much of a stretch to go from where he had been to being, you know, a farmer."

Two months after Hendrix returned from his last European tour with the Experience – and with a heroin bust from Toronto hanging ominously over him – Mike Jeffery asked Jerry Morrison to find the guitarist a house in the Woodstock area. With Juma Sultan in tow, Morrison took Hendrix to see at least four properties around Woodstock, including a large place that Johnny Winter had rented across the Hudson in Rhinecliff. Eventually they settled on an eight-bedroomed stone manor house at the end of Traver Hollow Road in Boiceville, four miles south-west of Woodstock. For a city boy it was quite the retreat, complete with horses in stables and a gatehouse where Sultan and his Chinese American girlfriend would soon install themselves. A half hour's drive away was the beautiful Peekamoose Road Waterfall, where Hendrix and his guests took acid trips.

When writer Sheila Weller visited the Traver Hollow house, she wrote that all the talk with Hendrix was about "puppies, daybreak,

Hendrix with Larry Lee (left) at "the Shokan House" in Traver
Hollow, early August 1969

other innocentia", and that she'd climbed down some rocks to an
"icy brook" with the guitarist. He told her he wanted to "write
songs about tranquility, about beautiful things". He put *John
Wesley Harding* on the turntable and played along to "The Ballad
of Frankie Lee and Judas Priest", "riding the rest of the song home
with a near-religious intensity". At the same time, he was leaning
towards the kind of avant-garde Afro-jazz rock espoused by Sultan,

who dressed in robes and pushed his friend to explore the fusion of jazz with tribal percussion.

If Hendrix was undergoing an identity crisis – did he want to be Bob Dylan or did he want to be Miles Davis? – he was keen to jettison the Experience, complaining to Sheila Weller that he didn't want to be a "clown" any more. 1968's sprawlingly eclectic *Electric Ladyland* had made his ambitions clear, though the sessions had so frustrated Chas Chandler that the genial Geordie quit and left Hendrix to the mercy of Mike Jeffery.

Jeffery himself was perturbed by any threat to the cash cow that was the Experience, which played its last show on 1 June. Used to regular income from the group's festival appearances, Jeffery watched with unease as a motley crew of musicians rolled up at the Traver Hollow house. Foremost among them was Gerardo "Jerry" Velez, a spunky New York bongo player who'd sat in on Hendrix's jams at Steve Paul's The Scene. Velez was a Puerto Rican street kid and former member of notorious gang the Young Lords; he showed up with two huge dogs that proceeded to defecate throughout the house. "Mike Jeffery . . . did not like me, did not like Juma, didn't like any of us," Velez remembered. "He was like, you know, 'What are you doing . . . why are you breaking up the Experience?'" When Jeffery entered a room, Velez said, "the temperature dropped by about ten degrees . . . we were all about peace and love and he was about making that dollar".

Hendrix ignored Jeffery's protests about the new musicians. "Jimi really picked up on my brother," says singer Martha Velez, who lived in Woodstock herself. "Because he had the resources, he just brought everybody up to woodshed in that house and ride horses and try that Woodstock meditative approach to writing and creating. He was a very intelligent person who was getting trapped in his own creation. It was important to break out of that, but on his own terms. And to do that he had to have a space where there wasn't a lot of observation."

When Martha visited the house, she found her brother hap-pily ensconced with a cook, together with two of the Experience's old roadies and a number of young women. "We tried to keep the groupies away from the place," Jerry Morrison told Hendrix biogra-pher Jerry Hopkins. "But Jimi went into Woodstock and brought a few girls back. That let it out, and after that they were always infil-trating." In early July Hendrix added two older friends to the mix. Bassist Billy Cox was a former army buddy and a steadying influence who avoided drugs; Larry Lee a rhythm guitarist from Memphis who had recently returned from Vietnam. Both had played in R&B groups with Hendrix in the early sixties. The final piece of the new jigsaw was Experience drummer Mitch Mitchell, who arrived with his girlfriend at the end of July. "[Jimi] could see the point of expanding a situation outside a three-piece band," Mitchell remem-bered. "There were so many opportunities . . . and he grabbed hold of what he thought would be comfortable." However, Juma Sultan didn't care for Mitchell, who – in the percussionist's words – was "drunk most of the time and . . . didn't know the concepts that Jimi was moving to". Mitchell, meanwhile, thought that neither Sultan nor Jerry Velez kept adequate time. "The band was grim and the house was grim," he later claimed.

Having coined the name Electric Sky Church for the new ensem-ble – a reference to the fact that the house sat high above the Ashokan Reservoir – Hendrix now changed its name to Gypsy, Sun and Rainbows. The name was suitably cosmic-bucolic but masked a lack of cohesion, as working titles such as "Jam Back at the House" and "Woodstock Improvisation" make clear. Hendrix may have abandoned the tight pop structures of the Experience, but he was floundering in his new role as improvisatory ringmaster. During one jam session in the house he became so frustrated that he hurled his guitar across the room.

He was also becoming ever more unhappy at his dependency on Mike Jeffery. With no control over his own finances, he constantly had to ask his manager for cash. "If Jimi wanted to buy a car, he had to go to them," Juma Sultan remembered. "And they always claimed he was broke. He was maintaining this whole cadre of people and he knew it, but there was no way he could go against it." To make matters worse, Jeffery was siphoning Hendrix's money off into a bank account in the Bahamas. The guitarist's sometime girlfriend Monika Dannemann maintained that Jeffery had even set up the heroin bust in Toronto "as a warning to teach Jimi a lesson".

"Jimi told me that he was trying to end management," said Claire Moriece, the cook who'd been hired to prepare healthy soups and stews for the household. Jerry Velez recalled Jeffery telling Hendrix he would "never get away" from him. "I do believe in my heart that Jeffery and his guys had Jimi manipulated, because I saw it there," says Lynne Naso, who visited the house with Philip Wilson. "It was a frustrated man I met that day. He talked about how black people were standing up to be their own persons." In "Sky Blues Today", a song begun at Traver Hollow that August, Hendrix sang despairingly that *"if I keep fucking around with you people / you gonna fell me like you fell a tree / That's why I got to keep moving all around / I wanna be alive but it's time for me to go and die . . ."*

In July Jeffery was approached by Michael Lang with an offer for Hendrix to headline the final day of the Woodstock Music and Art Fair. Supposedly he got the deal upped to $32,000 for two sets, more than twice as much as any other act was getting. With serious misgivings, Hendrix agreed to play and began rehearsing the band in earnest. "I was sitting with him," says Martha Velez, who'd just returned from recording her Joplin-esque album *Fiends and Angels* in London, "and he said to me, 'We're going to be playing at this festival at White Lake in August, would you like to come up and sing?' I said, 'Oh no, that's okay.' What was I thinking? But it was just too much for me."

On Sunday 10 August – three days after returning from a week's holiday in Morocco – Hendrix headed into Woodstock for a jam session at the Tinker Street Cinema, a former Methodist church converted into a movie house by Woodstock Motel owner Bill Militello. "I remember the music coming out of there," says Richard Heppner, a boy at the time. "My dad got so pissed about the noise. It was only later that I realised it was Hendrix." According to Alan Gordon, the jam took place the same night Johnny Winter played the Café Espresso and Van Morrison sat in at the Sled Hill Café. Also in town for a show at the Elephant were rising Latin-rock stars Santana, whose percussionists Michael Carabello and José "Pepe" Areas joined Hendrix, Sultan and fellow Aboriginal Society members Ali Abuwi and trumpeter Earl Cross for long workouts entitled "The Dance" and "JL (Earth Blues)".

The final number the sextet played that night was a spaced-out arrangement of a famous song that Hendrix had already played several times with the Experience – and which he was considering for his set at the Woodstock Music and Art Fair. "It was less than a week before the festival, and Jimi was practicing 'The Star-Spangled Banner' at the Tinker Street Cinema," Alan Gordon later reflected. "I said, 'God, look at this amazing place we're living in here!'"

9

BACK TO THE GARDEN

By the time Joni Mitchell got to Woodstock, we were about 30,000 strong. It was 15 August 1998, and the composer of "Woodstock" – who'd famously missed the original festival – was playing the second Day in the Garden at Bethel, sandwiched between Lou Reed and headliner Pete Townshend.

There were no campsites this time, but there were a lot more Portaloos. Baby-boomers had paid $70 to get in rather than break through chain-link fences. I'd driven the back roads of Sullivan County in the morning without hitting a single traffic jam. More surreally, I found myself roped into a Radio Woodstock panel discussion of the 1969 festival's legacy with Richie Havens – who'd kick-started the original gathering almost exactly twenty-nine years earlier – and an ectomorphic figure dressed in black. You might ask what Joey Ramone was doing there, since punk rock's brief had surely been to destroy everything the "Woodstock Nation" stood for. But then you'd also be entitled to ask what Lou Reed was doing there, since no one hated hippies more than he did. At least Pete Townshend had *been* there in '69.

A Day in the Garden was a restrained and civilised affair. Nobody was freaking out on brown acid or splashing naked in the lake behind the stage. Nearly three decades after dairy farmer Max Yasgur opened his floodgates to over 350,000 unkempt longhairs – no one has ever been sure of the exact number, which *may* have reached Joni's fabled half million – we were all so inured to the corporate business of rock fests that it was hard to imagine the tribal excitement (or trepidation) people felt as they swarmed towards Bethel in search of some heady communal climax to the sixties dream.

The Woodstock Music and Art Fair remains the defining congregation of rock's sixty-year lifespan, with "Woodstock" now a byword for all collective celebration and ersatz Dionysia. Woodstock was where the overheated rhetoric and psychoactive disturbance of the sixties hit critical mass. Watching Michael Wadleigh's great documentary *Woodstock* is like watching footage from a war zone: helicopters and medical tents, young men dazed and confused, muddy chaos. Vietnam hangs over the event like a shroud, permeating everything from the mess call that follows Wavy Gravy's famous breakfast invitation to Hendrix's closing de(con)struction of "The Star-Spangled Banner". One of the most significant interviews in the whole film is with a jovial Portaloo guy who has one son in 'Nam and another at the festival.

So were the half million really "stardust" and "golden", in Mitchell's lovely lyric, or were they hallucinating survivors of a middle-class disaster zone? Wadleigh's film – with camerawork by a young Martin Scorsese, among others – suggests the truth lay somewhere in between. Early intimations of the hordes advancing on O Little Town of Bethel had Bill Graham exclaiming that "there must be some way of stopping this influx of humanity", but no one – neither the bellicose Graham nor baby-faced hippie impresario Michael Lang – knew how to do it. "It looks like some biblical, epical, unbelievable scene," gasped the Grateful Dead's Jerry Garcia before Richie Havens had even been pushed out on the stage like some be-robed African chieftain about to be sacrificed.

As the threadbare remnants of the "ripped army of mud people" – Robbie Robertson's phrase – finally dispersed late on Monday morning, there was no clear sense of what the festival even meant. "Drugs and revolution, now it's all a little contrived," said one of the less fried hippies interviewed for the film. "People are really looking for some kind of answer when there isn't one."

✤

Forty-four years after he first rode around the festival site on his BSA motorcycle, Michael Lang sits in a restaurant on Tinker Street and talks of the complicated relationship between Woodstock and "Woodstock". Like everyone round here he knows how much the town owes to the festival that took place over sixty miles south-west of where we're sitting. And he knows there's a good and a bad side to that debt. The good side is all the tourists who pour into town and spend their hard-earned dollars on tie-dyed T-shirts and hippie knick-knacks. The bad side is all the tourists who pour into town and . . .

Well, you get the point.

Over the many years since 1969, Woodstock has become a kind of themed village of sixties hippie life, the culmination of the pop-cultural nightmare that Bob Dylan dreaded it would be. Where once the invaders came to seek *him*, now they descend on dinky Tinker Street to find the fields where Lang's festival happened – only to learn that it didn't happen there at all. "I used to sit on the back porch of Radio Woodstock on a summer afternoon," says Stan Beinstein, the station's former general manager, "and somebody would always walk up and ask in a German accent, 'Excuse me, vere vas de concert?' Constantly, constantly. Some people lied and directed them to the Andy Lee baseball field. Or they'd tell them the truth: 'Well, it's about a sixty-five-mile drive, take you about an hour and a half.'"

So why did Lang call it Woodstock? The short answer is that Dylan lived there, and that *Music from Big Pink* was born, if not recorded, there. The longer answer begins with the fact that Lang, a nice Jewish boy from Brooklyn, had first come to the town as a kid. "My mother liked the art galleries, so we'd come through Woodstock on the way back from visiting relatives in Canada," he says. He returned to the Catskills after running a head shop in similarly hippiefied Coconut Grove and – in May 1968 – promoting the first Miami Pop Festival. "When it was time to get out and move back north, I decided I'd like to live in that kind of community but somewhere nearer the city," he says. "So Woodstock was a natural place to come. The Band was in town, and I met those guys early on." He was all too aware of Albert Grossman as "the eye of the music storm that descended on Woodstock".

Moving with his girlfriend to a converted barn on Chestnut Hill Road, Lang began familiarising himself with the local music scene. He also learned about the history of the area, going all the way back to Hervey White's Maverick festivals. "There will be a village that will stand for but a day," White had written in a festival flyer in 1915, "which mad artists have hung with glorious banners and blazoned in the entrance through the woods." When Lang experienced the Sound-Outs on Pan Copeland's farm, their "joyous, healing feel" conjured visions of something on a far grander scale. And that something was encapsulated by the town of Woodstock itself. "The spirit of the festival was embodied in the people that lived there," Lang's friend Alan Gordon told writer Steve Turner. "Woodstock had become the Jerusalem of the new consciousness. There were people out here living in teepees and domes. Tie-dye stores started opening in 1966. Alternative food stores started here."

Gordon remembered Lang laying out maps of potential festival sites at Jim and Jean Young's shop, the Juggler, on Tinker Street. Jim dabbled in local real estate and took Lang to see the Winston Farm off Route 212, near Saugerties. "It was scheduled to become a golf course," says Lang, "but it didn't work." He adds that he "never found a piece of land around town that *did* work". The belief that he was "booted out of Woodstock" by the town board is, he says, a misconception.

It is true that by the early summer of 1969 Woodstock was all but overrun by barefoot children of the counterculture. "At the week-ends there was always an influx of hippies coming in," says Keith Reid. "There were people on the village green with acoustic gui-tars, and lots of pretty girls." The presence of these back-to-the-land

dropouts was now seriously unsettling long-time residents in ways that not even the Maverick revellers had done a half-century earlier. "The town was very paranoid about the potential overflow from our festival," Lang concedes. "There were a lot of people coming into town to try to get to Dylan, so it was difficult." One crusty old-timer, Peggy Egan, demanded at a town meeting that all undesirables arrested for loitering be "deloused and have their heads shaved to clean them up". Arrests of hippies for trespassing in Woodstock were soon averaging fifteen per day. When they couldn't pay a $15 fine, they were often packed off to Ulster County Jail for three days.

Yet just as Greenwich Village bohemians had brought much-needed business to Woodstock in the twenties, so now there were well-heeled hippies whose custom was welcomed by the proprietors of its new head shops. (One of those proprietors, Philadelphia importer Leslie Tobin, paid $54,000 for real estate near the village green, converting it into four shops selling hippie clothes and paraphernalia.) "Now they call them hippies," said plumber Adolf Heckeroth, who'd helped to build the Maverick. "Then they called us anarchists."

Some natives were more tolerant than others. Where Peggy Egan wanted Woodstock declared a disaster area, Town Justice Edgar Leaycraft told the *New York Times* that it was "no wonder" young people were being picked up for loitering when the town had failed to provide them with any recreational facilities.* Leaycraft was heavily criticised by old-timers for his "lace-panty justice" and the minimum fines he set for trespassers. Bob Dylan would almost certainly have sided with the apoplectic relics, whose fears were not allayed by notices in local papers that the upcoming "Rock Fest" had "NOTHING TO DO WITH WOODSTOCK N.Y." In the Kingston *Daily Freeman*, reporter Tobie Geertsema portrayed Woodstock as a small-town Sunset Strip with weekend parades of "teeny boppers and overaged juveniles, girls with straight-pressed blond hair and granny glasses, bearded youths in military coats and surfers' crosses, leather-garbed motorcyclists sputtering by on their choppers, high school dropouts in giant gilt earrings, stay-ins in General Custer hats, hundreds of elephant-cuffed legs flaunting rebellion".

Geertsema additionally listed examples of the impact of the hip-pie tide on Old Old Woodstock: the shoemaker forced out to make way for a "trinket shop"; the Woodstock Bakery, which was now a "mod clothing" store called Saturn. For Cindy Cashdollar, growing up in Woodstock was both exciting and disorienting. "It was like, 'Where did the little Italian shoemaker go? Where's the soda foun-tain?'" she says. "What I knew disappeared and was replaced by this exciting world of colours and characters and smells. I'd never smelled incense before. It was like the circus came to town and

---

* For four years Edgar "Pete" Leaycraft lived next door to me on Zena Road, and his son Matt was my landlord. You couldn't have asked for a nicer neighbour or a fairer landlord.

Rock Fest Not In Woodstock

The Aquarian Exposition, presented by the Woodstock Music and Art fair, HAS NOTHING TO DO WITH WOODSTOCK, N.Y.

The three day Aquarian Exposition is a production of "Woodstock Ventures, Inc." a New York firm using the title Woodstock as a corporate name. Neither the fair, nor a business office is located here.

LOCATION
The most recent location for the exposition, scheduled for Aug. 15, 16 and 17 is about ten miles west of Monticello, Sullivan county, in the White Lake area, near Bethel. OVER 60 MILES FROM WOODSTOCK, ULSTER COUNTY.

DIRECTIONS
For the general area locate Monticello on any map. Take exit 16 off the Thruway at Harriman, on to route 17 into Monticello and on to 17B to the town of Bethel.

Woodstock Week, 14 August 1969

never left." Barbara O'Brien says she understood "the anti-hippie thing" because she came from a long line of Irish cops. "But I saw the clashes on the village green and thought, 'Why are they doing that?'" she says. "My brain wanted to be where the hippies were."

In a *New York Times* piece entitled "Woodstock's a Stage, but Many Don't Care for the Show", Bill Kovach reported on the town's closure of Big Deep, the swimming hole in which art students had bathed in the twenties. "They shut off the swimming hole from 1969 to 1987 after some nude hippie gave a deputy the finger," says Ed Sanders. "Woodstock viewed headbands and fringed leather jackets as satanic. They weren't happy when the hippies feminised

masculinity with necklaces and long hair and kaftans." Richard
Heppner points out that Woodstock didn't become Democrat until
the eighties. "I don't think we had a Democrat on the town board
until 1980," he says. "And that's because it's an isolated town. The
artists had tried to stir things up, but they were outnumbered. And
now even some of the *artists* baulked at the hippies."

Bill Kovach's *Times* piece mentioned the upcoming "Woodstock
Festival", which was expected to draw 100,000 to Wallkill's Mills
Industrial Park the following month. Michael Lang was secretly
appalled by the soulless suburban location that he and his Woodstock
Ventures partners had been forced to settle for, but time was running
out. Recruiting the best team available – including Chip Monck, the
lighting director who'd once worked for Albert Grossman – Lang
set things in motion. By early June, it was clear they could not even
depend on Wallkill, where locals had mobilised to halt the festival.
Meanwhile, Woodstockers were still concerned that lawless hordes
would descend on their town on the assumption that "Woodstock"
was in, well, Woodstock. Republican assemblyman Clark Bell
accused Lang and his partners of "romanticising" the town and
deliberately making it known that "Bobby Dylan" lived there. Come
15 July, a month away from the festival, Woodstock Ventures no
longer had a site for their "Aquarian Exposition".

Michael Lang claims he was relieved by Wallkill's rejection. A
kind of divine intervention – a phone call from a motel manager
who'd been raised in the same Brooklyn neighbourhood as him –
took Lang to a remote and run-down part of Sullivan County, an
hour west of Wallkill. The manager's property was laughable, but
through him came Lang's first view of "the field of my dreams . . . this
perfect green bowl" on a 2,000-acre property near Bethel. "Michael
is desperately trying to find a site," says Stan Beinstein. "With dumb
luck he rides up to this Jewish farmer and says, 'Have I got a deal for
you.'" Max Yasgur, forty-nine, was no hippie, but he was no hillbilly
either. He thought Lang and his partners had been treated unjustly

in Wallkill. He also calculated he could make decent money out of them, whatever the risks to his land and the ire of his Bethel neighbours. "[Michael] has a way of ingratiating himself," said Yasgur's widow Miriam, not the first person to fall for Lang's combination of cherub and devil. "I think he's a born con man. Even though you know you're being had, you can't help but like him."

WOODSTOCK
MUSIC & ART FAIR
PRESENTS AN
AQUARIAN EXPOSITION
IN WHITE LAKE, N.Y.

Jimi Hendrix

*   *   *

3 Days of
Peace & Music
AUGUST 1969

Grateful Dead   Janis Joplin   *   *   *

Music Starts at 4:00 pm on Fri. and 1:00 pm Sat. & Sun.

Friday 15th	Saturday 16th	Sunday 17th
Joan Baez	Canned Heat	The Band
Arlo Guthrie	Creedence Clearwater	Jeff Beck Group
Richie Havens	Grateful Dead	Blood, Sweat & Tears
Sly and The Family Stone	Janis Joplin	Joe Cocker
Tim Hardin	Jefferson Airplane	Crosby Stills & Nash
Nick Benes	Santana	Jimi Hendrix
Sweetwater	The Who	Iron Butterfly
	Jack Harrison	Ten Years After

*   *   *   *   *   *   Jonny Winter

HUNDREDS OF ACRES TO ROAM ON
Ticket Prices, One Day $7.00
Two Days $13.00, Three Days $18.00

WE ENTERPRISES (201) 344-0604

Through a miracle, Woodstock Ventures had pulled it off. The festival was going to happen, and in the Edenic location Lang had always envisaged. Among those who began to believe was the man who'd played such a big part in establishing "Woodstock" as a countercultural state of mind. "He was a little sceptical about the festival," Lang recalls of Albert Grossman's initial response. "But when we moved to Bethel he came down with Rick Danko to see what was going on. We were standing at the top of the hill and I was describing what was going on. I said, 'Down there is the Hog Farm.'" Mention of the New Mexico commune set any remaining doubts to rest: Grossman had known the farm's founder Hugh "Wavy Gravy" Romney in the days when Romney did stand-up comedy in Greenwich Village.* "I'd gotten Bill Graham on board at that point," Lang says, "so it was just nice to have Albert on our side too." With Grossman's tacit endorsement came the bookings of The Band and Janis Joplin for $15,000 apiece, both crucial additions to the three-day line-up.

Lang felt more trepidation when it came to Woodstock's biggest star. "I didn't book Dylan," he states. "But I didn't book him for a bunch of reasons. I knew he didn't like the idea of being the prophet of the hippies, that that was onerous for him. It was known around here, and I knew it from the guys in The Band and other mutual friends. But of course I wanted him to be a part of it." With artist Bob Dacey, who'd filmed his Miami Pop Festival before moving to Woodstock, Lang went to see Dylan on Ohayo Mountain Road. As Sara prepared lunch, Lang made his pitch to the reluctant prophet. He even asked Elliott Landy to help him persuade Dylan to play the festival, or at least show up there. "Bob said, 'You'd have to bring guns,'" Landy says. "He didn't want to do it. He said he sensed danger." Yet Dylan told Al Aronowitz, who lunched with him on 11

---

* According to Bob Spitz, it was on Romney's typewriter that Bob Dylan had typed out the lyrics to "A Hard Rain's a-Gonna Fall".

August, that he'd "been invited, so I know it'll be okay to show up". Perhaps Dylan believed he was bigger than the festival; arguably he *was*. He told Aronowitz that he'd met Lang, "but I can't remember anything about him".

Later, Lang found himself wondering what would have happened if he'd offered Dylan more money to play. He wondered still harder when he learned that Dylan had agreed – for a whopping $50,000 – to headline an English Woodstock on the Isle of Wight, just two weeks after the Bethel festival. "They offered so much dough for Bob to play that nobody could turn it down," says Jonathan Taplin. Though Bert Block negotiated the deal, Grossman earned almost $16,000 from it, his last big Dylan commission before their contract expired. The hour-long set, with The Band backing him, was Dylan's supreme kiss-off to the hippie faithful – a low-key country-rock affair performed by six men in suits with short hair.

Though Dylan never made it to Bethel – notwithstanding rumours that he'd attended in disguise* – Joplin and The Band did. Albert Grossman, however, refused to allow either of them to appear in Wadleigh's film. "He had a kind of Dr No thing about him," Jonathan Taplin says. "He really liked to say no a lot more than he liked to say yes."

Joplin's set was only the second with her new Kozmic Blues Band, which was heavy on blue-eyed soul. The Band seemed thrown by the apocalyptic scale of the gathering and struggled to put their restrained mountain sound across to an audience that had had its collective mind blown by the Who and Sly and the Family Stone. "You sit on the big stage watered by the blue spotlights while The Band plays 'I Shall Be Released'," Al Aronowitz wrote, "and you look out into the eyes of the monster." Sandwiched between sets

* When he played the Bethel Woods Center for the Arts on the festival site in June 2007, Dylan muttered that "last time we played here, we had to play at six in the morning, and it was a-rainin' and the field was full of mud".

by blues-rock blasters Ten Years After and Johnny Winter, "Tears of Rage" and "I Shall Be Released" underscored the point that *Music from Big Pink* had been made in *reaction* to the subculture of rock festivals. "I looked out there and it seemed as if the kids were looking at us kind of funny," Robbie Robertson recalled. "We were playing the same way we played in our living room. We were like orphans in the storm . . ."

Equally unnerved by the sea of people in Yasgur's green bowl was Tim Hardin, who refused to open the festival on Friday 15 August. Michael Lang knew Hardin was on methadone and chose not to force the issue. When the singer finally stumbled onstage at twilight, he threw his musicians a major curveball by instructing them to perform a poem his wife had written about heroin but which had never been set to music. "He said, "'Snow White Lady' in F,'" remembered guitarist Gilles Malkine, "and he put this crumpled piece of paper on the keyboard and started playing, and so we just went along with him, but it was a disaster [. . .] Okay, you might do that in a café somewhere, but Jesus Christ, the whole world was looking at us!" More felicitous was the five-song acoustic set by John Sebastian, whose tie-dyed jeans and jacket became iconic symbols for the festival. The former Lovin' Spoonful star caught the vibe of togetherness that was the real story of Woodstock: as many subsequently reported, no one had known there were this many hippies in the entire country.

From Traver Hollow Road, meanwhile, came Jimi Hendrix and his entourage, driven to the site in a stolen pick-up truck by roadie Gerry Stickells after it proved impossible to arrange transportation by helicopter. Mike Jeffery quickly became embroiled in a heated discussion with Michael Lang about the timing of Hendrix's set, Lang warning that things were running chronically late and asking if Hendrix would consider playing earlier. Rigidly blinkered – or perhaps just nervous about how ragged the band would sound – Jeffery refused.

By the time Gypsy, Sun and Rainbows made it to the stage, it was 8.30 a.m. the next morning. "I see we meet again," Hendrix announced after the band had been introduced as the Jimi Hendrix Experience. "Dig, we'd like to get something straight. We got tired of the Experience, and every once in a while we was blowing our minds too much, so we decided to change the whole thing around and call it Gypsy, Sun and Rainbows for short. It's nothing but a Band of Gypsys." Most of the "half-a-million" had left, leaving around 40,000 exhausted stragglers who were treated to a sprawling set of loose blues-funk jams, retooled Experience classics and frequent delays for the retuning of instruments. At one point Hendrix announced a new song, "Valley of Neptune", only to realise that he couldn't remember its lyrics. "We only had about two rehearsals," he apologised, "[. . .] but, I mean, it's a first ray of the new rising sun anyway, so we might as well start from the earth, which is rhythm, right?"

If the supposedly unplanned "Star-Spangled Banner" – by turns blissed-out and mind-shredding – has long been overdetermined as a disturbing coda to a seismic decade, it was still a dramatic reinterpretation of America's national anthem. After closing with "Hey Joe", however, Hendrix walked offstage knowing the set had been an unholy mess. "We left by helicopter," said Leslie Aday, who accompanied him to the old borscht-belt hotel Grossinger's. "[He was] tired, cold, hungry . . . and unhappy with his performance."

After a long night of sleep and dope, Hendrix returned to Traver Hollow and asked Claire Moriece to keep the hangers-on at bay. Larry Lee, all too aware of the hostility emanating from Mike Jeffery, made his excuses and left. As Gypsy, Sun and Rainbows slowly unravelled over the ensuing weeks, Hendrix settled for more fluid jams with Philip Wilson and fellow Butterfield band member Rod Hicks, both loosely affiliated with Juma Sultan's Aboriginal Music Society. Another local musician was a jazz keyboardist who'd spent time in Woodstock since the mid-sixties. "At that time there was this

tremendous division between jazz musicians and rock musicians,"
says Mike Ephron, who first came to the house in mid-September.
"But I *loved* Jimi. I brought my electric clavinet, which fascinated
him because there weren't too many electric keyboards around. It
had a very funky groove, so we started playing, just the three of
us, at about four in the afternoon. And we didn't take a break till
midnight."

The notorious Mike Ephron bootleg, later released as *Jimi
Hendrix at His Best*

Ephron was part of a fertile avant-garde jazz scene in Manhattan, his loft on Broadway and Union Square a frequent hub for musicians like Pharoah Sanders, Marion Brown and Sam Rivers. In 1966 he'd rented a house on Woodstock's Meads Mountain Road, to which those same musicians were often invited. Three years later, living in Glenford with Garth Hudson as his neighbour, he received a call from Juma Sultan. "Juma had come by my loft jams in the city," Ephron says. "He contacted me to say Jimi had been trying to break away from the mould of the guitar player and all that theatrical stuff."

Ephron found Hendrix in good spirits. "It was just all about the music," he says. "He was doing stuff with feedback that I've never heard before or since. He was totally experimenting, going all the way out to lunch." Among the experiments were "amazing jams" with Sam Rivers and folk-rock duo Bunky and Jake. "Hendrix actually invited Sam to join his band," says trumpeter Steve Bernstein. "Someone once said to Sam, 'Wow, your life would have been a lot different if you'd stayed with Charles Mingus.' He said, 'Not really. What *would* have made a big difference is if I'd joined Jimi Hendrix.'"

One of Ephron's New York girlfriends told him she had a premonition Hendrix was going to die. "She thought the pressure from his management would drive him over the edge," Ephron says. "In fact, she proposed that we kidnap him and take him to my place in Woodstock – just to get him away from Jeffery." To Ephron, Hendrix was "a shy person, very sweet, who'd sit and write poetry and play his guitar", whereas Jeffery was "like something out of *Performance*", boasting that he'd "got Jimi signed up till 1999, mate, he ain't goin' nowhere!"

Ten days after the festival, Jeffery and Jerry Morrison turned up at Traver Hollow in a limousine. They had company – in Sultan's words, "some low-level Mafiosi who lived in Willow". While chauffeur Conrad Loreto engaged in intimidating target practice with a revolver outside the house, Jeffery and his new acquaintances talked to Hendrix and the others about life after Woodstock. Taking Sultan and Jerry Velez aside, they offered them contracts with a company fittingly named Piranha Productions, the terms of which promised no advance money and made it clear that they could never play with Hendrix again.* Jeffery was also insistent that Hendrix honour an upcoming commitment at Salvation, a mafia-owned New York club on Sheridan Square.

Neither Sultan nor Velez was easily intimidated – not by small-time hoods, not by a chauffeur with a revolver. "We had a lot of connections to the Young Lords and the Black Panthers," Velez said. "It was like, 'We're all about peace and love, but if you want to create a dark environment around the guy, you're messing with the wrong people.'" Hendrix, however, was genuinely scared by what these people could do to him. "He was a soft, lovable guy, [there was] nothing violent about him at all," said Velez. As a result, Hendrix did what he was told. On 10 September he played Salvation with Sultan, Velez, Billy Cox and Mitch Mitchell. "It was basically a disaster," Velez said. "The sound sucked. It was a small place, not really set up for a band like Jimi's. Jimi walked off after a while saying, 'This is bullshit.'"

What happened after that, only Hendrix really ever knew. He told his old friend and biographer Curtis Knight that, as he walked away from Salvation with its co-owner Bobby Woods – who also happened to be his coke dealer – he was forcibly abducted by four men who blindfolded him and drove him to an apartment in Brooklyn.† Some maintain the kidnapping was orchestrated by Mike Jeffery himself, who then came heroically to his client's rescue to prove he was on his side. Juma Sultan has said that when Hendrix returned

* There remains much confusion as to what actually happened at Traver Hollow that day. Electric Lady Studios engineer Jim Marron claimed "four or five mobsters came up to Shokan in a car, walked in with their guns out" and told Hendrix he was under house arrest, prompting Mike Jeffery to call in a favour from a Long Island mafioso. But Jerry Morrison told Jerry Hopkins it was *he* who had come to the guitarist's rescue.
† Almost five months later, Woods was found dead in Queens with five bullets in his head. It seems likely he paid the price for standing up to the mob.

to Traver Hollow, he laughed about how "Mike and his crew came in like gangbusters and rescued him".

If things had settled down by the time Sheila Weller visited Traver Hollow in mid-September, whatever idyllic moments Hendrix had experienced upstate were coming to an abrupt close. Soon he stripped Gypsy, Sun and Rainbows down to the three-piece Band of Gypsys, with Billy Cox and ex-Electric Flag drummer Buddy Miles playing behind him. After the first Catskills snowfall that autumn, Hendrix left the "Sky Church" and never returned. When owner Glen Markett came to inspect the house, it looked like an abandoned commune: one bedroom had been painted black, another boasted a mural of a flying saucer descending over a mountain; rugs had numerous burn marks, and wax from candles had spilled everywhere.

Back in Manhattan in the summer of 1970, Hendrix had a brief encounter with the author of "All Along the Watchtower", who happened to be cycling past the guitarist's limousine. "It was an eerie scene," Dylan remembered. "He was slouched down in the back [...] it was strange, both of us were a little lost for words. He'd gone through like a fireball without knowing it. I'd done the same thing, like being shot out of a cannon."

Relations with Mike Jeffery did not improve. When Hendrix played England's Isle of Wight festival that summer, he told Richie Havens his managers were "killing" him, that he couldn't eat or sleep. Havens recommended he speak with his attorney Johanan Vigoda, who had just bought his own Woodstock property off Ohayo Mountain Road.* "I told Jimi I would be glad to introduce him and

* Vigoda was a maverick New York lawyer who, amongst other things, renegotiated Stevie Wonder's contract with Motown's Berry Gordy. (It's his voice you hear as the judge sentencing the hapless protagonist of *Innervisions'* "Living for the City".) He also extricated Hendrix from an early contract with Sue Records, and represented Michael Lang and his partner Artie Kornfeld in the dissolution of Woodstock Ventures. "Even though he was an attorney, he kind of had this artistic soul where he wanted to do good things for artists," says Paula Batson, who

that I would be in London for four days after the festival," Havens wrote. "I told him to come by and see me when he left the Isle of Wight. He never showed up. The next thing I heard about him was some three weeks later. He'd been found dead."

After Hendrix's death on 18 September 1970, Mike Jeffery continued to spend time in Woodstock. "He'd become an embarrassment to many in town," wrote Paul Smart, "albeit one with a constant supply of drugs." A 1972 report on Woodstock in *Harper's* magazine referred to Jeffery's "financial problems" and said the local sheriff was "threatening to put his extravagant house up for sale to satisfy a bad debt".

After Jeffery died in a mid-air plane collision over Nantes on 3 March 1973, the high fences around 1 Wiley Lane stayed in place. They were, Smart wrote, "an odd memorial to the wild rock 'n' roll lifestyle hidden behind its quiet country façade".

worked for him. "He would do very funny things in his negotiations, like eating the contract as he was talking. And the other attorneys would just be like, 'Whatever you want, just stop eating the contract!'" Vigoda died in Nevada in 2011.

HE'S NOT HERE

For many, Woodstock ruined Woodstock. Though people had not descended on Tinker Street in the expected droves during the festival itself, they certainly showed up after the event had made "Woodstock" a global buzzword. "You see them arrive at the village green," said Lynda Sparrow, manager of the Happiglop leather-goods store. "They come in here and say, 'You mean, this is it? This is all there is?'"

As they had been before the festival, Woodstock's elders were up in arms about the hippie drifters. "We are not opposed to [them]," Town Supervisor Milton Houst said, before getting to the nub of the matter. "We want visitors and we don't want to keep anybody out, but this place is like everywhere else in the world: you need money to stay here."

"What concerned the town was that the musicians were bringing in people with no means of support," says Richard Heppner. "The way welfare rules worked here, the town was responsible for paying a good portion of any type of grant that you got. But it was such a mess that Woodstock took a stand and refused to allocate funds to these people." In 1970 the crisis-intervention centre FAMILY of Woodstock, run by Gael Varsi, was established at 13 Library Lane to help troubled kids who'd wound up in Woodstock – many of them runaways from abusive backgrounds. For most of the young seekers it was irrelevant that Woodstock hadn't taken place in Woodstock: the town by now was a sacred place and home not only to Bob Dylan but to The Band, Van Morrison and many more. "Kids would liter-ally get off the bus and say, 'Where's Bob's house?'" says Heppner.

"Woodstock turned into a place where a lot of young kids would come up and seek the ancillary aspects of being at the festival," says Martha Velez, who lived near Dylan's old house and even wrote a song, "Byrdcliffe Summer", about her life there. "Which was that if they were there, they were now part of the scene. And really they weren't; they were simply part of a commercial aberration for Woodstock." The upside of this was that the town's population grew large enough to support a vibrant live-music scene; the downside was the commodification of the counterculture itself. "Once Dylan had gone, what was presenting itself mimicked what he had done or been about," says Bruce Dorfman. "I didn't feel the community was vital any more, and it was becoming very commercialised. Suddenly all these little shops opened that sold fancy lollipops. It was turning into some sort of tourist place."

"There was nothing about the *place* that changed," says Daoud Shaw, who drummed in Martha Velez's band at the Espresso and the Elephant. "It was just what was happening in society at the time. Labels came out of the woodwork and signed anything that walked. If it's a rock 'n' roll band, sign it, wind it up, and it'll make money." Some of the visitors came and never left – or at least those willing to brave the Catskills winter. "With the phenomenon of the Woodstock Festival came the kind of accidental settlement of the town as a rock community," says Cindy Cashdollar. "It was as if everybody thought, 'Oh what the hell, we'll just stay here!'"

For Dylan himself it had all finally become too much. Even behind the gates of the Ohayo Mountain Road house he felt vulnerable and persecuted. In 1985 he spoke of "people living in trees outside my house, trying to batter down my door, cars following me up dark mountain roads . . ." When Charles Manson and members of his "Family" were arrested in connection with the savage murders of Sharon Tate and her friends (and of Leno and Rosemary LaBianca), Dylan was as freaked out as any of the musicians who'd crossed

Manson's path. Who *knew* what barefoot psychos might show up on the Dylans' doorstep. Though he continued to patronise such local establishments as Norma Cross's Squash Blossom Café – where he often breakfasted – he was desperate to destroy the messiah image that had made him such a magnet.° On one occasion he emptied a bottle of whiskey over his head and strolled into a department store, hoping the story would spread and deter the countless disciples he'd never solicited.

"Bob was more of a sitting duck out there," says Maria Muldaur, who often visited the Dylans. "People were walking onto his property. At first he was kind of nice about it, but it got old really quick." Trying to hold onto his sanity, Dylan socialised with old folkie friends like the Muldaurs and the Traums. One winter's night he appeared at Maria's door in a huge fur hat. "I said, 'What are *you* doing here, Bob?'" she says. "He said, 'Jim Rooney told me Bob and Betsy [Siggins] were here.† Can I come in?' So he would just kind of appear when there was something interesting going on."

Soon not even the presence of old friends who treated him like a normal person compensated for the hassles he regularly endured in Woodstock. "There was always the unseen presence of Dylan," says Keith Reid. "Everyone knew he was there, but no one ever *saw* him. It was always like, 'He was here, you just missed him.'" Dylan seemed to retreat ever deeper into himself. "There were some very good artists living on Ohayo Mountain Road, but Bob had very little contact with any of them," says Bruce Dorfman. "It was surprising to me, but I think at that point there were disruptions beginning to happen in his life. The amount of attention that was given to

---

° The Squash Blossom – on the Tinker Street site where former Blues Magoo Michael Esposito now runs his bicycle-repair shop – was one of Woodstock's great meeting places. "It was a sort of breakfast-and-lunch place," says Stan Beinstein. "Norma lived upstairs, and she had lace curtains and antiques around. We'd roll out of bed and go there, and that's where you saw everybody."
† Bob Siggins had been a member of the Charles River Valley Boys; Betsy had worked at Cambridge's Club 47.

him magnified things enormously – for everybody, but especially for him."

When Eric Andersen came to stay on Ohayo Mountain Road, he found a different Dylan from his previous visit. "He was definitely into his kids, but I didn't get the feeling he was relaxed," Andersen said. "He was trying to be nice, but you could tell things were going on . . . his mind [was] just flying all over the place." It was as if the three-and-a-half-year experiment in trying to be a regular guy was finally faltering. In *Chronicles* he was unequivocal: "Woodstock had turned into a nightmare, a place of chaos. Now it was time to scramble out of there in search of some new silver lining." He was more cryptic in a *Playboy* interview in 1978: "It became stale and disillusioning. It got too crowded, with the wrong people throwing orders. And the old people were afraid to come out on the street. The rainbow faded." He even contemplated a move to Nashville, viewing properties in the city with Bob Johnston.

To this day Dylan does not forgive the way Woodstock turned from being a sanctuary – both domestic and creative – to being a kind of prison. The festival was "the sum total of all [the] bullshit," he wrote, and "I got very resentful about the whole thing." When Larry Campbell played with him between 1997 and 2004, the two men periodically talked about the town they'd both lived in. "Bob laughed when I told him Garth Hudson still had his old station wagon, but there were never any conversations where he reminisced fondly about the place," Campbell says. "With Bob it always seemed like, 'Well, I did that and now I don't do that any more.' I do remember asking what he was doing up here, and he put it very simply. He said, 'I was raising a family. That's all I was interested in at the time.'"

Dylan continued to use the Ohayo Mountain Road house as a second home through the early seventies. Even then, with its owner mostly absent, the house attracted unwelcome visitors. George Quinn, who house-sat the property as a teenager, remembered "these really strange characters showing up at all hours – people who were not too mentally stable". By the summer of 1970, Dylan was wearying even of occasional visits to Woodstock. One afternoon he stopped by the Sled Hill Café and asked bartender Jeremy Wilber to fetch Oklahoman singer-songwriter Roger Tillison's acoustic guitar from the back room. No sooner had he struck a chord on it than two young women walked in and shrieked with disbelief. "Bob put the guitar down and left," says Wilber. "And that was the last time I ever saw him here."

One of the reasons the Dylans still spent time upstate was that their new life on MacDougal Street – where they'd moved shortly after the birth of son Jakob in December 1969 – wasn't quite working out the way Dylan had planned. With the notorious A. J. Weberman rifling through his garbage, and other mad radicals of the era accusing him of selling out, Dylan was soon regretting the nostalgic impulse that had taken him back to Greenwich Village. He later complained that "the Woodstock Nation had overtaken MacDougal Street", as though Woodstock itself had somehow corrupted the old Village he now longed for. "Albert Grossman was obviously very tough," says Ed Sanders. "When Dylan left him, he was left without a praetorian guard. People like Weberman and the Yippies could hound him." Interestingly, Dylan refrained from mentioning Grossman's name, even with people who'd known them both. "We never had any conversation about Albert at all, though I knew they'd fallen out," says Michael Friedman. "Albert never talked about it either, probably because he knew that the word was out there that he had overreached."

Dylan was also being serially unfaithful. "He was fooling around with other people, and that was pretty well-known," says one former employee. "When he came back from the Isle of Wight, he was very much the family man, but I distinctly remember being in Naomi Saltzman's apartment and there was a girl measuring him for a costume. They were in there with the door closed and I knew they were fooling around." Bruce Dorfman says he never saw Sara Dylan in the city. "It was pretty much Bob and his pinball machine in the living room," the artist remembers. "I can't imagine how Sara even stayed in the place."

Dylan tried to throw people off the scent again with the mischievously titled *Self Portrait* (1970), whose mixture of cornball-country and MOR-folk covers – including songs by old acquaintances like Bob Gibson, Tom Paxton and Eric Andersen – infuriated diehard disciples even more than *Nashville Skyline* had done. "Being at the *Self Portrait* sessions, I was like, 'What the hell is going on here?'" says Al Kooper, who lived near by and saw a lot of Dylan in this period. "I said to myself, 'Why is he doing *other people's songs?*'"* Decades later, much of *Self Portrait* and its better-received follow-up, *New Morning*, was rehabilitated and reclaimed when the box set *Another Self Portrait* offered stripped-down takes of tracks originally marred by cloying overdubs. Ironically, three of the set's highlights celebrated the country life Dylan had all but given up. Written for a play by Archibald MacLeish, "New Morning" itself might have hailed from the first flush of Dylan's love affair with Woodstock, while "Time Passes Slowly" – first recorded in New York with a visiting George Harrison – similarly evoked the pastoral charms of Dylan's Catskills hideaway.† Yet the ambiguity of "Time Passes Slowly" was hard to miss: as seductively peaceful as the

---

* In *Chronicles*, Dylan wrote that he'd urged Albert Grossman to pair Kooper with Janis Joplin. Grossman replied that it was "the stupidest thing" he'd ever heard. "I should have been a manager," Dylan hilariously concluded.
† Harrison, who'd spent further time with him on the Isle of Wight, wrote another song – "Behind That Locked Door" – about trying to reach out to Dylan. Along with "Time Passes Slowly", the two men recorded a number of other tracks at Columbia's New York studios, including the tongue-in-cheek "Working on a Guru" and a version of the Beatles' "Yesterday". On his ambitious triple-album debut *All Things Must Pass*, Harrison included not only "Behind That Locked Door" and the earlier Dylan co-write "I'd Have You Anytime" but "If Not for You", a Tex-Mex-flavoured song of amorous devotion that was *New Morning's* only single. The following year he used all his powers of unconditional friendship to coax a terrified Dylan back onstage at the Concert for Bangladesh.

picture looked ("We sit beside bridges and walk beside fountains"), the apathy ("Ain't no reason to go anywhere") and the mild desperation ("We stare straight ahead and try so hard to do right") were equally clear. One could have said the same of the gorgeous "Sign on the Window", a song of emotional thawing-out and desire for family that sounded like a man trying a little too hard to convince himself that "that must be what it's all about".*

Similarly struggling to convince himself that "that must be what it's all about" in Woodstock was the Ulsterman who lived at the top of Dylan's road. Van Morrison was trying to contain his own restlessness as he played Happy Families with Janet Planet and his stepson. Like Dylan, too, Morrison was instinctively repelled by the very idea of the Woodstock Festival. While he happily admits that Michael Lang never invited him to play at Bethel, he says that in retrospect he was "lucky" not to have been part of its "mythology and typecasting".

"Van just sensed that he didn't want to have anything to do with it," says John Platania. "He would speak in disparaging terms about it before it even happened." After the festival was over, Morrison claimed he'd moved to Woodstock to escape the scene, "and then Woodstock started *being* the scene . . . everybody and his uncle started showing up at the bus station, and that was the complete opposite of what it was supposed to be".

Despite the crabbiness he shared with Dylan, Morrison remained in Woodstock for another eighteen months. He was sufficiently taken with the town's spirit to piece together the quasi-communal Street Choir, expanding the *Moondance* line-up to include new players and singers. Assisting him in this was an ambitious new manager,

---

* Unconvinced by New Bob, of course, were the likes of Country Joe McDonald, who said he wasn't "fooled", and the deranged Weberman, who declared he'd "come to the conclusion that Dylan has turned into a HYPOCRITE AND A LIAR".

Mary Martin, who'd graduated from Albert Grossman's office after hooking Dylan up with the Hawks.

"Mary commanded respect and really got this whole thing moving," says Daoud Shaw, who'd replaced Gary Mallaber in Morrison's band. "I could see from the get-go that she was on Van's case to get him happening. She was constantly at gigs, constantly working." Janet Planet later claimed that Martin had urged her not to let Morrison "get too happy" lest his music suffer in the process. Janet was appalled, since her all-consuming obsession in life was to make her husband feel better about himself. "Hanging out with Van was like hanging out with someone from Mars," says Shaw. "But then again, it could be really fun, like getting a call at 3 a.m. saying, 'I heard there's a barber at this hotel who used to do Sinatra's hair. Let's get haircuts!'"

Coming together in the spring of 1970, the "Band and Street Choir" replaced a frustrated Jef Labes with keyboard player Alan Hand, and saxophonist Collin Tilton with Paul Butterfield's trumpeter Keith Johnson. The "Choir" itself consisted of Janet, Jack Schroer's wife Ellen and Johnson's pregnant girlfriend Martha Velez, along with Daoud Shaw, Larry Goldsmith and Andrew Robinson. "Initially it was just 'Come on up,'" says Shaw, whom Morrison heard jamming with some of Butterfield's musicians at the Espresso. "And I just kept going and playing. I would close my eyes and listen to him singing, and it was different every time."

Early demos for 1970's *His Band and the Street Choir* were done in a home-made studio that Shaw had built in nearby Hurley. "I had a two-car garage," he says, "and from that we built a studio right from the ground up. We called it Stone Sound." The feel of the demos was akin to the gypsy soul of *Moondance* but looser, more laid-back. On the surface the vibe was good, and Janet seemed to think she was "winning the battle" between the light and the darkness in her husband's brooding soul. In her liner notes for the album she wrote that she had "seen [him] open those parts of his secret self

– his essential core of aloneness I had always feared could never be
broken into – and say, 'Yes, come in here. Know me.'"

"Van really bought into the whole community aspect of trying to
have a big family feel," says Martha Velez. "To be up in Woodstock
and to have people sing choruses in that way was a very big step for
him." In a lengthy *Rolling Stone* interview that summer, Morrison
told Happy Traum that recording his third Warners album was "very
human . . . there was no uptightness about it". Yet behind the genial-
ity, he worried about losing control. "It was probably something he
got himself into by saying 'Okay'," says Shaw, who wound up with
a credit as Van's assistant producer. "The vibe was street-corner,
a bunch of guys singing together. It was like he couldn't say no.
Domestic relations took over from casting the film."

"It was too hippie for me," Morrison confirms today. "A lot of
it was well-meaning, but the people didn't get that I had been in
the music business for a long time. So it led to a lot of problems,
because they couldn't really take any direction." Having got his early
grounding on the ballroom circuit in his native Northern Ireland,
Morrison abhorred the sloppy jamming of late-sixties rock. "I was
coming out of the tradition of blues and R&B," he says. "I didn't
really play any rock gigs till I got over to America with Them, so it

took some time to get used to what that was." He became so impatient with the Choir's deficiencies that for the soul ballad "If I Ever Needed Someone" he reinstated the New York backing trio that had sung behind him on *Moondance*'s "Crazy Love" and "Brand New Day".

In true seventies rock parlance, Morrison even claimed that everything was ruined when "the old ladies got involved". One of those ladies, Velez, found Morrison "very enigmatic and very difficult to approach", often just because his thick Ulster accent was near impenetrable. "But I really respected his need to be a creative person," she adds. "He always said that the music channelled through him and he just had to catch it. When it's that much of a visceral experience, it really requires a lot of trust in the viscera."*
The problem with *His Band and the Street Choir* was that it wasn't visceral *enough*. Possibly because Morrison was producing his own music for the first time, the sound at New York's A&R Studios was flat and lacklustre. Even "Domino", which gave him a Top 10 hit at the end of the year, missed the feel and dynamics of *Moondance*: both it and another early Woodstock number, the funky "I've Been Working", suffer by comparison with their thrilling treatments on Morrison's live *It's Too Late to Stop Now* (1974). But the material in any case was weak next to *Moondance*. "Crazy Face" was no "Crazy Love", and the acoustic "I'll Be Your Lover, Too" sounded like an *Astral Weeks* reject. Uptempo R&B tracks "Blue Money" and "Sweet Jannie" never really got going, while "Gypsy Queen" unsuccessfully mated the gossamer soul of "Crazy Love" to a pastiche of Curtis Mayfield's Impressions. Only the closing "Street Choir" revived the Band-steeped feel of the previous album.

* After the dissolution of the Street Choir, Velez recorded her second album, *Hypnotized*, with the core of Morrison's 1970 band – plus her brother Jerry. "It's clearly a Woodstock album," she says. "We woodshedded it at Byrdcliffe and then at a little house in Glenford. The winters there were fabulous for woodshedding, because there was nowhere to go."

Morrison felt the deficiencies keenly and later complained that he'd been pushed into making the album too quickly. He also detested the cover, which displayed him in a comical kaftan he'd bought in one of Tinker Street's head shops. He wasn't even sure about the happy-feely pictures that David Gahr took of him with his band members in the woods behind Spencer Road. Missing from them was John Platania, who'd temporarily fallen out with his employer. "It was almost like a fight I'd get into with my brother," Platania says. "He put the road manager in the picture instead of me." In the photos, however, was Morrison's baby daughter Shana, who entered the world on a chilly night in April. Janet's long labour had been so traumatic that Morrison called the Gershen brothers from Kingston Hospital and asked them to help him make it through the night.

The Gershens' friendship with the Morrisons continued for the remainder of 1970; Morrison even posed with the Montgomeries for one of Gahr's outdoor shots.* "He would just call up and say, 'What are you doing?'" Jon Gershen remembers. "We'd get together and play Hank Williams records. We weren't looking for anything from him." The Gershens took Morrison to see their attorney Alan Bomser in New York, hoping he might be able to help him retrieve some of the money the singer was owed. "Van offered the example of 'Gloria' and said he'd never received a penny for it," says Jon Gershen. "Alan said, 'You mean the "Gloria"?' Within fifteen minutes he says, 'I'm seeing at least a quarter of a million dollars that should be in your pocket from that song alone.' It seemed to me that Van really didn't have a clue about the music-publishing business."

The brothers also witnessed the growing friendship between

* The photo session was arranged by Mary Martin, who was attempting to put together a nationwide package tour featuring Morrison, the Montgomeries and – as headliners – the Byrds. When the latter band dropped out, Martin lost her interest in managing the Montgomeries and eventually stopped managing Morrison.

Morrison and Richard Manuel. "They were close pals," Mary Martin told me in 1991. "For Van, Richard was the real *soul* of The Band." Alcohol apart, the two men had specific musical passions in common and talked of collaborating on an album of Ray Charles songs. Manuel also made Morrison howl with laughter. "Canadians had a different sense of humour than Americans, and I understood that more," Morrison says. "Richard was a very funny guy. His one-liners were killers." To Morrison's old sax player Graham Blackburn the two men were born soulmates – both extraordinary singers, both painfully introverted. "The basis of the friendship was that they could come together on equal terms," Blackburn says. "From my perspective as an English immigrant, The Band had a problem as Canadians who felt like second-class citizens. But for them it was irrelevant that Van was Irish and Richard Canadian."

Morrison's acceptance by The Band, and by Manuel in particular, almost compensated for his failure to befriend Bob Dylan. He did, however, have one long phone conversation with his Ohayo Mountain neighbour. "Bob was talking about a revue, sort of like the Rolling Thunder one he did later," Morrison says. "He said he was thinking about having different singers come out with him." Maria Muldaur confirms that Dylan was "all fired up about an idea of travelling across America on a train". She remembers him saying, "Why don't you guys and me and The Band and Butterfield and Janis ride across the country?" That summer of 1970 the tour happened exactly as Dylan had envisioned it – but without him, the Muldaurs or Van Morrison.

Quite how Morrison and Manuel weren't killed drunk-driving is a Woodstock mystery. "The drinking thing was a fixture of [Van's] existence at that time," Jon Gershen said. "He would come over with a fifth of Johnnie Walker Red and plump himself down on the floor. Driving back to his house on those back-country roads, it's a wonder we didn't get wrapped around a tree." When Morrison and Manuel did finally get around to recording together, fittingly it was

on a song whose title referred to the difference in alcohol percentage between Johnnie Walker Red and Johnnie Walker Black. "They
were totally drunk by the end of the session," says Jim Rooney,
who witnessed it. "Richard drove Van home, but Van had a circular
driveway, and after he let Van out of the car he just kept coming
round and round the circle. He almost ran Van over." A song about
an inebriated evening the pair had spent together in Los Angeles,
"4% Pantomime" was recorded in early 1971 in a new studio built
by Albert Grossman.° It was also one of the last things Morrison did
before following Janet and their kids back to her native California.
Just before the Christmas of 1970, he announced to the Street Choir
that he was forming a new group with guitarist Doug Messenger,
whom he'd just flown in from California. "I've got a problem," were
Morrison's first words to Messenger. "I've got to stop drinking." The
next morning, Messenger awoke to find Morrison sitting at the foot
of the bed and the entire group assembled around them. "Doug
and I are starting a band," Morrison informed them, "and you're all
fucking fired!"

The jury is still out on whether – after two "farewell" shows at
the Fillmore East in February 1971 – Morrison genuinely wanted
to leave. "I think he really loved Woodstock," says John Platania. "It
was Janet who wanted to go back to Marin County." Significantly,
Morrison included his paean to "Old Old Woodstock" on 1971's
Tupelo Honey, his first California album, and sang in it of the town's
"cool night breezes" and "shady trees". (The water "flowing way
beneath the bridge" was almost certainly the Sawkill passing under
Tannery Brook Road at the bottom of Ohayo Mountain Road.) He
also sang of his woman "waiting by the kitchen door", which may
have been one of the factors in the eventual breakdown of their

---

° At the end of the out-take version of "4% Pantomime" on The Band's *A
Musical History* box set, one hears the voice of Garth Hudson saying, "That
was *spectacular*." Equally spectacular was the ecstatic version of *Moondance*'s
"Caravan" that Morrison sang with The Band at "The Last Waltz" in 1976.

marriage: he was dead set against Janet pursuing a career as an actor. And yet the self-explanatory "Starting a New Life" was the plainest statement of a fresh beginning. "That was pretty much representative of what was going on," says *Tupelo Honey's* producer Ted Templeman. "Van had moved out of Woodstock and they were starting again."

Morrison claims he was welcomed in Marin County with a friendliness he'd never experienced in Woodstock. "California was very different," he says. "Everybody was very open, whereas Woodstock was very closed." Of the town he'd left behind on the East Coast, he says that "if you didn't buy into the hippie vibe, then you were *out*". But he also says that "everyone was very reclusive, and there was a lot of paranoia going around". Perhaps it's his own paranoia he is talking about: he may have underestimated how difficult it was for his Woodstock peers to understand the man Richard Manuel dubbed "the Belfast Cowboy" – or how intimidatingly grumpy he came across.

Years later, another British singer-songwriter who'd settled in Woodstock was touring Europe as Bob Dylan's support act. At a Belfast show, none other than Van Morrison showed up backstage. "He said to me, 'So you live in Woodstock,'" says Graham Parker. "I said, 'Yeah.' He said, 'Fuckin' horrible place. Well, whatever works for you.'"

Whether Tim Hardin felt the same way about his adopted home town we can't know. After the opiated debacle of his Woodstock Festival appearance he continued to operate in his usual desultory fashion. "He'd fire me," says Warren Bernhardt, often Hardin's sole backing musician, "and then I'd run into him on the street and he'd say, 'Hey, I got a bunch of gigs coming up, you wanna do 'em?' And this went on for, like, six years." During a show in San Diego, Hardin marched onto the stage and announced he had heartburn. "So here's Bernhardt," he added, before splitting to catch a plane.

"Leaves me on the stage with ten thousand people, just me and a clavinet," Bernhardt recalls with a chuckle. "Pretty interesting."

Managed by Jerry Wapner, a hip lawyer who'd swapped Brooklyn for Woodstock back in 1964, Hardin moved from Zena Highwoods Road into a place near Boiceville known as the Onteora Mountain House. "I drove him to the closing of the property," Wapner recalled in 2013. "We drove back to the place and he got out of the car and there was a huge flagpole right in the centre of the circular drive . . . [He] pulled down the American flag – I don't think he meant any disrespect – and he pulled out of his pocket a Jolly Roger flag [and] hoisted it high. I must say, that ingratiated him even more to me." Hardin regularly surfaced in Woodstock, where his eccentricities became the stuff of local legend. "Ten-thirty in the morning," Warren Bernhardt says, "you'd walk out and there would be Tim in a short bathrobe wide open, nothing else, in cowboy boots and a hat, walking through town. There were a million things like that." During a loose *musicale* at Jim Rooney's house in Lake Hill, Hardin got so drunk that he fell on somebody's upright bass and broke it. For his sins, Rooney's wife Sheila "dragged him by the ear and threw him out in the snow".

Against all odds, Columbia kept faith with Hardin, though they warned producer Ed Freeman what to expect of his new charge. Sensibly, Freeman recorded most of the instrumental tracks for Hardin's next album ahead of the singer's erratic visits to the studio. "It was a funny combination of thinking Tim walked on water and realising he was virtually impossible to work with," he remembers. "I had to piece a lot of stuff together with Scotch Tape, but at the same time he was unquestionably brilliant." Low on original songs, *Bird on a Wire* nonetheless stood up as one of Hardin's most focused collections, kicking off with a soulful treatment of the Leonard Cohen title song. The album ended with "Love Hymn", a maudlin account of Hardin's courtship of – and abandonment by – Susan Morss, who "drove off with a new friend out west to LA".

When *Bird on a Wire* made little more impact on the charts than its peculiar predecessor had done, Hardin decided it was time to leave not only Woodstock but America. With its registered heroin addicts, England had always looked attractive to him. In 1971 he uprooted to London, recording most of his last Columbia album there with ex-Shadow Tony Meehan producing and a cast of sidemen that included former Humble Pie guitarist Peter Frampton. This time not a single original song made the cut – probably because Hardin hadn't written any. *Painted Head* concluded with a long country-soulful working of Jimmy Cox's immortal blues "Nobody Knows You When You're Down and Out". Tim Hardin wasn't far off that.

11

OH LORD WON'T YOU BUY ME
A MERCEDES BENZ

For Geoff Muldaur of the Jim Kweskin Jug Band, the "big break-through" at the 1965 Newport Folk Festival wasn't Bob Dylan's scandalously amplified set on the Sunday night but Friday afternoon's performance by the Paul Butterfield Blues Band. "In the blink of an eye", Muldaur told Woodstock writer John Milward, "there would be two hundred thousand blues bands in the world based on that model."

Presaging the American blues-rock wave of the late sixties, just as the Yardbirds and John Mayall's Bluesbreakers were doing in England, the interracial Chicago group tore up Newport's Blues Workshop, with Butterfield's and Mike Bloomfield's searing licks solidly anchored by Howlin' Wolf's former rhythm section of drummer Sam Lay and bassist Jerome Arnold. "We were a little too chaotic for them," says Barry Goldberg, whom Butterfield had invited to join them at Newport. "It was white kids playing the blues, first of all, and they couldn't accept it. But it was really cool. Paul was a great entertainer, and Michael was never one to turn down: the more people resented it, the louder he got." Maria Muldaur, who watched open-mouthed with fellow members of the Kweskin band, had never seen anything like it. "I'd heard a lot of early R&B," she says, "but to see it live with the power and dynamics and energy those guys brought to it was something else. Plus it was the first integrated band I ever saw."

Crowning the whole event was the almost comical fistfight that erupted after the set, when a livid Albert Grossman confronted song collector Alan Lomax to berate him for the condescending way he'd

introduced the band.* "That was the *dumbest* introduction I have
ever heard!" Grossman yelled, before launching himself at Lomax
and shoving him to the ground. "We didn't know what had started
it," says Maria Muldaur. "All of a sudden these two big bears are
scuffling around in the dirt." For Barry Goldberg, Grossman's rage
towards Lomax made him an instant hero. "It was sort of obscene to
see these two old guys rolling in the dirt," he says, "but when Albert
went to that extreme and cared so passionately for his band, that
won me over."

Grossman had been turned on to Butterfield's trailblazing group
by Paul Rothchild, who'd seen them play in their native city at the
start of the year. "It was thrilling, chilling," Rothchild said in 1990.
"[It] changed my entire genetic code." Butterfield was a fiery Irish
American whose electrifying harmonica phrases were the only
answers anybody needed to the hoary question "Can white men
play the blues?" "I knew Paul was great, but I didn't know *how*
great," says Geoff Muldaur. "I was in Cleveland with him once, and
Cannonball Adderley turns to me and says, 'Do you know who the
fuck you're playing with?' Paul took it to a place where, if you have
the courage, you're risking death when you do it."

The same might have been said of the super-hip Bloomfield, who
was persuaded by Paul Rothchild to join Butterfield's band alongside rhythm guitarist Elvin Bishop. "Michael was a little intimidated
by Paul, because Paul was a tough guy," says Goldberg. "He was a
beer-drinker, he wore a black leather jacket." Butterfield's pal Nick
Gravenites was another tough guy, Goldberg says: "Those guys were
scary. Not the kind you could small-talk with. If you said, 'Hey, man,
how you doing?' they just glared at you."

---

* The only real account we have of Lomax's introduction came from the late Paul
Rothchild, who told Eric Von Schmidt and Jim Rooney that the revered blues
scholar had spoken words to the effect that there "used to be a time when a farmer
would take a box, glue an axe handle to it, put some strings on it, sit down in the
shade of a tree and play some blues for himself and his friends", whereas now
"we've got these guys, and they need all this fancy hardware to play the blues . . ."

Flying back to New York, Rothchild urged Jac Holzman to sign them to Elektra Records, despite the fact that the label had always shied away from electric music. Rothchild had only ever produced acoustic blues and folk for Holzman, and his initial attempts to capture the gritty Butterfield sound in the studio – and then in a faux-live setting at the Café au Go Go – were scrapped at considerable expense. At the third attempt Rothchild nailed the band's debut, with its home-town anthem "Born in Chicago" and its versions of Muddy Waters's "Got My Mojo Working" and Junior Parker's "Mystery Train".

Recommended by Rothchild, Grossman was instantly smitten, forging a bond with Butterfield that would last for the rest of his life. It was as though Butterfield grounded him in the Midwest that had spawned him, an earthy corrective to New York hype. It is even conceivable that the two men knew each other before Grossman left Chicago. "Before Albert was *Albert*, they were friends," claims Butterfield's son Gabe. "He, my dad and Nick Gravenites were like the kings of Chicago. They had a lot of history." Any misgivings Grossman might have had about straying from the folk path were rendered irrelevant by Dylan's embrace of electricity – especially after Bloomfield's performances on "Like a Rolling Stone" and the rest of *Highway 61 Revisited*.

Through Peter Yarrow, who was on the festival's organising committee, Grossman secured the group their Friday slot at Newport. They repaid his faith by cheering him on as he flailed around backstage with Lomax (though supposedly it was Sam Lay who pulled the two bears apart). The undignified showdown was, of course, symbolic of more than Grossman's anger at Lomax's condescension towards blue-eyed rhythm and bluesmen: it was a head-on collision between folk tradition and rock revolution.

The folk community's pervasive distrust of Grossman climaxed with Dylan's electric set forty-eight hours later, aided and abetted by Bloomfield, Lay and bassist Arnold. After that, there was no way back. As Pete Seeger, fellow folk activist Theodore Bikel and, yes, even Peter Yarrow knew in their bones, the utopian folk dream was over. "I would've plugged my guitar into Pete Seeger's *tuchus*", Bloomfield said uncharitably, "and put a fuzztone on his peter." Like Grossman and Holzman – and like Dylan, indeed – Bloomfield knew that "folk" culture meant nothing if it refused to evolve. Folk's future was electric, and the October release of *The Paul Butterfield Band* only confirmed it. Soon the band was experimenting still further with long jams – the "raga rock" classic "East–West" paramount among them – at such psychedelic ballrooms as the Fillmore in San Francisco. Bloomfield was America's first white guitar hero, a counterpart to the deified Eric Clapton across the water.

In 1967, following the release of the *East–West* album, Bloomfield split from Butterfield to co-found hybrid blues-and-soul outfit the Electric Flag with Buddy Miles, Barry Goldberg, Harvey Brooks and Nick Gravenites. (In due course Albert Grossman bagged them a $50,000 deal with Columbia.) With some of his new bandmates, the guitarist began using heroin, a disturbing development to which his manager turned something of a blind eye. "I told Albert he needed to call a meeting," says Goldberg. "One of the horn players had brought heroin into the band, and Albert knew that that was the one drug no one should mess with."

Butterfield's response to the loss of his guitar hero was to expand his line-up with a horn section, thereby moving the band's sound away from Chicago blues towards a funkier, more soul-oriented style. Produced by John Court and sounding like a Fillmore version of the great Bobby "Blue" Bland – whose "I Pity the Fool" was one of its cover versions – *The Resurrection of Pigboy Crabshaw* (1967) lacked the tight focus and urgency of the first two Elektra albums. "The further Butter moved away from the blues, the more he was moving away from what suited him best," said Elvin Bishop, who quit the group in 1968. "The other stuff just splattered out: too much formlessness."

Butterfield was undeterred, replacing Bishop with hotshot pretty boy Howard "Buzzy" Feiten and adding trumpeter Steve Madaio to the existing horn section of trumpeter Keith Johnson and saxophonists David Sanborn and Gene Dinwiddie. He also made the decision to uproot the entire band to the East Coast after visits to Grossman's lair convinced him that Woodstock would make a healthier base for the extended family his group had become. In late October 1968 the whole ensemble flew to New York with their partners and offspring. "We got off the plane from Chicago and went right to Albert's offices," says Lynne Naso, drummer Philip Wilson's girlfriend. "Albert was business and he was stern, and I sat outside and listened to raised voices. Paul was getting into the dollars – 'I'm not getting enough' – and Sanborn and Philip were telling him, 'He's not doing right by you, he's manipulating you.'"

Things had cooled down by the time Butterfield and his wife Kathy moved into what Naso recalls as "the next house down from Bob Dylan on Ohayo Mountain Road". Financially, matters were resolved to everybody's satisfaction. "You'd pass the Butterfield guys on the street," says drummer Christopher Parker. "It was like, 'Oh, he got a new Mercedes, their new record must have come out.'" When the band wasn't touring, its members were regular guests of the Grossmans. "The first time really sticks in my memory," says Naso. "There was a late snowfall and it was really chilly. We went to the house, which was like a mansion. We walk in the door and a party is raging. There's a lot of food and wine going around, and people are taking their clothes off. I didn't want to share my boyfriend, but a lot of the girls were getting naked and they would wander out of the room with some of the guys. I went for a wander and peaked in a room, and there was a very serious orgy going on involving a dog."*

---

* In a muck-raking item for the *New York Journal-American*, Walter Winchell wrote about "British rock and roll stars and touring recording people" gathering at a Woodstock hideaway, where they were ferried around in Rolls-Royces and treated to the favours of young women. One can only assume he was referring to Grossman's house, though it may have been Mike Jeffery's.

For Naso, Grossman was the Mr Big of Woodstock, an enigmatic chieftain pulling the strings that mattered. "He ran the show and we got a ticket to go," she says. "Paul went many years bickering back and forth with Albert, but somebody like him might not have made it without Albert."

With most of them living at the Peter Pan Farm – where their rehearsals took place – the Butterfield band was now a formidably funky outfit. "Paul brought a lot of the great players to town for the first time," Levon Helm remembered. "Those guys came in and made the town a more musical place." The group played the Woodstock Sound Festival in the early summer of 1969, frequently jamming with other local musicians at the Espresso, the Elephant and the Sled Hill. "Most of that band was musically literate," says Graham Blackburn, one of those who jammed with them. "It was such a big organisation that they could never really play around Woodstock, but they would all play individually. Different people would show up at the Sled Hill." Butterfield's harp even influenced the teenage Jim Weider. "It was the way he bent the notes," the guitarist says. "It was his attack."

In August the band played at dawn before Sha Na Na's and Jimi Hendrix's sets at Woodstock, though thanks to Grossman they weren't in the film and only the execrable "Love March" made it onto Atlantic's soundtrack album. For 1969's *Keep on Moving* Jac Holzman paired the band with soul producer-songwriter Jerry Ragovoy, and the ultra-funky result knocked *Pigboy Crabshaw* (and the subsequent *In My Own Dream*) into a cocked hat. "That horn-section band was one of the happiest times of my father's life," says Gabe Butterfield. "He was on fire."

By 1971, when the group released a de rigueur live album – recorded at the Troubadour in LA with Todd Rundgren at the controls – their personnel had changed again. Meanwhile, the Butterfields had found a measure of domestic bliss with their new baby Lee in a house out on Wittenberg Road. The group's final

Elektra album, *Sometimes I Just Feel Like Smilin'* – with the group posed against a mountain skyline that referenced Elliott Landy's group shot for *Music from Big Pink* – included an instrumental called "Song for Lee".

If Grossman was frustrated that he couldn't make a bigger star of Butterfield, he had no such problems with Janis Joplin. The careers of the two musicians, rooted in blues, ran on broadly parallel lines: they shared Fillmore bills during the first days of Big Brother, and both were infatuated by horn-driven R&B. Among Joplin's many love affairs was one she conducted in 1969 with Gene Dinwiddie; she even jammed with Butterfield's band while visiting Dinwiddie on the Peter Pan Farm. The following March she recorded the on-the-road song "One Night Stand" with them in Los Angeles.

Unlike Butterfield, whose primary voice was his mouth-harp, Joplin was an indisputably powerful singer. Combined with her spunky image – all feather boas and bellbottoms – her hair-raising voice made her what *West* magazine called the "shaman mama" of the new rock era. In Myra Friedman's words, "[she] was actually being merchandised as the symbol of everything that was against the very idea of merchandising". As with Dylan, everyone wanted a piece of her. *"Everywhere I go, the people wanna make some time with me,"* she sang on "One Night Stand". *"That's okay, if the next day I can be free . . ."*

Grossman did what he had done with his first superstar: he protected her, often bringing her up to Bearsville to keep an eye on her. He was also determined to up her game artistically: managing exceptional musicians like Butterfield and The Band made him ever less tolerant of Big Brother's shortcomings. "Albert wanted predictable technical competence, and that wasn't what Big Brother was about," says John Byrne Cooke. "He didn't want to deal with the vagaries of whether the band's magic was going to work one night or not." Joplin needed little persuading that a better band would help her to move beyond mere psychedelic freakery. "They didn't want to learn any new material, whereas she wanted to be better," says songwriter JoHanna Hall, whom Joplin had befriended in New York. "She wanted to grow." More than anything, she aspired to the same big-band soul sound that consumed Butterfield; she knew Big Brother would never get close to the funky precision of, say, the Stax house band. "I love those guys more than anybody else in the world," she told writer Michael Lydon. "But if I had any serious idea of myself as a musician, I had to leave. Getting off, real *feeling*, like Otis Redding had, like Tina Turner, that's the whole thing of music for me."

Elliott Landy saw the changes coming after he was assigned to do a Big Brother shoot in New York. "They were as important as she was, but the magazine wanted me to focus on *her*," he says. "It didn't strike me as right." In an essay on Joplin in *The Rolling Stone Illustrated History of Rock 'n' Roll*, rock critic Ellen Willis noted that "the elitist concept of 'good musicianship' was as alien to the holistic, egalitarian spirit of rock and roll as the act of leaving one's group the better to pursue one's individual ambition was alien to the holistic, egalitarian pretensions of the cultural revolutionaries". Within days of quitting Big Brother – whose loyal though equally addicted guitarist Sam Andrew she retained – Joplin was putting together a new group, complete with a three-piece horn section. "We were all crushed," fellow guitarist James Gurley remembered. "And the scars from that have lasted until this day."

Gurley was certainly not alone in seeing the sacking as a betrayal of the original Haight-Ashbury spirit – and resenting the covert anti-Big Brother propaganda that seeped out of Grossman's office. "The idea was that they were all pretty lame," says Donn Pennebaker. "But the fact is that they suited her and weren't competitive with her." Perhaps feeling guilty for breaking up the band, Grossman half-heartedly offered to help Big Brother after Joplin's departure, even packing John Herald off to San Francisco to sing with them. "[John] was very much a typical Albert Grossman kind of folk act," said drummer Dave Getz. "He came out and played with us one day, and [he was] so completely the wrong person for Big Brother . . . it really convinced me that Albert just never even had any idea what we were about."

"Janis was moving into a bigger league and saying goodbye to her Haight-Ashbury boys," says Peter Coyote. "She rebranded herself, but leaving them was like a divorce from her authentic roots." Invited to New York – where she installed them gratis at the Chelsea Hotel – Coyote and Emmett Grogan saw how desperately she wanted to stand as an equal alongside her African American peers. "We were walking past the Fillmore one night and Janis went off on how great Mavis Staples was," Coyote remembers. "I said, 'Well, Janis, *you're* the one who's got top billing.'" For him, on scorching versions of songs by Jerry Ragovoy and Van Morrison's old mentor/ nemesis Bert Berns, she worked too hard to prove her soul chops.

When Grossman learned definitively that Joplin was using heroin, he turned to an old ally to chaperone her through her only tour of Europe. "Bob Neuwirth was with us for part of it," says John Byrne Cooke. "I think Albert wanted to have another pair of eyes around. He thought Bobby – not having to do all the things *I* had to do as road manager – could hang out with Janis and get a better sense of where she was at." With Neuwirth on board, Joplin and her entourage – which now included actor Michael J. Pollard, fresh out of 1967's *Bonnie and Clyde* – replicated the scalding wit that Dylan and his cronies had patented a few years earlier. In London, where she played the Royal Albert Hall in front of a celebrity-studded crowd, Ian Kimmet was recruited as yet another "pair of eyes" to mind Joplin. When Richard DiLello of Apple Records showed up at her hotel, she was, says Kimmet, "hanging all over him and saying, 'Did ya bring me something, babe?'"

"Janis was certainly enabled, but back then we understood so little about alcohol and drug problems," says Cooke. "The whole business of codependency and enabling, none of that was in the language." As Myra Friedman wrote, "there was only the chasm of non-communication filled up by the argot of hipness". Some believed that, as with the Electric Flag, Grossman failed to confront Joplin as he should have done, even if ultimately he cared more about her than he'd ever cared about Mike Bloomfield – or even, perhaps, about Bob Dylan. When it later transpired that he had, in June 1969, taken out a life-insurance policy paying $200,000 in the event of her accidental death, it seemed to confirm the cold-blooded pragmatism of the man she trusted and loved.

"Janis was very insecure," says JoHanna Hall. "She would say to Albert, 'When no one wants me any more, will you give me a job in the office?'" If she couldn't reach Grossman in snow-bound Bearsville, she became as frantic as an abandoned child, protesting that he would never treat The Band or Butterfield like that. "She was a troubled being," says Peter Coyote. "And part of what troubled her was the difference between the throwaway Port Arthur pimpled girl and the image she had created." Joplin's relentless sexual liaisons were attempts to convince herself she was prettier than she believed herself to be. Being strongly attracted to men who quickly dumped her seemed to trap her in a cycle as addictive as her abuse of booze and drugs. As she only half jokily told Dick Cavett in a TV interview, "[men] just always hold up something more than they're prepared to give . . ." There was a painful paradox in Joplin's uninhibitedness: as Ellen Willis noted, "women endowed the idea of sexual liberation with immense symbolic importance [. . .] yet to express one's rebellion in that limited way was a painfully literal form of submission".

Joplin was becoming almost as insecure about her music as she was about her looks. Although she now at least had a band capable of performing the soul material she loved, she was terrified that African Americans would dismiss her as phoney. A poorly received performance at Memphis's second Stax–Volt Yuletide Thing in December 1968 – with Mike Bloomfield sitting in – confirmed her worst fears: the new stars of southern soul at best tolerated her, at worst resented her infiltration of their musical patch, their hostility to honkies stoked by the assassination in April of Martin Luther King in the very motel where Joplin was staying.

With the LA sessions for *I Got Dem Ol' Kozmic Blues Again, Mama!* (1969), Joplin came closer to realising her goals on versions of Jerry Ragovoy and Chip Taylor's "Try (Just a Little Bit Harder)" and the Bee Gees' "To Love Somebody". An aching interpretation of the Rodgers and Hart masterpiece "Little Girl Blue" seemed to pour from the pain inside her, a cry from the heart to anyone who was listening.*

At the Woodstock Festival, Yasgur's massed hippies weren't as gaga for Joplin's ersatz soul review as she had hoped. When Snooky Flowers took over the vocals for a Stax-by-numbers version of Otis Redding's "I Can't Turn You Loose", many of them wanted their old Haight sister back. It didn't help, either, that Sly and the Family

---

* Among the out-takes from the *Kozmic Blues* sessions was a curiously uptempo rendition of Dylan's "Dear Landlord". Can Joplin have been unaware that the song was rumoured to be about Grossman? At the very end of 1969 she met and chatted with Dylan after a Kozmic Blues Band show at Madison Square Garden.

Stone came on directly after her at 3.30 a.m. and all but obliterated any impression she had made. At the end of the year she disbanded the Kozmic Blues, retaining bassist Brad Campbell and new guitarist John Till but dispensing altogether with the horn section. What she (and Grossman) wanted more than anything was a crack unit of studio-quality players who could help her make a great album. In came Ken Pearson (organ) and Clark Pierson (drums), who'd played with Till in his own Full Tillt [sic] Boogie Band, and Richard Bell, an exceptional piano player who'd worked with Till in Ronnie Hawkins's Hawks. Almost all of them were based in Woodstock, where Joplin often rehearsed with them.

"I stole Richard from Ronnie," admits Michael Friedman, whom Grossman had asked to scout for new musicians. "He was just off-the-hook great, a killer piano player, so after a show I asked if he wanted to join Joplin's band. Ronnie comes over to me, pushes me against a wall and says, 'You tell Albert I'm sick and tired of being his fuckin' farm team!'" Worse for the Hawk's subsequent career was his confrontation with Grossman himself. "I'll whip enough piss out of you to scald a hog," he yelled while pulling on Albert's pigtail. It was probably no coincidence that, in his own words, Hawkins's "concert dates dried up" after that.

Joplin lopped the second "L" off Tillt, and the group became Full Tilt Boogie. She was finally satisfied with her backing band – happy enough, indeed, to try to get her life in some kind of order. "She bought a house in Larkspur and she was pulling it all together," says Maria Muldaur. She was also closer than ever to her manager. Even Sam Andrew, who'd been given the heave-ho, acknowledged Grossman's nurturing side. "I knew that he really liked Janis," he said in 1998. "He really understood her." Ian Kimmet says that years later, when critics compared singers like Pat Benatar to Joplin, Grossman would explode: "He'd say, 'What the fuck are they *talking* about?!'"

John Byrne Cooke watched the deepening relationship between Joplin and Grossman as Full Tilt came together in the spring of 1970.

"She never felt she didn't have his ear," he says. "They were like hangout buddies." Joplin's trust in Grossman was so implicit that for about five months she was even able to give up heroin. "She not only felt that her business was being handled properly", Cooke says, "but she knew more about it because she *talked* about it with Albert." Grossman was intent not only on helping Joplin but on improving her image. A *Rolling Stone* profile had compared her to the tragic Judy Garland; Grossman wanted people to know what a life force she was. "She was a reader, she was intellectual, she was funny," says writer David Dalton, whom Myra Friedman invited to meet her. As he walked into the East 55th Street office, Joplin was perched on the edge of a desk strumming an acoustic guitar and singing a wistful country song of love and wanderlust co-written by Kris Kristofferson. "Of course I know now that 'Me and Bobby McGee' wasn't her song," Dalton says, "but to hear her sing it then was an astounding thing."

The British-born Dalton hit it off with Joplin and was invited to join her as one of two *Rolling Stone* reporters on the "Festival Express", a train ride across Canada boasting an all-star mix of Americans and Canadians (and thereby making one of Bob Dylan's pipe dreams come true). "I was a card-carrying hippie in the sense that I didn't drink," he says. "But Janis insisted on it: two double Jack

Daniels at eight in the morning." Other entertainers on the train – The Band, the Grateful Dead, Delaney & Bonnie and Friends, and Ian and Sylvia's Great Speckled Bird – followed suit: the train was a virtual incubator of alcoholism. But it was also a magical last gasp of the communal-musical Woodstock spirit. "We left our egos at the train station," reminisced the lissome and quavery-voiced Sylvia Tyson, whose husband introduced Great Speckled Bird's cover of "Tears of Rage" as "a song Bob Dylan wrote about his kids".

Contagious jam sessions took place at all hours of the day and night. "One of the cars became very quickly devoted to electric music, whereas the other one was the acoustic car," says John Byrne Cooke, who doubled as participant and tour manager. "Rick Danko and I would trade Hank Williams songs. Richard Manuel said to me, 'You can't sing like that, you're a road manager!'" Joplin may never have been happier than she was during renditions of old bluegrass and mountain gospel songs led by the pickled Danko and accompanied by the Cheshire-cat-grinning Jerry Garcia. If she looked and sounded ragged at the riot-disrupted opening show in Toronto, by Winnipeg and Calgary she and Full Tilt had truly hit their groove.

Back in California, work commenced on a new Columbia album whose motif was an alter ego that Joplin had established for herself: "Pearl", a good-time gal and voracious man-eater, the extroverted public face of the lovelorn self-doubter from Port Arthur. With Paul Rothchild, who'd produced not only the Butterfield band but the Doors, she set to work on a batch of strong songs that included "Cry Baby" and "Me and Bobby McGee". The arrangements were slick, the playing of her Canadian henchmen tight and muscular.

Nowhere did that playing sound more fluent or funky than on "Half Moon", a song co-authored by Joplin's friends John and JoHanna Hall. "She was always looking for new material," says JoHanna, who had reviewed the *Kozmic Blues* album in the *Village Voice*. "As she was leaving one night, she stood in the doorway and said, 'Why don't you two write me a song?' I said, '*Me?*' She said to me, 'You're a woman, you're a writer. Write me a song!'" Along with two soaring Jerry Ragovoy classics – "My Baby" and the prophetic "Get It While You Can" – maverick soul man Bobby Womack stopped by the *Pearl* sessions with his song "Trust Me", later claiming it was a ride in his car that inspired an off-the-cuff novelty Joplin wrote with Bobby Neuwirth and poet Michael McClure. As flippant as it was, the a cappella "Mercedes Benz" perfectly articulated the escalating expectations of rock's new elite.

As the sessions began, Joplin was in a positive frame of mind. She'd even fallen in love with Berkeley student Seth Morgan. "She was talking about getting married," says Michael Friedman. Halfway through the sessions, however, Joplin reacquainted herself with heroin. "She was all excited about her wealth and said she might buy her own town in Texas," says Ed Sanders. "But I could see fifty or sixty gold bracelets around her wrists and forearms that were hiding her tracks." "Mercedes Benz" was the last song Joplin recorded before she overdosed and died at Hollywood's Landmark Hotel on 4 October, two weeks after the death of Jimi Hendrix. She had been due to record her vocal for Nick Gravenites's "Buried Alive in the Blues" the next day.

Grossman, who later claimed he had no idea she was back on smack, was at home in Bearsville when he got the call. "I can hear his voice as I'm talking now," says Michael Friedman. "He just said, 'Michael, Janis is dead.' I was breathless. I jumped in my car and went over to his house. There was nobody else there. And I saw a side of Albert I had never seen before. He was so deeply wounded. He was genuinely in touch with all of his feelings. It was a very moving moment for me."* Grossman immediately flew out to LA,

---

* None of which stopped Grossman claiming his $200,000 "accidental death" payout, though the San Francisco Associated Indemnity Corporation argued that Joplin's death was a suicide and he had to settle in the end for $112,000. In the civil trial he claimed, very disingenuously, that he had been unaware of the extent of her drug problems.

where a series of wakes was held at the Landmark. Neuwirth and Grossman's right-hand man Bennett Glotzer were in attendance, as was Kris Kristofferson, whose "Bobby McGee" would top the *Billboard* singles chart in the New Year. *Pearl* itself would reach No. 1 and remain there for nine weeks.

In a will signed on 1 October, Joplin had left money for two parties to be held in the event of her death. One was in San Anselmo in California, the other in a Bearsville restaurant that Grossman had recently opened near his home. "Bob Neuwirth and Rick Danko were walking around like hosts," says JoHanna Hall. "They were asking people, 'Is everything all right at this table?'" Also present was David Dalton, whom Myra Friedman had invited to the party. Grossman demanded to know who he was. "I said, 'Albert, I wrote the article about Janis in *Rolling Stone*,'" he recalls. "He said, 'How do I know that?' I said, 'Albert, why would I pretend to be him?'"

The belligerence was a displacement of Grossman's grief. Following the ugly rupture with Bob Dylan, Joplin's death made him wonder if it was time to get out of management altogether. "He was devastated," says Ronnie Lyons. "He kept saying, 'I'm outta the business.'"

Japanese magazine feature on Bearsville:
(clockwise from top left) Richard Manuel and
girlfriend Arlie Litvak; Elizabeth Barraclough
and Paul Butterfield; Randy Vanwarmer and Ian
Kimmet; bass maestro Tony Levin; and Vinnie
Fusco and Willie Mitchell

PART THREE

DANGEROUS FUN

It always looked real peaceful as you drove
through the mountains along those dusty
gravel roads that cut through all the greenery
but, man, was there some crazy shit going on
in those big houses back in the woods.

JOHN NIVEN, *Music from Big Pink:*
A Novella (2005)

1

IF YOU BUILD IT

On a starry summer night in early June of 1996 I am eating with the Vermont jam band Phish and their very British producer Steve Lillywhite. The group are recording their seventh album in the nearby Turtle Creek Barn, converted into a second studio in the seventies by Albert Grossman, but they're breaking for dinner in a pretty stone cottage built in 1917 for painter Caroline Speare Rohland. For many years the house was known as Goodbrooks, but these days it's more commonly referred to as "the Robertson house". For this is where Grossman installed Robbie Robertson after The Band's second album cemented their status as one of rock's most revered acts.

A year later I'm at Turtle Creek itself, watching Australian singer-songwriter Richard Davies at work on his album *Telegraph*. Among its fine songs is "Crystal Clear", written as the forests spectacularly changed colour during his first autumn in the Catskills. A photograph of Muddy Waters with Robertson's former bandmate Levon Helm hangs on one of the studio's walls, snapped on an icy day in February 1975 when the two men were recording here.

These convivial memories trump my recall of the main Bearsville studio just up the road. The first time I found my way there in 1991 I was asked to leave in no uncertain terms by a surly employee. The last time was twenty-two years later, after the shabby wooden structure had been bought by an eccentric hoarder from New York. In the company of John Simon, I drove up to see what was left of the place after Sally Grossman sold it in 2004. To our mutual horror we discovered that it had become a kind of trailer-trash dump.

Grossman had first thought about a studio when Dylan and the Hawks were using a portable reel-to-reel recorder in the basement of Big Pink in 1967. In a long interview two years later, Dylan himself told *Rolling Stone*'s Jann Wenner that "everyone's talking about that now", though he added that "some place like up in the country there, in the mountains, you could get a studio in, but that doesn't guarantee you anything else but the studio".

Indeed, Grossman was nearly pipped to the post by Michael Lang. "A couple of years before Bearsville was built, I had come up with this idea of building a studio," Lang says. "I don't think Albert and I interacted over that, but I'm sure it gave him the idea." Scouting around the town, Lang found an old Victorian house with outbuildings up on Yerry Hill Road. Until recently it had been a small hotel run by an Armenian family. "There was a big barn, a big studio building, as well as the main house where Alexander Tapooz lived," Lang says. "It was on thirty acres, and it was just an ideal defunct run-down property. So we made a deal to take an option on it." Pitching the concept to his Woodstock Ventures partners John Roberts and Joel Rosenman, he met with scepticism: they didn't believe there were enough rock stars in the town to justify the investment. By the time Lang's and Artie Kornfeld's "Aquarian Exposition" had got the attention of Roberts and Rosenman, the Tapooz studio was on the back burner.

As the Woodstock Festival plans got under way, Grossman seized his moment. Spending more and more time upstate, he sounded out his most trusted confidants on the subject of a studio. "Since John Court had gone, I was Albert's sort of A&R person who knew something about that side of the world," says John Simon. "He asked me what kind of studio he should build, and I told him my favourite one was the studio I broke in on, which was A&R's Studio A on Seventh Avenue." Simon obtained the dimensions and Grossman "went and tripled them". It was, Simon says, "typical Albert: 'I'll make one that's three times as big' . . . as a result it never got used for years".

Perhaps because he hadn't been to one, Grossman liked to surround himself with bright young graduates of Ivy League universities. Simon had been to Princeton, as had Jonathan Taplin. "Albert loved these button-down guys as much as he loved hippie kids like me," says Paul Fishkin. "If you had a suit and tie like Taplin, he was a real sucker for that. He was always calling and saying, 'Hey, I've got this guy I just met that you might like. He came from Princeton, he has an MBA.'" It was through Taplin that yet another Princeton graduate was approached to design the Bearsville studio. John Storyk was an architect who'd been in the right place at the right time when, in April 1969, Jimi Hendrix and Mike Jeffery – along with recording engineers Jim Marron and Eddie Kramer – commissioned him to design the new Electric Lady studio in Greenwich Village. Taplin got wind of the Hendrix project and invited Storyk up to Bearsville to meet his boss. "Albert hired me on a napkin," Storyk tells me in his office in Highland, an hour south of Woodstock. "He doodled out the site at the top of Speare Road."

Storyk swiftly became one of Grossman's indispensables: before long he had moved to Woodstock and would spend much of the next

decade working for him. He was another of the rustic potentate's
surrogate sons, coming to love him as a paternal mentor. "Albert saw
life through an extraordinary lens," he says. "He was not particularly
well versed school-wise, but he had tremendous street smarts and
was a pretty good judge of character – scrupulously honest, relent-
lessly tough in business." Storyk says he "learned a lot about patronage" from Grossman: "You need a crazy person with an extra dollar
or two. And when I had one or two down moments he was always
there with some nice advice."

Storyk doesn't think Grossman saw the Bearsville studio as a
money-making enterprise. "The original intent was just to be an
in-house recording studio," he has said – meaning a facility for
Grossman's own artists. Levon Helm certainly seemed to believe
the studio would function as a kind of clubhouse for The Band when
they first started using it. "They kind of parked themselves there for
a while," Storyk says. "It was definitely conceived as a place where
a group could park and make it feel like a rehearsal studio. It wasn't
funky, but it was rustic."

"When Albert really started to live up here in Bearsville more, his
focus became more into developing a recording situation," Bearsville
staffer Vinnie Fusco told *Billboard* in 1980. "After The Band did
Big Pink, the feasibility of recording in the country became more
realistic." Though Grossman was secretly more interested in his
tomato patches, he couldn't just walk away from the music industry.
This was the start of rock's boom years; there was serious money to
be made. Observing the tipping point was Paula Batson, who moved
up to Woodstock in 1971 after working in New York for Johanan
Vigoda. "The advances got crazy," she says. "I remember Johanan
doing international deals for Richie Havens that would have been
impossible earlier. And that had an effect on Woodstock because
people were now looking to cash in."

Along with the studio itself came an offer from recording-
equipment manufacturers Ampex for Grossman to start his own

label. "The accountants moved up," said Vinnie Fusco, "and the focus of the company began to move toward the record business." With its cartoon logo of a bear's head designed by Milton Glaser, the Bearsville label was one of a number of production deals that Ampex president Larry Harris struck in 1969. "They made two or three of them," says Paul Fishkin. "They did one with Gabriel Mekler's Lizard label and another with Phil Walden's Capricorn. They were all busy ripping off Ampex!"

"Bearsville was really Albert's grand vision of what was going to be the second half of his career," says Michael Friedman. "He wanted to create this whole community up there and he had the money to do it." It was, adds Fishkin, "Albert's baby and Albert's creation . . . he wanted to bring it all to Woodstock and create that whole musical community that he was the god of. He wanted his management success to translate into record success, and he wanted it to be an extension of the world he was in of Dylan and Butterfield – that amalgam of blues and folk, a hip, rural, anti-pop-star thing that would succeed on its own terms."

John Holbrook, a Brit who joined the Bearsville staff as one of its chief engineers, believes Grossman "put the whole studio together with his Ampex deal", adding that "Other People's Money" was one of his employer's mantras. Yet the studio was a long time in

the making. When Jim Rooney took up Grossman's offer of a job
as his studio manager, he arrived expecting to find, well, a studio.
"I'd come up to Woodstock two or three times that winter, but the
road to the studio was never ploughed so I never saw it," Rooney
says. "Robbie Robertson seemed to be involved in some way, but all
he would say about it was, 'Oh, it's gonna be great!' That was all I
knew, so I was really flying blind." When Rooney finally saw the site
in May 1970, it was nothing but a cinderblock shell; for the entire
summer, Bearsville Studios was a construction job. Even when it
semi-officially opened in September, the teething problems were
endless. "It had its unexpected challenges for Albert," says Michael
Friedman, who moved to Woodstock that same year. "To build a
studio is a specialty of its own, and there was a very steep learning
curve for that."

Jim Rooney claims the inaugural recording session at Bearsville
was John Hall's demo version of "Dancing in the Moonlight", pro-
duced by John Simon. "They needed to get the bugs out," says
JoHanna Hall. "So Albert said to Simon, 'You can have a month of
free studio time.'" The Halls stayed with the Simons before renting
their own cabin, and soon they too had fallen in love with Woodstock.
Another early session brought eclectic California bluesman Taj
Mahal to Bearsville with Columbia producer David Rubinson.
"Ours were, as I recall, the very first real recordings made [there],"
Rubinson wrote of the January 1971 sessions. "It was unbelieeeeev-
ably cold – mid-January upstate N.Y. – and it snowed about two feet
deep . . ."[*] When The Band finally got into Studio B to cut a version
of Marvin Gaye's "Baby, Don't You Do It" (aka "Don't Do It"), they
couldn't get the sound they wanted. "It was just horribly frustrating
for a long, long time," admits Michael Friedman. "Albert spent a
fortune on that building and it took a couple of years before it really

---

[*] Though the album was never released, three tracks from the sessions – songs
recorded more successfully on the 1971 live album *The Real Thing* – emerged
forty years later on *The Hidden Treasures of Taj Mahal, 1969–1973*.

Bearsville studios, summer 1991 (Art Sperl)

started working." Drummer Christopher Parker says the studio was "still very much under construction" when he first went there, adding that "everybody's complaint was that the two I-beams connected the two studios, so you couldn't use both at the same time". For years the far bigger Studio A served simply as one of Grossman's many storage spaces.

As it turned out, the studio was only a part of Grossman's grand scheme for establishing Bearsville/Woodstock as a music mecca. "The studio was just a business move," says Jonathan Taplin. "The second phase, with the restaurant and then the theatre, I trace to having what I would call heartbreak. It was like, 'Screw the business,' and that's when he began thinking about food and gardens and architecture."

The heartbreak Taplin discerned stemmed from several traumatic events. Bruisingly, Bob Dylan had declared war on Grossman, a legal conflict that culminated in an agreement signed on 17 July 1970. "Albert told me he offered to flip Bob for a quarter of a million dollars," says John Storyk. "I said, 'Did he go for it?' He said, 'Nope.' I said, 'Would you really have done that?' He said, 'Absolutely.'"

In the 1969 interview with *Rolling Stone*, Dylan had been circum-
spect about Grossman, telling Jann Wenner – on the subject of the
aborted ABC-TV special – that "I think my manager could answer
that a lot better" and even claiming Grossman was "a nice guy".
When Wenner pressed him later on whether he would continue to
be managed by him, Dylan replied that if Grossman "doesn't have
a hand in producing my next concerts or have a hand in any of my
next work, it's only because he's too busy". By 1970, however, he
hated his ex-manager so vehemently that he could no longer bring
himself even to speak to him. When Grossman requested the return
of the *shtender* on which Dylan had mounted his Bible at Hi Lo Ha,
Dylan asked Bernard Paturel – who'd been hired to run Grossman's
new restaurant – to deliver it to him.

The next blow for Grossman was the arrest of Peter Yarrow in
late August 1969 for "taking immoral and improper liberties" with
a fourteen-year-old girl in a Manhattan hotel. Though Yarrow was
later pardoned by Jimmy Carter, the damage to a man who'd been
a moral conscience of the folk movement was huge. Grossman
remained loyal to one of his first stars, who recorded tracks for his
first solo album at Bearsville, but it was another watershed moment
that left him questioning whether his heart was still in management.
And when Joplin died six months after Yarrow pleaded guilty, the
spirit seemed to go out of him. "He spent more and more time in
Woodstock, less and less time in New York," says Jonathan Taplin.
"He stopped being aggressive. It was more just like, 'We'll get it
done.' It was not as imaginative. He'd gotten hurt, that was clear."

On top of these stresses, Grossman's open marriage may have
taken more of a toll on him than he ever admitted. "When I first
went to work for Albert, he and Sally were living in the apartment
on Gramercy Park," says Michael Friedman. "She was around and I
found her to be really lovely. Then at some point she was just gone.
Albert said she was living in Oaxaca in Mexico. I said, 'Oh, are you
breaking up?' He said, 'No.' It was very matter-of-fact. He lived

his life and she lived her life." John Storyk told Paul Smart that Grossman "had rough edges but was also a soft, pretty lonely guy in many ways", while Odetta thought he was "a very private, very lonely and very alone person".

Grossman channelled his passion into a vision of Bearsville as a kind of personal fiefdom. "He had the idea of providing a healthy environment for the artists to live in, with good healthy food," says Peter Walker, another late-sixties import from Cambridge. "You take them out of the city, where they're eating ratburgers, and you bring them up here, where there's lots of fresh air. You feed them well in your restaurant, then you record them in your studio and have them showcase in your theatre, with the record-company executives flying in and staying in your cabins. That was the vision." To Jon Gershen, Grossman's plan was "to create something like a mini-Memphis or a Nashville, so that it became a centre . . . and then you'd have this sort of brand".

Among the musicians Grossman housed were the grieving members of the Full Tilt Boogie Band. "They were in a state of shock, they were paralysed," says Maria Muldaur. "They all knew *Pearl* was really good. And then it was like the world stopped. So Albert said, 'Well, pack up your stuff and come to Woodstock.' He was buying up all the land around Rick's Road, which included several farmhouses. And he put the band up there." Paul Fishkin claims Grossman "spent a fortune on Full Tilt . . . he just let them rack up ridiculous amounts of studio time". Yet little happened for the group in Bearsville. "We would have rehearsals trying to get songs together," says Graham Blackburn, a temporary member, "but they would invariably devolve into much more intellectual jazz jam sessions than the rock 'n' roll we should have been playing." When the band finally collapsed, Blackburn says, "everybody split up in disgust".

Grossman was more preoccupied by a fourteen-acre streamside farm at the bottom of Striebel Road that had recently come on the market. It included several barns and other outbuildings, as well as the nineteenth-century farmhouse itself. By December 1971, he had transformed two of the buildings into an upscale French restaurant. "These days a manager opening a restaurant is a normal thing, but at that time it seemed like a crazy and grandiose idea," says Paula Batson, who worked there. "And to do it in Woodstock and make it fine cuisine? I mean, this was the pre-foodie era." In Woodstock proper, the community looked on with mild amazement. "I thought, 'Wow, Albert's buying up the town,'" says Daoud Shaw. "For him it was like, 'Why go to Deanie's when I can have my own restaurant? I'm not that crazy about prime rib anyway.'"

Grossman took great pleasure in planning the Bearsville complex, recruiting the best local craftsmen to bring his dreams to fruition. He bought his lumber from Nelson Shultis's sawmill and hired copper-roofing master Otto Shue. "He started searching around for things to buy," says Dean Schambach. "We pulled those sheds together to form the Bear Café. Albert changed the town by building the Bear. The room with the fireplace had been a goat barn." Along with Schambach and David Boyle, Grossman hired Paul Cypert, a local giant who quickly became his right-hand man. "Paul and I hit it off right away," wrote Jim Rooney, who took over the books and payroll. "He was a master carpenter. He'd come to Albert's attention while building a spiral staircase for John Simon."

Rooney himself was soon co-opted into running errands for Grossman, driving down to the port of Hoboken to collect imported chairs or picking up stoves and coolers from bankruptcy sales on the Bowery. "Albert was nuts to work for, because he was so obsessed with quality at a good price," Rooney remembers. "He'd always say, 'The other side of a bankruptcy is a bargain.'" Assisting him on some of the runs was Jon Gershen, who watched as Grossman drove Rooney crazy with his demands: "He had a way of interacting that he'd perfected and that worked to his advantage. The most memorable thing was the silence: Jim asking a question and getting nothing back. It was like seeing a psychoanalyst." For Lucinda Hoyt, who worked for him as what she describes as his "good fairy" in the Striebel house between 1971 and 1975, Grossman had a "whammy" you could feel across a room. "It was like a hex, a mental projection that he emanated," she says. "It put people off, it undid them."

Paul Cypert, says Gershen, was "a prince of a guy married up to this hippie baron of Woodstock". He would often vent his exasperation to Gershen and Rooney. "He'd say, 'How am I supposed to do *that*?'" says Gershen. "He was frustrated by all the juggling." John Storyk was another who struggled with Grossman's reluctance to see things through to completion. "One day I said, 'Albert, why are we starting another project? Why don't we just finish the theatre and then we can start the next project after that?'" Storyk recalls. "And he turned to me and just said, '*Why?*' Which was quintessential Albert. And at that point I got it. It wasn't about finishing for him, it was about the journey."

By the mid-seventies, Grossman had a ten-man construction crew working exclusively on his projects. Nor did he limit himself to Woodstock and Bearsville. "Just when you thought the last project was done, he'd say, 'Hey, I got a house in Santa Fe,'" John Storyk says. "Or, 'I have two acres in Puerto Escondido . . . I wonder if you could take a look at it?' It was always, 'What does Albert have *this* week?'"

To Jonathan Taplin, Grossman was "really pulling back" from the music business at this point. "Bennett Glotzer did most of the booking and all the management stuff," Taplin says. "I don't think Albert was paying that much attention." Besides, carpenters and chefs were easier to manage than musicians. To John Holbrook, Grossman "maintained an interest" in the studio but little more: "He liked to drop in and say, 'Everything okay?' But there was more concern about decoration for the restaurants. Like, 'Do we have the right lights?'"

As "Albertsville" slowly took shape, even the doubters applauded the scale of Grossman's ambition. "It was a brilliant idea to come to a place close to New York where he could do what he wanted to

do," says Robbie Dupree. "That's why we called him the Baron. I
don't know how many houses he had, but I'm going to ballpark it as
fifteen, sixteen properties in Bearsville. What he did was import the
kind of people he needed, because they weren't here. He understood that 'If you build it, they will come.'" Grossman was no Midas,
however. Not only was the studio having problems, the Bear wasn't
quite working either. "Albert brought this guy over from France,
and he was not a great chef," says Michael Friedman, now a restau-
rateur himself. "We used to have dinner there three or four nights
a week for a long time – me and Taplin and the guys in The Band
– and the guy never got it right. But the demographics couldn't support that kind of place to begin with." As Robbie Dupree points out,
"the cops and the volunteer firemen who ate at Deanie's weren't
eating $29 entrées at the Bear".

"The World's Foremost Rock Music Tsar", Peter Moscoso-Gongora
wrote in a scathing *Harper's* magazine report on Woodstock, "has
dinner a quarter of a mile from *his* studio, at *his* kitsch, brocaded
'French' restaurant called the Bear, with its atrocious food, its cupolas,
its piped Bach chorales and its New York City prices [. . .] Parvenu,
like himself, it has been compared to a Bronx funeral parlor." The
plug was finally pulled on the Bear in 1972, when Grossman dreamt
up the idea of the less recherché Bear Café.

To Paula Batson, the Woodstock scene was slowly being overshadowed by Grossman's circle in Bearsville. "There were local
bands, and my husband's band Holy Moses was one that got a deal,"
she says. "But by this time The Band and Albert and the other successful people were kind of sequestered off in their own group.
Musically there was a kind of aristocracy." A schism of sorts opened
up between those in Grossman's world – one Fred Goodman
described in his seminal book *The Mansion on the Hill* as "a small,
terminally hip and incestuous universe, with Albert as the sun" –
and those outside it. "No one wants to admit it, but there was a
hierarchy in Albert's mind," Mercury Rev's Jonathan Donahue says.

"It was almost like an Indian caste system. I mean, how would *you* feel if you were a local and all of a sudden Albert announces that he's the new *rex* in town, and here's where the theatre's going to be and here's where the restaurants are going to be. Oh, and the laws are going to change a little bit too."

"Albert was the lord of the manor," says Maria Muldaur, who moved to Woodstock in the autumn of 1970. "He could afford to have the best of everything, including a restaurant that was practically at the end of his driveway. And some of the wives of the guys in The Band and various other people aspired to his lifestyle. Robbie and Dominique were in that crowd. The girls wore long flowing dresses and there was a certain amount of putting on airs. If Albert had a certain kind of furniture, they wanted that furniture. If Albert proclaimed that a certain imported cheese was the absolute best you could get, they wanted that too."

If many of Woodstock's working musicians resented him, Grossman's peers took a different line. "He gave Woodstock a new persona," Michael Lang has said. "He took us out of our quaintness and really brought us national attention." Happy Traum argues that "the whole Bearsville studio thing created a major vortex of high-end artists coming into town". And for Milton Glaser, who'd brought him to Woodstock in the first place, Grossman "made [it] attractive for musicians . . . [he] amplified a lot of what was already implicit in the town".

In the end, not even Bob Dylan was immune to his ex-manager's transformation of Bearsville. In the summer of 1971 he brought George Harrison in to see the studio Grossman had built. "I thought, 'That's interesting, what's *this* about?'" says Jon Gershen, who witnessed the visit. "Bob appeared to be showing George around the studio. It was like he was saying, 'Look what we have here in this town now.'"

It was certainly a very different place from the Woodstock that Harrison had visited three years before.

2

THE SHAPE THEY'RE IN

The Band had good reason to call their third album *Stage Fright*. On the eve of their live debut in San Francisco, on 17 April 1969, Robbie Robertson came down with a mysterious illness that almost scuppered the show, and even he wondered if fear wasn't a contributing factor. Here the group was, having played no more than thirteen minutes onstage in four years, headlining for the first time with their own material – and with no Ronnie Hawkins or Bob Dylan to hide behind. Headlining, moreover, in front of a crowd of hippies in the capital of acid rock.

Many people, when they heard *Stage Fright*'s title song, assumed Robertson was writing about Bob Dylan. But "Stage Fright" spoke as much for the five men who'd shied away from the limelight in the Catskills as it did for the man who'd mellowed into the reclusive bard of *Nashville Skyline*. The scale of the Woodstock and Isle of Wight festivals unnerved them, while the success of *The Band* had caught them by surprise, making them stars in their own right. On 12 January 1970 they were on the cover of *Time* magazine, with the misleading headline "The New Sound of Country Rock". "The Band appeals to an intelligent segment of this generation," William Bender said in the opening "Letter from the Publisher". "Many have tried the freaked-out life, found it wanting, and are now looking for something gentler and more profound."

Little did Bender know what was really going on behind the scenes. After touring for the first three months of that year, The Band returned to Woodstock to prepare for their third album. This time the fraternal spirit was tougher to summon: though they were

starting families, fame and money had disrupted the group's tenu-
ous chemistry, while drugs and alcohol were beginning to mess with
the health of at least three of them. Libby Titus would later describe
Richard Manuel as "the worst alcoholic I've ever met in my life",
claiming he drank "quarts of Grand-Marnier" every day. "Richard
was drinking too much from the very beginning, and his liver was
now pushing up into his stomach," says Jonathan Taplin. "Levon had
some serious problems with downers. Rick was like a hoover, he'd
take whatever was around. Garth would have a little toke once in a
while, but he was very moderate. At that point Robbie was Mister
Responsible." Fans of The Band who idealised them as peaceful
farm boys would have been shocked to learn that even opiates were
not off-limits to them. "I hope we didn't," says Peter Coyote, "but
I'm afraid Emmett Grogan and I might have been the people that
introduced Levon to heroin." Pictures that Elliott Landy took of The
Band outside Manuel and Hudson's Spencer Road house appear to
show Helm in an opiated state. "Heroin was a problem," Robertson
admitted. "I never liked it, never understood it, and I was scared
to death of it. But it came through, you know, like everything else
came through."

"After the *Time* cover, things got a little crazy," admitted Danko.
"Luckily, the people in Woodstock looked after us. The local judges
and the police called us 'The Boys'. And we felt that protection." If
police chief Bill Waterous referred to Woodstock's hippies as "bums
and freeloaders", he let The Band get away with everything but
murder. "Billy loved them," says Richard Heppner. "And he loved
them because they could cross over that redneck line very easily."
Today we'd say that Waterous was enabling The Band, as many other
Woodstockers did. "They were out of control and utterly indulged,"
admits Paul Fishkin. "It was all wrong and it was responsible for so
much of the destruction of lives and business entities."

When Danko and Manuel showed up at the Concert for Bangladesh in New York, Bob Dylan gave instructions not to admit them

backstage. "I was told, 'Bob doesn't want them here,'" says road manager Paul Mozian. "He didn't want serious carousers affecting George and Ringo."

It wasn't just The Band hell-raising around town. Joining them in their escapades was the hard-drinking Paul Butterfield. Another boozing buddy was Mason Hoffenberg, then on the methadone programme in Kingston. Woodstock was in any case filling up with assorted leeches and drug dealers. "There started to be a lot more insidious drugs than pot going on," says Maria Muldaur. "People were starting to snort coke, and a *lot* of alcohol was being consumed by virtually everyone: our band, Paul's band, everybody."

"This wonderful, nymphomaniac group of young rock stars became surrounded by these extremely charming and attractive vultures," Libby Titus recalled. "John Brent, Howard Alk, John Court, Larry Hankin. Some of them were brilliant, charismatic junkies, like John Brent, who was so magnetic you wanted to be a junkie ten minutes after you met him and heard his stories of beautiful girls in the Village and shooting up with William Burroughs. And that's what happened." Titus herself would struggle with addiction for years, while Alk would die in 1982 of an overdose – a suicidal one, according to his wife Jones – in Bob Dylan's Santa Monica rehearsal studio.

For the abstemious Robertson, the antics of his *compadres* were disappointing and frustrating. "Robbie always had the highest goal in mind, whereas the others were happy just to be playing music," says John Simon. "Robbie said, 'When I get out to Hollywood, I'm gonna get involved with films. I'm gonna work with Ingmar Bergman.' That's the kind of guy he was." Others thought the guitarist pompous and stand-offish. "He was the quintessence of super-cool and super-hip," says Paul Fishkin. "I hated the pretension of all that shit. There was this whole atmosphere of hipper-than-thou that pervaded Albert's and Robbie's world." Like Fishkin, Michael

Friedman was unimpressed by the airs that Robertson and others put on. "Everybody kind of sounded a bit the same, except for Levon, Rick and Richard," he says. "There was this kind of *whispering wisdom*, the way Robbie spoke and the way Jonathan Taplin spoke. They all got into this kind of Band-speak, and at a certain point it was like, 'Come *on*, guys!'"

The eccentric Hudson, meanwhile, kept to himself, moving into a house in the tiny hamlet of Glenford. "Just having a guy who could walk down the hill and sit at your piano and play Bix Beiderbecke's 'In a Mist', that didn't hurt," says Geoff Muldaur. "Of course he's a strange cat, but he couldn't be any sweeter." Musical genius that he was, Hudson was also something of a mountain man. One night after Helm hit a deer, Garth skinned the dead animal with a penknife in the car's headlights.

Once The Band accepted that their manager's studio wasn't going to be ready to use, the concept for *Stage Fright* became a live album to be recorded before an invited audience at the Woodstock Playhouse. "I thought, 'Let's have a little bit of a goof here,'" Robertson remembered. "It was, 'Let's do some touching things, some funny things. Let's do more of just a good-time kind of record.'"

It didn't take long for town officials to veto the idea of a live album. And by the time The Band had resigned themselves to using the theatre as another ad hoc recording studio, the music taking shape was anything but good-time. "I found myself writing songs I couldn't help *but* write," said Robertson, who up to this point had eschewed confessional writing. Along with the title track, songs like "The Shape I'm In", "The Rumor" and "Just Another Whistle Stop" did more than hint at the unrest behind the scenes. Even "Sleeping" – as wistfully lovely as it was – came a little too close to the truth about its co-writer Richard Manuel.

True, the set-up at the Playhouse was congenial enough when recording began in late May of 1970. Patti Smith, an all-but-unknown poet who came by in early June with her boyfriend Bobby Neuwirth, found the atmosphere friendly. In a Band profile written for *Circus*, she anticipated an album that was "pretty positive, looking at things with a friendly, ironic eye". She also bonded with Todd Rundgren, the hotshot young engineer on the session. One result of having him on board was that *Stage Fright* was more polished than its beloved predecessor. This time around, The Band sounded like an actual rock group, with each instrument clearly defined in the mix. Particularly prominent was Robertson's guitar, treated with effects and devices that pushed it into the foreground.* Also noticeable on *Stage Fright* was the relative lack of harmony singing. This time more of the songs were recorded with solo vocals, making the voices sound distant from each other. Only on "The Rumor", a troubling statement about a stiflingly incestuous community, did they really come together, weaving lines in the rough-hewn gospel style they'd mastered on their previous records. "That song was about Woodstock," John Simon says. "I had a line in one of my own songs that went, '*Rumours fly around this town / Like echoes around a canyon*'."

Not that there wasn't marvellous singing on the record: Helm sounded like a redneck Lee Dorsey on the boisterous "Strawberry Wine", and Manuel was at his most droopily soulful on "Sleeping". On "Stage Fright" Danko sounded genuinely spooked. Instrumentally, Garth Hudson was magnificent throughout: playfully fluttering on the accordion on "Strawberry Wine", dreamily evoking childhood on "All La Glory". Danko's fretless bass anchored the songs in a deep throb, Helm's drumming was organic and intuitive, and Robertson's needling Telecaster incisions on "Sleeping" and "The Rumor" were spine-tingling. But one could argue that the blithe

* The mix had its own curious history. Robertson wanted Rundgren to mix the album, but Helm argued for sending the tapes to British engineer and producer Glyn Johns. Rundgren flew to London with the tapes and started his own mix at Trident Studios, while Johns worked simultaneously at Olympic. "It turned into a game," Johns recalled. "It was like a competition, which I thought was howlfully amusing."

"Time to Kill" – "*We've got time to kill, Catskill, sweet by and by*" – masked a certain ennui. One question suggested itself: why was Manuel contributing less and less as each Band album rolled around? "I did everything to get him to write," Robertson claimed. "There's no answer. My theory is that some people have one song in them, some have five, some have a hundred." To John Simon, there was no question of Manuel being squeezed out: "Robbie certainly didn't consciously intimidate him, but then when you met Robbie he was so smooth and urbane and witty, whereas Richard was such a gee-golly-gosh kind of guy."

Received more coolly than *The Band*, *Stage Fright* still reached the Top 5 in the *Billboard* album chart after its release in September 1970 – the highest-charting album of their career. The group spent three months touring America, flying to north-eastern dates in a little turbo-prop airplane. "Some of the shows were real good," said Robertson. "Sometimes it got real accurate and sometimes we were just crazy rock and roll musicians. But when it was really good, when we all played well, it made us feel just tremendous." After wrapping the tour in Miami that December, the five men went into winter hibernation.

By the time they poked their noses out of the New Year snow, the Bearsville studio was ready for them to start work on their next album. "In my mind I had my own key to the studio and had drums set up everywhere that I never had to take down," Levon Helm later told me. "I had this wonderful world built up in my head where The Band would just be making music all the time, and it would just be hand over fist with money and albums, and who's got time to count it?"

What Helm hadn't reckoned on was Robertson hitting a nasty patch of writer's block and Richard Manuel drying up completely. "It was frustrating, a horrible feeling," Robertson remembered. "I just didn't have the spirit to write. A lot of the songs were half-finished ideas." More than ever, he was struggling to hold The Band together. "He became the leader because nobody else wanted to be," said Bill Graham. "Levon had been the leader, but he wasn't enough of a decision-maker."

Given all this, it's a wonder there was any decent music on their fourth album, *Cahoots*. "Life Is a Carnival" remains the funkiest track The Band ever recorded. Bob Dylan's "When I Paint My Masterpiece" was a droll fusion of *chanson* and Arkansas hoedown, and Helm's singing on "The River Hymn" – with Libby Titus harmonising behind him – was exquisite. Manuel's boozy sparring with Van Morrison on "4% Pantomime" was a soulful hoot. "Richard brought a real understanding of the Ray Charles thing to the whole thing," Artie Traum said. "I don't think he ever knew how good he was. He was very self-effacing and very modest."

Huge fans of New Orleans legend Allen Toussaint's R&B and soul productions, The Band couldn't believe their luck when he agreed to write the extraordinary antiphonal horn charts for "Life Is a Carnival", a song based on a sprung funk groove Helm and Danko had worked up at Bearsville. "When I heard that song . . . the intro was really strange," Toussaint said in 2011. "The way Levon plays is sort of upside down and sideways sometimes. When I first heard it, it was like turning on the radio in the middle of something and you don't know exactly where the 'one' is." For Toussaint, The Band's music was "another kind of genre that I couldn't put in a certain file cabinet". He was astonished by Garth Hudson, who would "tinker with things to get tiny different sounds and work ever so long to get a slightly different sound . . . you'd wonder was it worth it but when you heard the final things [you'd think], 'Oh yes, that's the difference in him and all the other players in the world.'"

For all the infectious propulsion of "Life Is a Carnival", *Cahoots* was an album of lamentation, mourning the passing of American traditions. Loss permeated "Last of the Blacksmiths" and "Where Do We Go from Here?" "The record poses the question, 'What are things coming to?'" said Robertson. "It dealt with the fact that things like carnivals and blacksmiths were vanishing from the American scene."* Jim Rooney, who witnessed the *Cahoots* sessions at Bearsville, felt that some of the group's creative energy was slipping away. "One day when I came in, Robbie was in the control room and Levon was out in the drum booth banging away," he wrote. "For what seemed like an eternity Robbie and [engineer] Mark Harman were labouring with the EQ knobs and various gadgets to get what they referred to as a 'drum sound'. It seemed simple enough to me. Put some mics on Levon's drum kit and let him play. As I watched them on that day and over the course of the next weeks, it became clear that the other band members were basically letting Robbie run the show."

Released to muted reviews in the autumn of 1971, *Cahoots* never made it higher than No. 21 and spent just five weeks in the Top 40. Some wondered if Robertson's elegies for the blacksmith and the eagle weren't sublimations of his feelings about The Band. "Everybody had been so easily satisfied before," he said in 1982, "and then it got harder to do what we did at ease. The inspirational factor had been dampened, tampered with, and the curiosity wasn't as strong." One of the dampening factors was the ill feeling between him and Helm, who had begun to realise that the guitarist was making significantly more money from the group's songs than he was. "Every band is a community effort," says Jim Rooney. "But then suddenly it isn't a community effort if you don't have a piece of paper to *say* it is. Levon found that out a little too late and was certainly very bitter about it."

"My opinion on this is very clear," Jonathan Taplin states. "Robbie wrote the songs. He got up every morning and worked on writing. I *saw* it. And it wasn't because he wanted to hog it, it was because nobody else was doing it. It's true that at that time nobody

---

* Woodstock's own last blacksmith was Henry Peper, born in 1859. His shop on Mill Hill Road became Peper's Garage.

understood how, years later, publishing income would be the *only* income you could really count on. But then the others were all around Dylan and they must have known how much money he was making from publishing. There was no need for this myth that they all got screwed by Robbie. It's the same as saying Bob got screwed by Albert." Sally Grossman would be the first to agree. "There's this alignment that goes on, that Albert and Robbie ripped Levon off," she said in 2014. "I don't know, maybe it could have been done better, however they had signed their deal. But I mean, there'd be these band meetings and the only one that would show up was Robbie. While Rick was going off the road and breaking his neck, Robbie was focused. Albert and Robbie set off to rip Levon off? Oh please."

Fortunately The Band overcame their inner tensions for long enough to record one of rock's finest live albums. "The only rock record I owned was *Rock of Ages*, and the reason I bought it was because I saw the horn players on it," says jazz trumpeter Steve Bernstein. "I think they're the greatest horn parts ever in rock 'n' roll." The double album, recorded at the very end of 1971 at New York's Academy of Music, was the culmination of the many great shows The Band had played that year – including two at the hallowed London venue where they'd been booed with Bob Dylan. "I remember they came out onstage at the Albert Hall and they were all wearing suits," says Keith Reid of the gig he saw. "And the way they had their set-up was so unusual, with the drums to the right and Garth in the middle. They'd play a couple of numbers and then all switch instruments. Levon got off the drums and picked up a mandolin, and Richard got on the drums. And it *still* sounded fantastic."

For the four Academy of Music shows, the group attempted something new and bold. After the syncopated thrill of the arrangements on "Life Is a Carnival", they invited Allen Toussaint up to a wintry Bearsville to write horn parts for a number of older songs.

"There were no houses around, just trees," he said in 2011. "It was so beautiful out there and I thought, 'It would sure be nice if it was snowing.' The next night it snowed and I put on a pair of pyjamas and kept going. It was one of the best times in my life." Toussaint's arrangements – played by a crack New York horn section – transformed songs such as "Rag Mama Rag", "Unfaithful Servant" and "The Night They Drove Old Dixie Down". "Don't Do It" was stupendously funky. "Across the Great Divide" and "The W. S. Walcott Medicine Show" swung like big-band jazz. On New Year's Eve, during the countdown to midnight, Garth Hudson turned the intro to "Chest Fever" into an extended keyboard fantasy that was equal parts Anglican hymn, Scottish reel, Charles Ives and Thelonious Monk. For the encore, the group was then joined by none other than Dylan, who launched into a rambunctious version of the basement song "Crash on the Levee (Down in the Flood)", followed by "When I Paint My Masterpiece", "Don't Ya Tell Henry" and "Like a Rolling Stone".

Exhilarating though the Academy shows were, the comedown felt grim. Where could they go from there?

3

MUSIC AMONG FRIENDS

In James Lasdun's story "Oh, Death", a white-collar professional moves into a house on a mountain road in upstate New York and commences a tentative friendship with neighbour Rick Peebles. Rick has lived in the next-door house since birth, and resents the second-home owners who've bought up parcels of land that used to be his boyhood "haunts". He is a kind of northern redneck: frustrated, Harley-riding, occasionally gun-toting. When he marries the unhappy Faye and takes in her two children, they celebrate their nuptials with a hog roast and music by a local bluegrass band: "Two fiddles, a guitar, a banjo and a mandolin, the players belting out raucous harmonies as they flailed away at their instruments."

The story's unnamed narrator tells us he is already a fan of this music, that he listens to Clinch Mountain Boys CDs on his daily commute to work. It's a sound, he says, that seems "conjured directly out of the bristly, unyielding landscape itself . . . arising straight out of these thickly wooded crags and gloomy gullies". Howling along with Ralph Stanley in his car, it's as if "a second self, full of fiery, passionate vitality, were at the point of awakening inside me". He could be speaking for all urban lovers of vintage Americana music.

A year after Rick and Faye's wedding, Lasdun's narrator unexpectedly runs into them at a party hosted by Arshin and Leanne, members of the local "healing community". Lasdun doesn't identify the place as Woodstock, but it may as well be, since "Oh, Death" beautifully illustrates the tension between the town's rural populace and the yoga-loving imports living out fantasies of getting away from it all. In due course, Rick's life itself becomes something like a Ralph Stanley song – an Appalachian tragedy in the Catskills.

On a warm autumn Saturday at his house in Shady, I sit with Lasdun over lunch and talk about the place he's based himself in for over two decades. "A lot of American towns are either just so entrenched in their own rural matters or they're too self-conscious," he says. "Woodstock is one of the very few places that has this combination of being real country and laid-back but where you can also take for granted that everybody's politically aligned."

He seems surprised, however, when I quote to him Richard Heppner's statistic that the proportion of second-home owners in Woodstock has grown to almost 70 per cent. He concedes that there is class tension in the area, citing the Confederate flags that used to appear on students' cars at his daughter's high school in Onteora. He also remembers a spate of barn burnings around town in the late nineties that had people "baying for blood" – till it transpired that the arsonist belonged to Woodstock's well-entrenched Shultis family. "All of a sudden it quietened down and the guy got an electric bracelet for a couple of weeks. When he was asked for his motive, he said something like he was fed up with not being able to get a cup of coffee for under two dollars."*

Surrounded by the very blue-collar people whose lives their music is about, middle-class folkies and bluegrass singers had made Woodstock their home since the early sixties. After *Music from Big Pink* fixed it in popular consciousness as a musical enclave, dozens of primarily acoustic – and often university-educated – players and songwriters began to settle in and around the town. "Happy Traum and John Herald lived there, and Artie Traum had just come up,"

* After we'd finished lunch, Lasdun asked if I was interested in seeing David Bowie's apple orchards, which were half a mile up the road. The notion would have been unthinkable in the era of Ziggy Stardust.

says Jim Rooney, who moved into his Lake Hill house in late 1970. "By the time I arrived it was quite a community."

Within a few months, banjo player Bill Keith – who'd played with Rooney in the early-sixties bluegrass duo Keith and Rooney – had joined them. So had Geoff and Maria Muldaur, who'd played with Keith in the Jim Kweskin Jug Band. "We were all still in Boston, so I said, 'Let's get down to Woodstock,'" says Geoff. "We looked at a very nice house on Glasco Turnpike, but it wasn't quite right for us. So I told Bill about it, and *he* went and got it. He still lives in that house today."

Keith is a regular at the weekly "Bluegrass Clubhouse" night held at Woodstock's Harmony Café, run by Sha Wu, the chef that Albert Grossman brought up to Bearsville in 1978 to run a Chinese restaurant called the Little Bear. (A signed photograph of Grossman still hangs behind the Harmony Café's till.) The Clubhouse is sparsely attended at the best of times, even when Keith sits in and picks along with singer-guitarist Brian Hollander, singer-mandolinist Tim Kapeluck and Stetson-wearing pedal-steel player "Fooch" Fischetti. Running through a repertoire of country classics – Patsy Cline's "Walkin' after Midnight", Lefty Frizzell's "Long Black Veil" – and close-harmony bluegrass beauties like the Louvin Brothers' "How's the World Treating You", the ad hoc group is heartily applauded by the handful of aficionados who've ventured out on this chilly October night. But it's a pale echo of the live roots-music scene that thrived in Woodstock's bars and clubs in the early seventies.

"There were four or five clubs in this one little town," says former Bearsville studio manager Mark McKenna. "In one place there'd be Paul Butterfield and in another Tim Hardin, in another Maria Muldaur. And all those people had a kind of fraternal sense and would play together and write together." Bill Keith, for one, must look back on those times and wonder what happened – especially when you consider that he revolutionised five-string banjo picking in the nine remarkable months he played with Bill Monroe's Bluegrass Boys in 1963.

Shortly before moving to Woodstock, Keith played pedal-steel guitar on 1970's *Pottery Pie*, the first album by Geoff and Maria Muldaur after their split from Jim Kweskin. Also playing on that earthy, easy-rolling record – produced in Boston by Joe Boyd – was Amos Garrett, a guitarist then coming to the end of a two-year stint in Ian and Sylvia's Great Speckled Bird. Keith himself had also done time in the Bird, unsung pioneers of "country rock". Still managed by Albert Grossman, Ian and Sylvia Tyson had reached a point of stagnation with their dated folk sound. They'd already recorded the countrified *Nashville* and *Full Circle* albums when – under the influence of the Byrds and the Flying Burrito Brothers – they started again from scratch. Already a local legend on Toronto's Yorkville folk scene, Garrett was the first musician they approached.

Almost overnight, Great Speckled Bird became a bona fide band of electric rockers. Having alienated their old folk fan base, they were passed over to John Court, who put them in a Nashville studio with the long-haired, satin-pants-wearing Todd Rundgren. "It was a peculiar marriage, God knows," Sylvia Tyson recalled. "You have to understand that we were doing that at Jack Clement's studio, right in the heart of Nashville, with all of the old boys that we'd played with dropping by."

The third release on Grossman's new label, *Great Speckled Bird* was equal parts Canadian country and hippie Bakersfield, shot through with the Tysons' folk harmonies. Playing off Buddy Cage's steel lines, Garrett excelled on the funky full-throttle opener "Love What You're Doing, Child" and the wistful waltz-time ballad "This Dream", sounding at moments like a fusion of James Burton, Clarence White and Curtis Mayfield. "I don't know anybody that plays like Amos," says Jim Colegrove, Great Speckled Bird's second bassist. Garrett was still in the band when they joined the Festival Express tour in that summer of 1970. "We were the darlings of that tour," drummer N. D. Smart II remembered. "We were the ones that everybody stood on the sidelines and watched."

By September, Garrett was living in Woodstock, with Smart and Colegrove following close behind. "After the *Pottery Pie* sessions I sent Amos a package," says Geoff Muldaur. "It had this thing rubber-stamped all over it that said, 'Leave Ian and Sylvia today!' And he did!" The first person Garrett encountered after moving into a cabin off the Wittenberg Road was John Herald, who, Garrett recalled, "came crashing out of the woods and shouted 'Hi!'" Smart and Colegrove drove up soon afterwards, searching for a guitarist to replace Garrett in Great Speckled Bird. "While we were there we thought, 'Well, this is a nice place and there's a lot going on up here,'" Colegrove says. "We knew Albert was building a studio, so we thought, 'Maybe we should look for a place up here and get in on the ground floor of whatever's gonna happen at Bearsville.'"

"There was a whole folk contingent that came in," remembers Happy Traum. "Jim Rooney, Bill Keith, Geoff and Maria, Amos, ND. And Johnnie Herald was already here with his bluegrass thing. So it was a very strong scene." Others who followed in their wake were John Sebastian and singer-songwriters Paul Siebel, Eric Kaz and Roger Tillison, the latter lured to Woodstock by Levon Helm (who fell out with him before Atco released *Roger Tillison's Album* in 1971).[*] For some, there was a clear line demarcating this folk crowd from the town's electric rock and blues musicians, though in reality there was plenty of overlap between the two camps. "You were either a *musician* or there were all these *folk* people," says Graham Blackburn, with a sniff of disdain. "Maria Muldaur had a little more spunk, and Geoff was kind of cool. But I've always liked stuff that struts, that's up there. And that was what I responded to in Van and Butterfield."

---

[*] Before moving to Woodstock, Eric Kaz played with Happy and Artie Traum in a New York band called the Children of Paradise. He later had several songs – including the co-authored "Love Has No Pride" – recorded by Linda Ronstadt and Bonnie Raitt.

With money from the Reprise deal that Grossman had negotiated for them, the Muldaurs paid $31,500 for a house on two acres off Boyce Road in Glenford, where they had an illustrious neighbour. "Every morning we'd hear Garth Hudson practising Bach on the organ," says Maria. "It would just come wafting across the treetops into our bedroom." The Muldaurs already knew Bob Dylan and had met Janis Joplin when Big Brother supported the Kweskin Jug Band in San Francisco. (They'd barely settled into their new home – dubbed "Hard Acres" – when Bobby Neuwirth called with the shattering news that Joplin was dead.) "You had this amazing community of our band, Butterfield's band and *The* Band," Maria says. "And meanwhile people like Johnnie Herald and Billy Faier were still active. Talk about the hills being alive with the sound of music. It wasn't the normal kind of rock-star lifestyle. We were happy hiding out in the woods and doing all that kind of earthy stuff, as opposed to hobnobbing around Hollywood. Our music was developing organically, like our gardens."

Keen to grow their own vegetables at Hard Acres, the Muldaurs sought the advice of Levon Helm. "He stood there with baby Amy in his arms and talked about fescue," Maria says. "It was touching to me that he knew the merits of one kind of ground crop over another." While they grew tomatoes and waited for gigs to roll in, the Muldaurs set to work on their second Warners album at Bearsville. *Sweet Potatoes* was a quintessential Woodstock recording of the period: rootsy, sexy, an eclectic mix of sultry blues and retro jazz. The Muldaurs were both great singers, and the backing from Amos Garrett, Bill Keith, Paul Butterfield and others was sublime.

"I took to hanging out with Amos and Paul," Geoff says. "I would also hang out with Albert, of course – that was a second home up the hill – and eventually with Danko, who was crazy enough to stay out all night with us." Drinking and drugging were endemic in the Butterfield circle, and Muldaur soon succumbed to the temptations

The Muldaurs' sophomore offering, recorded at Bearsville in 1972 (painting by Eric Von Schmidt)

on offer. "In my last Woodstock house on Ratterman Road", says John Simon, "there was a memorable pool game between Butterfield and Muldaur. Butterfield, with his typical braggadocio, said, 'I'm the best Chicago pool player ever!' Muldaur countered with, '*I'm* the best pool player!' They got a *gallon* of cocaine and were still playing when I woke up at seven in the morning. Butterfield went to Albert next day and said, 'I need five grand to pay Geoffrey.' Albert just said, 'Nope.'"

Hard Acres was itself something of a party house. On New

1 Bob Dylan in the "White Room" above the Café Espresso, August 1964 (Douglas R. Gilbert)

2 Dylan with Al Aronowitz (far left) and his son Myles and Allen Ginsberg in Albert Grossman's kitchen, Bearsville, August 1964 (Douglas R. Gilbert)

3 Dylan on his Triumph Bonneville with Victor Maymudes (left) and Bobby Neuwirth, Bearsville, summer 1964 (John Byrne Cooke)

4 Dylan with Sara Lownds at Peter Yarrow's cabin, Broadview Road, winter 1965 (Daniel Kramer)

5 Albert and Sally Grossman at the Monterey Pop Festival in California, June 1967 (Lisa Law)

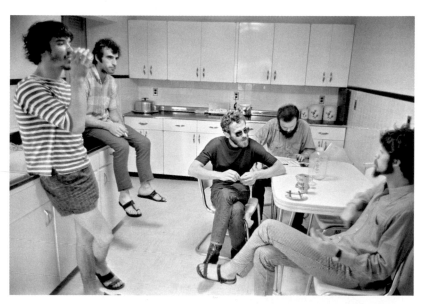

6 The Hawks (The Band) in the kitchen of Levon Helm and Rick Danko's house off the Wittenberg Road, late summer 1967. Left to right: Danko, Richard Manuel, Helm, Garth Hudson and Robbie Robertson (Elliott Landy)

7 Daddy Bob on the trampoline with stepdaughter Maria (left), son Jesse (foreground) and daughter Anna, Ohayo Mountain Road, summer 1969 (Elliott Landy)

8 Daddy Albert with Janis Joplin (right) and unknown woman, New York City, February 1968 (Elliott Landy)

9 Poster for the Woodstock Sound Festival, August 1968 (courtesy of Fern Malkine)

10 Tim Hardin and son Damion at the Onteora Mountain House, summer 1969 (Columbia Records)

17 Borderline on Sickler Road, Lake Hill, winter 1973. Left to right: David Gershen, Jon Gershen and Jim Rooney (courtesy of Jon Gershen)

18 A weary Todd Rundgren at the board during The Band's *Stage Fright* sessions, Woodstock Playhouse, early summer 1970. Left to right: Jon Taplin, Robbie Robertson, "the Runt" and a visiting John Simon (John Scheele)

19 Bobby Charles at Turtle Creek, Bearsville, 1972 (Bearsville Records)

20 John Holbrook at work in
Bearsville's Studio B, late seventies
(Shep Siegel)

21 Todd Rundgren and Bebe Buell,
Mink Hollow, summer 1975 (Bob
Gruen/www.bobgruen.com)

22 Ian Kimmet (far left) with Albert Grossman (far right) and executives
from Yamaha, early eighties (courtesy of Ian Kimmet)

23 John Simon outside the old Bearsville studio, October 2013 (Art Sperl)

24 Simi Stone and band at the Colony, Rock City Road, September 2013. Left to right: Zachary Alford, Stone, Sara Lee (Art Sperl)

25 The Bluegrass Clubhouse band at the Harmony Café, October 2013. Left to right: Bill Keith, "Fooch" Fischetti, Tim Kapeluck, Brian Hollander and George Quinn (Art Sperl)

Year's Day 1971, the Muldaurs hosted a bash to which most members of Grossman's circle were invited. Lubricated by Geoff's
bourbon-and-ice-cream punch, the menfolk watched football on
TV while the women slaved in Maria's kitchen making black-eyed
peas with cornbread. ("This was all sort of pre-women's lib," she
says.) Accompanying Grossman to the party were his house guests
Delaney and Bonnie Bramlett. When Eric Von Schmidt broke into
a bastardised version of the white-gospel standard "Will the Circle
Be Unbroken" – mischievously retitling it "Will the Serpent Be
Outspoken" – the Bramletts took southern umbrage. "It offended
their Baptist sensibility," Maria recalls. "They demanded that Albert
take them home."*

There were parallels between Woodstock and LA's Laurel Canyon,
where sixties bands broke up to produce seventies solo performers
who hung out – and sometimes slept – with each other. "Dylan's
song 'On a Night Like This' was a great little vignette of a winter-
night tryst in Woodstock," says Maria Muldaur. "There was a lot of
sneaking around through the woods and ending up in somebody
else's cabin – a lot of cross-pollinations going on besides the music.
And, dear God, it was fun before all the hideous diseases could
wipe you out for having a night like that." In 1977 Amos Garrett
said he couldn't "remember anyone with a steady old lady or wife
[in Woodstock] that didn't split up or divorce within a few years of
being there".

   One of the more damaging trysts was that between Maria
Muldaur's husband and Jim Rooney's wife. "I would see Geoff coming in the back door of the Squash Blossom, where Sheila Moony

_____

* Von Schmidt, who had spent time in London with Grossman and Bob Dylan in
January 1963, was another beneficiary of Bearsville Studios, recording his 1972
album *2nd Right, 3rd Row* there with the aid of the Muldaurs, Paul Butterfield,
Amos Garrett, Graham Blackburn, Jim Rooney, Garth "Campo Malaqua" Hudson
and more – as well as a second album, *Living on the Trail*, that didn't appear until
2002.

Rooney worked," says Stan Beinstein. One afternoon, Jim Rooney came home to find Geoff mowing his lawn, and "a tiny light bulb" went on in his head. Soon Sheila had moved out of their Lake Hill home and into a carriage house on John Court's property in Palenville. When Muldaur later covered Bobby Charles's "Small Town Talk", Maria hated "the way he sang it so innocently". "Geoffrey bought a Chevy Blazer and drove out of our driveway in a blaze of glory," she says, confessing that she went in tears to Grossman to ask for a waitressing job at the Bear. "I'd been waiting hand and foot on Geoffrey for years, so I figured I must have some skills in that department," she says with a snort of laughter. "Albert looked kind of sad, but I could tell he didn't have the fatherly instinct."

Maria laid low in Glenford, where her neighbour lent much-appreciated support. "Garth was so dear," she says. "He would come down the hill and say, 'Well, I'm getting my snowplough out today, you want me to plough you out?' He was a darling man." In the summer she drove to secret swimming holes with John Herald and Artie Traum. "I still make a pilgrimage to Palenville every year," she says. "The water that comes down from the Catskills is so pristine you can drink it."

In late September 1971 Happy Traum received an unexpected call from an old friend. "Can you come into the city tomorrow with your guitar and banjo?" Bob Dylan asked. "Oh, and do you have a bass?" The next morning Traum boarded a Trailways bus and made the trip into Manhattan. There was no one present at Columbia's Studio B besides an engineer and Dylan himself, who had decided to flesh out his forthcoming *Greatest Hits, Volume II* with new versions of "I Shall Be Released", "You Ain't Goin' Nowhere" and "Down in the Flood" (together with "Only a Hobo", a song he'd first recorded in 1963). The spirit of the session was quick and good-humoured: even "I Shall Be Released" was reworked as a jaunty singalong, while "You Ain't Goin' Nowhere" – with Traum wailing along and adding

what he calls "a frailing banjo part" – was a blast of fraternal fun. "At
the end of the session", Traum says, "Bob told me he felt stimulated
to prove himself again."

Whatever the reasons Dylan had for revisiting these particular
back pages, the recordings stimulated Traum as much as they did
his old friend. Disenchanted with the music business after a less-
than-stellar stint on Capitol Records, he and his brother Artie now
hatched the notion of a loose revue of the folk and bluegrass musicians they knew around Woodstock. "We just decided to go in a different direction," Traum says. "We said, 'Let's do the music we love
to do when we're sitting around at parties.'" In the recollection of
Jim Rooney, "I was working at Bearsville, but this other community
was all around me and we would get together for what we called
'picking parties' – Artie and Happy and Bill and me and Maria."

Rounding them all up in January 1972, the Traums booked a small
four-track studio north of Saratoga Springs and "literally camped out
on the floor" for a long winter weekend. From this extended song
circle came the album *Mud Acres: Music Among Friends*, with the
Traums accompanied by Maria Muldaur, Jim Rooney, John Herald,
Bill Keith, Tony Brown and others.* "I think Artie came up with
the name," says Rooney. "It referred to mud season in the country, when all the roads were dirt and everybody's car would be
covered with mud." Covering or adapting ancient favourites by
Gene Autry ("Cowpoke"), the Delmore Brothers ("Fifteen Miles
to Birmingham") and Blind Willie Johnson (Muldaur's solo showcase "Oh, the Rain"), the Mud Acres ensemble was a kind of folkie
Basement Tapes five years after Dylan's Big Pink summer. "It was
like, 'Okay, Johnnie, you take the lead on this one . . . Bill, you do this
banjo instrumental,'" says Happy Traum, who described *Mud Acres*
as "an album of songs that convey the sense of closeness, personally

* Tony Brown later became a member of Eric Weissberg and Deliverance,
playing bass on half of Dylan's revered 1975 album *Blood on the Tracks*.

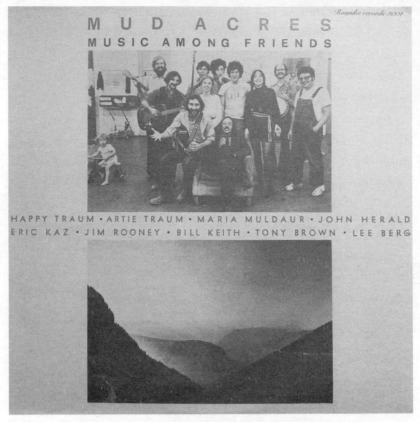

The first Mud Acres album, released on Rounder in 1972

and musically, that we feel, as well as the fun of doing something for its own sake, as opposed to doing it for financial or other ends".

Over the ensuing years, the Mud Acres concept evolved into the Woodstock Mountains Revue, rooted in the core unit of the Traums, Herald, Keith and Rooney, but embracing other friends new and old. "It was like an aggregator," says Stan Beinstein. "Some of the greatest folk music of the seventies is on the first two Rounder albums by the Mountains Revue."

"The second album was done at Bearsville in 1977," says Happy Traum. "We sort of expanded our group to include Pat Alger, who'd moved here from the south and became a very successful songwriter. Eric Kaz and Maria Muldaur moved to California, but John Sebastian and Eric Andersen became part of it, as did Rory Block, Gordon Titcomb and Rolly Salley, who wrote 'Killin' the Blues'. Paul Butterfield joined in, and he and Sebastian did this fabulous harmonica duet on 'Amazing Grace'."

Further albums followed, with Larry Campbell and Cindy Cashdollar augmenting the moveable feast. "The first day I got up here, John Herald introduced me to Happy and Artie," Campbell remembers. "He was doing a rehearsal with the Revue, so I met Bill Keith and Jim Rooney and all those guys. It felt like a utopian music scene. There didn't seem to be any egos involved. There was an aura of the ideal of the hippie scene that could actually come to fruition through music. And it seemed to permeate the whole town. Everywhere you went, there was this camaraderie and this easy flow of relationships."

The DIY nature of *Mud Acres* and the Mountains Revue reflected the challenge of sustaining careers as folk musicians in the seventies and eighties. Half the reason these Village and Cambridge veterans had moved to Woodstock was its affordability. Most weren't naturally ambitious. Paul Siebel, one of the most admired singer-songwriters on the Village scene of the early sixties, plugged into the Traums' circle but was diffident about playing live. "He was a brilliant songwriter, but he *never performed*," says Jeremy Wilber, who served him at the Sled Hill Café. "He was not rolling in any sort of dough, he was just shy about performing." Though Linda Ronstadt and Bonnie Raitt covered "Louise", his poignant song about prostitution, Siebel was depressed that his idiosyncratic country-folk style hadn't earned him more than cult status. Not even the bigger budget that Elektra allocated for 1971's *Jack-Knife Gypsy* stopped him sliding into heavy drinking. When he showed up for the *Woodstock Mountains* sessions, he didn't bring a single original song with him.

The music scene was equally difficult and painful for John Herald, who'd played such a part in bringing folk singers up to Woodstock in the sixties. "It really was hard on John," says Jim Rooney. "There was a group of Woodstock people that had some success, but there was another that didn't and was living hand-to-mouth. And it's no fun to live in a wintry place when you're broke. Ultimately he just couldn't take it – year after year of being told how talented he was and yet not being able to pay the bills." For Larry Campbell, Herald's tragedy was that he could never get out of his own way: "So many people tried to help him – chiefly Happy and Artie, who bent over backwards to get him some stability – but rather than take responsibility for the gift he had, he waited for somebody to come and offer him the world for it."

"I still like the 'back-to-the-country' idea, country music," Herald told the *Woodstock Times* in 1996; "some things Woody Guthrie might have talked about . . ." After the release of his final album, 2000's *Roll on John* – featuring "Woodstock Mountains", a plaintive song about his ex-wife Kim Chalmers – things deteriorated still further for Herald. In the early hours of 19 July 2005, after mailing farewell letters to friends, he took his own life.

Almost as reticent as Paul Siebel were fellow folkies Fred Neil and Karen Dalton. Neil had returned to his beloved Florida by the early seventies, but from 1970 onwards Dalton spent much of her time in Woodstock. "I think it was Freddy who brought her up there," says Harvey Brooks, who'd played on her 1969 album *It's So Hard to Tell Who's Going to Love You the Best*. "That was a big part of it – getting away from the city, and maybe away from your demons."

Dalton had been fleeing those demons for years. With her sometime partner Richard Tucker she would spend months out in Colorado, only for Tim Hardin to show up and kick off her heroin addiction all over again. "Tim and Karen hung out together a lot," says their friend Peter Walker. "They were just friends, really. Or shooting buddies. They saw each other up here in Woodstock." Dalton sang several of Hardin's best songs and may have been the first person to perform his "Reason to Believe".

In his *Chronicles*, Dylan called Dalton his "favourite singer in the place", while Fred Neil declared she was his "favourite female vocalist". (The three of them were pictured together in a famous photograph taken in early 1961, most likely at the Café Wha?.) An Amazonian beauty who'd acquired an unwanted reputation around the Village as "the hillbilly Billie Holiday", Dalton preferred to sing privately or jam in her kitchen with friends. "She's disappeared now," Neil told *Hit Parader* magazine in 1966. "No one knows where she is." Nor did Dalton care for recording, which was why producer Nik Venet virtually had to trick her into cutting *It's So Hard to Tell Who's Going to Love You the Best* by inviting her to drop in on a Record Plant session by Neil. Her harrowing performances reached back to her public-domain bluegrass roots. Her voice was horn-like, elemental and sparing of vibrato, each note a piercing straight line to the soul. "She wasn't Billie Holiday," Venet said, "but she had that phrasing Holiday had and she was a remarkable one-of-a-kind type of thing." On "Ribbon Bow", the aching plaint of a poor country girl who lacks the fineries of her big-city rivals, one heard the junkie stance in her every phrase and intonation.

Holy Modal Rounders singer Peter Stampfel, who acknowledged her as "the only folk singer I ever met with an authentic 'folk' background", claimed Dalton had been in hospital before moving to Woodstock with her two teenage children. Michael Lang signed her to his new Just Sunshine label, for whom Harvey Brooks produced her second album at Bearsville, drawing on a pool of musicians that included Bill Keith, Amos Garrett, John Simon and Full Tilt Boogie members Richard Bell and Ken Pearson.*

---

* Lang's label, bankrolled in a production deal by Gulf & Western's Paramount division, was also home to Brooks's Woodstock-based band the Fabulous Rhinestones and the pop-gospel group Voices of East Harlem, as well as to Betty Davis, who'd steered her husband Miles towards the avant-funk of 1970's *Bitches Brew* – on which Brooks played bass – before recording two lewd funk albums of her own for Lang. "The first two acts were Karen and Billy Joel," Lang says. "Harvey suggested Karen, and then the Rhinestones came together. The label lasted through 1974, when Gulf & Western sold Paramount."

Karen Dalton's second album, recorded mainly at Bearsville in 1970–1

Lang says of the *In My Own Time* sessions that Dalton "was introspective and damaged but very pleasant to work with". The album was a mixed bag: polarised between the stark bluegrass of "Katie Cruel" and "Same Old Man" on the one hand and the slightly awkward covers of soul staples "How Sweet It Is" and "When a Man Loves a Woman" on the other, it was – barring horn overdubs recorded in San Francisco – pure Woodstock. Dalton even posed for photographer Elliott Landy on the town's snowy back roads, elegant and graceful if somewhat ravaged. In places the album sounded like The Band, not least on its dreamy cover of their

"In a Station". More troubling was the version of her friend Dino Valenti's "Something on Your Mind" – with its nod to the junkie life in the line "who cannot maintain must always fall" – while the closing cover of ex-beau Richard Tucker's "Are You Leaving for the Country?" spoke for all those who, like Dalton herself, dreamed of leaving the city's "iron cloud" behind and moving to a "little country town / where dogs are sleeping in the cold and the flagpole's falling down".

The track that brings most people back to *In My Own Time* is the darkly chilling – and terrifyingly beautiful – "Katie Cruel", with Dalton's banjo accompanied only by Bobby Notkoff's spooky electric violin. She had been singing this traditional song for years, and it's hard not to hear it as the adopted autobiography of a fallen woman. (There's long been a rumour, incidentally, that The Band's "Katie's Been Gone" is about Dalton.) To newcomers, the timbre of her voice can come as a shock; some even find it hard to get past the catch in the throat that starts every phrase she sings. *"If I was where I would be, then I'd be where I am not,"* the voice of "Katie Cruel" sings with a kind of despairing Zen logic. *"Here I am where I must be, where I would be I cannot . . ."*

Peter Walker recalls seeing Dalton regularly at the home of their mutual friend Bob "the Brain" Brainen, on the Wittenberg–Glenford Road. "Bob was one of those people who kept a musical open house," Walker has written. "For years, whoever was in town would be up there hanging out: Freddy Neil, Tex Koenig, Tim Hardin, Bob Dacey, Becky Brindel, Bruce Gibson, Bob Gibson and a host of others gathered in the wee hours of the morning to share music, a beer, a bowl, and more music." According to Walker, Brainen "took care of [Karen] and tried to get her to reform". But when Michael Lang packed her off to Europe as a support act on a Santana tour, she imploded. "Mike hired John [Hall], with Bill Keith on bass and Denny Sidewell on drums," says JoHanna Hall. "Most nights they did not get a soundcheck, and every night

Karen got booed. And John would find her in the morning crying, 'I can't take it, I can't take it . . .' So finally one night they were in Montreux and she said, 'I'm not going on, I'm not doing it.' They had two thousand people sitting there." On a later occasion, when Dalton had a gig at Woodstock's Joyous Lake, JoHanna accompanied her into town: "She went onstage with her back turned to the audience, and I think she sang one song and just walked off. She was a very delicate flower." Dalton was happier sitting around the Halls' living room on Ohayo Mountain Road, singing Hardin's "Misty Roses" with John backing her on guitar. "That was the kind of thing that would happen then," JoHanna says. "It was such a shining moment."

As the years went by, Dalton divided her time between Woodstock and a rent-controlled apartment in the Bronx. Though her life remained chaotic, she maintained a stability of sorts upstate, even after contracting AIDS. Peter Walker remained a loyal friend. "I knew she was struggling to keep her apartment and would make small money passing out fliers and doing other subsistence work," he wrote. "At the end of the week when I would be leaving, she would come downtown and be ready to go back to Woodstock." In the late eighties a friend who'd been sentenced to a jail term gave Dalton the keys to his house on Eagles Nest Road in Hurley. It had a wood stove and a heated swimming pool. "She was there for quite a while," says Walker, "all the time people thought she was suffering and dying on the streets of New York. She had a good sense of what kept her healthy."

At the very end of her life, Dalton moved into a trailer on the same road. Rebuffing attempts by Kingston social services to force her into a hospice, she died in the trailer on 19 March 1993 – thirteen years after Tim Hardin fatally overdosed in Los Angeles and eight years before Fred Neil died of cancer in Florida.

4

THE BALLAD OF TODD AND ALBERT

In the autumn of 1997 Sally Grossman pokes at a plate of Chinese food in the Little Bear, a stone's throw from an abandoned video studio built by her late husband for Todd Rundgren, and talks to me about the goofy whiz-kid who first showed up in their world in the summer of 1969.

"Todd was this boy wonder," Grossman says. "To be such a renaissance man at the age of twenty-one was very striking. We were spoiled, of course, because we were so used to brilliant people. But he was like all of them, his talent was already full-blown. It wasn't like you heard him and thought, 'Gee, with the right songs and the right producer . . .'"

In truth, Albert Grossman was less convinced than his wife by the Philadelphia prodigy who'd tasted fleeting pop glory in a British Invasion-influenced band called Nazz, and whose whole sensibility – musical *and* sartorial – was so different from the earthy country funk of the artists Grossman loved. Rundgren had slipped into Grossman's world through the auspices of Michael Friedman, who'd worked with Nazz prior to being hired by Myra Friedman (no relation). "Albert was amenable to Todd but not very excited," Michael confirms. "I think he felt Todd didn't really fit in with the type of operation that he offered." Rundgren, however, kept coming to the East 55th Street office, often falling asleep in reception there. "One day Albert said, 'You've gotta get that kid outta here,'" says Friedman. "So I decided I would try and get Todd some production projects."

When he heard what Rundgren could do in a recording studio, Grossman changed his tune. "I knew Albert was supposed to be

this Allen Klein kind of guy," Rundgren says. "It wasn't too long
before he started to see something in me." Lucinda Hoyt believes
Grossman became "a paternal figure for Todd, just as he had been
for Bob and for Paul Butterfield". The very first album released on
Grossman's Ampex label was the eponymous release by a power-
poppish group from Rundgren's home town, produced by him at
New York's new Record Plant studio in August 1969. The American
Dream were managed by Paul Fishkin, who was palling around with
Rundgren in New York. "Todd said he was involved with Albert and
wanted to produce the American Dream for the new label," says
Fishkin. "So it was like, 'Okay, not only is my band gonna have a
record deal without me even trying, but it happens to be with the
god of all managers, the untouchable king of everything.'"

Rundgren also accompanied Robbie Robertson and Levon Helm
to Toronto to tape the debut album by a southern draft-evader who
had fled to Canada in 1967. Jesse Winchester had been making a
demo tape of his crisp, literate songs in Ottawa when Robertson
dropped by to listen. The Band guitarist not only persuaded
Grossman to sign him but heeded his manager's advice to take
Rundgren along as the engineer. "I think *Jesse Winchester* was a
kind of run-through for [*Stage Fright*]," Rundgren recalled. "I was
pretty quick to get the sounds, and they liked that." Though it was
more singer-songwriter poetic than *The Band*, *Jesse Winchester* was
still a close country cousin to that album. On the stare-you-down,
Walker Evans-style cover portrait, the bearded singer even looked
like a cross between Levon Helm and Richard Manuel, with whom
he shared a drink problem that Paul Fishkin soon encountered on
a visit of his own to Winchester's adopted home town of Montreal.
"The first night I got there, Jesse was playing a gig at a college,"
Fishkin says. "He was starting to catch on up there, but all of a
sudden he went into this insane alcoholic rage in the middle of a
song and walked off the stage." This didn't stop Fishkin believing in
the talent of a man later recognised by his peers as a songwriter of

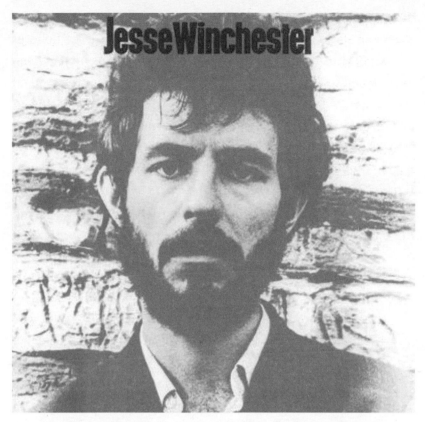

Jesse Winchester's 1970 debut for Bearsville/Ampex, produced by Robbie Robertson and engineered by Todd Rundgren

great depth and subtlety: "There was a lot of potential to turn him into something really special, but it just wasn't in him to become a big star."

Back in the US, Rundgren – whose production of Winchester's *Third Down, 110 to Go* was reduced to just three tracks* – continued functioning as Albert Grossman's pet producer of choice. After recording the Butterfield band at LA's Troubadour, he worked with

---

* Not including the sublime "Dangerous Fun", a song of carnal temptation that's among Winchester's absolute best.

them again on aborted sessions for Janis Joplin's third album. But as he had done with Ian Tyson in Nashville, he was beginning to piss people off. "He and his girlfriend Miss Christine were making faces behind Janis," says JoHanna Hall. "He was very arrogant and obnoxious and I thought he was making fun of her when I felt very maternal towards her." In truth, Rundgren was merely frustrated by fellow musicians apparently more interested in drink and drugs than in their music.

The same thing happened during the *Stage Fright* sessions at the Woodstock Playhouse. The painfully slow pace at which The Band worked made that album "one of the more maddening experiences" Rundgren had had to date. "They were hillbillies, or at least trying to *sound* like hillbillies," he says. "I remember the dichotomy of trying to do something that sounded concertedly folksy and creaky and dusty and not slick, and then at lunchtime Levon saying, 'Hey, order me one o' them lobster thermidors!' They had the best of everything and they had it both ways. And that was the germ of their demise." Helm in particular was riled by the St Mark's Place androgyne with his green hair and loon pants. Michael Friedman recalls the Band drummer chasing Rundgren around the Playhouse, enraged by his addressing the narcoleptic Garth Hudson as "Old Man". More sympathetic to Rundgren was the visiting Patti Smith, who was similarly bored by rock's pervasive hedonism. "We were both misfits, both wiry, skinny, hard-working people who didn't quite fit in," she says. "Neither of us was involved in drugs or anything at the time, so it was a relief to meet someone to talk to where you didn't have that kind of peer pressure to worry about."

Bruised by his experiences in Nazz, Rundgren was happy to sacrifice his own musical ambitions for a burgeoning career as a producer. By the early summer of 1970, however, he felt the creative itch and asked Grossman for a budget to record an album in Los Angeles. "I'd never thought of myself as a singer," he says, "but I continued to write as I had done in Nazz. I thought, 'There are other things to be written,' and I was very inspired by Laura Nyro and the possibilities of what you could say in a song." Using the sons of TV comedian Soupy Sales as his rhythm section, Rundgren cut *Runt* at I.D. Sound Studios on La Brea Avenue. Right off the bat, he proved he could turn his hand to anything he wanted: trashy rock ("Who's That Man?"), good-humoured pop ("We've Gotta Get You a Woman") and bittersweet Brian Wilson balladry ("Believe in Me"). Here were most of the blueprints for Rundgren's styles, stirred into a pot by an impish wizard not unlike the one pictured on the album's sleeve. Back in New York he added three tracks at the Record Plant, one of them ("Once Burned") surprisingly graced by the rhythm section of Levon Helm and Rick Danko. "I was imitating Richard Manuel on that song," Rundgren has claimed, "so I thought, 'Why not get Levon and Rick to play on it?'"

Another of the Record Plant tracks was "I'm in the Clique", a swipe at the in-crowd snobbery endemic in both Manhattan and his manager's social circle in Woodstock. "I was really punky about that," says Paul Fishkin, for whom the song also spoke, "because I had an attitude towards all Albert's Woodstock groupies and sycophants. There was a certain better-than-thou pretension in that whole era, and Todd and I had fun goofing on it." It was Fishkin, too, who inspired the song that gave Rundgren his first solo hit at the tail end of 1970. Based on their shared experiences of girl-watching (or frustrated lusting) from the stoops of St Mark's Place, "We Gotta Get You a Woman" was a perfect piano-pop song that made the Top 20 – despite enraging a phalanx of feminists with a silly line about women being "stupid" but "fun".

By the time Rundgren's second album came out in June 1971, Grossman had made the decision to leave Ampex for Warner-Reprise. Ever since the signing of Peter, Paul and Mary in the early sixties, Warners head Mo Ostin had watched as Grossman signed act after act to rivals like Columbia; there was even a rumour that

Grossman had intended to offer The Band to Ostin but had gone to
Capitol after learning that he was out of town. "We made the deal,"
says Fishkin. "And as bad and stupid as the Ampex deal had been,
the Warners deal was genius."

A casualty of the transition, unfortunately, was *The Ballad of
Todd Rundgren*, a collection of bittersweet ballads whose basic
tracks were again recorded at I.D. Sound. When N. D. Smart II
arrived at Rundgren's rented house off Nichols Canyon, he found a
wooden gallows in the living room. "I think it's because somebody
said, 'We're gonna give you enough money to hang yourself with,'"
Smart remembered. The noose duly appeared on the cover of the
Ballad album in a design by Milton Glaser, with Rundgren's back

to the camera and the rope around his neck. In an age of winsome singer-songwriters, it wasn't the smartest image to project.

If Grossman was disappointed that *The Ballad* produced no hits, consolation came in the fees he was now able to command for Rundgren's production skills. In September 1971 the boy wonder flew to London to take over Badfinger's *Straight Up* album from George Harrison. According to the band's Pete Ham, Rundgren "wanted four times the money he deserved". It was Grossman, however, who'd demanded it. "He asked for a shitload, more than any producer had ever been paid," Rundgren says. "And they paid it because it was Albert Grossman." Like Joplin and The Band before him, Badfinger's Joey Molland found Rundgren to be "rude and obnoxious". Michael Friedman says "the problem with Todd was that he was so difficult to work with that he almost never got to do a second album with anybody".

Failure though it was, *The Ballad* indirectly wove Rundgren deeper into the fabric of Woodstock. The album's exquisite multi-tracked vocals, for instance, were recorded at Bearsville's Studio B. "When the studio got running, this kid came in with long hair and took all my down time," says Jim Rooney. "He'd be in there all night long all by himself." Grossman told Rooney that Rundgren would be the most important artist of the seventies, and others felt the same way. "He could have been the biggest artist of the era," Paul Fishkin maintains. "If he'd taken a little more time to work with me, there's no question in my mind that we could have had it all." They very nearly did after 1972's sprawlingly ambitious double album *Something/Anything?* delivered the power-pop hit "I Saw the Light" and then, a year later, a Top 5 remake of the Nazz's "Hello It's Me".

Less supportive by this point was Michael Friedman, who was nurturing a new Bearsville artist named Jesse Frederick. "Todd didn't appreciate anything, and I'd really stuck my neck out for him," Friedman says. "I think he felt that I'd deserted him for Jesse, but I stopped being interested because he was pissing people off and I was putting my name on it. He was a good engineer, but I preferred John Simon's productions. With Todd, everything was sort of moulded after the Who and the British sound, which was a much harsher sound than the funky southern-blues style the Grossman artists were involved with." More appreciative than Rundgren, Frederick moved into Friedman's house in Shady and began rehearsing for an album made at the same Nashville studio where *Great Speckled Bird* had been recorded. 1971's *Jesse Frederick* – rootsier and more soulful than *The Ballad of Todd Rundgren*, though hardly as original – was the first Bearsville album released under the label's new Warners deal, while the second was a soft-rock effort by three long-haired Christians calling themselves Lazarus, produced at Bearsville by Peter Yarrow. The third in the Reprise 2000 series – not counting reissues of Rundgren's first two albums and of *Jesse Winchester* – was by eccentric Los Angeles duo Halfnelson, produced by Rundgren after he'd been introduced to them by Miss Christine. When Grossman suggested they rename themselves the Sparks Brothers, Ron and Russ Mael reluctantly compromised on Sparks, though success only arrived when they later signed to Island in London.*

Though *Something/Anything?* became the favourite Todd Rundgren album of many fans, it was never meant to be a double LP. "It was pretty much going to follow along the lines of *Ballad*," he says. "But it just went and went and went, fuelled by pot and Ritalin. The first three sides were done in three weeks. I was, like, Mr Music." *Something/Anything?* was a conscious display of tricks, flaunted with the chutzpah of a rock-and-roll jester. One minute Rundgren was the hard rocker of the slow, mesmerising "Black

---

* Following the 1971 release of *Halfnelson*, Miss Christine left Rundgren for Russ Mael, the more conventionally handsome of the two Maels. She was the subject of the Flying Burrito Brothers' unflattering "Christine's Tune" and a member of Frank Zappa's protégées/nannies/groupies Girls Together Outrageously. In November 1972 she died of a heroin overdose.

Maria", the next the power-pop brat of "Couldn't I Just Tell You". On the album's fourth side, he returned to Bearsville to record with various alumni of the Full Tilt, Butterfield and Great Speckled Bird bands: Amos Garrett, Jim Colegrove, Billy Mundi, Bugsy Maugh and Gene Dinwiddie. The tracks coincided with Rundgren's decision to leave California for good. "He slept on my sofa," says Colegrove. "He was different from all those people because he had no folk or country roots."

In February 1972 Rundgren began a relationship with a ravishingly pretty eighteen-year-old that would last five stormy years. For Bebe Buell he was close to being a father figure, while for him she became the conduit to a hipper-than-thou New York scene he would never have embraced on his own. Inevitably, he introduced Buell to his manager, bringing her to Bearsville. "The first time I met Albert, we went up for one of these amazing teepee parties he used to have," she remembers. "It was meant to be a bit of a spiritual moment, though it usually just turned into people going off and fucking." An early intimation of the relentless infidelity she would suffer – as well as perpetrate – came when Buell caught Rundgren with Lucinda Hoyt in the Grossmans' kitchen. After Grossman found her weeping in the teepee, she explained why. "Yeah, the guys really seem to like Cindy," he blithely replied.

To Buell, Grossman was like Santa Claus. "We were always going over to his house and eating good food," she says. "He would have Todd over or Butterfield and everybody would talk turkey. There was always a lot of discussion and debate." Though he'd disengaged from the day-to-day business of management, Grossman assiduously maintained his mystique. "The first time I met him was probably in October '71," says Paul Mozian, who became another of Grossman's tour managers. "I was working for Allen Klein, and Albert shows up in the office for a meeting with Allen's accountant to negotiate something for the *Concert for Bangladesh* album. He's wearing a gigantic fur coat, so this assistant says, 'Mr Grossman, shall I take your coat?' To which Albert says, 'No, that's fine,' walks into the office and throws it on the floor. I said to him, 'You really threw the guy off.' And he said, 'Well, that's the purpose, isn't it?'"

Grossman had a problem, though. He might have been a fearsome kingmaker as a manager, but he didn't quite grasp what it took to run a record company. "The label never really became what Albert envisioned," says Michael Friedman. "He was going to have all his bases covered and he would get income from every area imaginable. It was a brilliant concept, but The Band didn't want to leave Capitol, so the label never went anywhere. Todd had a couple of hits, but Jesse Winchester never really took off. You needed to have hit records, and Albert didn't know what hit records were. He just knew what hit *artists* were."

It was galling to Grossman that the first and only really big success chalked up by Bearsville Records came with Foghat, a meat-and-potatoes boogie band that Paul Fishkin signed from England. "It was like a cruel joke of fate," says Danny Goldberg. "Here was the ultimate music snob having a hit act with a band that had zero snob appeal." Graduates of sixties Brit blues stalwarts Savoy Brown, Foghat hit gold with their third album, *Energized* (1974), yet almost never recorded at Bearsville. In Grossman's eyes, there was nothing classy about frontman "Lonesome Dave" Peverett and his hairy henchmen, even if he liked the money that rolled into Bearsville's coffers from albums such as *Fool for the City* and singles like "Slow Ride". "Bearsville was a small company and a young company," Peverett said in 1995. "[Albert had] sort of almost semi-retired. He pretty much left it up to Paul Fishkin, and Paul, in conjunction with a budding agency, was the secret to our developing a following."

As snobbish as he felt towards Foghat, Grossman valued Fishkin and admired his refusal to genuflect to him. "For whatever reason, I had no fear of Albert," Fishkin says. "And I watched so many people around him fall by the wayside because they were doing what they thought they had to do." Grossman leaned increasingly on the younger man to steer the wayward ship that was Bearsville Records. "I'd become the cliché of the hip rock-and-roll executive working twenty hours a day," Fishkin says. "Albert loved that I was working so hard, but he was very frustrated I wasn't doing it on his terms. He really wanted me up in Bearsville more, but the phones never worked right and it would get flooded out."

Grossman's dependency on Fishkin was sorely tested when, in 1973, David Geffen headhunted the younger man to run his Asylum label in California. To keep Fishkin on the East Coast, Grossman offered him a third of Bearsville Records' stock. A year later, when Steve Paul tried to poach him for his Blue Sky label, Fishkin received a further 15 per cent. "The truth was that Albert never thought Bearsville was going to make any money anyway," says Fishkin. "I later found out he was borrowing tons of money against the label to build his empire."

That "empire" was itself fraught with complications and difficulties. Grossman's constant equivocation – and his tendency to start new projects before older ones had been completed – had become almost pathological. "There seems to be a general view that Albert was a bit of a bastard, but he was a lot more complicated than that," says John Holbrook, who was now working as a live-sound man for Todd Rundgren and Paul Butterfield. "The frustrating thing was that he wouldn't commit to anything. It was always like, 'Well, we'll have to just see . . . I dunno, y'know?'"

The pressure on Grossman's employees was palpable as he green-lit one initiative after another. At the studio, Jim Rooney suffered constant headaches as a result of the stress. When Paul Cypert told him, "I'm not dealing with [Albert] any more," Rooney wondered if it wasn't time to quit. Mark McKenna recalls that Grossman even had plans to build his own TV studio: "He was in discussion with developer Dean Gitter about getting a signal. Albert wanted to control his environment so much that he built a fucking town around

himself."* Grossman's scattergun approach to real-estate develop-
ment has its defenders. Jerry Wapner, the Woodstock lawyer who'd
tried to manage Tim Hardin, contends that Grossman brought only
good things to the town. "He was an interesting man and a great
client," Wapner said. "The people who attacked him are the same
people . . . whose base response consisted of a fear of anything new.
[And] that he was powerful and wealthy didn't help much."

With the studio's wrinkles finally ironed out, Grossman now
focused on the Bear Café – the 1973 successor to his failed French
restaurant – and on his plans for a Bearsville Theatre.† "The warm-up
was the Bear, but the theatre became a huge project," says John
Storyk, who moved to Woodstock to work full-time for Grossman
after returning from a stint in Colorado. Like the Bearsville studio,
however, the theatre was soon causing major headaches. "The problem was that Albert wasn't a town planner," says Michael Friedman.
"He couldn't put all the pieces together effectively. He would jump
from one person to another, whoever was reflecting in his aura at
that moment. If he'd had the sense to use professional people on
the theatre, it might have turned out differently."

Through all this feverish and not always effective activity, Grossman never lost his ability to astonish. When Friedman brought New
Orleans legends Snooks Eaglin and Professor Longhair to Bearsville
to make an album, Grossman took the tapes off him and then called
to say he was giving them to Robbie Robertson. "I said, '"Why?"'
Friedman recalls. "He said, 'I think it would be good for Robbie.'
I said, 'Maybe it *would* be good for Robbie, but so what?' And he
never put the record out."

---

* Grossman and Gitter went way back: the latter had produced Odetta's debut
album for Riverside and recorded his own *Ghost Ballads* (1957) for that label.
Later settling in the Catskills, Gitter became a classic Woodstock combo of
entrepreneur and spiritual seeker, as well as an unrepentant folkie – as his 2013
album *Old Folkies Never Die* attests.
† The Bear took its name not just from Bearsville itself but from a club – run by
Howard Alk – that Grossman had opened in Chicago in the early sixties.

Worse still was the treatment meted out to former Electric Flag keyboard player Barry Goldberg, who came to visit Grossman with his new wife, Gail. "We took the bus up and it was snowing, like *six inches* of snow," Goldberg says. "We got there about five in the afternoon and trudged through the snow. And we congregated in the kitchen, and Albert brought out the cheese and the salami." Just as Goldberg was starting to wonder when he and Gail would be shown to their quarters, Grossman turned to him and said, "By the way, where are you staying tonight?" When Goldberg gasped in disbelief, Grossman explained that the guest bedroom was unavailable and that no one was allowed in Janis Joplin's old room. "He said to me, 'You're a big boy now, Barry – you have to figure it out for yourself.' I broke into a cold sweat. We were stranded." Adding insult to injury, Goldberg's old Chicago homeboy Paul Butterfield also turned him down because his cat had just given birth to a litter of kittens in the spare room.

In the end it was the sainted Jim Rooney – who'd never even met Goldberg before – who put Barry and Gail up for the night. "I got really sick that night in the snow, because I couldn't believe what was happening," Goldberg says. "But Albert had that side to him. He loved to play games. He was always calculating."

5

"CREATIVITY AND FERMENT"

While the cluster of musicians around Albert Grossman dominated the Woodstock of the early seventies, another music community evolved in parallel to it. Yet the local avant-jazz scene was all but hidden from general view. "There are many musical Woodstocks, which gets lost in history," says Jonathan Donahue. "People come here hoping to see Janis Joplin's illegitimate child belting it out on the village green, but I've always found myself mated to the more underground inspirations there. Even today, if you include the local area of Kingston, there's Karl Berger, there's Pauline Oliveros, there's a lot of orchestral writers. And that's what's always kicking against the pricks."

Ed Sanders, who'd *always* kicked against the pricks, moved to Woodstock in 1973, drawn not by Albert Grossman but by the beauty of the place and the radicalism of its artistic heritage. "I came for the bluestone creeks and the history," he says. "I had a very turbulent sixties, and you've got to wash ashore somewhere. There were other leftists and radicals that survived here, so I knew that I could too." The immediate spur for Sanders's relocation was the heat that followed the 1971 publication of *The Family*, his chilling account of the Manson murders. "I had these satanic cults on my back, so my wife and I rented an old chicken coop out on Sickler Road," he says. "Then I got a big royalty payment for the book, so we decided to use the money to buy a place. Blame Manson for me becoming a permanent resident!"

Sanders was pleased to find not just artists and musicians in Woodstock but a smattering of writers. "There was a big poetry scene

Karl Berger and co. (1969)

going on when I moved up," he says. "There were over a hundred poets and a big network of readings in coffee shops and bars.* Plus Philip Guston was still alive, and there were lesser-known lights who got money from Jimmy Carter's CETA [Comprehensive Employment and Training Act] arts programme. Karl Berger and others got government grants. There was a lot of creativity and ferment."

Vibraphonist Berger and his singer wife Ingrid Sertso had come to New York from their native Germany in August 1966, having fallen

---

* For more on the local poetry scene, see Michael Perkins, "A Short History of Poetry in Woodstock, 1973–2008", *Woodstock Times*, 17 April 2008.

under the spell of radical free-jazz saxophonist Ornette Coleman. Initially homesick and disillusioned, the couple were dissuaded from leaving by Coleman himself. Though Berger played with the more radical figures in the New York and Brooklyn loft scenes – Archie Shepp, Roswell Rudd and others – it was only when he and Sertso moved permanently to America in 1971 that they began to feel at home. Hatching the concept of the Creative Music Foundation, they moved to Woodstock with their young daughters the following year. There they established the Creative Music Studio, initially in Mount Tremper and then in a converted Woodstock barn on Witchtree Road, inviting their old loft friends from the city to stay and participate in formal music classes.°

It helped that there were already jazz players living at least part-time in the Woodstock area. Maverick violinist Betty MacDonald had made the town her home in 1969, while husband and wife Carla Bley and Mike Mantler had moved their rural base from Maine to a house-cum-studio in Grog Kill, near Willow. Among the huge cast of players on Bley's and poet Paul Haines's epic 1971 "chronotransduction" *Escalator Over the Hill* were Berger and Don Cherry – along, more improbably, with Jack Bruce and Linda Ronstadt. "Talk about someone who connected rock and jazz," says trumpeter Steve Bernstein, who recorded at Grog Kill in the early eighties. "Carla was really one of those people meeting people from both scenes." Two of the key sidemen on Miles Davis's revolutionary albums *In a Silent Way* (1969) and *Bitches Brew* (1970) now also made their homes in Woodstock: English bass player Dave Holland was in Mount Tremper, while drummer Jack DeJohnette lived in Willow with his wife Lydia. Harvey Brooks, another of Davis's musicians, similarly straddled the spheres of Woodstock's rock and jazz scenes, and befriended both Holland and DeJohnette.

° Living just a few houses along on the same road was none other than Charles Mingus. "We didn't know him that well, and he didn't come by," Karl Berger recalls. "He was mostly in a state of not being approachable."

Woodstock proved fertile for serendipitous hook-ups. John Simon remembers driving along Tinker Street with folk-bluegrass singer-songwriter John Hartford when they spotted Dave Holland lugging his laundry back from Sam's Laundromat. "We stopped and said, 'Hey, Dave, wanna play bass on a bluegrass album?'" Simon says. "He said, 'What's bluegrass?' But he signed up for it anyway." Recorded at Bearsville, Hartford's *Morning Bugle* album came out in June 1972 and was, says Simon, "the kind of thing that could only have happened in Woodstock".

Holland was just one of the illustrious "guiding artists" at the Creative Music Studio, a place of refuge for battle-scarred jazz veterans. Established by Berger and Sertso with the help of their great free-jazz mentor Coleman, CMS took root in the autumn of 1972. "Ornette never came up, but he was basically the spirit behind it," says Berger. "I asked him why he wasn't coming to teach, and he said, 'If I came to teach, people would think I *know* something!'" The Bergers relished the fact that jazz factions prevalent in New York seemed to break down in Woodstock: alto saxophonist Lee Konitz jammed with violinist Leroy Jenkins, bassist David Izenson collaborated with flautist-composer Harvey Sollberger. "People were more relaxed up there," Berger told Ludwig Van Trikt. "They didn't think in terms of the PR quality or the career situation or whatever it was."

The Bergers' non-hierarchical, non-bureaucratic approach to creativity was refreshing to the bolder spirits on the New York scene, as well as to such notionally mainstream players as Konitz and Jimmy Guiffre. Another participant was Howard Johnson, the tuba player who'd been a key member of the horn section on The Band's *Rock of Ages*. Later came Don Cherry, who taught inspiring CMS classes through the summer of 1976, and the cerebral, pipe-smoking Anthony Braxton, who settled in his own place on Chestnut Hill Road. There were more intermittent visits from the minimalist Steve Reich and local composer Pauline Oliveros. "Some

of the best people in the world would come . . . right to our house,"
Berger said. "Also, all these musicians who lived in the Woodstock
area at the time . . . were actually looking to do some work at home
that was creative, and not have to be on the road all the time."

Most of these remarkable player-composers had experienced the
freedom of the scene in Europe and wanted to recreate it in the
Catksills.* "The CMS became a woodsy outpost of the city's loft
scene," Will Hermes wrote in his *Love Goes to Buildings on Fire*
(2011), "a sort of new-jazz ashram developing a tradition of freely
improvised music that aspired, among other things, to draw every
form of world music into its vocabulary." Among the "world musicians" who regularly participated in the CMS were percussionists
Naná Vasconcelos and Babatunde Olatunji, along with saxophonist
Ismet Siral and the kora player Foday Musa Suso. "Even before
you get to CMS, you know that your whole attitude is changing,"
Olatunji told Robert E. Sweet, author of the CMS history *Music
Universe, Music Mind* (1996). "Coming from a city like New York,
a concrete jungle, you pass through woodlands, you hear birds singing – it's country. You become aware of all the things that nature has
given us to admire that we seldom take a look at."

To pianist Marilyn Crispell, who was closely involved with the
Bergers between 1977 and 1982, CMS was "a totally unique place
in the world . . . a hands-on experience, free and creative". Indeed,
the Studio was almost an *un*music school: Dave Holland came to
teach not bass playing but his own ensemble work. Albums such as
his 1973 ECM release *Conference of the Birds* and Braxton's 1976
work *Creative Music Orchestra* were rooted in the CMS experience. "It's not like you go to a music school or conservatory and
then you find these nasty, cranky teachers that have a job until they
retire," Ingrid Sertso said. "CMS was the opposite."

* For a perfect example of what one might term Woodstock's bucolic fusion,
hear "Back-Woods Song", the first track on the 1976 debut by Gateway, a trio
comprising Holland, DeJohnette and guitarist John Abercrombie.

"Karl and Ingrid were somewhere between mom 'n' pop and gurus," says Steve Bernstein, who took a CMS course in the summer of 1977. "They were like hippie parent figures, very spiritual and into Buddhism. They'd talk about things other people weren't talking about, about enlightenment and pure sound and the power of rhythm." Central to CMS "teaching" were breathing and body-awareness classes – not to mention Buddhist meditation, which Don Cherry had practised for many years. Indeed, the Woodstock jazz scene became somewhat intertwined with the town's alternative community. "Healers tell me that Woodstock is on blessed land," says Lynne Naso. "Jack and Lydia DeJohnette became centrepieces of that community." (The DeJohnettes were close to Robert Thurman, father of actor Uma and a leading American Buddhist whose Menla retreat is located in the mountains west of Phoenicia.) "My teaching was basic practice," Berger says. "It started with the principle of sound and silence – and there *was* no silence in New York. Nature really helps, and from the start we had a rather spiritual approach to music. We wanted to make sure that music was understood not just as a business or as entertainment but as a lifeblood of mankind."

In the autumn of 1974 the Bergers moved CMS back to its original home of Mount Tremper, striking a deal with a Lutheran summer camp that enabled them to use an old monastery in the spring and autumn. After two semesters there, they moved to West Hurley in the autumn of 1976, taking over Oehler's Mountain Lodge motel on forty acres of land. After initial teething problems – a culture clash between the musicians and the Lodge's established German clientele – in 1977 the Bergers asked the Oehler family if they wanted to sell. Though it would become a financial millstone for them, the Lodge provided CMS with its first secure home. "We could really house people there year-round," says Berger. "It became like a live-in college."

During its late-seventies heyday there were eight-week CMS semesters in the autumn and spring, along with two five-week semesters each summer. Many of the earlier "guiding artists" maintained their involvement with CMS, and there were poetry workshops held by Ed Sanders and Allen Ginsberg (who brought cellist Arthur Russell with him as a musical accompanist). There were also what the Bergers called "intensives" at Easter and at the turn of each year, the most celebrated of which featured the illustrious Art Ensemble of Chicago and – in the winter of 1979/80 – the wildly experimental pianist Cecil Taylor. "Students" such as Steve Bernstein, Marilyn Crispell and multi-instrumentalist Peter Apfelbaum became part of the Bergers' family, even when some of them became willing participants in Woodstock's rock culture. "In the rewrite of jazz history, they make it seem like avant-garde jazz was this weird kind of phenomenon that ruined jazz," Bernstein says. "But if you think about Hendrix and people like that, it was very related to Coltrane and Pharoah Sanders. There were a lot of cross-currents between what young people wanted to hear, and that was really what CMS was about."

With grants from the Ford Foundation and the National Endowment of the Arts, CMS was able to employ upwards of thirty people – a boom period for Woodstock arts that recalled Roosevelt's Federal Art Project of 1935–43. As fundraiser Marianne Boggs told Robert Sweet, "we really were running . . . more than a half-million-dollar organisation, annually, out of those bizarre half-bedrooms over at Oehler's". Sadly, the boom came to a crashing halt when, two years into the Reagan administration, all the programmes set up by Jimmy Carter were slashed. With European students now obliged to attend the CMS as tourists, the Bergers were forced to close the Studio in 1984.* The legacy of the CMS remains for all

---

* Though not before the Woodstock Jazz Festival, held in September 1981 in an adjacent field to mark the tenth anniversary of the birth of the Creative Music Foundation. The gathering featured performances by Anthony Braxton, Jack DeJohnette, Pat Metheny, Chick Corea, Lee Konitz, Howard Johnson, Naná Vasconcelos and Marilyn Crispell.

to see and hear, however. "The avant-jazz community grew pretty fast in the seventies, and some of the people who came up to study stayed here," says Berger. "There are over forty or fifty musicians that came up then who still live around Woodstock."

Berger continues to lead the Creative Music Studio Orchestra, comprised of former members and specialising in old pieces by Don Cherry, Ismet Siral and others. "Peter Apfelbaum and I still play with Karl," says Steve Bernstein. "The sad thing is that CMS doesn't have a physical base any more." In 2011 downtown avant-jazz star John Zorn offered Berger a weekly series of CMS Orchestra shows at his East Village space the Stone. In the same year non-profit label Innova released a compilation of archival CMS recordings from the late seventies and early eighties.

In the nineties, in need of steady income, Berger entered the groves of academe, teaching at the University of Massachusetts at Dartmouth and becoming dean of the music department at Frankfurt Conservatory. After the CMS years, he found the experience enervating. "The kids of the nineties particularly were very goal-oriented," he said, "in the sense of having a profession, being music teachers, getting a diploma so that they could teach . . ." But he also found a new lease of creative life as a writer of arrangements for such artist-producers as Bill Laswell. "I got to know Bill as a nineteen-year-old who was starting to produce in New York," he says. "A few years later I had this idea: why can't we have strings playing rhythmic lines like horn sections in funk productions? He loved the idea and we did many records for Sly and Robbie and Yellowman, over fifty albums."

Through Laswell's association with Sony/Columbia, Berger was brought to the attention of one of the label's rising stars. "They invited me to write for Jeff Buckley at Bearsville," he says. "It turned out that he was one of those CMS-style guys who would listen to Shostakovich and Bill Evans and any kind of music he liked."

Footage of Berger with Buckley in Bearsville's vast Studio A – and of Berger conducting members of the Hudson Valley Philharmonic as they played his swirling string arrangements – was included on the bonus DVD accompanying the tenth-anniversary edition of Buckley's *Grace*. In an interview for the DVD, Buckley described Berger's work on the album as "kind of like a regal visitation". Like so many before him, moreover, Buckley found Woodstock highly conducive to music-making. "I've lived in pretty rural places before, so this is familiar," he told director Ernie Fritz. "The setting itself is great, but the best thing about it is that it's outside Manhattan, and I'm an easily distracted person sometimes when it comes to the city . . . [Woodstock] is a great place to get focused. It's like a pirate ship. There's nothing to do but make this ship sail."

Along with the Creative Music Studio "graduates" who still call the town home, other jazz stars – from clarinettist Don Byron to the legendary Sonny Rollins – either reside in Woodstock or use it as a rural base to recharge their creative batteries. "At a time when I was very busy with sessions in the city, I'd come back here to decompress," says Warren Bernhardt, who toured with Jack DeJohnette in the mid-seventies. Carla Bley is still in Grog Kill, and was even lured out of her hideaway in April 1993 for a rare performance at the Bearsville Theatre. "It was a duo concert with her second husband Steve Swallow," says Mark McKenna, who booked the date. "She was reluctant, because she said she didn't want the guy who ploughed her driveway to have to come and see her in concert. But as it turned out, she loved it."

For Karl Berger, the jazz scene in Woodstock – like its music community in general – is in a sad state. "There are so many musicians here, yet there's so little music in town," he says mournfully. "The musicians play all over the world but they don't play here. I haven't seen Dave Holland or Jack DeJohnette play here in years. It's really a sorry situation."

6

IN A GOOD PLACE NOW

Woodstock would not be complete without an Artist Road, though technically the cul-de-sac of that name is in Saugerties. In the early summer of 1971 Paul and Kathy Butterfield were living at the end of it, while Amos Garrett rented a small cottage on the same road closer to Route 212. Across the way from Garrett, in a larger single-storey house, lived Jim Colegrove and N. D. Smart II, the rhythm section that, until lately, had played with Garrett in Great Speckled Bird.

With their lease up for renewal in July, Colegrove and Smart agreed to allow viewings of the property while they made up their minds about whether or not to stay. One day there was a knock at the door. A local realtor stood there with two men who clearly were not employees of IBM or Rotron. Both had beards and longish hair, and one wore bib overalls without a shirt. Out in their car was a shaggy-haired golden retriever named Willie. As they strolled about the house, the guy in the overalls was heard to say, in an unmistakably southern accent, "Ah see y'all are musicians." When Colegrove requested his name, the man said it was Bobby Charles Guidry. Colegrove did a double take. "You mean Bobby Charles, the guy that recorded for Chess and Imperial?" Guidry nodded. "Don't tell anybody," he said.* What were these swampy characters, grizzly men out of *Deliverance*, doing at large in a Yankee arts town? How had Charles, author of the timeless "See You Later, Alligator" and

---

* The other man was also a southerner named Bobby. "Bobby Lynn Shehorn was a songwriter from Texas," says Colegrove. "He was doing all the chauffeuring, because Bobby Charles didn't have a driving licence."

"Walking to New Orleans", fetched up in the Catskill mountains, fifteen hundred miles from the bayous of Louisiana?

It transpired that Charles was on the run from the law in Nashville, where he'd worked as a writer-for-hire in the stable of WLAC DJ John "R" Richbourg. With a drugs charge hanging over him – a neighbour had stashed some speed in his apartment – he'd fled town and hidden out in Texas and the south-west. "You learn to live with the underground, you know, with the street people," he said in 1995. When things got too hot in Austin, someone told Charles about a safe house in upstate New York. He commandeered Shehorn and told him to point his car north. For a while the two men holed up like fugitives in the tiny Sullivan County village of Jeffersonville, later described by Patty Hearst – who was held there after her kidnapping – as "remote and near nowhere in particular".

"One morning I was at the laundromat," Charles recalled. "I had long hair, looked like a clump of shit in a piece of snow, sticking out real bad, and these old ladies there were looking at me and saying, 'Well, I'm sure glad we got all these state troopers living in this town.' And I ran out of there and got [Shehorn] and said, 'Man this is a cop town, I'm getting my ass outta here.'" Charles claimed he'd never heard of Woodstock and didn't even associate the name with the world-famous festival that had taken place only a few miles from Jeffersonville.

Colegrove is sceptical about the claim and thinks someone had tipped off the Cajun songwriter that Albert Grossman might be able to get him out of his Nashville jam. If that was true, Charles played it cool and wormed his way slowly into Grossman's inner sanctum. Having found a house out in Wittenberg, he and Shehorn took to visiting Artist Road and hanging out with Colegrove and Smart, who soon introduced their legendary new acquaintance to their Woodstock peer group. "One afternoon, Colegrove and N.D. showed up at the studio with another fellow in tow," Jim Rooney wrote. "He had [. . .] a weathered look – a little like Jesus. He had a beautiful smile and a lovely soft way of speaking, very laid-back. After work that night a few of us wound up over at Bill Keith's with Bobby. In the course of the evening he picked up a guitar and sang us a song."

The song was "Tennessee Blues", which Bobby had written in Jeffersonville as an expression of his yearning to leave his troubles behind him. Like the others gathered at Keith's place, Rooney was floored: "It entered my heart and stayed forever," he would write years later. Others have been just as affected by the song's dreamy melancholy. "We once did a cover of it," says Mercury Rev's Jonathan Donahue. "I took it as my own, as something I would have written about the Catskills. And then a friend told me it was written here. I began to see the thread that runs through the place and was able to connect myself to it. It hit me like a ton of bricks."

Word soon leaked through to The Band that Charles was in town. From there it was only a matter of time before the whisperings reached the ears of their manager. "Woodstock was a very stratified community," says Paula Batson, then waitressing at the Bear. "But when somebody like Bobby came to town, he was just so immensely talented and such a wonderful character that he acquired a special kind of status."

Along with Rick Danko, Maria Muldaur was at Grossman's house the night Charles came by to sing some of his songs. "She's such a free spirit," Charles remembered. "We started singing some songs together, and Albert liked it. He just sat there with his fingers crossed, twiddling his thumbs, like dollar signs were going through his mind." Though he hadn't performed live since scoring mid-fifties R&B hits with "Alligator" and "Time Will Tell", Charles had a voice as rich and soft as molasses, a little like Danko's. And if Danko thought Charles was cool, that was good enough for Grossman, who soon assured the Louisianan that he could get the drugs charges dropped. "Albert said he would get me out of my problem if I would sign a contract with him," Charles recalled. "He guaranteed me that

I would be making all kinds of money and all that bullshit, you know." After Grossman got Mo Ostin and Joe Smith at Warner-Reprise to vouch for Charles's character and commercial prospects, the singer was put on a five-year probation order in New York state. "Albert was the guru," Charles said. "He carried a big stick. If Albert said yes everything was fine. If Albert said no you had a big problem."

Fittingly, it was Rick Danko who expressed the most interest in collaborating with Charles when Grossman green-lit some demo recordings at Bearsville in November 1971. "They became the fastest of friends," says Jonathan Taplin. "Levon loved Bobby too, but Rick was up for any party, any time, anywhere." To Paula Batson, who watched Danko and Charles drinking at the Bear – often with Paul Butterfield in tow – Danko was "the member of The Band that people knew, the one who was more out-there and friendly to anybody". Charles was equally sweet-natured, though the company of Butterfield often got him into trouble around town. "I actually had a fight with Bobby," says Robbie Dupree, whose band the Striders were then making waves in Woodstock. "We were in the Espresso one night, and my bass player Greg Jackson was awestruck. He told Butterfield he'd seen him play in Central Park but said the sound man hadn't done a good job. And for that he got a smack right in the face. So I grabbed Butterfield's hand and Bobby grabbed me, and then *we* went at it. They were drunk and liked to think of themselves as tough guys, so I said, 'Go to Kingston – there's a whole *town* to fight down there!'"

Despite the scrap, Dupree felt a sneaking admiration for these "tough guys", who seemed to model themselves on local icon Lee Marvin. "They were real *men*," he says. "And that was really prevalent in the Bearsville scheme of things: Butterfield and Bobby Charles and the Band guys. They were all hard-drinking everymen, and that was why they liked Lee so much. It was a blue-collar vibration that was happening. They were not to be trifled with."

Less of a real man, and more of a baby-faced crazy man, was actor

Michael J. Pollard, who also took up with Charles in Woodstock. "He used to follow me around the house," Charles remembered. "Man, he was really out there. He lived in a balloon, he lived in his own world." When Jim and Sheila Moony Rooney hosted a party for Charles's thirty-fourth birthday in February 1972, Pollard staggered into their house on Sickler Road with Bobby Neuwirth. "Someone brought Fred Neil along," Rooney recalled. "Here he was in our living room opening his guitar case, getting ready to sing Bobby a song. Suddenly I heard a crash in the kitchen." Pollard had upended a wicker planter, strewing broken pots and soil all over the floor. "Sheila came over to him and boxed his ears," wrote Rooney, who threw the actor out into the snow. "As I turned around, Fred was quietly putting his guitar back in his case. All the commotion was too much for his quiet soul."

Bobby Charles may be the quintessential Woodstock album of the early seventies. The key to its swampy charm may be that none of the musicians thought they were cutting anything more than demos. The sleepy, sensual nature of its country funk comes from its early-hours, booze-loosened provenance. "I was tending bar when Bobby made that album," says Jeremy Wilber, "and I can tell you that the entire record was made between the hours of 4 a.m. and whenever they finally collapsed." Like everyone else, Wilber fell in love with the bayou bard. "There was just something so *blithe* about Bobby," he says. "He would walk into our establishments and run up these enormous bar tabs without any means of paying them."

The special magic of *Bobby Charles* also stemmed from the input of the players rounded up for the sessions. "The basic band was N.D. on drums, me on bass, Amos on guitar and John Simon on piano," says Jim Colegrove. "Bobby had a lot of songs and would *transmit* them to us, because he didn't play an instrument. If you made a wrong change he'd say, 'No, it dunt do that.' And that's how you learned the song." Bolstering the core unit was an all-star assembly of the town's finest roots musicians – the Band boys, Geoff Muldaur,

Bobby's Bearsville classic (1972)

John Till, Billy Mundi, David Sanborn and Nashville pedal-steel maestro Ben Keith, then newly arrived in town – along with visitors Bobby Neuwirth and Mac "Dr John" Rebennack, who contributed an insouciant organ part to "Small Town Talk", one of two songs Bobby co-wrote with Rick Danko.* "John Simon started out as the producer," says Jim Colegrove. "But then Bobby said, 'I don't think we're going in the right direction with this, I'd like to get somebody else involved.' And that somebody was Danko."

* Years later, with Charles looking on, Rebennack co-produced Sharon McNally's album *Small Town Talk (The Songs of Bobby Charles)*.

"Bobby and Rick used to come to our house at three in the morning," says Christopher Parker. "I had drums and a Wurlitzer piano and a really cool Gibson violin bass, so they knew they could jam there. It was like, 'Hey, man, we got this idea for a toon, man!' My wife would say, 'Oh my God!' But we always let them in, and some good music came out of it." "Small Town Talk" was Bobby's wry portrait of Woodstock as a kind of rock-and-roll Peyton Place. "It was about the class system there, the gossip," says Paula Batson. Other highlights on the album included the opening "Street People", a languorously funky homage to Charles's years on the run; "Long Face", a Lee Dorsey-esque track featuring Levon Helm on drums; and "I Must Be in a Good Place Now", with its happy evocation of blissful love and "wild apple trees".

"He's Got All the Whiskey", meanwhile, was a song of hilarious envy that spoke for everyone in Woodstock trying to keep up with the Albert Grossmans of the world. "That was another song we did in one cut," Charles said. "We went and woke Billy Mundi up. It had snowed and hardly anybody could get up to the studio. Billy was staying in one of Albert's cabins so I went and asked if he felt like going into the studio with me. He jumped out of the bed into his pants." When they got to Bearsville, Todd Rundgren was trying to fix the mixing desk. "We had to sit there for a couple of hours," Charles remembered. "I said, 'I'm not leaving till I've put this fucking song down.' Ben Keith said, 'Well, I'm sticking with you,' and Billy said, 'Well, I ain't going nowhere.' And now here come two other people up the hill, Buzzy Feiten and John Till – they walked up that fucking mountain with their guitars and when Todd finally got the board fixed we put down the song in one take."[*]

Another track, "Grow Too Old", revived an old chestnut Bobby had co-written with Fats Domino in the fifties. "There was a great

[*] Both Mundi and Feiten had played – alongside Harvey Brooks and the album's de facto producer Al Kooper – on Dylan's *New Morning* album.

deal of disagreement on how it should go," says Jim Colegrove. "We were almost at each other's throats. But someone pulled out a bottle of cocaine and then everything was fine!" Amos Garrett was magnificent throughout the album, never more so than in the shimmering shapes he sprinkled over "Tennessee Blues", which additionally featured heartbreaking accordion counterpoint from Garth Hudson. Delight though it was, *Bobby Charles* sold poorly. "Bobby didn't care about promoting his album," says Paul Fishkin. "Aesthetically there were a lot of great songs, but we couldn't put the machine behind it. He was just drinking up at the Bear every night."

Meanwhile, Mac Rebennack's brief sojourn in Woodstock ended unhappily after he got wise to a deal that Grossman and his management partner were using to blindside him. "The very first thing [Albert] did was hand me over to his hand-chosen flunky Bennett Glotzer," Rebennack wrote. "[He] informed me that Albert and company now owned one-third of my publishing rights. 'The hell you do,' I said, and I got out of his office fast." Rebennack resorted to some "basic voodoo", placing a dead bird on Glotzer's New York doorstep and lighting black candles around it. Later, outside the Troubadour in LA, he thought he saw Glotzer reach inside his coat for a gun and "busted the shit out of him".

Beckoned up to Woodstock by The Band and Bobby Charles, Rebennack accepted Grossman's hospitality in one of his Turtle Creek cabins but quickly soured on his hidden agenda. "You need to un-sic this fucking asshole off me," he complained to Grossman of Glotzer. Getting only an airy and noncommittal response, he reached over to a peyote plant on Grossman's desk and yanked off one of the buttons. Grossman flipped out, saying he'd been growing it for years. Rebennack shrugged: "As far as I was concerned, he was trying to screw me three ways to Christmas and he'd earned his doom and destruction."

Grossman resorted to a time-honoured tactic, insinuating that he would destroy Rebennack's career. The two men yelled at each other for twenty minutes before Grossman had Rebennack thrown out of the room. The experience seemed to bear out what Bob Dylan had been through: "They'd take money *from* me, on top of the percentage they were taking for handling me," Rebennack recalled. "As soon as I grasped this deal and all that it was about, I said 'Fuck you' and I walked."

Jim Colegrove remembers Bobby Charles introducing him to Rebennack at Deanie's, the social meeting place of choice for Woodstock's music community. "As it got later, the families who'd been having their dinners would leave," says Barbara O'Brien, who waitressed at the restaurant. "And then the party people would come in to start their evenings."

"Deanie's was where the drinking *began*," confirms Maria Muldaur. "For the *serious* drinking, we'd all go to the bar at the Bear." The Bear's handsome bartender Michael Word poured generous shots for the Muldaurs – and for Bobby Charles, Paul Butterfield and Amos Garrett. "They invented a drink called 'The Pretty Bad'," says Maria. "It was fresh-squeezed orange juice, Bacardi rum, tonic and lime, and they would each have some of those while Richard Manuel drank hideous amounts of Cointreau. I'd have a few sips of Grand Marnier and be three sheets to the wind. And that's when we all discovered margaritas."

The Muldaurs, Garrett and Butterfield were hanging at Deanie's one night when Albert Grossman unexpectedly walked in. "He took one look at us", says Garrett, "and he said, 'Well, *there's* a band.'" Butterfield might have been forgiven a certain wariness at the remark. Though Grossman had managed and supported him for over five years, their relationship had been tested during the last days of the Butterfield Blues Band. "Bills weren't getting paid," says Jim Rooney. "Bennett was down in New York running the office and Albert was just not paying attention. The band went away in a flash and Paul never recovered." While horn men David Sanborn,

Trevor Lawrence and Steve Madaio split to join Stevie Wonder's group, three others – Buzzy Feiten, Philip Wilson and Gene Din-widdie – formed Woodstock fusion band Full Moon with keyboard player Neil Larsen. "Full Moon played the Sled Hill, doing jazz rock before it was even labelled," says Jim Weider. "For me it was eye-opening, because they really stretched stuff out, doing funk but with jazz technique over the top of rhythm and blues." After one eponymous 1972 album of Steely Dan-ish instrumentals, the group disbanded. "Clive Davis *loved* Full Moon, but they didn't make it out onto the road," says Lynne Naso. "They couldn't even get out of their hotel rooms." Twenty years later, on 25 March 1992, Wilson was murdered in a drug-related execution in the East Village. "He'd become addicted to bad things," says Naso. "He was always around bad, crazy people, and one of them took his life."

In Woodstock, Butterfield drowned his disappointment in dope and booze rather than reproach his home-town protector. "Paul never called Albert on that whole debacle of the band going down," says Jim Rooney. "And they'd been making good money." Maria Muldaur recalls visiting Butterfield on icy winter nights at his Wittenberg house and finding him "banging away" at an out-of-tune piano. "The only thing that kept him together was his wife Kathy," says Graham Blackburn. "I don't know why he was out of control, other than that he was a basic inner-city Chicago kid."

Grossman may have felt guilty about Butterfield: Michael Friedman has claimed that he "knew that Butterfield was his ward for the rest of his life". More likely, he saw an opportunity to get a deal for a Woodstock supergroup – and in the process get Butterfield and the Muldaurs back out on the road. As it turned out, Maria would soon withdraw from the nucleus, and not just because her husband had taken up with Sheila Moony Rooney. "Paul and Geoffrey and Amos wanted to have a real macho, rock-'em-sock-'em high-energy electric R&B band," Maria says. "So that's what they went off and did."

To his credit, Butterfield wanted the new group to be a properly democratic unit, a sum of equal parts. When they settled on the name Better Days – from a phrase of Bobby Charles's – Butterfield battled Grossman and Paul Fishkin not to have it prefixed by his own name.° With Warner Brothers ponying up a generous $250,000 advance, Butterfield, Muldaur and Garrett took their time assembling a super-hot band. Much of the autumn of 1972 was spent auditioning drummers, bassists and keyboard players, none quite right for the rootsy sound the trio wanted. Billy Mundi tried out on drums, former Jerry Garcia sideman John Kahn auditioned on bass. Garcia acolyte Merl Saunders was the band's first organist. Even Rick Danko tried out.

In October Butterfield and Muldaur found their drummer, nineteen-year-old Christopher Parker. "I was playing around Woodstock in power trios, gospel groups, any band that would have me," Parker says. "I started to notice this guy with a full beard and a big fur hat who was often in the audience. He looked like some wacko Eskimo. I never put it together that it was Butterfield." Parker's first rehearsal with Better Days was at the Muldaurs' place in Glenford, with Kahn and Saunders still in the line-up. "Geoff and Paul were singing together and there was a good friction there," Parker says. "Garth Hudson came by to check it out, and Albert came to check what was happening." This iteration of Better Days played about a dozen shows and even posed for Bearsville publicity pictures at Butterfield's house. Within a month, Kahn had been replaced by Taj Mahal's bassist Billy Rich and Saunders by an old acquaintance of Mac Rebennack's. "Maybe Mac suggested Ronnie Barron, or it might have been Bobby Charles," says Parker.† "Butterfield was

° Muldaur wanted to call the band Success. "There's a couple of publicity photos of us in front of this Nash Rambler automobile with the name Success on it," says Christopher Parker. "I think Kathy Butterfield took the pictures."
† Along with his other grievances against him, Mac Rebennack claimed Bennett Glotzer stole Barron from his band following the release of *Dr John's Gumbo* (1972). It was Barron who'd developed the original "Night Tripper" persona, a

coming from his horn band, which was a virtuoso blues and jazz thing, and he wanted a very different kind of band, with all these disparate influences coming to bear."

Meanwhile, Muldaur was busy reinventing himself, sloughing off his jug-band folkie past and toughening up as a singer. "Geoff brought a lot of music in – Bix Beiderbecke, Nina Simone," says Parker. "He was very eclectic and an excellent piano player and taskmaster. It was like, 'This is how we're gonna do it, and we've got to get the vocals right.' When he'd get his teeth into a tune like Percy Mayfield's 'Please Send Me Someone to Love', he'd research it and really live the song before he felt he could sing it properly." Then there was Garrett, whose playing was the band's secret weapon. "Amos wasn't as funky as some of the guys Paul had played with," says Muldaur, "but the sound he was getting was obviously history in the making."

By the time Better Days started work on their debut album at Bearsville, they had no fewer than four singers: Butterfield, Muldaur, Barron and even Garrett, who added his eccentric vocal tones to the brew. And that's without factoring in the floating presence of Bobby Charles, who supplied the rueful "Done a Lot of Wrong Things" for the record. Charles certainly made a difference to Ronnie Barron, who'd first pitched up in Bearsville on a dark autumn night. "It was remote, cold and creepy," Barron told Tom Ellis III. "I'm a city guy and it was this quaint little town. Then I'm being driven down this long dirt road, and I arrive at this villa in the middle of nowhere. It's Grossman's place." Initially bridling at Muldaur's and Butterfield's manner – "I picked Paul up over my head, and that shocked everybody there" – Barron was soon mollified by Charles. He even came round to Muldaur, saluting him as someone who "helped me find myself again". "People like Bobby

---

character he called "Reverend Ether" who then morphed into the "Dr John" of 1968's exotically sinister *Gris-Gris*. Years later he played on Tom Waits's albums *Heartattack and Vine* (1980) and *Swordfishtrombones* (1983). He died in 1997.

and Ronnie were people we had never seen before," says Maria Muldaur. "We were just hippies, whereas Ronnie had this whole old-school R&B showbiz thing that he did and used to wear all this hairspray." Charles, meanwhile, endeared himself to Christopher Parker by giving him a bejewelled crayfish brooch. "Bobby was an absolute sweetheart," Parker says. "Plus he had a reputation as a killer songwriter, so everybody wanted to sing with him or jam with him or, ideally, co-write with him." Geoff Muldaur was equally entranced: "Bobby said more things during a day than you could have written in five songs. The way he talked, you'd think, 'Fuck, why am I not writing this down.' So that was another flavour that came into the band."

With the album finished, the group embarked on a punishing sixty-date tour of the States that confused many promoters: was this the Paul Butterfield they knew or a totally new entity? Or what? "That whole thing was the worst of Albert," says Paul Fishkin. "He managed them, but he wanted to show Butter that he could be Albert. So he did his classic thing of forcing the promoters to pay high guarantees. He pissed off *everybody*, and he did it because he was Albert. And then ten people showed up in every market because they didn't know that Better Days was Butterfield. The promoters ate it bad and they hated Albert for it." Adding to the friction was the fact that most of the Warners advance went to Butterfield instead of being shared between the band members. "They were bitching and moaning," said Nick Gravenites, whose "Buried Alive in the Blues" – unfinished on Joplin's *Pearl* – was a highlight of the Better Days album. "Albert just said, 'No, forget it. If you're gonna do that, I'm not gonna get you the deal.'"

"Paul and Albert were close in a very measured and secretive way," says Geoff Muldaur. "And that was actually a problem for the band. Our eyes were so closed to business." To Christopher Parker, Bearsville Records was deeply dysfunctional: "By that time it had too many kinds of artist and not enough budget. There was also a lot of peer pressure among the artists, like who got the new Mercedes and was that based on record sales or was it based on who could manipulate Albert to their advantage."

Released in March 1973, *Paul Butterfield's Better Days* was a cracking collection. "New Walking Blues" reworked *East–West's* "Walkin' Blues" as a throbbing cousin of The Band's "The Shape I'm In". "Rule the Road" and "Baby, Please Don't Go" were sultry bottleneck blues, the latter featuring Maria Muldaur on fiddle and backing vocals. Rod Hicks's "Highway 28" was a clarion call to Woodstock itself, complete with namechecks for Garrett, Barron and "Topher" (Parker). If Butterfield was never the most accomplished singer – his growl of a voice remains the template for a thousand mediocre white bluesmen – his harp playing was nonpareil, and Geoff Muldaur was a revelation. "We're the only band around that's playing rooted American music," Muldaur told an interviewer. If it wasn't quite true, it was still a great boast. "It was definitely the furthest Paul ever got away from the Chicago harmonica or horn band sound," Amos Garrett said. "That band was a very unique rhythm and blues band. It incorporated blues influences of Paul's, but it had an acoustic Delta influence of Geoffrey's and a heavy New Orleans feel from Ronnie. My playing was just so strange. It kind of fit in everywhere, in every context."

A second Better Days album, *It All Comes Back*, appeared within months of the first. This time Bobby Charles had four co-credits, including a new version of the beloved "Small Town Talk". He wrote the karmic title track and – with Butterfield – the lustily funky "Take Your Pleasure Where You Find It", a virtual credo for the debauched life of seventies Woodstock: Butterfield himself was in the grip of a cocaine habit, and the rest of the band were hardly immune. "Things were getting difficult for Paul," says Graham Blackburn. "But as long as you could still stand up and play, everything was justified."

"There was a musical evolution but a character *de*volution," says Geoff Muldaur. "That's the sadness of some of this era. The second

It all came back: the second Bearsville album by Butterfield's Better Days, released in 1973

album had too much cocaine on it. There were people who seemed to be able to handle coke, but maybe they didn't do it the way *we* did it." Muldaur had in any case left Woodstock with Sheila Moony Rooney and would eventually – after four solo albums – give up music altogether for several years.*

"Maybe my survival instinct was kicking in," Muldaur says. "The problem with leaving was that I took myself with me, but it really

---

* Muldaur's long silence would be broken in 1998 by the release of a glorious blues and gospel album called *The Secret Handshake*. The album featured such Woodstock/Bearsville alumni as Amos Garrett, Billy Rich and Howard Johnson.

might have saved me. Because it was just getting too funky in Woodstock." Meanwhile, his estranged wife took a chance on a solo deal of her own when she moved to California and – with Amos Garrett playing gloriously behind her – scored a huge 1974 hit with the coolly beautiful "Midnight at the Oasis".

With the Muldaurs gone and Butterfield sinking into addiction, even Bobby Charles fell out of love with Woodstock. Though Grossman offered him a deal for a second Bearsville album, Charles heard too many bad things about his business practices and so extricated himself from his contract. "He and I didn't get along at all," Charles recalled. "He'd say one thing and then do another. When I'd go to sign the papers, he'd have something else on it." Local legend has it that Charles's parting words to Grossman were "*Adios*, motherfucker!"

In 1975 Charles returned to his native Louisiana and spent the remainder of his days there. "I've been to his house recently," swamp-pop legend Johnnie Allan said in 1979. "He lives out in a secluded area of Abbeville, way back in the woods. Bobby's always been a loner." Jim Rooney thinks Charles had got everything out of Woodstock that he was ever going to get. "He was a very sweet person, but he was hard to help," Rooney says. "A friend of mine engineered for him to get his royalties for 'See You Later, Alligator' and he took Bobby up to meet the fellow in some penthouse apartment. Bobby goes, 'So *this* is what you've been doing with all the money you've stolen from me!' That was the end of the conversation."

"Bobby always had someone who was screwing him," says Geoff Muldaur. "He said Levon was screwing him. I'd tell people, 'Levon's always complaining about Robbie, and now Bobby's complaining about Levon!' But we had some times. He once took me to a roadhouse near Lafayette and we watched a cockfight. Then we went around the corner and there was a marquee that said 'Blues Tonight'. Inside the club were Jimmy Reed and Lightnin' Hopkins. That was pretty amazing."

7

"DOPE, MUSIC AND BEAUTY"

In a withering critique of Woodstock published in September 1972 in *Harper's* magazine, writer Peter Moscoso-Gongora declared that "the Woodstock pop-music boom is imploding, eating into itself, trying to stave off the entropy at its core". The town's streets, he wrote, were full of "sad, pathetic people, drawn to Woodstock by the myth", while its few remaining stars wished these "street people" would "disappear somewhere, like under a rock".

Moscoso-Gongora argued that once Dylan, Van Morrison and others had left Woodstock, there was no one to take up the slack. He wrote of "engineers with newly-built studios, waiting for the boom that never came" and noted that both Albert Grossman and Mike Jeffery had "burned their fingers" with performers who were "too wiped-out to put an album together".

"A series of cocky flak-catchers – John Gardner, Jim Rooney, Al Schweitzman, Jon Taplin, Mark Harman, all faceless – exist to keep people away from [Grossman] and say nothing about anything," Moscoso-Gongora observed. "They can all be seen on a late night at the Bear Café next door to the restaurant, with its own kitchen and its own moniker: 'The Cocaine Palace'." John Simon told Moscoso-Gongora he couldn't even go into town any more. "Everyone is plying his tapes," the former Band producer said. "You come up here for privacy and you're bombarded by the lousy groups. The whole town is full of a bunch of poopbutt musicians. Muscle Shoals can offer backup musicians, Grossman's studio can't offer *anybody*."

Outside the immediate orbit of Grossman's mini-empire, however, the Woodstock scene continued to thrive. "There were some very good groups," says Happy Traum, who released *Hard Times in the Country*, his third album with brother Artie, in 1975. "There were the Striders with Robbie Dupree, the Fabulous Rhinestones, NRBQ, Chrysalis, Billy Batson and Holy Moses. You could spend a lot of time talking about all the interrelationships."

"In those days you were able to cluster," says Dupree. "Most of the bands had their own houses: the Rhinestones, my band, and a band called Crackin' that came from the Midwest and were all set to go when Albert picked Bugsy Maugh to be Full Tilt's new bass player." At the Striders' house on Glasco Turnpike, Dupree would regularly come home to find a new set of strangers sprawled on the couch watching TV. "They'd say, 'Who are *you*?' and I'd say, 'I *live* here!' So that was the vibe in Woodstock." According to Dupree, there was a circuit of at least ten decent venues in and around Woodstock – north to Albany and south to New Paltz, east to Saugerties and west to Hunter Mountain – and the Striders played all of them.

Still another home-grown outfit was Bang!, brainchild of former Cyrkle bassist Tom Dawes and briefly the employer of departed Butterfield band guitarist Buzzy Feiten. "Tommy had worked in advertising and made a lot of money by coming up with the 'UNCOLA' campaign for 7 Up," says Jeremy Wilber. "As a consequence he was forced to show up at the Sled Hill every afternoon with a snow shovel's worth of cocaine just to keep those boys in the band. It was the most coked-out group anybody ever saw."[*]

Also forming in Woodstock was Holy Moses, pieced together by guitarists Teddy Speleos and David Vittek with bass player Marty David. "The town was overrun by hippies and tourists and people sitting on the Green," says Christopher Parker, whom Holy Moses had coaxed upstate to be their drummer. "There were multiple leather shops and candle shops, bakeries run by hippies." Soon fronting

---

[*] Along with Wilber himself, Bang! can be seen on YouTube in an ABC News clip about the Sled Hill Café, shortly before it closed in August 1971.

Holy Moses was Billy Batson, who'd surfaced in Woodstock back in 1965 after leaving his native California. Gigging as a solo act at the Elephant one night in 1969, he hung around to catch Holy Moses and got chatting with them after their set. Moving from the Peter Pan Farm to Batson's place on Ohayo Mountain Road, the band was scouted by Albert Grossman, who pencilled in Rick Danko to produce their debut album. "They were kind of like The Band, real funky roots-rock stuff," says Jim Weider. Before Grossman could get them in his clutches, however, they were spirited away from him by Mike Jeffery. "We saw Mike a lot and he would come to

The Mike Jeffery-managed Holy Moses, whose first and only album was released on RCA in 1971

rehearsals," says Parker. "We had our own house on Wiley Lane with a bunch of different bedrooms and walking distance from the town. We played in all the clubs there, and we'd play Port Ewen, Saugerties and Hunter Mountain."

Blending heavy guitar rock with the southern influences of The Band, 1971's *Holy Moses!!* was recorded for RCA at Hendrix's Electric Lady studio in the city. Batson played tack piano and sang in a ragged baritone, while Speleos blazed away on fuzzy guitar lines – a kind of East Coast Crazy Horse with neo-psychedelic edges. "It's hippie rock with these guys who don't really know how to sing," says Parker. "The songs are not that bad, reminiscent of The Band but with darker themes – nothing like 'Rag Mama Rag'."

"The Sad Café" was Batson's snapshot of the Café Espresso, the closing "Bazaraza Bound" an intense epic. "Billy wrote some great tunes," says Jeremy Wilber. "He was a strikingly handsome man with many qualities, except for one little defect, which was that he could not drink a thimble of whiskey without turning into the meanest, most insulting sonofabitch that ever walked the earth." That might not have mattered had Mike Jeffery not lost his clout with the death of his most famous client. "When Hendrix died," says Wilber, "Holy Moses was dropped like a stone."

By the time that band had unravelled – Speleos sloping off with Great Speckled Bird, Parker joining Paul Butterfield – Woodstock was rife with home-grown groups. Like Holy Moses, Hungry Chuck only got to make one album, an eponymous 1972 release on Bearsville that leaned closer to countrified roots rock than *Holy Moses!!* did. Fresh from commitments to Great Speckled Bird, the group's core members – Jim Colegrove, N. D. Smart II and pianist/singer/writer Jeff Gutcheon – teamed up with Amos Garrett and added Ben Keith and trumpeter Peter Ecklund to the mix. *Hungry Chuck* might have been The Band had The Band *really* been "The New Sound of Country Rock", as *Time* described them. "I signed them to Bearsville and we made an album," says Michael Friedman. "I thought it was

terrific, but Albert didn't embrace it. They put it out but didn't promote it, didn't put out any singles. So I was disillusioned at that point,
and the guys were crestfallen because I could probably have got them
a deal with a major label." Though the *Hungry Chuck* album stiffed,
the group's members evolved into a kind of floating session unit at the
Bearsville studio. "People like Colegrove and Garrett were great ad
hoc session musicians," says Jon Gershen, then assisting at the studio.
"They were fast on the uptake and very tasteful."

Hungry Chuck should have gone on to greater things and did start
work on a second Bearsville album, but Garrett's continued involvement was blocked once he'd been recruited for Butterfield's Better
Days. "Albert was shoving his weight around," says Colegrove. "We
had a disagreement at Michael Friedman's apartment in the city,
and it got pretty heated. Michael said to me, 'You were offering to
go out in the hall with him – I'm surprised he didn't go out there
with you.' Because Albert was pretty pugnacious." When Colegrove
demanded to know why Bearsville hadn't pushed *Hungry Chuck*
harder, Grossman protested that the album had been "mixed like it
was a folk record and not a rock-and-roll record". Colegrove countered that "we did it in *your* studio with *your* engineers, so it must
be *your* fault". The longer he knew Grossman, the less he liked him:
"He had a sly, sneaky side to him. He didn't operate on the level and
he had this manipulative power he liked to use on people."

From Hungry Chuck's ashes came an even more ill-fated band.
Jook was formed by Colegrove with Billy Mundi, guitarist David
Wilcox and pianist/guitarist/singer Joe Hutchinson. "They were
real good, the favourite band in Woodstock during 1974 and 1975,"
Amos Garrett said. "But for some reason they couldn't get a recording contract." Despite regular shows at the Espresso and the new
Joyous Lake club, Jook demos made at Colegrove's Artist Road
house never led to anything. Perhaps their progress was blocked by
the unseen hand of Albert Grossman.

⁂

Jim Colegrove played in an early incarnation of yet another local band. Formed in West Saugerties by John Hall – who'd played guitar in the late-sixties band Kangaroo with Teddy Speleos and N. D. Smart II – Orleans was the result of Hall and his wife JoHanna upping sticks from the East Village after their apartment was burgled. After renting for a few months on Ohayo Mountain Road, the Halls used royalty payments from Janis Joplin's "Half Moon" to make a down payment on a house just off Route 212. Soon they were ubiquitous on the Woodstock scene.

While the Halls wrote for other artists, John toured with Taj Mahal and with Karen Dalton.° "I met John through Harvey Brooks," says John Simon. "They'd both played on a Seals and Crofts album I produced, and then I got a call from Taj's manager saying he wanted to put together this tuba band. Howard Johnson was going to assemble the horn section and they wanted me to assemble the rhythm section. So I called John and I asked Billy Rich to play bass and Greg Thomas to play drums." The result was Mahal's delightful live album *The Real Thing*, recorded at the Fillmore East in February 1971.†

As much as he loved Mahal and touring, Hall was keen to make his own mark. "He came home from playing with Karen in Europe," JoHanna Hall told me in the kitchen of the house they bought together in December 1971. "He said, 'I have to start a band.'" That winter, drummer Wells Kelly moved down to Woodstock from his native Ithaca, gigging with Hall and urging

° One of the Halls' songs, the Tymes' "Ms Grace", topped the UK singles chart in January 1975.
† Hall also played on Simon's Warner Brothers solo debut, 1970's *John Simon's Album*, recorded with an all-star cast that included Band members and sat somewhere on the piano-man/songwriter spectrum between David Ackles and Van Dyke Parks. *Journey*, Simon's second (and rather less expensive) Warners album, appeared in 1972 and included both the instrumental "The 'Real' Woodstock Rag" and opening track "Livin' in a Land o' Sunshine", a ten-minute epic about a Catskills summer that featured Dave Holland on bass and David Sanborn on sax.

fellow Ithacan Larry Hoppen to join them. For several months Orleans played around town, switching instruments onstage as The Band had done. "They were doing Hendrix stuff and 'Knock on Wood', different funky things," says Jim Weider. "John's guitar playing was amazing back then."

"They played every weekend, alternating between Ithaca and Woodstock," says JoHanna Hall, who as her husband's co-writer was the group's de facto fourth member. "John and Wells and I would travel back and forth in an old white station wagon." With Jim Colegrove unable to commit long-term to the bass spot, Hoppen's younger brother Lance joined after graduating from high school that summer. Meanwhile, Hall continued to work as a session guitarist at Bearsville, playing with Bonnie Raitt when she came to town to record *Give It Up* in June 1972.

"That summer was one of the coolest, most fun and most creative and most sparking scenes I've ever been part of," Raitt remembers. "It was such a hotbed of creativity and romance. To me at twenty-two, to come from Cambridge and hang out with people like John, it was like Paris in the twenties. I can't say we got a lot of sleep. Jean-Luc Ponty had the daytime session, and we had midnight till 10 a.m. So you can imagine what it was like. I did the whole record on NyQuil and Freihofer's coffee. We would have breakfast at Deanie's and crash, then wake up and have steak and go back into the studio. I probably saved myself from some pretty damaging partying, because we were sleeping when everybody else was revving up."

"Taj Mahal introduced us to Bonnie in New York at the Bitter End," says JoHanna Hall. "I loved her, and she was always the voice I was writing for in my mind." Hall was at Bearsville the night Raitt sang the album's closing track, "Love Has No Pride", a bruising ballad of masochistic need that Libby Titus had co-written with Eric Kaz about Emmett Grogan. "'Love Has No Pride' was what 'I Can't Make You Love Me' has become for me," says Raitt. "It was the

ultimate heartbreak ballad at that point, and I meant every word of
it. I had just been in the middle of a terrible break-up, and my heart
was aching for this person to come back."

By early 1973, Orleans had signed with ABC-Dunhill and were
making their first album in Muscle Shoals. In 1975 they hit big with
the re-recorded "Dance with Me" – originally from the *Orleans II*
album cut at Bearsville – and established a breezy soft-rock style
that earned them a deal with David Geffen's Asylum. Anathema to
the hipper critics, the Top 5 smash "Still the One" – with its creamy
dual lead guitar lines – made Orleans one of Woodstock's major seventies success stories. "They were really the house band here in
town," says Stan Beinstein. "Wells Kelly was the heart and soul of it,
the humour of that band."

"We felt part of the scene," says JoHanna Hall. "We loved *Astral
Weeks*, but we tended to do more three-minute pop songs. What we
were doing was very different – more urban – than, say, the Mud
Acres group." For JoHanna, being a woman in the Orleans set-up
was problematic, especially when the royalties began to roll in. "As a
female on the scene, you were disregarded if you were not a player,"
she says. "There was a lot of resentment towards me." Drugs didn't
help the situation: "John was Mr Clean, but some of the others were
doing cocaine." In 1984, seven years after John Hall left the band,
Wells Kelly died of his excesses in London. "He took a gig with
Meat Loaf," says Stan Beinstein. "He was stone drunk and just had
too much fun. They found him in an alley."

Another of Woodstock's "house bands" was the similarly soft-
rocking Fabulous Rhinestones, led by singer-guitarist Kal David,
who'd moved to Woodstock from California in late 1970 and joined
forces with Harvey Brooks and keyboard player Marty Gregg.
Signed to Michael Lang's Just Sunshine label, for which they made
three albums between 1972 and 1975, the Rhinestones were –
like Orleans – a Woodstock institution. "Their vibes were similar,
and their harmonic sensibilities were similar," says Beinstein. On

the cod-Latin groove of "What a Wonderful Thing We Have" the Rhinestones seemed to pick up where Brooks's former band the Electric Flag had left off.

"There were a lot of musicians and bands in Woodstock that weren't signed to Albert or Bearsville," says Amos Garrett. "Bands like Orleans and the Rhinestones pretty much woodshedded on their own, made their own records and stayed on their side of the mountain." Yet the connections were there all the same: members of both Orleans and the Rhinestones fraternised with – and played on albums by – Grossman-associated artists like John Simon and Paul Butterfield.

An act hatched at Bearsville was Borderline, a trio conceived by Jim Rooney and Jon and David Gershen after Jim and Jon had worked together at Grossman's studio. The Montgomeries having folded, Jon Gershen began working up songs with Rooney at the Cooper Lake home of his girlfriend Barbara. A deal with Avalanche, a label distributed by United Artists, followed. "Obviously Jim was rooted in bluegrass and folk, which was not my thing," says Gershen. "But in a way it was a good thing that I didn't know about the whole Club 47 story, because I might have thought this wasn't a guy I'd have enough in common with."

Borderline's *Sweet Dreams and Quiet Desires* (1973) was a rootsy mix of folk, country funk and pining waltz-time ballads that utilised several of the stellar sidemen who'd played with Bobby Charles: Ben Keith, Jim Colegrove, John Simon, Billy Mundi, David Sanborn et al. Also smuggled into the sessions, under wry aliases, were The Band's Richard Manuel ("Dick Handle") and Garth Hudson ("Campo Malaqua"). "It didn't seem such a stretch to say, 'Let's get Richard and Garth in,'" Jon Gershen says. "Richard got it right away, yet he kept saying things like, 'Are you sure this is good enough?'" Kicking off with Rooney's adapted traditional "Handsome Molly" and concluding with Gershen's aching "As Long as It's You and Me", the album was another example of Woodstock's proto-Americana sound. "I think it's a pretty good document of the Woodstock sound at the time," Rooney says. "It was this neat sound that The Band was the leading example of, but all these great players were around and most of them were on the Borderline album."

After United Artists failed to release their second album, Rooney decided he'd had enough of managing Albert Grossman's studio.[*] In late 1973 he moved to Nashville, where he enjoyed a successful career as the producer of artists such as Nanci Griffith, John Prine and Iris Dement. "I had an instinct that it was time for me to move on," he says. "The local legend is Rip Van Winkle. I had the feeling that the Catskills is a very enchanting place but you could wake up twenty years later and still not be getting anywhere."

Another album featuring a star-studded cast of Woodstockers was the third by British import Jackie Lomax, who had followed in the footsteps of his mentor George Harrison and fallen in love with the town. Lomax's *Three* (1972) was a blue-eyed rock 'n' soul set graced by members of The Band and much of the horn section employed on *Rock of Ages*. "Jackie had a great band," says Christopher Parker. "They played the Sled Hill and it was really powerful, solid English rock." In Woodstock, Lomax took up with former dancer Norma Kessler, who numbered Jimi Hendrix and Kris Kristofferson among her former lovers and was, in Parker's words, "kind of a mover and shaker on the scene". Kessler's eccentric cowgirl outfits so reminded Lomax of Little Annie Oakley that he renamed her Annie. The couple were arch-scenesters in Woodstock, though hardly ideal parents for her seven-year-old son Terry, whose own father – cult fashion photographer Bob Richardson – was a schizophrenic drug abuser and periodic visitor to Woodstock with his young girlfriend Anjelica Huston. "My mom left New York in 1970 and moved up to Woodstock," Terry

---

[*] Borderline's *The Second Album* was finally released by Capitol in Japan in 2001, and then by Real Gone Music/Razor & Tie in 2013.

Richardson said in 1998, by which time he was himself a controversial photographer. "[It was] just to get away from the city and not have to deal with the system or fashion anymore. Be a hippie, grow out her armpit hair, get a job as a waitress in a health-food restaurant. She was like, 'Enough of this fucking city.'"

As amusing as Richardson claims it was to be seven years old in Woodstock – "all the little kids would be running around at one o'clock in the morning . . . I remember making out with Maria Muldaur's daughter Jenni" – the experience was hardly a formula for lasting emotional health. Lomax and Annie Richardson frequently abandoned Terry in order to go out partying. "I remember that I never had a fucking babysitter when I was a kid," Terry said. "And we lived in this fucking house in the woods, which is very scary for a child."

The world of Woodstock's most feted rock group wasn't a lot less dysfunctional than Terry Richardson's childhood. 1972 was a lost year in the life of The Band. All five members went their separate ways. Rick and Grace Danko divorced. Garth Hudson worked on his Glenford house. Levon Helm detoxed from heroin at his parents' home in Arkansas before spending a semester at the Berklee School of Music in Massachusetts. "That winter was great," Libby Titus told me. "Levon was the greatest father, couldn't wait for Amy to wake up in the morning. He even read some books."

Robbie and Dominique Robertson, weary of Woodstock's entrenched self-destructiveness, moved for a period to Dominique's home town of Montreal. She told *Rolling Stone*'s Greil Marcus that Woodstock was "everything people ought to want, and I hate it" – that there was nothing there but, in Marcus's words, "dope, music and beauty". Perhaps overly influenced by the Robertsons' disenchantment, Marcus – whose chapter on The Band in his groundbreaking *Mystery Train* (1975) did much to enshrine the (mostly) Canadians in the pantheon of American music – wrote that Woodstock felt "like a private club, inhabited by musicians, dope dealers, artists, hangers-on . . . it seemed like a closed, smug, selfish place".

As for Richard Manuel, he pretty much did nothing but drink and crash cars, usually in the company of his new crony Mason Hoffenberg. "Mason was still caught up in the whirlwind of the sixties," recalls Robbie Dupree. "He was cloistered in a real small world and he lived with Richard, which was something that was not even *imaginable*." When *Playboy*'s Sam Merrill visited the Manuel–Hoffenberg lair off the Wittenberg Road, he found two chronic alcoholics and a house strewn with dog faeces. Hoffenberg had kicked methadone but was penniless and loudly self-piteous. Manuel, he said, was "really fucked up . . . I was in better shape before I moved in with him, and the idea was that I was supposed to help pull him out of the thing he's in". The latter appears to have been Albert Grossman's bright notion, but then Grossman's track record with junkies was hardly stellar. Hoffenberg further informed *Playboy*'s readers that it was his role "to head off all the juvenile dope dealers up here who hang around rock stars"; instead he and Manuel "sit around watching *The Dating Game*, slurping down the juice, laughing our asses off, then having insomnia, waking up at dawn with every weird terror and anxiety you can imagine".

Jane Manuel had kicked her husband out that summer. "He didn't have the coping skills to survive," she told me in 1991. "People thought it was amusing to watch this guy drowning." With no Band commitments to give him either structure or a simple *raison d'être*, Manuel was disintegrating. When Bob Dylan came by to say hello, he made a swift about-turn after stepping in dog shit.

To fulfil their contractual obligations to Capitol, The Band reconvened at Bearsville Studios in the spring of 1973. This time there was no new material in the can: Robertson had been labouring on an ambitious symphonic piece called *Works* but had nothing tailor-made for The Band's voices. Instead they did what many of rock's sated stars did in the early seventies: they made a covers album. *Moondog Matinee* wasn't terrible but its primary purpose was to tread water while Robertson figured out what to do next. That turned out – after the group's summer appearance at the huge Watkins Glen festival* – to be a reunion with none other than Bob Dylan, who came to Woodstock that summer to discuss plans for a new album and tour. Dylan was impressed by the scale of Watkins Glen and felt a renewed zeal for live performance. The first rehearsals for what became the mega-hyped "Tour '74" took place in Woodstock in early autumn, by which time Robertson had persuaded his bandmates to move with him to Los Angeles. "My thought was, 'Let's get out of Woodstock, we've burned down these woods,'" he told me. "The idea of being by the ocean, it all sounded good. LA was a decadent place, but Woodstock had become that too. Over the years a lot of undesirables had come up there."

Could there have been a more pointed rejection of Woodstock than The Band's relocation to Malibu in October? To leave the woods and mountains of the Catskills for glitzy oceanfront California seemed almost like a betrayal. "It was effectively an act of leaving Albert," says Jonathan Taplin, who accompanied them. "Occasionally Sally would come through California on her way to Mexico or wherever she was travelling. But Woodstock was really not on our radar any more." Robertson had claimed The Band still had "managerial ties" to Grossman, adding rather disingenuously that "I don't know about Dylan . . . they may have something going, but I don't know what it is." The truth was that Robertson – like Dylan himself – was busy being seduced by David Geffen, who'd lured Dylan away from Columbia and was keen to add The Band to his trophy cabinet. In

* For an amusing account of an apoplectic Albert Grossman, see Rock Scully's memory (in *Living with the Dead*) of him threatening Grateful Dead tour manager Sam Cutler at New Jersey's Roosevelt Stadium, just after Watkins Glen. "You cocksucking little limey sonofabitch," Scully claims Grossman yelled. "Your mother fucks sailors in a Buick!" The reason for Grossman's rage? The Dead were being paid more than The Band.

the end, the group were forced to pay $625,000 to get out of their management contract with Grossman.*

Recorded on the hop between rehearsals for "Tour '74", Dylan's *Planet Waves* was no masterpiece but was given unfairly short shrift by critics. "On a Night Like This" galloped along nicely, and "Tough Mama" was satisfyingly funky. "Forever Young" was a more than credible hymn to childhood innocence, while "Dirge" – like other songs hinting at painful cracks in Dylan's marriage – may be the most tortured vocal he ever put on tape. As for the sound of "Tour '74", heard on the double album *Before the Flood*, Dylan's own dismissal of it as "an emotionless trip" has rather sealed its fate. Pampered and coked-out the six men may have been, but onstage they cooked up a din that Ralph J. Gleason – the *éminence grise* of *Rolling Stone* – rightly described as "pulsing, cracking, shaking", driven by Levon Helm's charging grooves and Rick Danko's stubby, undulating bass lines. "The most significant thing about the '74 tour to me was proving that we hadn't been crazy," said Robertson. "It was not incredibly different from what we'd done with Bob before. It was just this kind of dynamics – it got loud and it got soft. We'd come way down when the singing came in, and when the solos started we'd go screaming off into the skies."

That's a fair description of *Before the Flood*'s "All Along the Watchtower", one of the most intense pieces of live rock ever recorded and almost the equal of the Hendrix version. Perhaps power was what Dylan needed after drifting for the better part of eight years. Yet old friends found it as bludgeoning as Dylan himself did. "I found the show powerful in a certain way," Happy Traum noted after seeing one of the three Madison Square Garden shows. "Maybe it was anger that I felt, which is very powerful, but maybe

---

* Geffen claimed he'd made a $10,000 bet with Grossman that he could get an album out of the impossible Bobby Neuwirth. For the full chaotic story, see Al Aronowitz, "A Movie for David Geffen", in *Bob Dylan and the Beatles*, pp. 339–88.

it was a lack of gentleness." Mimi Fariña, who saw the show in Oakland, heard "a branch of that old nastiness coming through, by the intonation of his voice".

"The tour was very lavish," Libby Titus recalled. "It was lots of dope and lots of girls. Occasionally the wives and girlfriends were brought in for shows, but it was all so sad and pathetic." After the LA wrap party for the WAGs and children, the tour was finally over. "Bill Graham had set aside a room for the offspring of all these lunatics," Titus remembered; "for the wives who'd been cheated on and the kids who were destined to be scarred . . ." Dylan, ever restless and never one for commitments that limited him, did not look back.

The Band's exodus from Woodstock marked the close of a chapter in the town's musical history. Grossman was still there and Bearsville was still busy, but the lo-fi, backwoods spirit of Big Pink had gone. "The last time I went back was after I met Jim Rooney in New York," Amos Garrett said in July 1975. "We decided to go up and see how many old friends we could round up. We arrived on a Saturday night, but we couldn't find a soul that we knew. It felt horribly like the end of an era."

8

A HERMIT, A TRUE STAR

Todd Rundgren was always out of step with rock's prevailing trends. While everyone else in his peer group was doing drugs, he refused them. When they stopped doing LSD, he started tripping on mescalin and mushrooms. For him it was a badge of honour to be different.

More than anything, Rundgren liked to challenge his own internal limitations. After 1972's *Something/Anything?* produced a second Top 20 hit, the gorgeous "I Saw the Light", he raced ahead of himself and began constructing his very own sonic laboratory, Secret Sound, in keyboard player Moogy Klingman's loft on West 24th Street in New York. There he set to work on the extraordinary *A Wizard, A True Star*, a stunning roller-coaster ride of genre mutations that to this day sounds more bravely futuristic than any supposedly cutting-edge electronica made in the twenty-first century. Where *Something/Anything?* was full of winsome micro-ballads and boy-in-his-bedroom doodles, *Wizard* was Todd going into full-on prog-psych overdrive.

"Psychedelics brought me to an awareness of myself that I'd had no comprehension of previously," Rundgren told me of his first trips. "I began to see my ego elements as weird, goofy, aberrational appendages." Though he never entirely abandoned the pop-ballad mode of his work to date, the Secret Sound sessions propelled him into a new realm of experimentation. "I had the idea that a synthesizer was supposed to sound like a *synthesizer*, instead of sounding like strings or horns," he says. Along with the electronics and hallucinogenics came an immersion in mystical literature that supported his radical new ideas. "Todd started seeking," says Bebe Buell. "He was asking a lot of questions."

At Bearsville, Rundgren's new path was greeted with mild consternation. For Albert Grossman, the label's resident genius was straying ever further from the blueprint of Dylan, The Band and Butterfield. Not that Rundgren gave much of a damn about that. "Todd just wanted Albert to make everything easy for him so he could be creative," says Paul Fishkin, himself exasperated by Rundgren's wilful disregard for pop pragmatism. "He was off on his psychedelic adventure. And then a year later 'Hello It's Me' becomes a hit, at which point we're up against Todd in a completely different mindspace. With five more potential hits on *Something*, he says, 'No fucking way am I releasing anything else off that album.'" The climax of Rundgren's defiance came in December with a kamikaze performance of "Hello It's Me" on TV show *Midnight Special*, on which he was dolled up like a glam-rock drag queen. "He had iron fucking balls, that I will say," Fishkin laughs. "This is his chance to be Elton John and the Beatles, and he goes on TV with his eyes painted as multicoloured teardrops."

"Todd wouldn't take any advice," confirms Michael Friedman. "And the bottom line was that the public didn't buy it. He wasn't Stevie Wonder, another guy who could do it all but knew how to make commercial records." Equally frustrated was young Marc Nathan, an ardent Rundgren fan who'd dropped out of NYU in 1972 to work as a Bearsville promo man. "Todd's willingness to self-sabotage his pop career was tough," Nathan recalled. "I don't think I ever believed in anybody more than I believed in him, and boy did he become a tough sell at radio."

As he had with Dylan, Grossman indulged Rundgren and trusted in his talents. Besides, he was making big money out of his prodigy's production work. "I don't think Albert kept that kind of distinction between star producer and star artist client," Rundgren told Paul Myers. "I was always problematic that way and it probably would have been worse for a different kind of manager than Albert, who was used to dealing with people who could be very self-directed, temperamental or mercurial." In the summer of 1973 Grossman vowed to make Rundgren the best-paid producer in the world and then delivered on the promise. For Grand Funk Railroad's *We're an American Band* he secured him an unheard-of advance of $50,000. "That was definitely the record that got us out of our East 13th Street apartment," says Bebe Buell, who found a three-storey townhouse on Horatio Street. Soon she was dragging her reluctant beau around town to meet the right scenesters and tastemakers. On her urging he agreed to see a shambolic glam-rock band called the New York Dolls, deeming them a joke but producing their debut album anyway.

Not content with expanding the *Wizard* palette on early 1974's equally diverse and thrilling *Todd*, Rundgren was keen to start a new band as a side project. "Everybody expected him to continue in the realm of *Something/Anything?*," says Buell. "So when he dropped the Utopia bomb, it really caused a lot of unhappiness within the Bearsville hierarchy." Sally Grossman said that the group lost not only her but "hundreds of thousands of people", adding that all they did was "drag Todd down, in my candid opinion". Utopia was nothing short of Todd's own prog-rock band, inspired by Yes and the Mahavishnu Orchestra and featuring both Moogy Klingman and keyboard player Jean-Yves Labat, an eccentric Frenchman as passionate about synthesizers as Rundgren was.

Labat had played with John Holbrook in the obscure Anglo-French group Baba Sholae, staying in touch after Holbrook landed a job in London with synth manufacturers EMS. Hyping Holbrook to Albert Grossman as "the new Glyn Johns", Labat arranged for him to move to Woodstock. Falling in with the Grossman crowd at the Bear, where he had a job washing dishes, Labat even persuaded Grossman to bankroll a recording session in May 1973, agreeing to become "M. Frog" in the process.

Featuring an assortment of players from The Band and Paul

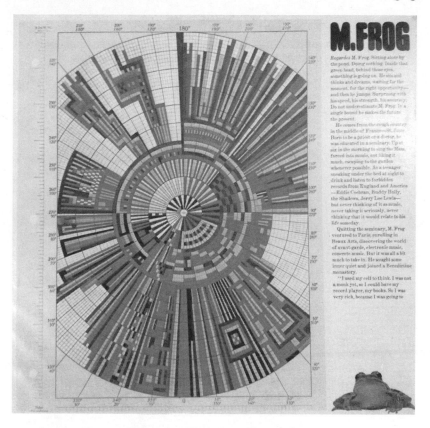

Butterfield's Better Days – as well as Rundgren, who mixed it at Secret Sound – M. Frog remains one of the stranger items in the early Bearsville catalogue. "It had nothing to do with the earthy Band aesthetic," says Holbrook, who engineered and played guitar on it. "I don't think anyone knew what the hell to make of Jean-Yves, but he somehow got people like Todd, Rick and Garth to play on the record." That is doubtless why Julian Cope – no fan of Woodstock earthiness – later championed M. Frog so breathlessly, describing the daft opening track "We Are Crazy" as sounding "like Jean-Pierre Massiera backing a spirited, three-chord/three-IQ band of heavy metal kids by blasting holes through their efforts with excruciating Synthi-A zappings, squiggles and explosions . . ."

"We Are Crazy" formed part of the live set on the first Utopia tour in the spring of 1973, when Rundgren and the band all sported multicoloured hairstyles. Unfortunately the tour ground to a premature halt after an onstage fiasco that inspired one of the most painfully funny scenes in 1984's *This Is Spinal Tap*. "We played one memorable show in Cleveland," Rundgren says, "but we had a disastrous gig in Philadelphia when this big elaborate intro built to a point of thunderous loudness and there was no sound coming out of the guitar amps." More humiliatingly, Jean-Yves Labat was trapped, like Derek Smalls, inside a Perspex geodesic dome that refused to open. "They all walked off stage, and Todd was extremely upset," says Bebe Buell.*

Undeterred – and as stubborn as ever – Rundgren assembled a new line-up for 1974's part-live *Todd Rundgren's Utopia*, an album consisting of three epic prog pieces and the token four-minute pop-rocker "Freedom Fighters". Through it all he was driven and restless, his mind working at five times the speed of everybody else's. "Todd could be quite cutting and sarcastic," says John Holbrook, who mixed the live sound for the Utopia tours. "The road crew had T-shirts made up that said, 'Fear and Loathing in Utopia'." For Buell it was painful to witness Rundgren's withering putdowns. "He did not suffer fools gladly and had very little tolerance for anybody that didn't match his intellect," she says. "Patience was not his strongest virtue."

Though no one could have accused Grossman of being a fool, even *he* was now getting short shrift from Rundgren. "There was a love–hate relationship between them," says Mark McKenna. "Todd was Albert's golden goose – at one point Albert bought him a Lotus for selling so many copies of 'Hello It's Me' – but then he wouldn't lay any more eggs." Things deteriorated so much between the

---

* Labat was eventually fired from Utopia, to be replaced by the more sober and capable Roger Powell. In 1978 the "Frog" man cut the unreleased *Froggy Goes a-Punkin* at Rundgren's Utopia Sound.

two men that Grossman handed over managerial responsibilities to Susan Lee, Paul Fishkin's assistant and the wife of local singer-songwriter Robert Lee. "Susan was the liaison between Albert and Todd," says Buell. "I think she was in love with Todd, as were about seventy-five other women." The twist in this dysfunctional tale was that Susan Lee had recently become Grossman's mistress. "She'd been the manager of the Bear," says Lucinda Hoyt. "She was always inveigling her way into Albert's business deals."

Lee offered Grossman consolation of a sort for his wife's persistent absences. "I never understood the marriage anyway," says John Storyk, who was busy on designs for Grossman's Bearsville Theatre. "Sally was never there. For the longest time I didn't even know they were married." Grossman moved Lee into the Striebel house, the first time he had ever done such a thing. Linda Wortman, rehired by Grossman to run his publishing arm in New York, was no fan of Lee's. "She didn't do anyone any favours, and she certainly didn't do *Albert* any," she says. "I think she screwed around with his head, not only with his body." Lee also ceased managing Rundgren after a screaming fight between her and Bebe Buell at Mink Hollow. "Susan had a hammer and Bebe had a pair of scissors," says Kasim Sulton, Utopia's new bass player. "Todd was in the middle saying, 'Everybody please just calm down!'"

It was Lee who urged Rundgren to invest some of his newfound wealth in a property upstate. Initially he was against the idea: despite the time he'd spent in Woodstock, he did not wish to be part of Grossman's cabal up there. "I thought it was kind of a cop-out moving to Bearsville, and I wanted to keep my New York City edge," he says. "But I was making so much money as a producer and spending so little of it that finally Susan said to me, 'You're just gonna have to buy a house or else the IRS will take your money away.'" In the summer of 1975, with the mystical *Initiation* in the record stores, Rundgren found a house north-west of Bearsville in Lake Hill. "Mink Hollow Road was very isolated, and I liked that," he says. "Plus it had a barn where I could put my studio." The reality of home ownership soon hit him, however: "When I moved in, it was completely unfurnished. It was just me and a sleeping bag. I had to go bed shopping, and I went through little antique shops throughout the Hudson Valley."

Much to his own surprise, the urban wizard took to his new rural life. When *Creem*'s Robert Duncan visited Mink Hollow in the early autumn, Rundgren – with a pair of dogs at his heels – was "squirreling about in the backyard visiting his saplings and his would-be-saplings, his corn, tomatoes and cauliflower, his eggplants". He was even constructing an ornate garden on the property, becoming almost as obsessive a horticulturalist as Grossman. "Todd really worked hard to make that house beautiful," says Buell, who posed for photographer Bob Gruen on the back of Rundgren's lawnmower. "He built a Chinese water pond behind our house. We would go around in the woods looking for moss to attach to the rocks. He was constantly doing things to make the property Zen-like." Rundgren told Duncan he was bored by rock 'n' roll and by "the scene". He was disappointed that "the generation that six years ago was into peace marches" was now "strung out on speed and fucked up". He says it was "time for me to leave the city – to make a full commitment to being by myself and learning about myself".

"Todd was on a kind of spiritual quest at this point," says Buell, who did her best to adjust to country life. "A lot of the songs he wrote were very introspective and extremely complex." In 1976 Rundgren developed his most high-concept Utopia project yet, the Egyptian-themed opus *Ra*. Joining him in the latest line-up was Kasim Sulton, who – against Rundgren's wishes – had been drafted into the group by Roger Powell and drummer John "Willie" Wilcox. "Todd begrudgingly accepted me but didn't talk to me for a year and a half," Sulton says. "The first day I went up to Woodstock, we drove from Manhattan to Mink Hollow in total silence." A giant fan of Rundgren's early pop-rock work, Sulton was thrown by the bombastic pretension of *Ra*. "When I joined the band, the New York scene was glam rock and punk, and here I was in a prog-rock band," he says. "When they told me I had to dress in a toga for the album cover, I cried."

"I wasn't being stubborn for the sake of stubbornness," Rundgren says in his defence. "I considered *Ra* to be a serious relaunch of Utopia, and that was when we got as big as we ever got. But the changing style of music eventually eroded that whole audience. To me, punk was a particularly British phenomenon, albeit inspired by bands like the New York Dolls. In Britain it had a specific political component, and we didn't have the same thing happening in America."

If Grossman was hardly supportive of the stripped-down punk sound that had declared war on mid-seventies excess, he nonetheless couldn't get his ponytailed head around *Ra*. "There was an electric winch that would slowly let Todd down to the stage," says Paul Mozian, road manager on the *Ra* tour. "One night it starts coming down and Tommy Edmonds, the engineer, lets him dangle there for a few seconds." It was all a long way from Dylan at the Gaslight or The Band at Big Pink. "Albert *put up* with Utopia," says Kasim Sulton. "IIe did not care a whit about the group. But I don't think he wanted Todd to leave, because at that point he didn't have that big a stable of artists."

With Bearsville Records at something of a crossroads, Grossman was too distracted to know what to do about it. "I think he could see that the future for records was going to dwindle," says Donn Pennebaker, who remained his friend. "But when you're on a downward slope, nobody wants to help you." Significantly, the main Bearsville office now moved from New York to Los Angeles, home of Warner Brothers. While Paul Fishkin and Susan Lee relocated to the Greif-Garris building on LA's Beverly Boulevard, Grossman expanded the label's offices in Bearsville itself. Assisting him there as his new head of A&R was the straight-talking Scotsman he'd known from London trips dating back a decade.

Billboard's Bearsville spotlight, March 1980

Ian "Ralf" Kimmet had fronted the glam-era UK band Jook – no relation to the Woodstock quartet of the same name – before giving up his pop-star dreams to run Bearsville's UK office out of the Warners building in London. "Albert came to London with Susan Lee," he remembers. "She showed me some recent Bearsville

album covers, and I said, 'They're not very good, *are* they.' I was
a little punky at that point. She wasn't very pleased." In February
1978 Kimmet moved with his young family to Woodstock. Installed
at Bearsville in the middle of winter, he did everything in his power
to make the label more relevant. On the one hand he signed new-
waveish acts such as the Johnny Average Band and Pam Windo
and the Shades, along with soft-rock singer-songwriter Randy
Vanwarmer; on the other he catered to Grossman's vestigial taste
for roots rock and R&B by reviving the flagging career of Paul
Butterfield and putting legendary soul producer Willie Mitchell on
retainer. "My first day at Bearsville, Albert divvied up everything,"
Kimmet says. "It was like, 'Butterfield's yours . . . you deal with
the promo people at Burbank,' and so on. So I started running the
label while he was busy renovating the Bear and building the Little
Bear. I'd constantly have to run around looking for him: 'Albert!
Albert!'"

"I don't think Albert knew which way the wind was blowing," says
John Holbrook, by now the main engineer at Bearsville. "He came
out of the fifties and sixties, when he had a grip on music, but now
it was like, 'What *is* this new-wave bullshit?' He signed Pam Windo
and the Shades because it didn't cost him anything, but he'd say,
'Why are we working with *this* act?' And Ian or Paul Fishkin would
have to answer that question." Bearsville even entered the hitherto uncharted waters of disco, signing both Hot Chocolate's Tony
Wilson and Norma Jean Wright, whose Chic-produced "Saturday"
was a masterpiece of the Studio 54 era and an R&B hit in July 1978.

With Fishkin and Lee three thousand miles away, a schism of
sorts opened up between Woodstock and LA. Despite Vanwarmer
giving Grossman the biggest hit single Bearsville ever had – 1979's
maudlin earworm "Just When I Needed You Most" – Fishkin looked
down on him. "I thought Randy was a lame signing," he admits.
"I was disconnected from it." From the viewpoint of Kimmet –
who'd specially remixed the track with Holbrook, overdubbing an

autoharp part by John Sebastian* – "it became Albert and me here, and 'What the hell's happening in LA?'" Hardly blind to Grossman's flaws, Kimmet remained unflaggingly loyal to him. "Albert had great respect for Ian, who I always thought was a very brilliant person," says Cindy Cashdollar, by then Bearsville's receptionist. "He was almost like Albert's muse. I think he was one of the few people Albert truly trusted."

Perhaps the most divisive Bearsville signing of the period was the bluesy singer-songwriter Elizabeth Barraclough, who happened to be Paul Butterfield's new girlfriend. "Albert was very excited about her," says Danny Goldberg, who briefly did PR work for Bearsville in this period. "He said she was a combination of Dylan and Janis, and insisted that I get high before listening to it." Fishkin, on the other hand, was unimpressed. "Albert thought she was the next Dylan or Joni Mitchell, but she was a wreck," he says. "I hated her and her music. I didn't want money being wasted on his projects." When Grossman flew to LA to ask Mo Ostin to commit to a proper budget for Barraclough – a decent songwriter if an unremarkable singer – he accused Fishkin of neglecting Bearsville acts in favour of his new girlfriend, Stevie Nicks. Fishkin tried to placate Grossman by saying he planned to sign Nicks to Bearsville as a solo artist. Grossman didn't buy it, and additionally blamed Fishkin when Foghat – Bearsville's most dependable cash cow – stopped selling. Secretly he was scared that Fishkin would abandon him. "Susan Lee said to me one day, 'You have to understand, Albert is *terrified* of you leaving,'" Fishkin recalls.

In the end Fishkin *did* leave Bearsville. More painfully for Grossman, it was to start a new label, Modern Records, with Danny Goldberg. "Albert was *extremely* pissed off and threatened legal action," says Goldberg. "He looked at me as having taken Paul away

---

* Sebastian had moved to Woodstock after a period in California, buying a house with the royalties he earned from the theme song to TV show *Welcome Back, Kotter*, a No. 1 hit in the spring of 1976.

from him." It would be Modern, not Bearsville, that launched the solo career of Nicks. "She decided her boyfriend could run her career for her, and Albert sued their asses," says Ian Kimmet. "Paul gave up everything for that."

"Right before I left", says Fishkin, "Albert wanted to leave Warner Brothers for RCA. I was so appalled that he would consider leaving Mo Ostin, because RCA was such a toilet in those days. So that was another thing that made me decide to leave. After he sued me, I went to David Geffen and told him the story. Before I've even finished it, David calls Mo and says, 'Did you know Albert was going to fuck you?' I was like, 'Woah!' I got the best of Geffen in that moment. He was like an animal." After the smoke cleared, Grossman bought Fishkin out for a million dollars. "He was really upset," Fishkin says. "He never got over it, according to Susan. I would see him at conventions, but he was very cold towards me."

Bearsville Records was certainly never the same after Fishkin's departure and replacement by Howard Rosen as VP and general manager. "Albert had Elizabeth Barraclough, Randy Vanwarmer, Jesse Winchester and a few others," says Kasim Sulton. "But it was hardly the stable of Bob Dylan and The Band and Janis Joplin." Though he had worked hard to present a positive image to the industry – going so far as to host a special "Bearsville Picnic" filmed by the BBC for its rock show *The Old Grey Whistle Test* – Grossman's eye was no longer on the prize.* "There was no money left," says Ian Kimmet. "Albert was using it all for the buildings, so he wasn't

---

* Padding around the Bearsville complex in one of his classic buttonless Native American shirts, Grossman informed *Whistle Test* presenter Bob Harris that he preferred working with "more personal artists, even if what they do may not be really important in the historical sense". The hour-long film, shot in the summer of 1977, featured live footage of Foghat, Elizabeth Barraclough, Utopia's *Ra* tour and even the reclusive Jesse Winchester. There were cameo appearances by John Sebastian, a sheepish-looking Paul Butterfield and a visiting Mick Ronson – soon to move to Woodstock – as well as music from Levon Helm and a skeleton version of his new RCO All-Stars. Finally there was footage of Rundgren at work on primitive computer videos in his new Utopia Sound studio.

putting any money into promoting the records. The music wasn't turning him on."

"Albert Grossman was very stand-offish up here," says Ed Sanders, to whom Grossman had always been something of a capitalist ogre. "He had his little empire out there and he kept pumping money into the studio so that big artists would come up to record."

None came bigger than the Rolling Stones, who in the late spring of 1978 booked the Turtle Creek Barn to rehearse for their forthcoming American tour, simultaneously hiring Bearsville's Studio B for their pal Peter Tosh to mix his new album *Bush Doctor*. Keith Richards had just been busted for heroin possession in Toronto when the Stones' circus rolled into town in late May: he had to be carried up to a bedroom by one of the "executive nannies" Mick Jagger hired to mind him. Jagger himself was determined to get healthy ahead of the tour and was often sighted jogging on Bearsville's back roads, tailed by a minder in a Jaguar. Richards did not jog, and played too loud into the bargain. "The first chord Keith played in the Barn, there were a hundred phone calls complaining," says Kimmet. "So we moved them into Studio A."

Periodically the Glimmer Twins poked their heads into Tosh's mixing session. "Keith came in with a big bottle of pharmaceutical coke and dumped a small mountain of it on the table," says John Holbrook, who was engineering the session. "He said, ''Ere, that'll keep you going.' The rastas weren't too keen, though. They didn't really approve." One of the more unlikely guests on *Bush Doctor* was Happy Traum, who received a call from studio manager Griff McCree asking him to come in with his autoharp. Plied with lethally strong ganja, Traum "tried desperately to keep the room from spinning out of control" and to put out of his mind the fact that Mick Jagger was "slouching in a corner". Tosh and his Rastafarian friends also disapproved of their food being prepared by local cook Linda Sheldon, in case she was having her period. "Jagger swings into the kitchen one day", Sheldon remembers, "and shouts, 'Where's this *unclean woman* I've heard so much about?'"

The biggest drama during the Stones' week of rehearsals came when Richards realised his US visa was about to expire. "They had to move all the farm equipment out of this nearby field so a helicopter could land," Kimmet recalls. "Keith climbed aboard, and then they flew him to Paris on the Warners jet. Forty-eight hours later he was back. So that was all very exciting."

Even more exciting for Utopia crew member Tommy Edmonds was being hired as Richards's guitar tech. "When Tommy left he was maybe a hundred and ninety pounds," says Kasim Sulton. "When he came back he was a hundred and twenty-five. I said, 'Tommy, what happened?' He just said, 'Keith.'"

Utopia continued to compete for Todd Rundgren's attention as he juggled the band with his "solo" work. "There was a whole period where I continued to make Todd Rundgren records but only toured with Utopia," he says. "So it became this double life where Utopia was the live thing and drew giant crowds. There was a split in the audience, but there was also a big overlap." Kasim Sulton says he would have given his eye teeth to junk *Ra*'s bombastic "Hiroshima" in favour of power-pop songs like "Couldn't I Just Tell You".*

"Todd felt under duress," says Bebe Buell. "I noticed his boyishness began to diminish. He toughened up and lost a lot of his sensitivity. He became an angry young man." Some of that anger had to do with the affair Buell conducted with Aerosmith singer Steven Tyler – whose daughter by her, Liv, was born in July 1977 – though Rundgren had himself been persistently unfaithful and had recently taken up with a striking Texan redhead named Karen

* When I saw Utopia in 1977, I clung not just to Rundgren's early-seventies gems but to the heavenly songs ("Cliché", "Love of the Common Man", "The Verb 'To Love'") from the previous year's *Faithful*.

"Bean" Darvin. "He never had a shortage of partners," Buell says. "I was just trying to keep up."

Money continued to pour into the Rundgren coffers, especially after he took a punt on former *Rocky Horror Show* star Meat Loaf and his songwriter accomplice Jim Steinman, who'd been turned down by every label (including Bearsville) before landing a deal with Epic subsidiary Cleveland International. "It was one of those circumstantial things," says Rundgren, who assumed Meat Loaf's music was meant to be a parody of Bruce Springsteen. "If any one of the elements was different, we wouldn't even be talking about it. At no point did it look like any sort of slam-dunk commercial success." Recorded partly at Bearsville and partly at Rundgren's new Utopia Sound studio at Mink Hollow, *Bat Out of Hell* – ridiculous and over-blown though it was – went on to sell over 43 million copies. "It's the record I have the fondest memories of, because I was pregnant with Liv," says Bebe Buell. "I had a craving for doughnuts, but every morning I would look in the fridge and they'd all be gone. Meat had eaten them."

Meanwhile, Utopia released the Armageddon-themed *Oops Wrong Planet*, which mixed proto-AOR ("The Martyr") with delirious prog ("The Marriage of Heaven and Hell") and heartfelt anthemics ("Love Is the Answer"). Not that Rundgren's apocalyptic politics ever aligned with those of his peers. "Around 1978 I happened to be on a bus to New York with him and Bebe," says JoHanna Hall, who was getting busy in the No Nukes movement. "I thought, 'This is my chance!' So I went over and pitched him about being part of No Nukes. And he said to me, 'Nuclear waste? We'll just shoot it into outer space!'"

1978 brought the release of *Hermit of Mink Hollow*, a feast of Rundgren melodiousness that included three aching break-up songs about Buell. Ever diffident about the music his fans treasure the most, he now rather disavows the album. "A lot of people are hung up on *Hermit*," he says. "While it has songs I still like to perform, I don't have the same feeling about it as most of the fans who like to hear it performed." By the time the album's bittersweet "Can We Still Be Friends?" cracked the Top 30 in July, Rundgren had in any case moved on to his new obsession: video. Using Bearsville's Studio A as an audio-visual workshop, he monopolised the space where the Stones had rehearsed – and which John Holbrook and others were now keen to retool as a proper recording studio. ("We got so tired of being in the claustrophobic Studio B," says Holbrook, who made his own tongue-in-cheek Bearsville albums as "Brian Briggs". "Here they were in the middle of a forest, and they hadn't even put a skylight or a window in.") When Ian Kimmet asked if they could take over the big room, Grossman demurred. "I can't move Todd out of there," he protested. In the end he gave in, but at the cost of building a hugely expensive state-of-the-art facility for his sometime golden boy.

"Todd told me he wanted to build a video studio and needed me to manage it," says Paul Mozian. "I started looking for spaces in Manhattan, but he said, 'No, you've got it all wrong – I wanna be able to drive down my driveway and go to work.' I said, 'But it's not going to be a commercial venture in Woodstock.' He said, 'We'll figure something out.'" The next thing Mozian knew, Grossman was up and running with the Utopia video studio, just across from his restaurants. "Albert had stayed so far away from commercial pop music that I was so surprised to see his relationship with Todd go on for so long," says Robbie Dupree. "But then Todd was really different from *anyone*. He had a whole planet around him – the women he was with, the studio, his video thing, the Utopia people. It was ToddWorld."

Funded largely by royalties from *Bat Out of Hell*, Rundgren's video studio was a classic case of his being too far ahead of the curve. Despite an early and lucrative commission from RCA – to create a synchronised film for Holst's *Planets* as a vehicle for demonstrating their new SelectaVision CED player – the studio was soon haemorrhaging money. By 1982, when Rundgren's

surrealist-inspired "Time Heals" was the second-ever video broad-
cast on MTV, the operation was causing serious friction between
him and Grossman. "There are people who think Albert should
have kept a tighter rein on Todd's spending," says Bebe Buell. "And
Todd spent a *lot* of money on that place." The following year things
got so ugly between the two men that Rundgren arrived at the studio one morning to find Grossman had superglued the locks shut.
"We were all paying attention to Todd's career," says Ian Kimmet.
"And then he wasn't paying his rent and it got to fighting." One
night when he was onstage, Rundgren said that life as a Bearsville
act was like "being tied up in a bag in a hotel room and having
someone shove an electric curling iron up your ass, turning it on,
and then walking out the door".

Rundgren hardly helped his own cause: after *Adventures in
Utopia* crept into the Top 40 early in 1980, spawning the minor
hit "Set Me Free", his response was to follow it up with *Deface the
Music*, an album of Beatles parodies. With uncannily bad timing, the
album came out three months before the shooting of John Lennon
by a deranged young man whose preferred target for assassination
had been Rundgren himself. When Mark Chapman was arrested
for the ex-Beatle's murder, he was wearing a *Hermit of Mink Hollow*
T-shirt.

Rundgren had other reasons for falling out of love with Woodstock. On 13 August 1980 four masked men broke into the Mink
Hollow house, binding and gagging him and the pregnant Karen
Darvin and then robbing them while whistling his songs. "It was
a horrifying violation," he told Paul Myers, "and it started to make
us feel kind of creepy about living up there." 1981's entirely solo
Healing was written as a therapeutic response to the trauma they
had suffered. Rundgren remained at Mink Hollow, paying the bills
by producing artists at Utopia Sound. For all the years that had
passed since his arrogance rubbed The Band and Badfinger up the
wrong way, little had changed in his modus operandi. Even those

visitors who loved the location were treated with veiled disdain
by their host. "His people skills are like Hermann Goering's," said
Andy Partridge, for whose band XTC Rundgren produced the brilliant *Skylarking* (1986). "I remember talking briefly to a couple of
the Psychedelic Furs," says John Holbrook. "They were like, 'That
fucking guy, we're never going to work with him again.' With Todd
it was always like, 'That sucks, let *me* do it.'" Utopia Sound clients
would often climb the stairs to the studio's control room to find their
producer with his feet on the console reading a book. "I *can* read
and listen to music at the same time," Rundgren protests. "When
you're in the middle of a session where the band is dithering, you
can make suggestions or you can let the whole thing run its course."

"Working with Todd wasn't really great," admits Jules Shear,
whose 1983 album *Watch Dog* was recorded at Mink Hollow.
"Producing probably wasn't what he really wanted to do. We did the
whole record in two and a half weeks, including the mixing. I kind
of liked the way he worked. A lot of people seemed to feel slighted
by it, but I didn't." Indeed, Shear was so taken with the Woodstock
area that after the sessions he decided to stay there. "Todd was
really nice to me," he says. "He said, 'Just stay in the house till you
find a place.'"

By 1986, the writing was on the wall for Utopia. With the group
playing to half-empty houses, Rundgren spent increasing amounts
of time in the Bay Area, where the computing industry was evolving
in leaps and bounds. After the vocal-only *A Cappella* was shelved
by Bearsville in 1984, he decided enough was enough. "Albert
connived that the album was not acceptable," he says. "I'd worked
really hard on it and thought I'd achieved as complete a concept as
I'd ever visualised, and yet he refused to accept it. This went on for
a year, and I was just freaking livid." The last time Kasim Sulton saw
Grossman was at the last meeting to discuss Utopia. Afterwards,
when the band left Bearsville, Mo Ostin signed Rundgren to
Warners – with Grossman retaining the publishing. "I settled for

that," says Rundgren. "It meant I didn't have to deal with him any longer."

Rundgren continued producing at Utopia Sound before making a permanent move to California and recording the R&B-infused *Nearly Human*. Sally Grossman loved the album and threw parties for him on its May 1989 release. "People were not interested," she said a decade later. "And they're still not interested. It's like this complete perception problem. I mean, it gets scary when you can't sell a hundred thousand records."

"The fact that Todd did exactly what he wanted, and didn't bend to trends, is admirable," Patti Smith says in his defence. "He's always had very revolutionary ideas. He's not just rebellious, he actually has a very strong, articulate philosophy and he backs it up with action." Though he's influenced a hundred acts from Prince to Hot Chip and Tame Impala, Todd Rundgren remains the cult hero's cult hero: Albert Grossman's last prodigal son and Woodstock's last true star.

9

TUESDAY NIGHT FEVER

Walk through the centre of Woodstock at night and it's difficult to picture the scene that would have greeted you forty years ago. The place is not quite a graveyard, but it can be eerily quiet after dark. Back in the early seventies the little Catskills town buzzed with nightlife, street people, the assorted flotsam and jetsam of the post-sixties counterculture. "There were bars everywhere and no cable television," says *Woodstock Times* editor Brian Hollander. "People had to come out at night if they wanted entertainment."

Though the Elephant and the Sled Hill Café were gone by 1972, the Café Espresso still featured live music, and new venues popped up to fill the vacuum. On the site of the old Brass Rail, on Rock City Road, Rosa's Cantina hosted folk singers and poetry readings. On the same street was Richie Mellert's Village Jug, which had opened in the spring of 1968. Out in Mount Tremper was the White Water Depot, while close to Bearsville sat the Watering Troff – in Hollander's words, "a bucket-of-blood kind of bar, with fights in the parking lots and a lot of people drinking really hard and playing country music". The Troff had taken over the premises from Bernard and Mary Lou Paturel's Country Pie and drew an eclectic mix of bohos and local working people. "The rednecks and the artists would get together there and drink," says Hollander. "It wasn't as chic as the Bear, but there'd be city transplants, gay guys sitting at the bar and drinking with the cowboys." Hollander's future wife, Fran Bruno, rounded up aspirant performers for the bar's Sunday jam sessions. One was Cindy Cashdollar, who in 1975 returned from eighteen feckless months in Florida. "The Troff was a really good

education in just playing with people," she says, "as well as playing whatever form of western swing there was in Woodstock at that
time. It was where I started playing dobro. Everybody was very nice
and very generous in allowing you to sit in."

One establishment, however, defined Woodstock's live music
scene in the seventies. "The Joyous Lake was wild," says Michael
Lang, "in a country kind of way." The Lake was an archetypal
Woodstock story. Ron and Valma Merians had begun visiting the
town in the late sixties, renting a house on Plochmann Lane that
became a weekend hangout for the likes of Mike Jeffery and Bob
Richardson. "Cass Elliot came to stay," says Valma. "We were very
friendly with Peter Max when he was working for Milton Glaser.
There were people who were living in the Woodstock area that were
not hippies, who were very special and educated people. Plus we
were rich! We weren't walking around putting flowers in our hair."

Ron Merians was the Brooklyn-born son of Russian and Polish
Jewish immigrants, his father a manufacturer of orthopaedic shoes
in Manhattan. In swinging sixties New York he'd veered away from
podiatry and fallen in with the beautiful people. A marriage to his
high-school sweetheart broke up when he met Valma at the Dakota
on Central Park West. "He was a very magnetic personality," says
the woman who'd worked as a model in London and been photographed by David Bailey. "He had a good rap and he took my
breath away." Through Valma, Merians landed a job with ad agency
Ted Bates, for whom Valma had modelled in a campaign for Kool
cigarettes. In a storyline straight out of *Mad Men*, the agency's then
president Barry Ballister dropped out of the rat race and moved up
to Woodstock, later opening the farmers' market Sunfrost Farms
near Bearsville. "Ron had been working with Barry," says Valma.
"One day he says to me, 'How would you feel about moving up
to Woodstock full-time? I don't want to raise our children in the
city.'" The Merianses were already living on Plochmann Lane when
Michael Lang invited them to the Woodstock Festival. "We had a

BMW motorbike we'd imported from Munich," says Valma. "We decided to take a ride down to the festival, where Michael gave us backstage passes." The festival confirmed they were in the right place at the right time: Woodstock had become the East Coast vortex for the Aquarian Age.

The following year the Merianses opened a macrobiotic food store and juice bar on Mill Hill Road. Naming it the Joyous Lake after throwing the *I Ching*, they quickly attracted the town's in-crowd. "Lots of people came up to Woodstock after the festival," says Valma. "And it was like, 'Where do you go?' Well, you went to the Lake, where there were great vibes and good food and everyone was friendly. It

Opening Mid-August

Joyous Lake

was kind of like hanging out on the King's Road in Chelsea."

Along with the influx came Albert Grossman. "People were always complaining about him, but to me he was a special soul," Valma says. "I adored him, though I never had anything to do with him business-wise." Rather less adorable was Tim Hardin, who often dropped in to demand that Valma cook for him. "He just seemed like such a pathetic person," she says. "So I cooked him sautéed chicken with grapes and brown rice, and he fell in love with it. A couple of days later he comes in with a guitar and asks for more food." Another customer was Charles Mingus, who came with his wife Sue. "They ate at the Lake a lot," Valma says. "He'd show up in the morning and say, 'I need some of your oatmeal, lady!'"

Both Hardin and Mingus performed at the Lake after Ron decided in 1972 to build a small stage in the restaurant. Inspired by the Trident in Sausalito, the Merianses took a leaf out of Grossman's book and hired the finest local carpenters to fit the place out. They also installed the best sound system money could buy, with speakers embedded in the ceiling to disperse the music. "The sound would rain down on you," says Jim Weider. For Martha Velez, whose son Taj played with the Merianses' daughter Three, the Lake was "a very prestigious venue, with good sound and good lights". The food from the open kitchen was great and the underdressed waitresses almost as edible. "I only hired beautiful women, it's terrible," says Valma. "No, it's not terrible, it's *true*!"

"The Lake was jumping when I moved here," says Ian Kimmet. "I'd sit outside with Albert and Barry Feinstein, and there were people queuing round the block. It was the centre of everything." For many people, weekends entailed a ritual of starting at Deanie's and heading up to the Lake – and then ending up back at Deanie's for breakfast.* To folk guitarist Peter Walker, Ron Merians was "the

---

* After his original restaurant burned down in 1974, Deanie Elwyn bought the old Town House, a gay-friendly establishment opposite the Woodstock golf course, and reopened Deanie's there.

same kind of hero that Albert was . . . he created something out of nothing, and it was the best scene in the world".

Though regular live attractions at the Lake included local favourites Orleans, the Striders and the Fabulous Rhinestones – along with the Traums, the Muldaurs, Paul Butterfield and more – the place also became an essential stop for touring stars like Bonnie Raitt, Dr John, Johnny Winter, Taj Mahal, Joe Cocker and John Hammond. Jazz, blues and funk acts, too, were well received. "Ron and Valma were very wise to the New York scene," says Christopher Parker, who played at the Lake with Raitt, John Hall and others but was also part of a super-hot jazz-funk band that had recently formed in the city. Dubbing themselves the Encyclopedia of Soul, bassist Gordon Edwards, pianist Richard Tee and guitarist Cornell Dupree had all contributed to landmark R&B sessions in New York studios. In 1974 they began playing Mondays through Thursdays at Mikell's on Columbus and 97th, bolstered in due course by the additions of guitarist Eric Gale and drummer Steve Gadd. "When I came back to Woodstock, Butterfield said, 'Gordon ruined you!'" Parker says with a laugh. "I said, 'Whaddya mean?' He said, 'Well, you had this great feel and now you're like a metronome.' Which was the point: I wanted to play perfect time, rather than in that looser Chicago groove."

One night in 1975 Michael Lang walked into Mikell's and was blown away by the Encyclopedia of Soul's slick Crusaders-meets-Steely-Dan grooves: Tee's churchy chords, Dupree's biting fills and the double rhythmic dynamo of Parker and Gadd. Lang paired the band with Joe Cocker, whom he managed, and subsequently made a deal for them – as Stuff – at Warner Brothers. When he pointed them in the direction of Ron Merians, Stuff became a fixture at the Joyous Lake, spending whole weekends upstate. "I loved that band," says Jim Weider. "The grooves were ridiculous: Steve and Chris together were mind-blowing, and Richard Tee's rhythm would just float with the gospel influence of his chords. That band was giant for me in this town, and they liked it up here."*

Along with Stuff, jazz icons such as Jack DeJohnette, Gary Burton, Chico Hamilton, Dexter Gordon and Chet Baker all played the Lake. Mingus's 1976 set took place on a December night so cold he arrived with snow in his beard. Lake jams, meanwhile, became semi-legendary. "I saw a lot of them," says Jim Weider. "Bobby Charles would sit in with John Hall and Stuff. Butter would always come down and jam." Harvey Brooks says wintertime was prime jamming season, since no one had anything else to do. He singles out as a special memory a "snowy evening" that involved himself, fellow Fabulous Rhinestone Kal David, Jack DeJohnette, Howard Johnson and David Sanborn: "We played till breakfast." The Lake also hosted shows by Chicago blues stalwarts Muddy Waters, Willie Dixon, James Cotton, and Sonny Terry and Brownie McGhee.

"Everybody talks about the Lake as a big party place, and it was, but the music was incredible," says Jane Traum. "The people that played there, in this little town, it was staggering. If we were coming back from New York, we'd say, 'Let's just stop by and see who's playing at the Lake.' And nearly always it was somebody you really wanted to see – whether it was Stuff, who were sensational, or little bands like Country Cooking. It was so eclectic."

To describe the Joyous Lake as a "party place" is one of the great understatements. Like a rural outpost of Manhattan's most decadent haunts, the club quickly succumbed to the cocaine epidemic ripping through mid-seventies America. "I probably spilled more coke in that place than most people snort in their lives," says Kasim Sulton. "It's not something I'm proud of, but at that point cocaine, marijuana and alcohol were all you did all day and night. If you want to see my first house, get a camera and stick it up my nose."

* Among the more unlikely artists that Stuff backed was Fred Neil, whom Michael Lang still managed. They played behind him on an unreleased album cut in New Jersey in 1978.

For local writer Martha Frankel, who worked as the Lake's cashier, it was as if all Woodstock's grown-ups had vanished and left a bunch of insane children to run the show. "Almost all the business owners, chefs, bartenders, and town officials were play-acting at being adults," she later wrote, "and yet there they were, out front and in charge." Like everyone else who worked for the Merianses, Frankel witnessed scenes of hedonism and promiscuity that would make her hair curl today. "The waitresses at the Joyous Lake wore tiny little short-shorts and bandanas tied strategically around their breasts," she wrote. "When they went missing for fifteen minutes, you knew they were either getting high in the walk-in or giving blowjobs in the bathroom." The sex-for-cocaine culture then rife in rock 'n' roll was in full flow at the Lake, particularly in the infamous Green Room upstairs. "When you went through that door, you never knew what you were going to see," says Linda Sheldon. "Nine times out of ten it was somebody getting a blowjob. Lotta girls got in for free that way." Nobody talked about sexual harassment, Frankel wrote, because "nobody cared".

Things became markedly more debauched in the bacchanalian era of disco. Though Woodstock was a long way from the world of *Saturday Night Fever*, the Lake's weekend clientele brought a touch of Studio 54 glamour to Mill Hill Road. In the words of Catskills jeweller Robin "The Hammer" Ludwig, "it was where Woodstock met the jet set . . . elite counterculture". If the seventies had begun as a post-radical Me Decade, cocaine – the ultimate ego enhancer – turned it into the Me First decade. Never one to pass up a commercial opportunity, Ron Merians introduced the Lake's first "Disco Night" in 1976. Spinning the discs was Linda Sheldon, who'd deejayed in a club in Rochester and befriended the Woodstock bands that played there. "The Rhinestones would say, 'You gotta come to Woodstock,'" she says. "They kept talking to Ronald, who called me and said, 'They tell me I have to have you.'"

Woodstock shocked Sheldon. "You have to remember what the

town was like in 1976," she says. "There were crazy people *every-where*." Characters with nicknames like Juicy Brucey, Liquid Lloyd and Magic Markie were stuck in a lysergic time warp while the new funky-but-chic crowd colonised the Lake and – when they hadn't hoovered up too much appetite-suppressing powder – ate steaks at the Bear. "The Lake was only three bucks at the door, which people from the city would laugh at," says Sheldon. "But everybody drank when they danced. It's hard to believe now, but there would be two or three hundred people in that little building."

Sheldon's Tuesday "Disco Nights" took off so quickly that Merians was forced to start a bigger night on Fridays. "The thing that made me a little different was that I played the Stones and Elvis Costello, because I felt all that stuff was danceable," Sheldon says. "I was a little miffed at the beginning that I was having to spin disco records, because I was, y'know, too good for that!" She soon got the twelve-inch bug, however. One night, "high as a kite", she looked down from her booth to see a half-soused Paul Butterfield shouting up at her. "I wanna hear 'The Rubberband Man'!" he yelled through the music. "That was Paul's favourite song," she says. "So whenever I saw him I'd mix the Spinners in." One morning Sheldon picked up the latest *Woodstock Times* to find Merians had placed an ad announcing "Dance Night! With Disco Linda!" It's a tag she's never quite shaken off: "Even today, if I go in the meat market, it's like, 'Hey, Disco, how's it goin'?'"

Sheldon was at the Lake the night the Stones booked it to celebrate the birthdays of Charlie Watts and Ronnie Wood. "Ron Merians was no fool," says Stan Beinstein. "He said, 'They're gonna leave town in five days and I'm gonna get stuck with five grand's worth of food and booze. If they're gonna throw a party, they're paying for it.' Everybody went, 'Are you crazy?' But Jagger respected it. And that night I wound up in a conversation with Charlie, Artie Traum and Albert Grossman. I got Charlie's ear by telling him about the night Mingus played."

Though Merians hated punk rock and would have kept it out of the club if he could, he was obliged to make the occasional concession to the abrasive new sounds coming up from the city. "One rainy Thursday night Ron put the Talking Heads on when they were still a trio," says Beinstein. "There's, like, eight people in the room and he says, 'Get this shit off my stage.' People said, 'Ron, these are the darlings of CBGBs! They're the Talking Heads!' He said, 'I don't care if they're the Flaming Assholes, get 'em off the stage!'" In time, however, the Lake became home to local new-wave acts like the Johnny Average Band, fronted by English guitarist Mick Hodgkinson and his wife Nicole "Nikki" Wills.*

Merians and his wife were a volatile combination. "When I first met them, they were living down at the end of Deming Street and they were all lovey-dovey," says Linda Sheldon. "Ron was this cool guy from the city and Valma was really beautiful. They had three kids. But things started going bad, and when they went bad they went *really* bad."

"There were extraordinary nights with Butterfield and Danko and Orleans and Richie Havens, but Ron was having too much fun," says Stan Beinstein, who promoted Lake shows on Radio Woodstock. "He and Valma were coming apart at the seams. I would get a phone call from him at ten-thirty in the morning: 'I'm comin' down with some cash, I gotta get this on the air.' At eleven o'clock *she's* calling: 'Cancel everything!' It was like nobody was in charge any more." Martha Frankel wrote that the Merianses fought like "demented, brain-damaged boxers, throwing pitchers of beer at each other", yet minutes later they'd be "kissing while they sautéed garlic and shrimp with lemon and tomatoes". The Lake's staff were

---

* Hodgkinson had moved to Woodstock to play with Elizabeth Barraclough. He then formed the retro-slanted Johnny Average and the Falcons, a fluid fixture of late-seventies Woodstock whose members included fellow Brits Ian "Little Roy Watson" Kimmet, John "Brian Briggs" Holbrook and Mick "Shane Fontayne" Barakan.

a drug-crazed family, forced to take sides in the marital wars. "You always felt you were being dragged into the middle of this melo-drama," says Sheldon. "At the end it got really, really fucked up."

In 1978 Valma Merians took up with record producer Eddy Offord, who'd been brought over from England by Albert Grossman to engineer tracks on Utopia's *Ra*. Smitten by the beau-tiful Mrs Merians, Offord watched her marriage unravel and then "just swooped in and went for it". The couple's elopement signalled the end of the Merians era in Woodstock. Interviewed at the Lake as he was "about to tear it down", Ron talked of wanting a better quality of family life. Within a year he'd moved to California. "He never even said goodbye," says Linda Sheldon. "The next thing you knew, Valma and Eddy were in the city. And after they were all gone, nobody much talked about them any more."

Valma Merians disputes that the Lake closed because of drugs and divorce. "It closed because it was over," she says. "Ronald and I drove this comet across the sky for ten years, and then it was the eighties. The whole business was changing. I remember talking to Albert about how bigger venues were coming in. People weren't just coming up the road and playing at the Lake on their way to somewhere else." Under new management the Lake reopened, but it was never the same. "The Sanchez family took it over from Ron," says Sheldon. "And then the next owner ripped everything out, all the beautiful carving, all the mahogany, and turned it into, like, a bar in Newburgh. 1986 was when everything seemed to go by the wayside. The last three years were horrible. A job I had absolutely loved had turned into something I detested."

Ron Merians died in 1989, aged just fifty-five, after suffering a massive brain aneurysm. He'd moved back to the East Coast and was even talking to his old Woodstock friends – Peter Max, Michael Lang – about starting again in the town with a new club. Fifteen years later film-maker David McDonald made a documentary about the town's wild countercultural history, *Woodstock: Can't Get There from Here* (2005), in which he trained a laser beam on the torrid life of the Lake using black-and-white photographs by Howard Greenberg to tell the story of the Merianses and their infamous establishment. One of the more salacious images showed Ron snorting cocaine. After showing the film in Saugerties, McDonald received a call from a New Jersey lawyer threatening to keep him in litigation for the rest of his life. "The guy said, 'This film will never see the light of day,'" says Stan Beinstein. "So the wheels of paranoia continue to spin." McDonald was even accused of anti-Semitism by people demanding to know why he'd targeted Merians but hadn't condemned Ralph Whitehead. "I got this feeling that I'd touched some kind of nerve," he says. "But I also thought I was just telling the truth."

Still married to Eddy Offord, Valma prefers to remember the crazy fun of those high times. "Everybody loves negativity and sensational journalism, but that wasn't what it was about," she says. "I don't want to hear about the bad drugs. Everybody was having a good time. Whatever his faults, Ron was a great guy. They'd never seen the likes of him in Woodstock before, and he always loved people. He was a good soul."

10

FORBIDDEN FRUIT

On Valentine's Day in 1975, a hundred or so hardy souls huddle together on Woodstock's frigid village green to witness an unusual event. America's greatest living bluesman, McKinley "Muddy Waters" Morganfield, is being presented with the keys to the town. "To see the whole place turn out for Muddy, right on the green, was really something," Levon Helm will recall years later. "He got out of the car and everybody started applauding. And I swear he had a tear in his eye."

Helm has just wrapped a two-day recording session with Waters at the Turtle Creek Barn. For the Band drummer, bringing the Chicago bluesman to Woodstock is almost the crowning moment of his own career as a musical disciple. To him, Waters is the real unvarnished thing, a high priest of the blues. "He had a face like a king," Bobby Charles, whose song "Why Are People Like That?" will kick off *The Muddy Waters Woodstock Album*, will say. "He *was* a king."

The Turtle Creek sessions, produced by former King Records legend Henry Glover for his and Helm's new production company RCO, are also a bracing tonic for a southerner who feels sated by the overly sweet life of southern California – a chance for Helm to get back to his roots not only with Waters but with Paul Butterfield, who jammed with Waters as a teenager. Joining those three men in the barn are Garth Hudson, who plays organ and accordion on the album, and The Band's go-to horn man Howard Johnson.

If Helm has enjoyed the fringe benefits of Bob Dylan's "Tour '74" – not to mention the Malibu lifestyle that Dylan has plugged The

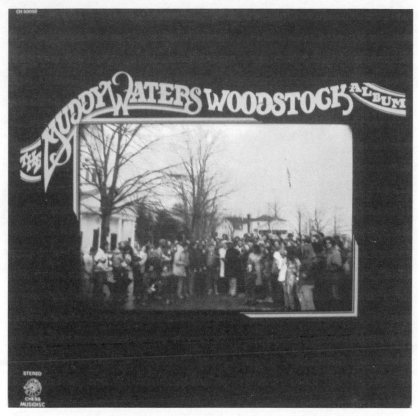

A blues titan comes to the Catskills, February 1975

Band into – in his gut he feels uneasy about all of it. The problems
the group suffered in Woodstock are only exacerbated in California.
"Levon knew it was all wrong, and he wanted to get the fuck away
from it," Libby Titus will say. "On the surface it was all so beautiful,
and underneath everything was so rotten." (Titus's own addiction is
in full flow at this time. According to Al Aronowitz, she embarks on
an affair with Eric Clapton while still with Helm.) By the spring of
1974, not only have Titus and Helm split – Titus taking up with Mac
Rebennack, Helm with his future wife Sandy Dodd – but Helm
has come to believe that Robbie Robertson was only lobbying for
The Band to switch coasts out of self-interest. Long intrigued by

film, Robertson now has an in with Martin Scorsese, whose *Mean
Streets* was co-produced by Jonathan Taplin. "Robbie was obviously very ambitious and socially very adroit," says Peter Coyote.
"At Emmett Grogan's wedding he was wearing a turtleneck sweater
and jacket. And I thought, 'Wow, this is a very sophisticated guy, this
isn't Scruffy Eddie on the hill at Woodstock.'"

The Band's other members have found it trickier to adapt to
the chic milieu of Malibu. "We were like fish out of water," Libby
Titus will say. "It was a floating gold iceberg, white beach houses
and $3,000-a-month rents, but it was all completely unreal."
Especially displaced is Richard Manuel, who was never cut out for
the Hollywood rock lifestyle and who has begun a chaotic relationship with new girlfriend Arlie Litvak. "Richard was renting a place
Goldie Hawn owned at Point Dune, near where Dylan had his
domed house," says Ronnie Lyons. "He tried to kill himself several
times there. He almost burned the house down after trying to set
himself on fire. Then he shot himself in the head with a BB gun. I
don't know how he went so crazy."

Nor is it just Manuel who experiences the dark side of La-La
Land. Rick Danko will tell Al Aronowitz that someone came to his
house and killed himself right in front of his second wife Elizabeth.
"They were rolling in the excess of the time," says Peter Yarrow.
"Not all of them. There was sane Robbie and there was Garth. But
Rick was one of the looniest people I've ever known. The results of
improvident living had come home to roost."

By the time Muddy Waters's Woodstock album was released
in April 1975, Levon Helm had returned to LA, where Robbie
Robertson was finishing up a new project: the exhumation of the
fabled basement tapes, hitherto available only in selections on
bootlegs like *Great White Wonder*. Did Dylan want those tapes
released or had Robertson pressured him into doing The Band
a favour? And was the double album Columbia released in June

1975 an authentic document of what Garth Hudson had taped at Big Pink?

In time it transpired that Robertson had not only cleaned up the sound but overdubbed new parts onto the original reel-to-reel tracks. More disingenuously still, the songs featuring Helm post-dated the 1967 basement recordings and were taped either at the Wittenberg Road house he shared with Rick Danko or during demo sessions for *Music from Big Pink*. (Robertson and engineer Rob Fraboni even remixed tracks such as "Yazoo Street Scandal" to make them sound muddier than they actually were.) Yet "the Historic *Basement Tapes*" made for a rollicking good listen all the same, vin-dicating the underground hype that had followed them around for seven years. The best Dylan songs exuded the spirit of stoned glee that he and his Canadian henchmen experienced as they opted out of the Summer of Love. Though the Dylan cognoscenti bemoaned the absence of "I'm Not There", "Sign on the Cross" and "I Shall Be Released", reviewers warmed to the soaring choruses of "Goin' to Acapulco" and "Open the Door, Homer".

Robertson was simultaneously supervising sessions for The Band's next album. Both projects were worked on at Shangri-La, the group's new studio-cum-clubhouse at Zuma Beach, though get-ting all five of them together under one roof proved as challenging as it had been in Bearsville. It was no coincidence that the opening song on *Northern Lights–Southern Cross* was a coded commentary on heroin addiction called "Forbidden Fruit".

Touring the album in early 1976 turned out to be the last straw for Robertson. Fired up by the sideline career he'd started as a producer – working with Neil Diamond on *Beautiful Noise* – The Band's de facto leader felt growing resentment from Helm and growing alarm at the state of Manuel. "I was really concerned about Richard," he told me. "His health was failing. And it was like, 'We've got to figure out how to avoid putting him in situa-tions he can't live up to.'" Tired of being the group's only grown-up,

Robertson pondered ways to wind The Band down: "I said, 'Maybe we should take a period of time and really concentrate on writing and helping Richard to get his health organised.'" Perhaps he even realised that Los Angeles was not the wisest choice of environment for Helm and Danko, let alone for Manuel. "The whole atmosphere over the music scene at that time, there were some dirt clouds going over," he said. "I was seeing a lot of people in bad shape, and we weren't doing so good ourselves. I just thought, 'We've gotta get off the road.'"

In the summer of America's bicentennial year, Robertson aired the idea of a farewell show that would give him the exit he needed. His bandmates may not have grasped the full implications of the event he was planning with Bill Graham at Winterland, where The Band had played its first show. "I thought, 'Why don't we have this celebration where we do something really musical with a bunch of our friends that we really love?'" Robertson says. "It all just felt really good, and it started out that it was just going to be Ronnie Hawkins and Bob Dylan. And then it was like, 'Well, if we're gonna invite them, we should invite him and her . . .' So it naturally grew and then took on this thing of wanting to represent the different flavours of who we were."

Through Jonathan Taplin came a meeting with Scorsese, who instantly said yes to the idea of filming the Thanksgiving Day show. Everyone except Helm was excited. "It wasn't really his thing," Robertson says. "He was just going along with all of this." Ironically, many viewers of Scorsese's film of "The Last Waltz" thought that – for all the camera's feasting on Robertson's smouldering good looks – it was Helm who stole every scene he was in. "*He* was the one who garnered all of the Band charisma," says Robbie Dupree. "*He* was the one who always said something that was quotable, while Robbie just appeared to be lip-synching."

What really irked Helm about "The Last Waltz" was the last-minute decision to shoehorn Neil Diamond into the show. ("What the fuck is *he* doing there?" asked Albert Grossman, who'd flown in from New York.) For Robertson to justify Diamond's inclusion because it "represented that Tin Pan Alley, Brill Building period" was one thing; to ask that Muddy Waters's contribution be trimmed to make room for him made Helm apoplectic. In the end both men got to perform – as did Dylan, Paul Butterfield, Bobby Charles, Mac Rebennack, Van Morrison and others who'd spent time with The Band in Woodstock – but Helm never forgave Robertson for getting his priorities so wrong. And it only further convinced him it was time to return to Woodstock, where – in Libby Titus's words – he'd "staked out this swampy Ponderosa off Plochmann Lane".

By the spring of 1977, when The Band's lamentable last album *Islands* was released, Helm's new RCO studio had been built on the Plochmann Lane property. He'd also pulled together the RCO All-Stars, comprising Butterfield, Rebennack, the three surviving members of Stax powerhouse Booker T. and the M.G.'s, and a group of horn players led by Howard Johnson. Helm was as happy as a pig in clover. "What a group *that* was," says Geoff Muldaur. "How did *that* not work? You hear that music and you go, 'Well, there's the best band in the world right now, so . . . where *are* they?!'" The answer to that riddle was that most of those All-Stars, like Helm

Levon and his all-stars at the RCO barn, 1978

himself, had succumbed to the slothful self-indulgence so endemic to late-seventies Woodstock. It was easier to tread water rehashing good-time blues songs – while abusing the usual cocktails of drugs and alcohol – than to attempt something vital or innovative.

The supporting cast of Woodstock hangers-on didn't help. "The thing that struck me about the place", says Kasim Sulton, "was all these wannabe rock stars and wannabe managers and wannabe drug dealers. The vast majority of those people wanted to present themselves as having a fabulous time when really they were just mooching off somebody else. It wasn't so much nepotistic as incestuous. I was twenty-two and had just come from New York City, and now I had to spend my time in this bucolic do-nothing town where if you weren't an alcoholic or sleeping with somebody else's wife, you weren't accepted. So naturally I became an alcoholic and started sleeping with somebody else's wife!"

When *Village Voice* writer Perry Meisel came to town in early 1976 to visit his friend Dolph Menzies, a roadie who was house-sitting Helm's unfinished RCO studio, he found the experience deeply disillusioning. Where once a "hip tension" had reigned in Woodstock, with Dylan's and The Band's doors necessarily closed to outsiders, the departures of the town's biggest stars had exposed the sad reality behind its rock dreams. "Woodstock seems to have been woven out of so many contradictions that it couldn't have held on for long in any case," Meisel noted. "The sweet country setting got cancelled by big city tensions; the ambience of a retreat by the prevailing deference and cool; the number of musicians by a lack of studios and clubs in which they could play. And, to top it off, a massive pop investment in the myth of Woodstock got cancelled by the dearth of real musical activity there. No wonder the air festered and people began to clear out."

When Meisel went to the Bear for dinner with Menzies, he observed that the place was "full of flannelled scenoids who converse in a quiet, cool hush like the one that prevails in the deserted roads of the village". Returning to Manhattan the next day, he wondered if what he'd witnessed wasn't something like the death knell of rock's sixties promise. "I wondered why I kept hanging out and kept playing", he wrote, "even after the music and the people had both become absurd."

At the Bear, Perry Meisel had waited twenty long minutes for Paul Butterfield to vacate the men's room. The thirty-three-year-old harmonica master may not have been absurd, but he was a pale shadow of the force he'd been in 1965, or even in 1973. After Better Days unravelled, he got to make his first solo album. Produced at Bearsville by Henry Glover, the big-budget *Put It in Your Ear* featured an all-star scrum of musicians supplying slinky grooves behind him. But the songs – whether funky, slushy or just routinely bluesy – were dull, with only the weary southern-soul ache of Bobby Charles's "Here I Go Again" offering redemption. Butterfield simply wasn't a strong enough singer to carry the material, and there was too little harmonica on the record. When Ian Kimmet met him for the first time, he was ballsy enough to say he didn't like *Put It in Your Ear*. "[Paul] looked me right in the eyes and asked, 'You didn't like my record with Henry Glover?'" Kimmet recalled. "[He said] 'Do you know who he *is*?'"

To Kimmet, Butterfield "seemed asleep" in the late seventies. "He was at the bar at the Joyous Lake 24/7," says Valma Merians. "He couldn't play the blues until he got sad and stoned, and then you'd have no idea how he would play." Old friends were appalled to learn that Butterfield's addiction had progressed to a full-scale heroin habit. "It blew my mind how he got into the drug thing when he'd been so *down* on drugs," says Barry Goldberg. "It was as if he'd dwindled down egotistically in Woodstock and lost his identity." Lynne Naso remembered Butterfield as "such a beer guy, Chicago Irish all the way". When she visited him in Woodstock, she was "horrified and terrified" by his drug use and tried to help him get straight.

"Paul's insides were dissolving," says Jim Rooney, who drove all the way from Nashville after hearing that Butterfield was close to death. "He wound up in the Kingston hospital and almost bought it. He suffered from an Irish disease I call 'terminal cuteness'. He always thought he was exempt, but eventually he was only fooling himself." Diagnosed with peritonitis, Butterfield underwent several gruelling operations at the turn of the decade and was forced to wear a colostomy bag. "One time I saw my dad get upset, so I followed him around the back of a club he was playing," says Gabe Butterfield. "I said, 'Dad, are you all right?' And he goes, 'Fuck off!' And I noticed that he was opening his shirt and emptying his bag in the gutter."*

Through all of this, Albert Grossman stayed loyal. "On the few occasions I saw him with Butterfield," says Danny Goldberg, "Albert treated him with the greatest respect as someone who, regardless of whether he was making money from him or not, was to be regarded as a major figure. And when I knew Butterfield as a Bearsville artist, he was *long* past that." Mark McKenna witnessed Grossman's pain up close: "He really loved Paul, and it broke his heart to see him fall apart the way he did. But Albert never presumed to tell people how to live their lives. His philosophy was self-reliance."

In the autumn of 1978 Ian Kimmet set up a Butterfield appearance on the German TV show *Rockpalast*, with a band featuring Buzzy Feiten on guitar. "It was a spirited performance, but Paul wasn't fit and he didn't have any material ready when Buzzy arrived for rehearsal," Kimmet says. "We edited the entire performance down to perfection back in Woodstock, but when we listened to it, Albert said it was substandard." Grossman tried to rekindle the Butterfield magic with the help of Todd Rundgren. "Paul comes in

* There was a grim but unheeded warning for Butterfield when, in mid-February 1981, Mike Bloomfield was found dead – dumped by his drug buddies in the front seat of his car – after overdosing at a party in San Francisco. Just three months earlier, Bloomfield had joined Bob Dylan onstage at the city's Warfield Theatre to perform "Like a Rolling Stone".

and Todd says, 'Whaddya got?'" remembers Kasim Sulton. "Paul says, 'I don't have *anything*.' Todd says, 'Well, we're supposed to record something.' So Paul says, 'Why don't you guys come up with something?' Todd goes, 'Oh my God, this is just torture.'" Butterfield was in such poor shape that he even declined an opportunity to support Eric Clapton on a European tour.

As a last throw of the Bearsville dice, Grossman packed Butterfield off to Willie Mitchell's studio in Memphis. He had signed up the Hi Records producer as Bearsville's "Executive Director of Memphis Operations" in 1979. "I did a lot of projects with Willie," says Kimmet. "He liked coming up to Woodstock, and we looked after him here. In Memphis it sounded exactly like the old Hi Records, but we had moved on. Things were bolder and brasher." Butterfield's 1980 album *North–South* was neither bold nor brash, just sterile and irrelevant. Only the slow closer "Baby Blue" sounded like authentic Butterfield. "It would have been nice to say to Paul and Albert, 'Let's wait a year and get some good tunes together,'" said Elizabeth Barraclough, who accompanied Butterfield to Memphis. "[But] Albert was always ready to go with an artist if he said he had the songs together. [His] final word was often, 'I don't care – let them make the record. And if it doesn't work out, well, whatever.'"*

Back in Woodstock, Butterfield saddled up with Rick Danko, who'd returned to the East Coast after the failure of his self-titled solo debut.† Throughout the early eighties the two reprobates

---

* Another Bearsville artist who made the pilgrimage to Mitchell's studio was Jesse Winchester, whose *Talk Memphis* (1981) at least spawned a minor hit in "Say What". For Winchester it was actually a homecoming: he had spent his formative years in the city of Sun, Stax and Hi.
† Recorded at Shangri-La, 1977's *Rick Danko* featured three co-writes by Bobby Charles – including "Small Town Talk" – and four by Emmett Grogan. "Emmett moved into The Band's bailiwick because they were the hippest guys he had access to," says Peter Coyote. "But they were also junkies, and I'm sure he was their connection." A year after the release of the album Grogan was found dead of a heroin overdose on the F train to Coney Island. Bob Dylan, always partial to an outlaw, dedicated *Street Legal* to his memory.

played numerous gigs together, usually in any north-eastern bar that would have them. "My dad and Rick loved each other," says Gabe Butterfield, "but they were not a good couple." Paul Mozian, who booked gigs for them at venues such as New York's Lone Star Café, says Butterfield was forever scamming: "He'd say, 'Mozian! You got fifty bucks?' And I'd say, 'After the first set, Paul.' Rick, no matter what shape he was in, could always perform. Butterfield I was never so sure about."*

Butterfield eventually left Woodstock, though not without a protest. "He didn't want to sell his house, but he had to," says Gabe Butterfield's wife Liz. "When the listing agent showed up at the front door, Paul opened it in his underwear with a shotgun."

Having made three undistinguished albums of his own – and after surviving a bitter custody battle with Libby Titus over their daughter – Levon Helm began talking about a Band reunion in early 1983. The very notion appalled Robbie Robertson, who felt it made a mockery of "The Last Waltz", but he opted not to block the "Band Is Back" tour that kicked off at the Joyous Lake on 25 June 1983. "Instead of coming up with new material they just repeated all their old material," John Simon said. "Whereas the audience when they first came out was intellectual-thinking people, [. . .] the younger people were just, 'Play "Take A Load Off Fanny"!' It had gotten to be what I call the vomit-and-sawdust crowd."

By the following spring, Richard Manuel too had returned to Woodstock, with Arlie Litvak in tow. Both were in bad shape; Manuel even thought he had AIDS. "They were almost like poor stepchildren," says Mark McKenna. "Richard used to come up to the studio, very meekly, and say, 'Is anybody working today? Can I play the piano?' And we'd say, 'Sure, of course.' Honestly, they were

---

* "An unsuccessful alcoholic doesn't have any fun," Danko quipped in October 1980. "A successful alcoholic looks *forward* to not having any fun."

just adrift. The music business in its infinite wisdom had passed them by."

"There were some times when it didn't seem like very many people were pulling for us at all," Helm said in 1998. "Except when we would go and play, and the people that showed up to hear us play wanted to hear 'Cripple Creek' and 'King Harvest' and all those old songs. That's what got us through." Intermittent gigs didn't make a lot of difference, though, when Danko and Manuel were struggling with heroin habits. "I came home one time about three in the morning, and Richard was loading up his car with boxes," remembered Al Aronowitz, whom Grossman had installed in one of his Turtle Creek cabins. "I didn't realise what it was until I got into my house and saw that he'd stolen my record collection."

Aronowitz believed Danko had burgled him too. "I was in Al's apartment and he was showing me a picture of Dylan and Lennon together," says Stan Beinstein. "Rick came over and started to noodle on this Mexican *guitarrón* that Al had. Al said, 'You took something from me.' Danko said, 'I didn't take nothing.' Al said, 'You're a fuckin' liar.'" Though Aronowitz became notoriously bitter in his later years – often grouching about how Dylan had cut him off – he certainly didn't deserve to be robbed by junkies. "I didn't talk to Rick for a long time after that," he told me. "We were supposed to be friends."*

Ian Kimmet was present when Manuel told Grossman that Robbie Robertson was going to produce a solo album for him. "Albert just rolled his eyes at me," Kimmet says. Yet it was thanks

---

* Aronowitz, Bearsville's Vinnie Fusco wrote, "has been defamed, humiliated, persecuted, tormented and driven insane, [but] Albert Grossman has just rescued him . . ." Fusco's letter was included in the photocopied *Blacklisted Masterpieces of Al Aronowitz*, launched at the Bearsville Theatre in June 1981. "Tom [Pacheco] came and sang me some of his songs," Aronowitz wrote of the evening. "Listening along with me was my old friend Levon Helm." Pacheco opened his 1997 album *Woodstock Winter* with the nostalgic "Hills of Woodstock", a song that described Grossman as "a feudal lord . . . smiling most inscrutably".

to Grossman that Manuel underwent detox and eventually stayed sober for a period. For a while he held down a regular spot at the Getaway Lounge on Route 212 between Woodstock and Saugerties. There he specialised in his favourite Ray Charles songs – and in Tin Pan Alley classics like Cole Porter's "Miss Otis Regrets" – going so far as to tell the *Woodstock Times* that he was "irked to the point of telling [my bandmates], 'Fellas, this is it, I'm going on with my own career.'"

"It was like they never really left Turkey Scratch in Arkansas or some barnyard in Ontario," says Jonathan Donahue. "Rick and Richard went crazy, but they probably would have been crazy whether they had a hundred dollars or a hundred thousand." For Michael Friedman, who'd known them since 1969, Danko and Manuel were "two of the nicest people" he'd ever known: "There were no pretences or phoney bullshit with them. I felt so bad when things went wrong for them."

In the summer of 1985 – with Garth Hudson and his Mormon wife Maud having made their own move back to Woodstock from LA – The Band toured as support to Crosby, Stills and Nash. Depressed that they were resting on their laurels and not moving forward, Manuel had already fallen off the wagon. Now he was drinking to dull the futility every alcoholic knows. "The last time I saw him was at a dealer's house," says Jeremy Wilber. "What I remember most is these big gleaming store-bought teeth he had. They were just so out of place." The following spring The Band set off to play two shows in a lounge on the outskirts of Orlando. "It didn't look good to me," says pianist-producer Aaron "Professor Louie" Hurwitz, who'd worked with them for a year. "They didn't look too healthy." In the early hours of 4 March, after playing a second set at Winter Park's Cheek-to-Cheek Lounge, Manuel hanged himself in his motel room. "He was one of the greatest singers ever," says Peter Yarrow. "The loss of him was crushing to all of us."

For Helm, the suicide was proof of the sheer unfairness of

Robbie Robertson taking the lion's share of The Band's royalties. For the rest of his days the drummer railed against the guitarist for not doing right by his musical brothers. "That's really what broke the Band up, and made everybody go to drugs and dope and death and nuts," he said in 2000, the year Robertson landed a plum gig as a "creative executive" at David Geffen's new DreamWorks label. "[It] made everybody into a has-been."

For years the opposing camps have continued to debate the rights and wrongs of the Helm/Robertson feud. With some validity, those on Robertson's side point out that it was he who got up in the mornings and wrote (most of) the songs; those on Helm's think a "band" is by definition a collaborative entity. "One guy writes the song, but they all add something to the process," says Michael Friedman. "It was very uneven and very unfair, and I'm sure Albert made more money than anybody except Robbie."

If anything, Paul Butterfield was in worse shape than even Richard Manuel had been. "A lot of people worried about [Paul]," Bonnie Raitt said. "The Eighties were a very rough decade for a lot of us. Our kind of music was completely off the air. We really felt disenfranchised." But where Raitt bided her time – and stopped drinking and snorting – Butterfield piled it on. "He looked terrible and seemed very weak," Sally Grossman recalled of a dinner with him at Deanie's early in 1987. "He kept falling asleep at the dinner table. After he left, I called Rick Danko and told him I thought Paul was very close to death."

She wasn't wrong. On 7 May, aged forty-four, Butterfield overdosed and died in an apartment in North Hollywood. "I went to his funeral in Westwood," said the LA-based writer Eve Babitz, who'd had an affair with him. "It was a huge gathering – the entire music business was there. All the people that loved Paul, his family and all the women in his life." Sally Grossman told Mark McKenna that it was a Buddhist ceremony. "Apparently they tried to burn a picture of Paul in a fire," McKenna says. "But it wouldn't burn."

11

BROKEN HEART

When the playfully irreverent Paul Morley visited Woodstock in the late winter of 1982 – ostensibly to report for the UK's *NME* on Todd Rundgren's video studio – a blizzard stranded him in town and delayed his return to New York. Taking pity on the English journalist was, in his words, a "creased old man with the crotch of his jeans hanging round his knees and the dusty grey hair tied into a long pony tail" who drove him back to his Bearsville pile and plied him with cognac and "some fruit bread" flown in from California.

Also being plied by Albert Grossman that afternoon was Al Aronowitz, a hero of Morley's whom Grossman had saved from penury in Washington DC. "Albert was pretty kind to me when I was broke on welfare," Aronowitz told me in 1991. "He brought me up to Woodstock and gave me a free house to live in." Grossman had done the same for Barry Feinstein, who moved to Woodstock after divorcing *Tonight Show* star Carol Wayne. "Barry stayed in one of Albert's cabins, but he got terribly bored," says Ian Kimmet. "He'd say, 'Nothing ever happens here.' But then he never *went* anywhere." Feinstein, who later married local painter Judith Jamison, was part of Grossman's inner echelon – in Kasim Sulton's recollection, "constantly at Albert's side". He would accompany Grossman to boxing matches, the two men acting out a kind of Mailer-esque machismo together.*

Another Woodstocker invited to fights was Robbie Dupree,

---

* Ian Kimmet also recalls Feinstein and Grossman chuckling after their initial exposure to Dylan's first Christian album *Slow Train Coming*.

who'd moved back east after a stint in Los Angeles that brought him a Top 10 hit with 1980's slick "Steal Away". "The phone would ring and Albert would say, 'Thursday night there's a fight, you wanna come?'" he remembers. "Then a shitty-looking old limousine would pull up with a guy in a flannel shirt driving, and we'd pile in and go down to the city or Newburgh, or just to Kingston. Albert was fascinated by that kind of physical prowess. He was a sedentary man himself, but he got a vibe off people like that, just like he'd gotten a vibe off all the hard-edged guys he managed or had on his label."

Many saw Grossman's largesse towards Feinstein and Aronowitz as proof of his essential goodness – or at least of his good *side*, since he continued to be a perplexing mix of generosity and vindictiveness. "It's like there was Albert, and then there was his evil twin," says Cindy Cashdollar, who'd graduated to working as Ian Kimmet's assistant. "And I never knew which one I was going to get on any given day. He could be very gruff and cranky, but I also saw kindness from him towards Elizabeth Barraclough and Randy Vanwarmer. He genuinely cared about people who'd moved to the area and were trying to get settled there." Grossman's evil twin seemed to manifest itself when Lucinda Hoyt returned to Woodstock in 1981 after living for a few years in Greece. She had come back to help Yvette, a former housekeeper of Albert's who was dying in a nearby hospital. "I asked him if he wouldn't do something for her," she says. "It would only have required a little bit of money. His reaction was, 'Well, do *you* want to pay for it?' I can't forget him doing that to someone who'd been so loyal."

Then there was Grossman's perennial vagueness. "Albert was incredibly cryptic," says Mark McKenna. "A typical encounter would be him coming in and saying, 'Did you take care of that thing?' And you'd say, 'What thing?' And he'd say, 'Whaddya mean, "What thing?" That thing we *talked* about!' And you'd be like, 'Can you give me more than two syllables?'" More than anything else, though, what made Grossman memorable was his refusal to conform to social norms, dress codes above all. On the occasions when he could be bothered to attend industry gatherings in Manhattan or Los Angeles – or Cannes, where he always went for the annual MIDEM conference – he pointedly declined to wear suits or tuxedos. At a T. J. Martell Foundation dinner honouring his friend Bob Krasnow, he made zero effort to smarten up. "Everybody has to go in black tie, and Albert shows up in a peasant shirt with blue jeans and the cuffs rolled up," says McKenna. "That was his uniform. He was even nuts about getting a certain kind of wire to wrap his ponytail in."

Yet behind the fuck-you front was a sadder and lonelier man whose love of rich foods was more gourmand than gourmet. "I remember going with him to the Bearsville market, and he bought a Sara Lee pound cake from the freezer," says John Holbrook. "He said, 'You have to eat it while it's still cold.' So he took it back to the office and ate the whole thing." Though he'd given up smoking, Grossman was chronically unfit – "the only exercise he got was jogging to the refrigerator", quips David Boyle, who was still doing carpentry jobs for him – and ate red meat like there was no tomorrow. "Once he was making one of his famous hamburgers," says Ronnie Lyons. "I said, 'Albert, how *big* is that thing? Half a pound?' He said, 'A pound.' This girl who was there said, 'That's two dozen heart attacks waiting to happen right there!'"

If Grossman was comfort-eating, one of the reasons may have been unvoiced pain over his marriage. "All I knew about Albert and Sally was that he really loved her," says Mark McKenna. "He doted on her, but there were a lot of periods when they just weren't together." Ian Kimmet was chatting with Grossman one day when, out of nowhere, he said, "Worst fucking mistake I ever made." Kimmet asked what he meant. "Susan Lee," his boss replied. In that moment, Kimmet got the poignancy of Grossman's situation: "It fucked up his life. He became very lonely. He would ask me to come up to the house just to talk." Occasionally Grossman requested that

Kimmet drive him to the city to have dinner with Sally. "I could tell that he really cared for her," Kimmet says. "He was just soft and receptive around her. And then she'd float off again and we'd drive back up to Bearsville."

Perversely, Grossman actually set Sally up with Ronnie Lyons, his friend since the sixties. In the winters Grossman even joined them at the house he'd bought years before in Oaxaca. "That's just the way he was," Lyons says. "He had his girlfriends, but Sally was his wife and he *treated* her like his wife." Lucinda Hoyt, however, has a more prosaic theory to explain it. "Sally was very afraid of being dumped by Albert and having to go back to work," she says. "And I'm sure the reason Albert never divorced her was because he would have had to give her half his assets."

In Bearsville, Grossman at least had the consolation of knowing his studio was thriving. "It was a who's who of recording artists," recalled Peter Cantine, who worked at the Bear as a teenager. "We'd get a phone call saying, 'We'll take four shrimp cocktails and four bottles of Piper-Heidsieck to go.' It was a whole different world." Run like a boot camp by ex-marine Griff McCree, Bearsville became a destination studio for acts that wanted seclusion and fresh air. "A lot of people went to Bearsville to record simply because it wasn't Manhattan," says Kasim Sulton. "You could concentrate on your work and not worry about the phone ringing."

Thanks to McCree, Grossman's relationship with the studio was essentially hands-off. "He'd come up once in a while, but the younger guys on the staff were encouraged to avoid him," says Mark McKenna. "It was like, 'Don't interact with Albert, you'll say something stupid and get into trouble.' They had a camera on the driveway so we could see when he was coming, and everybody was supposed to look busy when he did."

One act that used Bearsville regularly was funk-soul institution the Isley Brothers, who owned a nearby cabin they used as a base for hunting. "I think they liked the studio because they could doodle around and nobody would be any the wiser," says John Holbrook, who began engineering for the group on 1977's aptly titled *Go for Your Guns*. "They were always five hours late. The three younger guys worked out the tunes, and then the older brothers would come in and argue and mess around with the lyrics." In the age of P-Funk and Earth, Wind and Fire, the brothers loved the sound Holbrook got for them in Studio B. "There was a polyrhythmic funk between the drums, the popping bass and the guitar and keyboard parts," he says. "For me the thing was to keep the impact of the rhythmic attack, so my approach was to keep everything super-clean."*

At times the atmosphere on the brothers' sessions got more fractious. "They were big scary guys, and they'd be yelling at each other," Holbrook says. Biggest and scariest of all was Rudolph Isley, who was rumoured to carry a revolver in his briefcase. "One time they're at Bearsville and there's a big row," says Holbrook. "We see Rudy storming into the control room and going for the briefcase. And he opens it and takes out . . . a *cassette*!" When Todd Rundgren clipped Isley's El Dorado as he bombed down Mink Hollow Road in his new SUV, Rudolph was incensed. "I called Cindy Cashdollar and told her what happened," says Paul Mozian. "She said, 'Rudy's not very happy.' Two days later the Isleys were in Studio B and they saw me coming down the hallway. Rudy said, 'D'you know Paul Mozian?' I said, 'I think I saw him back there.'"

Bearsville's boot-camp atmosphere abated somewhat after Grossman fired Griff McCree. "When Griff went, we all said to Albert, 'Why can't we talk to you? What's the big deal?'" says Mark McKenna. "And he said, 'Oh, I dunno.' Eventually the younger guys got to be friendly with him." Grossman thawed still further after

---

* In 1980 the brothers recorded tracks for a "live" album at Bearsville, the intention being to add crowd noise after the fact. Columbia rejected *Wild in Woodstock*, which finally saw the light of day in 2015 as one of the twenty-three CDs that made up *The RCA Victor and T-Neck Album Masters, 1959–1983*.

agreeing that Studio A should become a proper recording room. "The acoustics became legendary," says Holbrook, who baffled the room's sound with packing blankets. "Within a few days Paul Cypert put in these diffusion things I'd designed on a napkin, sort of like a boat. It was just luck that it worked out."

"Holbrook was a genius," says McKenna. "He set up the studio and completely revolutionised it. When the whole drum-sound-sampler thing was happening in the eighties, we had it better than anybody else." Producers such as Rhett Davies and Bob Clearmountain began block-booking Bearsville. After Simple Minds came to mix 1985's *Once Upon a Time* there, singer Jim Kerr was asked if he liked the studio. "I guess we must," he replied. "The last time we were supposed to come for five days and stayed five weeks." Grossman was delighted. "He loved the action," says McKenna. "He'd come in and shoot the breeze with Chrissie Hynde. It was hard to get close to him, but in general there was a lot of affection going both ways."

As re-energised as Grossman felt by the studio, he was rapidly losing what interest he still had in his label. Rundgren, Butterfield and Willie Mitchell had gone. Foghat weren't selling any more, and Randy Vanwarmer hadn't followed up "Just When I Needed You Most". "I had the feeling Warner Brothers were frustrated because the label wasn't delivering," says McKenna. "Bearsville was doing Pam Windo and the Shades, stuff nobody gave a shit about. They did some very weird things. At one point Krasnow sent in this thing by an act called the Human Body."

The latter's *Make You Shake It* (1983) – the last album released on the label – was actually the work of black funk eccentric Roger Troutman, who decided to make a visit to Bearsville. "We spent a couple of hours in the studio with him," McKenna says. "He'd never seen an AMS sampler before, so that blew his mind. Then Albert said, 'Let's go get some lunch.' We're walking into the Bear, and all of a sudden Troutman stops and goes, 'Do they let coons in here?'"

As Bearsville Records limped on, Grossman increasingly left the hard work to Steve Constant, the label's financial controller. Mark McKenna says the workaholic Constant would always be at his desk, "no matter what time I arrived at the studio or what time I drove home". But the busiest hive of Bearsville industry was the accounting office, whose job it was to collect royalties trickling in from deals Grossman had made all over the world. "There were about five accountants working for him," McKenna says. "I guess he needed them just to keep track of it all and call people to say, 'Where's the money?'"

In 1981 the accountants were asked to assist Grossman's lawyers in a $450,000 lawsuit he'd brought against Bob Dylan for non-payment of royalty commission. In response, Dylan stopped paying his ex-manager altogether and filed eighteen counterclaims, arguing that Grossman had "exploited and mismanaged" him from the get-go. "Albert's only comment to me was that he just wanted what he was entitled to contractually," Sally Grossman said diplomatically in 1987. She added that Dylan had recently called her, offering to settle. The following year Dylan paid the Grossman estate $2 million.

Aside from Roger Troutman, the very last acts signed to Bearsville were Nicole Wills, the Saugerties-based NRBQ and neo-power-pop band the dBs. "I'd loved Bearsville's output over the years," dBs leader Peter Holsapple recalled. "Todd Rundgren . . . was a huge influence on [drummer] Will Rigby and me as teenagers, and I'd even sewed the Bearsville logo on to my book bag when I was sick at home with mononucleosis in the tenth grade." But producer Chris Butler encountered only indifference when he enthusiastically pitched his vision for the dBs' *Like This* to Albert Grossman. "After listening to me silently for a while", Butler recalled, "he stopped me mid-sentence and said in a rather nasal baritone, 'Chris, all I am interested in these days is restaurants and wood.'" *Like This* was barely out when Warners terminated its relationship with Bearsville, and the album's distribution ceased overnight. "You couldn't get it in the stores when we were touring with R.E.M.," said Holsapple, "so it was all kind of distressing."

Nicole Wills's *Tell Me* was a mechanical-sounding album of cover versions – including Rundgren's "It Wouldn't Have Made Any Difference" – that was left similarly high and dry. *Tell Me's* last track, "Never Take the Place of You", was a song by Al Anderson of NRBQ, whose *Grooves in Orbit* was released by Bearsville in 1983. After the band clashed with Grossman over the song "Daddy-O", he refused to release further singles from the album or to let them go. "Barry Feinstein said to me, 'Albert was always trying to get the best deal, and he best-dealed himself out of the business,'" says Mark McKenna. "I thought that was a great line." In a last desperate move, Grossman turned to none other than Rundgren. "Albert announced that he was making him head of A&R, which was very awkward for Ian Kimmet," says McKenna. "I don't know if it was an attempt to breathe new life into the label, but Todd became an A&R figure, which was totally out of character. I don't think it lasted more than a couple of months."

After Bearsville Records folded in 1984, Grossman was at something of a loose end. *Musician* later described him rather fancifully as "rock and roll's Citizen Kane", roaming alone through the halls of a rural Xanadu. "One time near the end, Albert and I went for dinner in New York with Krasnow and Barry Feinstein," says Kimmet. "Krasnow asked me, 'So what are you doing up there, Ian?' And I said, 'Not very much. Barry drives Albert down here and I drive him back.' And Albert and Barry just cracked up. Bob didn't know where to look, and we all just started eating again. But it was almost true." In 1985 Grossman asked Kimmet if he wanted to run the studio. "I said I needed a break, and he was upset," Kimmet says. "I said, 'I think I'm gonna try something else.'" When Kimmet left Woodstock for a new life in Nashville, Grossman experienced it as the latest in a long series of abandonments.

As detached as he'd become, Grossman was still trying to pull deals together; it was like a muscle memory for him. He even retrieved the Professor Longhair sessions that Michael Friedman had recorded over a decade earlier. "He had me rough-mix all the songs," says Mark McKenna. "I spent a couple of days on them, drove up to his house and gave him the cassettes." To McKenna's mild amazement, Grossman told him he wanted to resurrect Bearsville in a new deal with Capitol-EMI Music president Bhaskar Menon.

In January 1986 Grossman prepared to make his usual trip to Cannes for MIDEM. On the eve of his departure he went with Ronnie Lyons to the first Rock and Roll Hall of Fame dinner at New York's Waldorf-Astoria hotel. "Albert said, 'Krasnow's having a rock 'n' roll dinner, ya wanna go?'" Lyons says. "Everybody was in black tie, but Albert and I were in Mexican shirts. The only person who didn't look at us like we were crazy was Ray Charles."

The following day the two men were driven to Kennedy airport. "We were laughing and telling jokes," says Lyons. "We were going to get together when we got back. He said he wanted me to run the studio." While Lyons flew to Mexico to travel through Central America with Sally, Grossman flew on Concorde to London to meet Krasnow and other music-biz cronies. "They were having a Super Bowl party at the Savoy," Lyons says. "Albert said, 'I've been waiting thirty years for the [Chicago] Bears to get to the Super Bowl.'"

Next morning Ronnie and Sally were woken in their Mexico City hotel room by a phone call from Krasnow: an air stewardess had been unable to wake Grossman on the flight. When the Concorde landed at Heathrow, the *Cumulus Nimbus* was pronounced dead from a heart attack.

Woodstock went into shock. Though Grossman hadn't looked after himself, no one expected him to die at the age of fifty-nine. "It was super-devastating to me," says Peter Yarrow, who rarely returned to the place he and his manager had put on the musical map. "I let my cabin in Woodstock go to rack and ruin. It was just too painful to go back there."

At the memorial service in Bearsville, which Yarrow organised, friends and clients were inconsolable. "Artie Traum was sitting in front of us and just sobbing," says Mark McKenna. "A lot of people were like that." Dean Schambach says "there were real tears shed, because Albert really connected with you on a deep level". Some, however, were unmoved by the eulogy given by Robbie Robertson. "He blew my mind," says John Simon. "He said, 'In this life we have teachers.' And I thought, 'Wait a minute, what in the world did Albert teach *you*?' What he taught him was how to be a ruthless businessman." Rick Danko, however, found it hard to summon the bitterness that Simon and others felt for Grossman. "All this stuff that Albert perhaps didn't tell me about, I didn't really hold it against him," he told me in 1995. "The man had to do what the man had to do. I hope he's happy, wherever he may be."

A stone's throw from the restaurant, Grossman was already in the ground, buried in a grave dug by Paul Cypert against the town's express orders. "They said he couldn't be buried there," says Ed Sanders. "They said they would freeze him for six months while they decided where to put him. The family just said, 'Go to hell.' He had a nice shiny-topped coffin, a huge thing, and they just plopped him down there." Standing at the graveside, John Storyk glanced around him. "It was winter and there were no leaves," he says. "I looked around and virtually every building I could see, Albert owned. And I'd either built them or renovated them."

There were conspicuous absentees. Ian Kimmet was in Nashville. Levon Helm was too nauseated by the thought of Robertson's homage to attend. "I ran into Levon once in the studio and he couldn't even say Albert's *name*," Sally Grossman said in 2014. Inevitably, there was no sign of Bob Dylan, whose rise to superstardom might have been very different without Grossman. But the most stinging verdict of all came from Todd Rundgren. "He got what he deserved," the former Runt said to Kasim Sulton. "Good riddance to bad rubbish."

Thirty years after his death Albert Grossman continues to elicit ambivalent feelings from those who knew him. "There was Albert the businessman and Albert the guy, and I liked them both," says Michael Friedman. "He never yelled at me once, he always treated me with respect."

But Barbara O'Brien, the woman who salvaged the career of Levon Helm, speaks for many in her very different view. "Maybe Albert *was* a wise businessman, but I think he's the model for what managers *shouldn't* do," she says. "I was a pit bull for Levon, but there are ways to do it so you don't piss everybody off. Albert wanted to be as big as Dylan or Janis were, and he took too much from them. The guy was an empire, but his personality stopped you from wanting to embrace it."

No one has ever summed up the puzzle of Albert Grossman better than Mary Travers, one of his first real stars. "He wasn't a very nice man," she told Dylan biographer Bob Spitz, "but I loved him dearly."

EPILOGUE

"HOW DOES THAT OLD SONG GO?"

> Sometimes I walk through town and look at
> all these places where I used to play or get
> laid, and part of me thinks they must still be
> there. But they're not.
>
> GRAHAM "MONK" BLACKBURN

In one of the Elliott Landy images that hang in the foyer of the
Bearsville Theatre, Albert Grossman is grinning affectionately at
Janis Joplin. The iconography of Woodstock is all around us as we
await a performance by Rickie Lee Jones. The audience is late-
middle-aged and shabbily affluent in pastel colours and jeans and
fleeces. I'm guessing there aren't many Republicans here. Ninety
minutes later Jones rounds off her set with a rendering of "The
Weight", dedicated to what she terms "all the Woodstockings" in the
tasteful 250-seat venue. There can't be many more pleasant nights
out in North America than an early dinner at the Bear followed by a
show in the venue that would have been Grossman's pride and joy.

The fact that the theatre opened at all, three years after Grossman's death, was testament to the resolve of his widow – as well as
that of John Storyk – to see it through to completion. "I'd promised
Albert we'd finish it," Storyk says. "When the dust had settled, I
finished the parking lot and got all the paperwork done by the end
of that summer." Meanwhile, Paul Cypert completed an ambitious
double-helix staircase in the theatre, and David Boyle put in a fireplace based on the hearth at George Washington's headquarters in
Newburgh. "Sally sold Warhol's *Double Elvis* to pay for it all," says

The Bearsville Theatre, October 2013 (Art Sperl)

Mark McKenna. "She sank about three-quarters of a million dollars into it to get it open. She'd talk about Albert's dream – whatever *that* was, because he never told anybody."

For a few years after it opened in July 1989 – with a concert by Happy Traum – the venue's programming switched between theatre and live music. "Albert had a vision for the place," says JoHanna Hall, who served on its ad hoc board of directors. "We got together and brainstormed about how to make it into a going concern, but it all came to naught." Subsequent plans to make the theatre a loss leader for a small hotel in the Petersen House building next door were blocked by Sally herself. "Every time they got to the altar", says Hall, "she bolted." Michael Lang thinks Sally "felt obligated to keep things going, but it was a bit of a white elephant . . . and eventually too much for her". JoHanna Hall lays out the central problem that's beset the theatre ever since: "You need to bring in acts you can't see every day in town, but because it's such a small theatre you can't really pay an Emmylou Harris to play there. The two theatres at either end of town could have been the bookends for something international and certainly national. But where was the person, once Albert was gone, to make that happen?"

The hole left in the Woodstock community by Grossman's death was immense. "When he was up there, it was an incubator," says Mark McKenna. "It was sort of like the Laurel Canyon of the East Coast. And then after he passed, it just started to diminish." JoHanna Hall agrees: "A lot died with Albert. Things began to fray. There wasn't a nightlife. You'd go into town and it would be shut down."

Though Sally Grossman stepped up to the plate in Bearsville, she was soon antagonising the very people trying to help her. "I love her," says Peter Yarrow. "She has a lot of Albert's insight and wisdom, but she also has a lot of his terseness and dismissiveness." Ian Kimmet, who returned from Nashville in 1988 to work for her, soon found himself on the receiving end of both those traits. Grossman also fired a number of people who worked for her. "She threw Sha Wu out of the Little Bear, and I have no idea why," says Ronnie Lyons, whose own relationship with her did not survive the relocation to Bearsville.

Another Bearsville employee who felt the heat of Sally's wrath was Steve Constant, who still owned a stake in Bearsville Records. "She cut Steve out of her life," says Kimmet. But Constant knew something other insiders did not: that Grossman's non-probated will would have prevented Sally gaining control of any assets beyond his residencies and personal effects. One clause stipulated that the theatre and surrounding properties should not pass into her ownership. "She said to me, 'The day of Albert's funeral, Steve was trying to get me to sign papers!'" Kimmet says. "He was telling her she had to give him power of attorney. She said, 'Get the fuck away from me!' And she never did sign them." Another vexing legal matter was that of Grossman's former partner Bennett Glotzer. "Glotzer had cut himself in for a piece of *everything*," recalls Ronnie Lyons. "Sally said to me, 'What, I'm gonna have to pay Bennett for the rest of my *life* now?'"

Kimmet took seven more years of Sally Grossman before quitting the music business altogether. On a drive to St Tropez while they were attending MIDEM, she told him she felt like a failure. Says Kimmet today, "I didn't have much to say to that."

Driven almost as crazy by Sally was Bearsville Theatre manager Dan Griffin. He too fell out of favour with her, though not before booking a series of shows whose primary purpose was to supplement the meagre income of Rick Danko. "It was a bit puzzling that Sally always made the calls for Rick," Griffin recalled. "I came to learn that every time he was tight on money he would play the theatre, and that happened about once a month."

Joining Danko at Bearsville were some of the singer-songwriters who'd moved to the Woodstock area after its halcyon days. One evening Jules Shear and Marshall Crenshaw arrived at the theatre for a "songwriters' circle" of the kind that had become popular at New York's Bitter End. The problem was that there was no sign of Danko, forcing them to start the show without him. "Suddenly the engineer signals that Rick is on the telephone," Griffin remembered. "He says hello to us all and proceeds to tell us – on air – a hilarious story of how he'd been driving to the station when he hit a deer on one of Woodstock's mountain roads."

"We were wondering if Rick would ever show," says Crenshaw. "And then he came lumbering in with a six-pack in his hand and I thought, 'Okay, here we go.' But then he sat down, and it was a six-pack of ginger ale, and he offered me one. Instantly I just really dug him."

Like Garth Hudson, Danko had been roped into a Bearsville

session for the 1987 solo debut by his former bandmate Robbie Robertson. Signed to a generous deal by David Geffen, Robertson spent a huge amount of money on a set of bloated and overproduced songs that included the Richard Manuel tribute "Fallen Angel". "I think the record cost a million bucks," says Mark McKenna. "When Bob Clearmountain mixed it, he had a hell of a time just arranging it so he could *hear* everything." Naturally, Levon Helm was nowhere to be seen during the Bearsville overdubs for "Fallen Angel" and "Sonny Got Caught in the Moonlight".

Jules Shear had his own mini-adventure with Danko after offering songs to The Band for their first album since the departure of Robertson and the suicide of Manuel. "Rick I got along with better than anyone else in the group," Shear says. "He seemed to have the most grasp on the fact that you actually had to write the song. He even came to my house a couple of times to write." Paul Mozian confirms that Danko "could be very offputting with his shenanigans" but was genuinely committed to keeping The Band together. "He'd say, 'Hey, you gotta pay the rent,'" Mozian says. "Whereas for Levon it would be, 'If Garth's willing to do it, *I'm* willing to do it.'"

Sitting in with the reconstituted Band – the line-up comprising Helm, Danko and Hudson, with Jim Weider, drummer Randy Ciarlante and keyboardist Stan Szelest – Shear soon got the measure of the boss man. "Levon says, 'Jules, I really wanna talk to you in private,'" Shear remembers. "When everybody goes, he starts explaining to me how Robbie ripped him off and how he wants to split everything between me and the guys in The Band. So it would be one-seventh mine and six-sevenths to the other guys." Shear's manager, Mike Lembo, politely told Helm where he could stick it. In the end, the only song of Shear's that made it onto *Jericho* (1993) was "Too Soon Gone", a tribute to Manuel that started life as a piano doodle by Szelest. "And then one night I came home and I got a call from Rick telling me Stan was dead," says Shear. "So a tribute to Richard became a tribute to Stan as well." Szelest's replacement in the new Band was former Full Tilt member Richard Bell.* "He had this huge sound, so Garth could just do his thing," says Jim Weider. "After *Jericho* The Band did really well. Everyone was in good physical shape. But then we did *High on the Hog* and everything started to decline."

Like Shear, Marshall Crenshaw was something of a fish out of water in Woodstock, which he'd first visited when Ian Kimmet tried to sign him to Bearsville. "It was a freezing-ass winter and the place was buried in snow, but I really dug it," he says, sitting in the yard of his home in Rhinecliff. "My wife and I came up and saw this beautiful house on eighteen acres off Tinker Street, and I could rent it for less than half of what I was paying for my duplex in the East Village." Moving into the house in early 1987, Crenshaw began an ambivalent relationship with the town. "The place didn't seem to have any kind of identity," he says. "You couldn't tell what had happened there." As time passed, he became increasingly disenchanted. "There's a provincialism there," he says. "Just being in this isolated place could turn you into a zombie. I started to call it 'the Woodstock glaze'. But I guess we loved it too. When we moved away we felt nostalgic for it."

Equally ambivalent was British import Graham Parker, who – like many – moved to the area because he didn't want to raise his child in the city. "For me there wasn't any premeditation about a music community," he says. "When I go to a party and guitars come out, a feeling of dread comes over me." Worse still for Parker was the "benefit fatigue" that afflicted so many Woodstock musicians. "Whenever I'd go to the Grand Union supermarket, somebody would come up and say, 'Hey, Graham! We're doing a benefit for the sewers!'" he says with an English chortle. "I'm not sure I *ever* got paid for playing there."†

---

* Shear had rather more fun collaborating with Ed Sanders in 2009 on a hilarious song suite entitled *The Surreal Wives of Woodstock*.
† John Sebastian told author Mick Brown that benefits were "the spirit" of Woodstock: "Nobody really wants to charge their friends anything when they play,

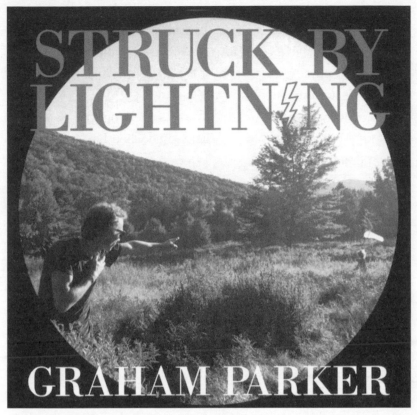

An Englishman in upstate New York: Graham Parker's *Struck by Lightning*
(1991), featuring the genius of Garth Hudson

When Parker recorded 1991's *Struck by Lightning* at West
Hurley's Dreamland studios, he asked John Sebastian, Garth Hudson
and Orleans's Larry Hoppen to play on it. "I had the Woodstock
experience without going into the actual town," he says. Mixing the
album at Chris Andersen's Nevessa studio – located in the Artist
Road house where Jim Colegrove and N. D. Smart II had once lived
– Parker had Hudson overdub organ and accordion on three tracks.

---

but we're always looking for excuses. The minute somebody's loft burns down or
anybody falls ill, you've got a benefit on your hands."

"I wanted him on at least five, but it didn't quite work out like that," he says. "In the end I wasn't even thinking about the money I was losing. There's a bit Garth played in 'Kid with a Butterfly Net' that still sends shivers down my spine. It's like the angels come down and touch you." At one point Hudson fell fast asleep on a couch. "We sort of crept around and I think we brought in some tuna fish," Parker says. "Garth woke up to the smell of food and went, '*Who are all these women?!*' And it was just me and Chris in the room."

Parker also befriended – and toured with – Rick Danko in the early nineties, not long after opening for The Band at Kingston's UPAC Theatre. "It was awesome to do 'Watch the Moon Come Down' and hear him doing background vocals way up there with that feathery angelic vocal," he says. "But the rehearsals were terribly sloppy. He'd turn up late and the bass wouldn't work. At our first gig at the Bearsville Theatre, people were walking in during the soundcheck. I thought, 'This is so fucking unprofessional. We're not in the sixties now.'"

When I met Danko in London in 1995, his life had become a train wreck. Six years earlier he had suffered the loss of Eli, his son by his first marriage. He was surviving on bar gigs and sporadic royalty payments. "I get paid for 'This Wheel's on Fire'," he told me. "I wish I'd had a few more of *them*." He had even fewer after Robbie Robertson bought out his publishing, an ill-advised example of the short-term thinking that Helm – as a matter of belligerent principle – avoided. In 1997 Danko was arrested in a Tokyo hotel after receiving an envelope of heroin mailed to him by his wife Elizabeth. Evicted from a farmhouse off Route 212, just outside Woodstock en route to Saugerties, the Dankos were forced to move into a motel near Kingston.

"My last recollection of Rick was on the Labor Day weekend of 1999," says Robbie Dupree. "I was sitting in with John Hall's band. There'd been a comedy of errors, and Danko came pretty high. He opened up his guitar case and it was empty. Yet at the end of the day, John said, 'Let's have Rick come up and let's do an encore.' I said, 'What do you wanna do?' So we played 'The Shape I'm In' and it actually was good. I remember him standing a little bit forward and singing it really good. And there was just this moment where he looked over at me and it was like he got in touch with better times for that moment."

On 10 December, after a short tour of the Midwest, Danko was found dead in his bedroom in Marbletown, near Kingston. "He ended the way he came into it," says Jonathan Donahue. "He was a mess, as innocent as the day is long, a country boy, a child." Danko was just three weeks shy of his fifty-seventh birthday.

When I met Donahue and Sean "Grasshopper" Mackowiack for lunch in Woodstock in May 1998, they had just completed the fourth Mercury Rev album. Yet they already seemed resigned to its commercial failure, since 1995's intoxicating *See You on the Other Side* had died an unwarranted death and they'd been dropped by Beggars Banquet Records.

But there was something different about their new one, released by Virgin offshoot V2, and it had more than a little to do with the fact that Levon Helm and Garth Hudson were playing on it. "There were people who were very nonplussed that we were working with them," Donahue told me. "Well, I *like* people from that era. You go to the source, you don't go to somebody who says they can play like Levon."

"Levon would be sneaking off to the bathroom now and then, but it made no difference to his playing," Grasshopper recalls. "Garth was harder. He'd bring out one horn and play a few notes, and then he'd play another horn and play some other notes. It was all in his head. And after an hour all the parts fit together into this melody line. We were flabbergasted. It was like, 'How did he *do* that?'"

Deserter's Songs was an album filled with haunting refrains: "How does that old song go?" Donahue sang on the opening "Holes". Quaintly exotic non-rock sounds – of harps, bowed saws, flugelhorns – offered beguiling backdrops to sweet, almost fragile

"Opus 40" from the classic *Deserter's Songs* (1998)

vocal lines. Coming after the bluster of grunge and the posturing of Britpop, it tapped a new nerve in pop's collective psyche. To the amazement of all in Rev's world, it was voted in several polls – including the *NME*'s – as the album of the year. The front-parlour feel was still there on 2001's *All Is Dream*, but this time the mood was darker, more steeped in Donahue's occult obsessions. Here lurked serpents, monsters surfacing from the depths of nightmares.

With 2005's *The Secret Migration*, the Rev made their most pastoral album to date: a "dark country ride" through the seasons of the Catskills, a hymn to nature's mysteries in the face of materialist artifice. Sadly, Mercury Rev's moment had passed: the fad for *Deserter's*

Songs' spectral neo-Americana was over. "*The Secret Migration* pas-toralised its way right into the budget bin," says Donahue. "A lot of people who'd been listening tuned out."

A decade on, Donahue and Grasshopper remain proud Kingston-ians with mixed feelings towards their famous neighbour. "Wood-stock looks at us like we're the dirty half-sister," says Donahue, picking at a plate of fries in Kingston's ancient Hoffman House. "There are a lot of well-meaning people there, but it's not a clear picture to say that Woodstock is this fountain of well-being. In a way it's very much a self-cherishing self-preservation: 'We'll let the outside world run its course, but here we'll make sure there's no McDonald's.'" Ironically, Kingston is now semi-hip in a way that Woodstock may never be again, attracting as it does a spillover of middle-class twenty-somethings who can no longer afford to live in New York City. "The hipsters here are interested in Woodstock, and they know where Dylan crashed his motorcycle," Grasshopper says. "But a lot of them hang out in places like Phoenicia because Woodstock is too tie-dyed and hippie-touristy."

The same goes for the offspring of Woodstock's original hip-pies. "Because the town is so famous for what it was and what it's traded off, it becomes hard for the younger generation to turn it into something else," says Tony Fletcher, a British writer who lives in Phoenicia. "The venues aren't there, and the ones that survive are those dominated by open-mic nights with older guys doing blue-grass. The bigger question is: does music still play the same role for the younger generation?"

"I don't want to hurt anybody's feelings, but this is not Seattle," says Simone Felice, whose side project the Duke and the King recorded its 2009 album *Nothing Gold Can Stay* in a Bearsville cabin. "There aren't seven or eight amazing bands playing in Woodstock. The decline of the Bearsville-style studio has occurred during my own ten years as an artist. That's been part of what's driven people into their own spaces. It's more about people hiding away. We're in the woods here."

Grasshopper dates the dawning of a new curiosity about Woodstock to the 1985 release of Bob Dylan's career-spanning box set
Biograph. "There was all this interest in the basement tapes and
Bearsville Studios," the guitarist says. "And then later, after R.E.M.
and Nick Cave recorded up there, it gave the place a new credibil-
ity. People wanted to go see Big Pink."

R.E.M.'s use of Bearsville to record tracks for *Green* (1988) – and
for the consciously "pastoralised" albums *Out of Time* (1991) and
Automatic for the People (1992) – was certainly a high-water mark
in the studio's life. "At the time of Albert's passing, Sally wasn't a
very significant presence in the life of the studio," Mark McKenna
says. "None of us was really sure what would happen next. But then
she got gradually more involved and it just went on. And there was
a big blossoming in the late eighties."

The initial omens weren't great. When Ronnie Lyons took over
the running of the studio – as per Albert Grossman's wishes – he
alienated the majority of the staff. "Ronnie was the kiss of death,"
says John Holbrook. "He had no feel for anything. People said he
was just looking after Sally. He drove everybody away, including me.
Bob Clearmountain said, 'I'm never working in this fucking studio
again.'" For his part, Lyons claims Bearsville had its biggest year to
date on his watch. "It had an SSL board in the smaller room, and
Clearmountain was there all the time," he says. "I had Chris Kimsey
in for three and a half months with the Psychedelic Furs." Eventually
Lyons was ousted by Steve Constant and Peter Hoffman, a fellow
executor of Grossman's estate and later the husband of Susan Lee.

Mark McKenna deserves much of the credit for Bearsville's resur-
gence. "I took out an ad in *Billboard*," he says. "It was an aerial shot
of the studio and it said, 'Would you believe that five of the albums
in the Hot 100 were recorded in this building?' Because it was just
a place in the woods. I told Sally we needed to create a brochure for
the studio, and we got Milton Glaser to do it. On the first page he
put 'The Magic of Woodstock'."

By the time McKenna returned in 1992 from a few years in Los Angeles, "Bearsville" was synonymous with a particular kind of away-from-it-all studio. "You had to want to be in a place where ideas could coalesce," he says. "R.E.M. did those two albums, and Dave Matthews did *Under the Table and Dreaming* in 1994. Jeff Buckley did *Grace* there." Bearsville was even used by rapper Nas, thrash-metal deities Metallica and Björk-fronted Scandi oddballs the Sugarcubes.

The studio's burgeoning popularity coincided with moves to mark the twenty-fifth anniversary of the Woodstock Festival – this time at Winston Farm, the Saugerties site first proposed for the original Music and Art Fair. Once again Michael Lang met with muted fear and loathing from Woodstock's town board, who dreaded a mass invasion. "They were very paranoid," Lang says. "I kept saying, 'Look, no one will be coming here, everybody will be going *there*.' And of course nobody showed up in town, and the business community was upset by it. But they should have embraced it."

On the weekend of 12–14 August 1994, over 300,000 people descended on Winston Farm in what turned out – after rains that made the 1969 downpour look like a passing shower – to be a mass mudbath. Lang and his partners had scheduled a mix of high-testosterone nineties hands and veterans of Max Yasgur's farm. Orleans, The Band and John Sebastian represented Woodstock itself, while Santana, Joe McDonald, Crosby, Stills and Nash, and Lang's client Joe Cocker dusted themselves down to rekindle the spirit of '69. On two stages Metallica, Green Day, Nine Inch Nails, Cypress Hill and Red Hot Chili Peppers braved the elements. More elderly entities included Traffic, Aerosmith, the Allman Brothers, Peter Gabriel and – giving multimedia performances in an area dubbed "the Surreal Field" – Todd Rundgren.

But Lang's biggest coup was persuading Bob Dylan, at long last, to play Woodstock. "The fact that he played and The Band played had some reflection back on the town," says Lang, who doesn't pretend that Woodstock '94 matched the Aquarian vibes of its world-shaking predecessor. Among the songs Dylan sang on the closing evening were "All Along the Watchtower" and – rather more passionately – "I Shall Be Released". He was performing the latter song just a few miles from the pink box where it had first been recorded in the far-off summer of 1967.

Twenty years after Woodstock '94, Michael Lang sits in Tinker Street eatery Oriole 9 and takes stock of the place that etched his name in pop-culture history. "Woodstock's roots have endured," he tells me. "It's still a haven for artists and musicians, and people still leave you alone. There are lots of places where people can record, even if there are no major studios any more. The club scene has diminished, but I think there's a basis for some sort of renaissance up here."

Lang speaks of opening a $10 million music college in the building that formerly housed Zena Elementary School, in partnership with Paul Green, founder of the original School of Rock and latterly of the Paul Green Rock Academy near Saugerties. "That could change things," comments Karl Berger, who's been invited to participate. "We've had some talks with Michael and Paul, and they do want to have it broad enough for us to be engaged as sort of devil's advocates."

Not everybody agrees there is a "basis for a renaissance" in Woodstock. Since the 1994 festival, the town has all but ossified into a musicians' retirement home. "When Albert moved up, there was actually a butcher and a cobbler and there were tradespeople in the town," says Jim Rooney. "Now you can't get anything: there's nothing there but knick-knack shops." While Rooney's old friends Happy and Jane Traum have carved out the lucrative niche that is their instructional-video business Homespun Tapes, there is no longer a live music scene to speak of. Even in the nineties, when Radio Woodstock became a regional flagship for alternative rock, few bands beyond Shivaree and the Push Stars made more than local waves. "When I programmed music for the Bearsville Theatre, I was able to bring in Astrud Gilberto and Lindsey Buckingham,

Billboard ad for Radio Woodstock, summer 1981

Phil Woods, Boozoo Chavis," says Mark McKenna. "It was totally eclectic and provided a focal point for music in the area. But the actual native music scene? Nothing was happening."

There were also ongoing drug problems in town. "I studied the heroin epidemic here," says Ed Sanders, who covered it for his *Woodstock Journal.* "I wanted dealers to promise not to sell to kids, because there were a bunch of overdoses in the nineties. It just came up from the city on the Trailways buses. There was always a dealer in town. We had a guy right near the art-supply store, and he was impervious."*

---

* One summer afternoon in 1996, I was sunning myself in our Zena Road backyard when an enormous St Bernard ambled across the lawn. When I returned the good-natured brute to its owner, in a backwoods shack off Route 212, I was confronted by a scene of appalling squalor – and a wall bedecked

Not only did the great live venues close, but even the Bearsville studio fell victim to the vicissitudes of the music industry in the digital era. "People couldn't afford the rates, which were something like $2,500 a day," says Ian Kimmet. "Seymour Stein said, 'I can't pay that, Sally.' She said to me, 'What the fuck are we gonna do?'" In 2004 she sold the studio building – together with all its audio equipment – for the knockdown price of $725,000. "Woodstock became a sleepy town," says Jim Weider. "The music scene was shifting." As far back as August 1991, Artie Traum told me his fellow musicians had replaced drugs with health foods. "Most of the ones I know are in bed by 10.30," he'd said. "They do jobs and they're sober." In a review of a Band show that year, the *Woodstock Times* argued that the town was "a pariah in the music industry at this point".

With the diminishing of the place as an incubator of actual music, Woodstock slowly reached an uneasy truce between its resistance to change and its powerlessness in the face of rising property values. By the late nineties, a new crowd of affluent urban scenesters was pouring in, many of them claiming it was precisely Woodstock's downhome character they treasured. After 9/11, the flood only increased. "We had a ton of people moving up out of the city," says Richard Heppner. "Second-home prices went through the roof. And that's kind of where we are now. There's not much you can do about it."

"When Albert died, it took the wind out of me for a while," says John Storyk. "And what I saw after that was not as interesting to me. It was a depressing mix of leftover hippies and New Yorker yuppies. I didn't see any real music coming out of Woodstock." For Robbie Dupree, Woodstock used to be a place where you came to realise your dreams; now "you have to have had your dream already to come here". Those who've had their dreams include A-list celebs

---

with images of Andy Warhol and his acolytes. The man turned out to be Factory photographer Nat Finkelstein, who'd apparently enjoyed a second wind as – in Al Aronowitz's words – the "cocaine king" of eighties Woodstock. The St Bernard was named Gucci.

from David Bowie to Daniel Craig. And yet there's still a "funkiness" to Woodstock that will never exist in Rhinebeck. "If you want to paint your house purple, you can," Heppner says. "Woodstock still maintains that independence, and God forbid you try to legislate it." Ed Sanders, who chaired the committee that rewrote Woodstock's zoning laws in 1988 and 1989, says that in thirty years the town will still "look somewhat the same" – and still be McDonald's-free.

"I don't think the Woodstock spirit is ever going to change," says Tony Fletcher. "It's a liberal, progressive community that understands the history of the town. There will come a point when the vast majority of the people from the sixties are no longer with us, but I don't see that spirit changing. The Democrats outnumber Republicans five to one on the town board." For Milton Glaser, whose wife inadvertently triggered the town's rock revolution in the first place, there is still an "unspoiled bucolic sweetness" to Woodstock: "Shirley and I always compare it to our friends in the Hamptons, who are busy all the time and where the idea of a protective enclave doesn't exist. I think that's one of the reasons Albert went there. He hated that kind of social activity, it wasn't natural for him. And he wasn't impressed by people who had a lot of money."

Along with its purple houses, however, Woodstock has settled for life as a tourist trap – and a somewhat meaningless one at that. When the summer crowds pour into town, lured by a half-digested myth of the place, the merchants who flog them T-shirts and crystals are slow to disabuse them of their illusions. "Remembering Woodstock the way it was and seeing the T-shirt shops and the pictures of Bobby all over the town", says Peter Yarrow, "is like the selling of something precious. It's as if the real substance has now evolved into a cartoon version of what it once was."

"What's the difference between Giuliani's Times Square and Woodstock's village green?" says Jonathan Donahue. "Not much. People wax poetic about a Woodstock that isn't there any more – not Deanie's and not the Pinecrest Motel, let alone Richard Manuel's

Woodstock, which was more of a Wild West. It's like they're wor-
shipping ghosts, creating devotional deities that didn't operate the
way we think they did." Yet paradoxically it may be the tacky pathos
of Woodstock that saves it. "It's almost a caricature of what you
think it ought to be," says Tony Fletcher. "Which ultimately makes
it quite authentic." Geoff Muldaur thinks the inherent scuzziness of
Woodstock's centre is exactly what redeems it. "I think it keeps the
place good," he says. "I say to Happy Traum and John Sebastian,
'What saves this town is all those scuzzbags in the middle of it.
Everybody takes one look at them and keeps going to Vermont!'"

Artist Bruce Dorfman, who taught Bob Dylan to paint in an
unassuming cube of a Byrdcliffe studio, believes Woodstock is actually morphing into something that bears true witness to its artistic
past. "It looks to be turning on the efforts of the Artists Association
Museum," he says. "There's an attempt to try to get deeper about
things, and that's got to be helpful to the place." For Dorfman,
Woodstock will always be special: "It offers something more than
beautiful landscape. It offers an emotional thing as well. At its best,
it's comfortable and comforting to be around people who are living
their lives in a way that is somehow related to your own beliefs. It
reduces the sense of isolation."

Woodstock Times editor and bluegrass guitarist Brian Hollander
struggles to think of another place where he could "do these two
things the way I like doing them" and suggests I leave my last words
to a 1989 song by the Texan troubadour James McMurtry:

> *I'm not from here, but people tell me it's not like it used to be.*
> *They say I should have been here back about ten years*
> *Before it got ruined by folks like me.*

CODA

DIDN'T HE RAMBLE

On a mild autumn night in 1998, Levon Helm sits in almost pitch darkness in the Barn, his home-cum-studio off Woodstock's Plochmann Lane. He's wirily thin and ashen-grey-faced, very different from the grinning roustabout he was in the great days of The Band. His pupils look pinned, though the only drug he consumes in my company takes the form of a hash cookie. More shockingly, his voice is faint to the point of near inaudibility. I feel guilty asking him to talk at all.

A few months back, Helm was diagnosed with – of all the cruel things – cancer of the vocal cords. Subsequently he's undergone twenty-eight brutal doses of radiotherapy. "I didn't have to have any chemo," he rasps. "They tell me they think they got it, and God, I pray they did." Next to living and dying, he admits his biggest concern now is being able to sing again. "I never thought much about it, because Richard was always The Band's lead singer," he says. "But now that I can't, fuck, I really want to!"

Helm talks with a deep appreciation of his adopted northern home town. "Woodstock has been very forgiving," he says. "It's a town full of good people. Without having any kind of regular scene except a couple of studios, it's really good because there's no commercialism, and it just makes it quieter. People aren't apt to come bothering you. Every now and then somebody'll pull in looking for Dylan, but that's about it."

"Levon has always sought out the locals more than the artistic types here," Happy Traum tells me a few days later. "He used to have these Fourth of July barbecues, and there would be at least as many of the local plumbers and carpenters and stonemasons there as musicians and artists." For Traum, Helm's diagnosis has had only a positive impact on his mental attitude. "I've rarely seen him so gregarious and cheerful since he's come through the other side," he says. "He seems to have been given a new lease on life."

One thing, though, hasn't changed in Helm's attitude, and that is his rage towards The Band's former guitarist. "Robbie Robertson's got people who'll say he wrote everything," he says, fixing me with a steely glare. "Those are the same people that are helping him spend the fucking money, but he knows it ain't right, it ain't fucking true . . . And it damn sure ain't fair for him and Albert Grossman's estate to spend all The Band's money." Some of his friends, aghast at his boy-cotting of The Band's 1994 induction into the Rock and Roll Hall of Fame, have urged him to get over his grievances. "Ronnie Hawkins told Levon he should bury the hatchet, and I kind of agree," says Ian Kimmet. "But there's a working-class part of me that digs it and says, 'Good for him!'"

What I didn't quite grasp as I wandered around the Barn in October 1998 – and when I visited him again the following January – was just how broke Helm was. He and his wife Sandy had, in fact, been declared bankrupt, and the Barn was in serious danger of being repossessed. Within a decade, though he was still in debt, almost everything had turned around. He had kept the cancer at bay and was even singing again. With the help of his new right-hand man, Larry Campbell, he'd recorded the widely hailed comeback *Dirt Farmer* (2007), a Grammy-winning album of Americana – part Muddy Waters, part Dock Boggs – that made far more sense than anything he'd released previously as a solo artist.

More triumphantly still, he had turned the Barn into the live venue he'd always fantasised about. "Levon and I built houses at the same time," says Garth Hudson. "He said to me, 'We'll have a show and we'll call it Uncle Remus, and we'll have various groups and singers and we'll televise it.'" Stan Beinstein remembers Helm voicing a similar dream: "He told me he was going to set a stage up at the Getaway and have Chuck Berry and Bo Diddley come up to play. I thought, 'A hundred and eighty people in the place, and these people are coming up *here*?' And then I went to the Barn years later and thought, 'Holy shit, he did it. In his own living room.'"

In 1991, when I visited the original RCO barn Helm had built in the mid-seventies, it was literally a smouldering ruin. A fire had recently gutted the place, though some locals thought he might have torched it himself to collect the insurance money. Rebuilt in the same spot and to the same specifications, by the summer of 2005 the Barn was home to a weekly "Midnight Ramble" hosted by Helm and featuring his daughter. "Amy being part of the band, as well as part of the family, really made it special," says Mercury Rev's Grasshopper. "Playing with her dad and helping him, it all came together."

"I was always wary of being around my idols, and I'd heard Levon could be a little mercurial," says trumpeter Steve Bernstein. "The first Ramble I played was in November 2004. I wrote some quick horn charts and said to [saxophonist] Erik Lawrence, 'I don't want this to sound like a wedding band.' When Levon got on the drums, it was like the purest free improvisation ever."

The Ramble owed almost everything to the crusading belief and commitment of Barbara O'Brien. Saddened by the deaths of Richard Manuel and Rick Danko – and distraught at the depressed state in which she found Helm in 2003 – she set about making the drummer's dreams come true. "I always felt I could straighten The Band out," she says, sitting outside the Barn on a balmy autumn afternoon. "I didn't want to be their girlfriend, I just wanted to help them." When I went to the Ramble in July 2009, it was immediately clear she had done just that. "She's the first manager he's ever had that you could call a manager," said John Simon, who was himself performing that night. "She's stable and not crazy, and the fact that Levon's put his trust in her is a wonderful thing."

Levon Helm's barn, home of the Ramble, on Plochmann Lane (Art Sperl)

As I sat with Helm's band members in a ramshackle den off the Helmses' homely kitchen, I noted framed pictures of former comrades on its walls. (Rick Danko and Richard Manuel were there; Robbie Robertson, predictably, was not.) Slouched on the sofa, raking his fingers across an acoustic guitar, was Larry Campbell. Wedged in a corner and almost obscured by a vast tuba was Howard Johnson. "Someone gimme an A?" requested Byron Isaacs, the dapper bassist who anchored the band's sound – to which Johnson responded by producing a subatomic fart from his instrument. Laughter – from Isaacs and Steve Bernstein, and from Campbell and his Tennessee-born singer-guitarist wife Teresa Williams – rippled across the room.

Rumours had drifted around that Helm wouldn't be singing at that night's Ramble. Underlying them was the faint dread that his cancer had returned. "It's only the second time this has happened," he told me. "Before that we haven't had to worry about it. What voice I've got, I've always been able just to push it on out there." The Ramble was enormous fun anyway. After short sets by John Simon and octogenarian bluesman Little Sammy Davis, Helm and band kicked off with "The Shape I'm In", the first of six Band songs included in the show. Stick-thin and ghostly pale in a loose pink shirt, Helm was still – in Campbell's stage announcement – "the greatest drummer in the world". And that was true whether he was channelling the second-line spirit of New Orleans on Jelly Roll Morton's "I Thought I Heard Buddy Bolden Sing" or supplying clipped country-soul rim shots for his daughter's rendition of William Bell's "Everybody Loves a Winner". As he'd so often done with The Band, he switched periodically to mandolin – in this case for the country waltz "Did You Love Me at All?". If there was something a mite contrived about the way he had been positioned as a patron saint of Americana – *O Levon Where Art Thou*, anyone? – Helm himself was as genuine an article as American music could boast.

At that point, Larry Campbell had been playing the Rambles for four years, ever since quitting Bob Dylan's road band. "Levon and I had a two-hour conversation about the similarity of our experiences with Bob," he says. "At the end he said, 'Well, whyn't you come up to Woodstock and let's make some music together!' So I came up and never looked back." When Campbell moved back to town, Helm finally had himself a proper bandleader. "It sort of rounded out the rhythm section plus the extra voices we needed," he said. "And then with Barbara coming in, that kind of took care of everything on the *other* side of the desk."

That night, Helm talked again of Woodstock. "There's something about it," he said. "For me it's part of the south. It's one of the best towns I've ever known, and it still looks and acts the way it did when I first got here."

"Levon personified the spirit of the place, musically and in his country manner," Larry Campbell tells me today. "You could never get him to say a bad word about this town. From 1968 to the day he died, he said there was nowhere he'd rather be. He said, 'Woodstock is the one place where you can just be who you are.'" For Steve Bernstein, Helm was "kind of the symbol of what Woodstock meant . . . it was like he was one of *us*, not like some untouchable rich guy that got separated".

Anyone who ever saw a Ramble will tell you what an intimate and organic experience it was. "Levon ended up doing exactly what he wanted to be doing, and he was *right*," says Paul Fishkin. "Everything I ever revered about the music world and how it should be was manifest in the Ramble." For Marshall Crenshaw, who guested at the Barn in November 2009, there *was* no scene in noughties Woodstock before the Ramble. "It galvanised people," he says. "I took my eight-year-old son and he sat right behind the drum kit. At one point Levon turned around and gave him this great big grin. And then he handed him a set of drumsticks. He's never gotten over that."

Among the other luminaries to play the Ramble were Elvis Costello and Allen Toussaint; Ralph Stanley and Charlie Louvin; Gillian Welch and David Rawlings; the Grateful Dead's Phil Lesh and Bob Weir; Jackson Browne and Ramblin' Jack Elliott; Bill Frissell and Billy Bob Thornton; Kris Kristofferson and Kinky Friedman . . . along with John Prine, Norah Jones, Hubert Sumlin, Taj Mahal, Mavis Staples and far too many more to mention. Among those with a direct connection to Woodstock were Happy Traum, John Sebastian, Donald Fagen, Jesse Winchester, Maria Muldaur, Natalie Merchant and Cindy Cashdollar.

Garth Hudson, who guested at the Ramble "four or five times over the years", says he felt an almost paternal pride in what Helm achieved at the Barn. *Woodstock Times* editor Brian Hollander shared in that pride. "There's no Big Daddy like Albert in town any more, but Levon enjoyed that role," he says. "He enjoyed having a twelve-piece band coming up to his barn and getting a good payday." At the turn of the decade, Barbara O'Brien began inviting younger acts – bands such as Drive-By Truckers and My Morning Jacket – to the Ramble. "I'd read the bios of Mumford & Sons and Dawes and they always mentioned The Band," she says. "They were getting that scruffy look, with the wrinkled white shirts and the vests and the hats. To see these kids in absolute awe of Levon was beautiful."*

On 31 March 2012 – with Los Lobos as his special guests – Helm played his last Ramble. The cancer had returned with a vengeance, and he was soon back in Memorial Sloan-Kettering, the hospital which had saved his life. This time there was nothing they could do except make the end as comfortable as possible. Word got around to everyone who needed to know and wanted to say goodbye. Among them was Robbie Robertson, contacted by the woman now known – after her marriage to Donald Fagen – as Libby Titus-Fagen.

In 2005 I'd asked Robertson how pained he felt by the bad blood between him and the man who'd been like an elder sibling to him. "I do feel deep in my heart that my brotherhood with Levon is untouchable," he'd replied. "I just wish him well and hope he doesn't have to live a life of bitterness and anger. He was like my closest friend, so I just want the best for him and hope he finds a way to relieve himself of having to deal with everything through negativity."

On the surface, therefore, it was moving to learn of Robertson's visit to Memorial Sloan-Kettering on 15 April. "I sat with Levon for a good while, and thought of the incredible and beautiful times we

* Drive-By Truckers, scions of Alabama, had included a harrowingly beautiful song about Rick Danko and Richard Manuel on their 2004 album *The Dirty South*. "Fifteen years ago we owned that road," its author Jason Isbell had sung. "Now it's rolling over us instead . . ."

had together," he wrote on Facebook. Though Robertson did not claim he'd spoken with Helm, the wishful thinking of others turned the deathbed scene into a touching moment of reconciliation. "Amy told us she went in and said, 'Dad, is it true you patched things up with Robbie?'" says Jonathan Donahue. "Levon said, 'We didn't patch up *shit*.'"

Yet Titus-Fagen, who sat outside the hospital room during Robertson's visit, wrote this to me six days after Helm died: "The story is much more complex than the bloggers and the press understand. I can tell you that, for the years I was with Levon – from 1968 to 1974 – they each shared a part of the other's soul. One would start a sentence, pause, and the other would finish it. They had their own alphabet, their own clock, their own DNA, a Levon–Robbie double helix. When I called Robbie to say Levon was dying, he was stunned, shattered – he thought Levon had beaten the cancer."

"Robbie flew to New York to say goodbye," Titus-Fagen added in her email. "Amy, Donald and I were in the waiting room, and I don't know what Robbie said to Levon for the long time he spent by his bedside. All I know is that there's a side to this life-and-death song that no one has heard. Levon wouldn't want this bitterness to ramble on any longer."

Over two thousand Woodstockers paraded past Helm's coffin at the Barn before his burial in the town's Artist Cemetery, where everyone from Ralph Whitehead to Rick Danko lies in peace. Afterwards I remembered some words Danko had said to me in 1998: "Levon and I have known each other nearly forty years and we've never once slapped one another. We've never come to blows. We've always maybe been smart enough to talk it out. And we've always protected one another."

All three of the addicts in The Band are gone now, and it seems such a waste, not only of their exceptional talent but of their touching brotherhood. "I keep telling my son that those guys were no role models for how to live life," says Marshall Crenshaw. "I say, 'You can't miss the fact that they're all dead, and they're all dead because they lived their lives in a fucked-up way. They were good people but they were childlike in all the wrong ways.'"

A year after Helm's death, the New York State Legislature approved a resolution to name Route 375 – the main artery connecting Woodstock to Kingston and the New York Thruway – Levon Helm Memorial Boulevard. At least one Woodstocker found this risible. "I don't wish to denigrate the fame or name of Levon Helm and The Band," Carl Van Wagenen, a police chief who frequently arrested them in their heyday, wrote to the *Daily Freeman*. "But [. . .] wouldn't it have been wonderful if they had donated all the money they stuffed into their noses to more appropriate venues? Does having an alternate drug-fuelled lifestyle, interspersed with occasional bankruptcies, really qualify one to have a road named after him?"

When you've made some of the greatest American music of the past half-century – and been the wild life and troubled soul of Woodstock, New York – then yes, Mr Van Wagenen, it does.

Formerly known as Route 375 . . .

TAKE YOUR PLEASURE: TWENTY-FIVE TIMELESS TRACKS

1 The Band: "In a Station" (1968)
2 John Martyn: "Woodstock" (1969)
3 The Band: "Time to Kill" (1970)
4 Bob Dylan: "Time Passes Slowly" (1970)
5 The Band: "The Rumor" (1970)
6 Bob Dylan: "Sign on the Window" (1970)
7 Van Morrison: "Old Old Woodstock" (1971)
8 Karen Dalton: "Are You Leaving for the Country?" (1971)
9 The Band (with Van Morrison): "4% Pantomime" (1971)
10 Holy Moses: "The Sad Café" (1971)
11 Bobby Charles: "Tennessee Blues" (1972)
12 Martha Velez: "Byrdcliffe Summer" (1972)
13 John Simon: "The 'Real' Woodstock Rag" (1972)
14 Bobby Charles: "Small Town Talk" (1972)
15 The Fabulous Rhinestones: "Big Indian" (1972)
16 Jesse Winchester: "Dangerous Fun" (1972)
17 Paul Butterfield's Better Days: "Highway 28" (1973)
18 Borderline: "As Long as It's You and Me" (1973)
19 Paul Butterfield's Better Days: "Take Your Pleasure Where You Find It" (1973)
20 Muddy Waters: "Why Are People Like That?" (1975)
21 Tom Pacheco: "The Hills of Woodstock" (1997)
22 Drive-By Truckers: "Danko/Manuel" (2004)
23 Mercury Rev: "Hudson Line" (1998)
24 John Herald: "Woodstock Mountains" (2000)
25 The Duke and the King: "Hudson River" (2010)

ACKNOWLEDGEMENTS

Thank you once again to Lee Brackstone and Angus Cargill at Faber, and to Jonny Geller for making this book happen. Likewise to Ben Schafer at Da Capo and to Dan Kirschen at ICM. Thank you additionally to Ian Bahrami, Amber Morris, Beth Wright and Julie Ford. Also to Kevin Freeborn for his perfect Woodstock map.

Thank you to my darling wife, Natalie, for her unwavering love and support, and to all our offspring: Jake, Fred, Nat, George and Freddie.

My gratitude to the following for granting interviews – most specifically for this book, a handful for my earlier Band biography *Across the Great Divide*, or for older magazine pieces about Levon Helm, Todd Rundgren, Van Morrison, Tim Hardin and Mercury Rev: the late Al Aronowitz, Paula Batson, Stan Beinstein, Karl Berger, Warren Bernhardt, Steve Bernstein, Graham "Monk" Blackburn, David Boyle, Harvey Brooks, Bebe Buell, Gabe Butterfield, Liz Butterfield, Larry Campbell, Cindy Cashdollar, Jim Colegrove, John Byrne Cooke, Peter Coyote, Marshall Crenshaw, Norma Cross, Arline Cunningham, David Dalton, the late Rick Danko, Jonathan Donahue, Bruce Dorfman, Robbie Dupree, Mike Ephron, Billy Faier, Simone Felice, Paul Fishkin, Tony Fletcher, Michael Friedman, Amos Garrett, Holly George-Warren, Jon Gershen, Milton Glaser, Barry Goldberg, Danny Goldberg, Sally Grossman, JoHanna Hall, the late Levon Helm, Richard Heppner, John Holbrook, Brian Hollander, Lucinda Hoyt, Garth Hudson, Aaron "Professor Louie" Hurwitz, Ian Kimmet, Al Kooper, Daniel Kramer, Elliott Landy, Michael Lang, James Lasdun, Ronnie Lyons, David McDonald, Mark McKenna,

Sean "Grasshopper" Mackowiak, Fern Malkine, Ken Mansfield, Mary Martin, Beverley Martyn, Valma Merians, Van Morrison, Paul Mozian, Geoff Muldaur, Maria Muldaur, Lynne Naso, John Niven, Barbara O'Brien, Eddy Offord, Larry Packer, Christopher Parker, Graham Parker, D. A. Pennebaker, John Platania, Bonnie Raitt, Keith Reid, Robbie Robertson, Jim Rooney, Todd Rundgren, Ed Sanders, Dean Schambach, Daoud Shaw, Jules Shear, "Disco" Linda Sheldon, John Simon, Patti Smith, John Storyk, Kasim Sulton, Jonathan Taplin, Ted Templeman, Libby Titus, the late Artie Traum, Happy Traum, Jane Traum, Martha Velez, Peter Walker, Jim Weider, Jeremy Wilber, Linda Wortman and Peter Yarrow.

In addition, my thanks to all the following:

To Ian Worpole – for providing the perfect base in Woodstock.

To Edward Helmore and Alastair Bates – for their gracious hospitality in New York.

To Ian Kimmet – who supported (and amused) me throughout my research.

To David Boyle, John Byrne Cooke, Jon Gershen, Douglas Gilbert, Bob Gruen, Ian Kimmet, Dan Kramer, Elliott Landy, Lisa Law, Monique Paturel, John Scheele, Shep Siegel, John Simon, Art Sperl and Getty/Michael Ochs Archives for providing the wonderful images.

To Fern Malkine – who generously shared her archive of Woodstock history.

To JoAnn Margolis – for her meticulous assistance at the Woodstock Historical Society.

To Clinton Heylin – the ultimate Dylan fact-checker.

To Paul Smart and Weston Blelock – Woodstock experts who generously shared contacts and suggestions.

To Fred Goodman and James Motluk – for helping to shape my thoughts about Albert Grossman.

To Johnny Black – for sharing the transcripts of his interviews about Jimi Hendrix's "kidnapping".

To Pete Frame – for sending the family tree to end all family trees.

To Holger Petersen and Nick Bollinger – for their interviews with Bobby Charles.

To Edward Helmore (again) – for the transcript of his interview with Sally Grossman.

To Gayle Jamison – for her hospitality on Ohayo Mountain Road.

To Charlie Boxer – for sending Ezra Titus's stories.

To George Slater – for some impeccable transcriptions.

And to all those who provided assistance, encouragement and/or simple favours along the way: Kerry Adamson, Keith Altham, June Harris Barsalona, Dean Biddle, Loraine Alterman Boyle, Beth Bradford, Eve Brandstein, Bonnie Brooks, Tim Broun, Peter Stone Brown, Val Brown, Martin Colyer, Ted Cummings, John and Jan Cuneo, Ben Edmonds, Steve Farina, Martha Frankel, Mick Gold, John Griffin, Craig Harris, Will Hermes, Ken Hunt, Nicholas Jennings, Gordena Jesson, Duncan Jordan, Harvey Kubernik, Michael Naso, Joe Pickering, Simon Reynolds, Henry Scott-Irvine, Pal Shazar, David Simpson, Jim Sullivan, Alana Tyson, Julia Wrenn and Dusty Wright.

To my colleagues at Rock's Backpages for bearing with me through the research and writing: Mark Pringle, Tony Keys, Paul Kelly and Kate Allen.

Finally, to all the good friends made in Woodstock over many years: Mark and Maria Larson, Richard and Parveneh Holloway, Ian and April Worpole, Barry and April Price, Scott and Sari Grandstaff, Paul and Liza Mones, Ras T and family, Nic Harcourt, Abba Roland, Dennis Collins and too many more to mention.

BIBLIOGRAPHY

"AllMusic Review: *Paul Butterfield's Better Days*", AllMusic.com, n.d.: www. allmusic.com/album/paul-butterfields-better-days-mw0000312871

Alterman, Loraine, and Ben Fong-Torres, "Bob Dylan's Star-Studded Homecoming", *Rolling Stone*, 14 March 1974

"An Interview with Phil Ochs", *Broadside*, 15 October 1965

Anson, Robert Sam, *Gone Crazy and Back Again: The Rise and Fall of the* Rolling Stone *Generation* (Garden City, NY: Doubleday, 1981)

Aronowitz, Alfred G., *The Blacklisted Masterpieces of Al Aronowitz* (self-published, 1981)

—— *Bob Dylan and the Beatles*, Volume 1 of *The Best of the Blacklisted Journalist* (Bloomington, IN: 1st Books Library, 2003)

—— "Eyewitness: Dylan Turns the Beatles onto Dope", *Q*, May 1994

—— "Friends and Neighbors Just Call Us the Band", *Rolling Stone*, 24 August 1968

—— "Tom Pacheco Honors Al Aronowitz with a Heartfelt Tribute", Tom Pacheco, 2005: www.tompacheco.com/cgi-bin/news/newsmanager. pl?action=show&id=11

—— "Woodstock . . . Well, Dylan Likes the Name", *New York Post*, 11 August 1969

Atlas, Jacoba, "Interview with Tim Hardin", *Hullabaloo*, October 1968

Baer, Joshua, "The Band: The Robbie Robertson Interview", *Musician*, May 1982

Baez, Joan, *Daybreak* (New York, NY: Dial, 1968)

Batson, Billy, "The Original Woodstock 1960s Rock & Roll Band [review of *Holy Moses* (Audio CD)]", Amazon.com, 17 April 2010: www.amazon. com/review/ROXI0X6OZIF9M

Bauldie, John (Ed.), *Wanted Man: In Search of Bob Dylan* (London: Penguin, 1990)

Bell, Ian, *Once Upon a Time: The Lives of Bob Dylan* (Edinburgh: Mainstream, 2012)

Bender, William, "The Band: Down to Old Dixie and Back", *Time*, 12 January 1970

Black, Johnny, "The Kidnapping of Jimi Hendrix", *Classic Rock*, October 2011

—— unpublished interview with Claire Moriece, 2011

———— unpublished interview with Jerry Velez, 2011

———— unpublished interview with Jim Marron, 2011

———— unpublished interview with Juma Sultan, 2011

Blelock, Weston, and Julia Blelock (Eds), *Roots of the 1969 Woodstock Festival: The Backstory to "Woodstock"* (Woodstock, NY: Woodstock Arts, 2009)

Bollinger, Nick, unpublished interview with Bobby Charles, 3 May 1995

Boyd, Joe, *White Bicycles: A Memoir of the Sixties* (London: Serpent's Tail, 2005)

Brend, Mark, *American Troubadours: Groundbreaking Singer Songwriters of the '60s* (San Francisco, CA: Backbeat Books, 2001)

Broven, John, *South to Louisiana: The Music of the Cajun Bayous* (Gretna, LA: Pelican, 1983)

Brown, Mick, *American Heartbeat: Travels from Woodstock to San Jose by Song Title* (London: Michael Joseph, 1993)

Browne, David, *Dream Brother: The Lives and Music of Jeff and Tim Buckley* (London: Fourth Estate, 2001)

Buell, Bebe, with Victor Bockris, *Rebel Heart: An American Rock 'n' Roll Journey* (New York, NY: St Martin's Griffin, 2002)

Chapple, Steve, and Reebee Garofalo, *Rock 'n' Roll Is Here to Pay: The History and Politics of the Music Industry* (Chicago, IL: Nelson-Hall, 1977)

Cohen, Scott, "Don't Ask Me Nothin' About Nothin', I Might Just Tell You the Truth: Bob Dylan Revisited", *Spin*, December 1985

Cooke, John Byrne, *On the Road with Janis Joplin* (New York, NY: Berkley Books, 2015)

Cornyn, Stan, with Paul Scanlon, *Exploding: The Highs, Hits, Hype, Heroes, and Hustlers of the Warner Music Group* (New York, NY: Rolling Stone Press/Harper Entertainment, 2002)

Cott, Jonathan, "Bob Dylan: The *Rolling Stone* Interview, Part II", *Rolling Stone*, 16 November 1978

Cross, Charles E., *Room Full of Mirrors: A Biography of Jimi Hendrix* (London: Sceptre, 2006)

Crowe, Cameron, essay for the Bob Dylan box set *Biograph* (Columbia Records, 1985)

Daley, Dan, "John Storyk: Thirty Years of Studio Design", *Mix*, 1 June 1999

Dallas, Karl, *Singers of an Empty Day* (London: Kahn & Averill, 1971)

Dalton, David, *Who Is That Man? In Search of the Real Bob Dylan* (New York, NY: Hyperion, 2012)

———— with Jonathan Cott, "The Million Dollar Bash", *The Rolling Stone Rock 'n' Roll Reader* (New York, NY: Bantam, 1974)

Dannemann, Monika, *The Inner World of Jimi Hendrix* (New York, NY: St Martin's, 1995)

Davis, Clive, with James Willwerth, *Clive: Inside the Record Business* (New York, NY: William Morrow, 1975)

Delehant, Jim, "Impressions of Bob Dylan by Michael Bloomfield", *Hit Parader*, June 1968

DeLillo, Don, *Great Jones Street* (Boston, MA: Houghton Mifflin, 1973)

Duncan, Robert, "Todd Rundgren: Veg-o-Matic into the Void", *Creem*, October 1975

Dylan, Bob, *Chronicles: Volume One* (New York, NY: Simon & Schuster, 2004)

────── *Writings and Drawings* (London: Panther, 1974)

Einarson, John, *Desperados: The Roots of Country Rock* (New York, NY: Cooper Square, 2001)

────── with Ian and Sylvia Tyson, *Four Strong Winds: Ian and Sylvia* (Toronto: Emblem, 2011)

Ellis III, Tom, "Paul Butterfield: From Newport to Woodstock", *Blues Access*, spring 1997: www.bluesaccess.com/No_29/butter.html and www.blues.access.com/No_31/butter.html

Escott, Colin, liner notes for Paul Butterfield's *Bearsville Anthology* (Castle Records, 2000)

Evers, Alf, *Woodstock: History of an American Town* (Woodstock, NY: Overlook, 1987)

Fagen, Donald, *Eminent Hipsters* (London: Jonathan Cape, 2013)

Festival Express, directed by Bob Smeaton and Frank Cvitanovich (Apollo Films, 2003)

Fleming, Colin, "The Secrets of the Sessions that Produced Some of Bob Dylan's Best Songs", *Vanity Fair*, 17 November 2014

Fong-Torres, Ben, "Knockin' on Bob Dylan's Door", *Rolling Stone*, 14 February 1974

────── "A Restful Farewell to Tour '74", *Rolling Stone*, 28 March 1974

Fowles, Paul, *A Concise History of Rock Music* (Pacific, MO: Bill's Music Shelf/Mel Bay, 2009)

Frame, Pete, "Muldaur, Garrett, Keith 'n' Rooney", *Even More Rock Family Trees* (London: Omnibus, 2011)

Frankel, Martha, "The Joyous Lake", 2014: marthafrankel.com/the-joyous-lake

"Fred Neil: Where's It All Going?" *Hit Parader*, January 1966

Friedman, Myra, *Buried Alive: The Biography of Janis Joplin* (New York, NY: William Morrow, 1973)

Gabites, Lee, "The Truth, the Whole Truth and Nothing but the Truth: An Interview with John Simon", 2000: thebandhiofno/articles/the_truthhtml

Geertsema, Tobie, "The Scene at Woodstock", *Daily Freeman* (Kingston, NY), 19 June 1969

Gilbert, Douglas R, *Forever Young: Photographs of Bob Dylan* (New York, NY: Da Capo, 2005)

Gill, Andy, "The Band: Back to the Land", *MOJO*, November 2000

Gleason, Ralph J, "Bob Dylan: Like a Rolling Stone, Again", *Rolling Stone*, 28 March 1974

Glover, Tony, "The Band: A Wonderful New Group", *Eye*, October 1968

Gold, Mick, "The Band: A Tree with Roots", *Let It Rock*, April 1974

Goldberg, Danny, *Bumping into Geniuses: My Life Inside the Rock and Roll Business* (New York, NY: Gotham Books, 2008)

Goldberg, Michael, "Albert Grossman: 1926–1986", *Rolling Stone*, March 1986

Goldstein, Richard, *Another Little Piece of My Heart: My Life of Rock and Revolution in the '60s* (New York, NY: Bloomsbury, 2015)

Goodman, Fred, *The Mansion on the Hill: Dylan, Young, Geffen, Springsteen, and the Head-On Collision of Rock and Commerce* (New York, NY: Times Books, 1997)

Gray, Michael, and John Bauldie (Eds), *All Across the Telegraph: A Bob Dylan Handbook* (London: Sidgwick & Jackson, 1987)

Griffin, Dan, "Rick Danko's Woodstock, Part One: Wit and Wisdom in the Midnight Hours", Blinded by Sound, 28 December 2011: blindedbysound.com/rick-dankos-woodstock-part-one

—— "Rick Danko's Woodstock, Part Two: A Canadian and a Brit Keep Woodstock Alive", Blinded by Sound, 1 January 2012: blindedbysound. com/rick-dankos-woodstock-part-two

—— "Rick Danko's Woodstock, Part Three: A Mullet, a Baby Deer and a Joyous Noise", Blinded by Sound, 2 January 2012: blindedbysound.com/ rick-dankos-woodstock-part-three

—— "Rick Danko's Woodstock, Part Four: New Year's Eve at the Bearsville Theater 1991", Blinded by Sound, 9 January 2012: blindedbysound.com/rick-dankos-woodstock-pt-4-new-years-eve-at-the-bearsville-theater-1991

Griffin, Sid, *Million Dollar Bash: Bob Dylan, The Band and the Basement Tapes* (London: Jawbone, 2007)

Grossweiner, Bob, and Jane Cohen, "Industry Profile: Marc Nathan", Celebrity Access, 1 July 2005: www.celebrityaccess.com/news/profile. html?id=256

Hajdu, David, *Positively Fourth Street: The Lives and Times of Joan Baez, Bob Dylan, Mimi Baez Fariña and Richard Fariña*, 10th anniversary edition (New York, NY: Picador, 2011)

Harris, Craig, *The Band: Pioneers of Americana Music* (Lanham, MD: Rowman & Littlefield, 2014)

Haust, Jan, liner notes, Bob Dylan and The Band, *The Basement Tapes Complete, The Bootleg Series, Vol. 11* (Deluxe Edition), box set (Columbia Records, 2014)

Havens, Richie, *They Can't Hide Us Anymore* (New York, NY: Avon, 1999)

Hawkins, Ronnie, with Peter Goddard, *Last of the Good Ol' Boys* (Toronto: Stoddart, 1989)

Hedin, Benjamin (Ed.), *Studio A: The Bob Dylan Reader* (New York, NY: W. W. Norton, 2004)

Heil, Jane, "Dave Van Ronk: Big Daddy of the Blues Singers", *Hit Parader*, July 1966

Helm, Levon, with Stephen Davis, *This Wheel's on Fire: Levon Helm and the Story of the Band* (New York, NY: William Morrow, 1993)

Helmore, Edward, "Dylan's Basement Tapes: It Sounded Like Nonsense, Says His 'Cover Girl'", *Observer*, 1 November 2014

—— unpublished interview with Sally Grossman, October 2014

Heppner, Richard, and Janine Fallon-Mower, *Legendary Locals of Woodstock, New York* (Charleston, SC: Legendary Locals/Arcadia, 2013)

Hermes, Will, *Love Goes to Buildings on Fire: Five Years in New York that Changed Music Forever* (New York: Faber & Faber, 2011)

Heylin, Clinton, *Bob Dylan: Behind the Shades* (20th anniversary edition) (London: Faber & Faber, 2011)

—— *Can You Feel the Silence? A New Biography of Van Morrison* (Chicago, IL: A Capella Books, 2003)

—— *A Life in Stolen Moments: Day by Day, 1941–1995* (New York, NY: Schirmer, 1996)

—— "What's Reel & What Is Not: Some Historical Notes on Those 'Basement Tape' Tapes", in Bob Dylan and the Band, *The Basement Tapes Complete, The Bootleg Series, Vol. 11* (Deluxe Edition), box set (Columbia Records, 2014)

Hollander, Brian, "The Survivor: Levon Lives to Ramble On", *Woodstock Times*, 2 July 2008

Holsapple, Peter, "Anatomy of a Flop", Measure for Measure (blog post), *New York Times*, 18 November 2008

Holzman, Jac, and Gavan Daws, *Follow the Music: The Life and High Times of Elektra Records in the Great Years of American Pop Culture* (Santa Monica, CA: FirstMedia Books, 1998)

Hopkins, Jerry, *Hit and Run: The Jimi Hendrix Story* (New York, NY: Perigree, 1983)

Hoskyns, Barney, *Across the Great Divide: The Band and America*, expanded edition (London: Pimlico Books, 2003)

—— "The Eden Project: Van Morrison and *Astral Weeks*", *MOJO*, November 2001

—— "In Her Own Time and Ours: The Cult of Karen Dalton", eMusic, August 2007: www.wonderingsound.com/spotlight/in-her-own-time-and-ours-the-cult-of-karen-dalton

—— "Mercury Rev: 'Most People Wait Till Later for Substance Abuse'", *Guardian*, 17 August 2001

——— "Tim Hardin: The Unforgiven", *MOJO*, February 2012

——— "Todd Rundgren: 'Go Ahead, Ignore Me!'" *MOJO*, November 1997

——— "Various Artists: Woodstock 40", *Observer Music Monthly*, July 2009

Houghton, Mick, *Becoming Elektra: The True Story of Jac Holzman's Visionary Record Label* (London: Jawbone, 2010)

——— *I've Always Kept a Unicorn: The Biography of Sandy Denny* (London: Faber & Faber, 2015)

How Sweet the Sound, documentary directed by Joe Berlinger, produced by Radical Media, 2009

Hund, Peter, "Taj Mahal", Good New Music, 21 August 2012: goodnewmusic.com/?p=3201

Iachetta, Michael, "Scarred Bob Dylan Is Comin' Back", *New York Daily News*, 8 May 1967

"Interview with Howard Alk", *Take One*, March 1978

Israel, Steve, "Dylan Returns Home with Friends", *Times Herald-Record* (Middletown, NY), 17 July 2009

James, Billy, *A Dream Goes on Forever: The Continuing Story of Todd Rundgren* (Bentonville, AR: Golden Treasures, 2002)

Jennings, Nicholas, *Before the Gold Rush: Flashbacks to the Dawn of the Canadian Sound* (Toronto: Penguin Books, 1998)

Jimi Hendrix: The Road to Woodstock, BBC4, 11 October 2014

Jordan, Scott, "Backtalk with Levon Helm", *Offbeat*, December 1998

Kaufman, Michael T., "Woodstock Up Tight as Hippies Drift In", *New York Times*, 19 June 1970

Kooper, Al, review of the Band's *Music from Big Pink*, *Rolling Stone*, 10 August 1968

——— with Ben Edmonds, *Backstage Passes: Rock 'n' Roll Life in the Sixties* (New York, NY: Stein & Day, 1977)

Kovach, Bill, "Woodstock's a Stage, but Many Don't Care for the Show", *New York Times*, 9 July 1969

Kramer, Daniel, *Bob Dylan: A Portrait of the Artist's Early Years* (London: Plexus, 2001)

LaBruce, Bruce, "Terry Richardson, 1998", *Index Magazine*, 1998: www.indexmagazine.com/interviews/terry_richardson.shtml

Landy, Elliott, *Dylan in Woodstock* (Guildford, UK: Genesis, 2000)

——— *Woodstock Vision* (Hamburg: Rowohlt, 1980)

Lane, Dakota, "Band Stand", *Woodstock Times*, 1 August 1991

Lang, Michael, with Holly George-Warren, *The Road to Woodstock* (New York, NY: Ecco, 2009)

Larkin, Philip, review of *Highway 61 Revisited*, *Daily Telegraph*, 10 November 1965

Lasdun, James, "Oh Death", in *It's Beginning to Hurt: Stories* (London: Picador, 2010)

Lefsetz, Bob, "Cowboys and Indies", The Lefsetz Letter: First in Music
    Analysis (blog), 6 March 2014: lefsetz.com/wordpress/index.php/
    archives/2014/03/06/cowboys-indies
Leviton, Mark, "Badfinger at the Crossroads", *Phonograph Record*, May 1972
Loder, Kurt, "Bob Dylan: Recovering Christian", *Rolling Stone*, 21 June 1984
Lost Songs: The Basement Tapes Continued, documentary directed by Sam
    Jones, produced by Beware Doll Films, 2014
Love, Robert, "Bob Dylan: The Uncut Interview", *AARP: The Magazine*,
    February/March 2015
Lucas, Gary, *Touched by Grace: My Time with Jeff Buckley* (London:
    Jawbone, 2013)
Lydon, Michael, *Flashbacks: Eyewitness Accounts of the Rock Revolution,
    1964–1974* (New York, NY: Routledge, 2003)
——— *Rock Folk: Portraits from the Rock 'n' Roll Pantheon* (New York, NY:
    Delta, 1971)
McDermott, John, and Eddie Kramer, *Hendrix: Setting the Record Straight*
    (New York, NY: Time Warner, 1992)
MacDonald, Ian, *The People's Music: Selected Journalism* (London: Pimlico
    Books, 2003)
McGregor, Craig (Ed.), *Bob Dylan: A Retrospective* (London: Picador, 1975)
The Making of Jeff Buckley's "Grace", DVD feature by Ernie Fritz, 10th
    anniversary reissue of *Grace* (Sony, 2004)
Marcus, Greil, *Invisible Republic: Bob Dylan's Basement Tapes* (New York,
    NY: Henry Holt, 1997)
——— *Mystery Train: Images of America in Rock 'n' Roll Music* (4th revised
    edition) (London: Plume, 1997)
——— *When that Rough God Goes Riding: Listening to Van Morrison* (New
    York, NY: Public Affairs, 2010)
Martyn, Beverley, *Sweet Honesty: The Beverley Martyn Story* (Guildford,
    UK: Grosvenor House, 2011)
Marvin, Pamela, *Lee: A Romance* (London: Faber & Faber, 1997)
Maymudes, Victor, and Jacob Maymudes, *Another Side of Bob Dylan: A
    Personal History on the Road and off the Tracks* (New York, NY: St
    Martin's, 2014)
Medenbach, Deborah, "A Beacon in Bearsville", *Ulster*, September/October
    2013
"Meeting Held on Hippie Problem", *Ulster County*, 12 December 1968
Meisel, Perry, "The Woodstock Myth: Dues City Is a Roadie's Reality",
    Village Voice, 16 March 1976
Merrill, Sam, "Mason Hoffenberg Gets in a Few Licks", *Playboy*, November
    1973
Meyer, Musa, *Night Studio: A Memoir of Philip Guston* (London: Thames &
    Hudson, 1991)

Miliard, Mike, "The Go-Between: Al Aronowitz", *Boston Phoenix*, 3
    December 2004

Milward, John, *Crossroads: How the Blues Shaped Rock 'n' Roll* (Boston,
    MA: Northeastern University Press, 2013)

Miss Information, "Woodstock – Re: Atlas" (email message), the Dylan Atlas,
    15 November 2004: expectingrain.com/dok/atlas/woodstock.html

Morley, Paul, "Utopia in Woodstock", *New Musical Express*, 24 April 1982

Morrison, Van, *Lit Up Inside: Selected Lyrics* (London: Faber & Faber,
    2014)

Moscoso-Gongora, Peter, "Woodstock Was: Dylan's Dream Is Dying Hard",
    Harper's, September 1972

Myers, Paul, *A Wizard, a True Star: Todd Rundgren in the Studio* (London:
    Jawbone, 2010)

Niven, John, *Music from Big Pink: A Novella* (New York: Continuum, 2005)

Obrecht, Jas, "Jimi Hendrix: From Toronto to Woodstock", Jas Obrecht
    Music Archive, 2010: jasobrecht.com/jimi-hendrix-woodstock

O'Conner, Rory, "Albert Grossman's Ghost", *Musician*, June 1987

Panken, Ted, "Karl Berger and Ingrid Sertso: Interviews", Ted Panken (blog),
    October 2008: tedpanken.wordpress.com/category/karl-berger

Pareles, Jon, review of Bob Dylan at Bethel Woods, *New York Times*, 2 July
    2007

Pearl, Mike, "The Mystery of Folk Singer Bob Dylan", *World Journal
    Tribune*, 14 October 1966

Perkins, Michael, "A Short History of Poetry in Woodstock, 1973–2008",
    Woodstock Times, 17 April 2008

Perry, Tim, and Ed Gilnert, *Fodor's Rock & Roll Traveler USA: The
    Ultimate Guide to Juke Joints, Street Corners, Whiskey Bars and Hotel
    Rooms Where Music History Was Made* (New York, NY: Fodor's Travel
    Publications, 1996)

Petersen, Holger, *Talking Music: Blues Radio and Roots Music* (London,
    Ontario: Insomniac, 2011)

—— unpublished interview with Bobby Charles, 23 May 1997

—— unpublished interview with Allen Toussaint, 18 October 2011

"Philip Roth Unleashed, Part One", *Imagine*, season 23, episode 2, directed
    by Sarah Aspinall, BBC, 20 May 2014

Ratliff, Ben, "Creative Music Studio: A Ferment of World Jazz Yields a Trove
    of Tapes", *New York Times*, 21 October 2008

Rebennack, Mac (Dr John), with Jack Rummel, *Under a Hoodoo Moon: The
    Life of the Night Tripper* (New York, NY: St Martin's, 1994)

Roeser, Steve, "Do What You Love: Big Brother and the Holding Company",
    Goldmine, 25 September 1998

Rogan, Johnny, *Van Morrison: No Surrender* (London: Secker & Warburg,
    2005)

Rooney, Jim, *In It for the Long Run: A Musical Odyssey* (Champaign, IL: University of Illinois Press, 2014)

Rosenbaum, Ron, "The Playboy Interview: Bob Dylan", *Playboy*, March 1978

Roth, Philip, *American Pastoral* (Boston: Houghton Mifflin, 1997)

―――― *Shop Talk: A Writer and His Colleagues and Their Work* (New York, NY: Vintage, 2002)

Rotolo, Suze, *A Freewheelin' Time: A Memoir of Greenwich Village in the Sixties* (London: Aurum, 2009, Kindle edition)

Roxon, Lillian, "The Woody Guthrie Concert", *Sydney Morning Herald*, January 1968

Saal, Hubert, "Dylan Is Back", *Newsweek*, 26 February 1968

Salvo, Patrick William, "Playing in the Band: A Conversation with Robbie Robertson", *Melody Maker*, 7 October 1972

Sander, Ellen, *Trips: Rock Life in the Sixties* (New York, NY: Charles Scribner's Sons, 1973)

Scaduto, Anthony, *Bob Dylan* (London: W. H. Allen, 1972)

Schier, Johanna, "Woodstock, NY – A Quiet Festival of Life", *Boston After Dark*, summer 1972

Scully, Rock, with David Dalton, *Living with the Dead: Twenty Years on the Bus with Garcia and the Grateful Dead* (New York, NY: Little, Brown, 1996)

Sheff, Will, "Suite for Tim and Damion Hardin", WillSheff.com, 23 December 2013: www.willsheff.com/suite-for-tim-hardin-and-black-sheep-boy

Shelton, Robert, *No Direction Home: The Life and Music of Bob Dylan* (revised and updated edition, edited by Elizabeth Thomson and Patrick Humphries) (London: Omnibus, 2011)

Shepard, Sam, "A Short Life of Trouble", originally published in *Esquire*, 1987, reprinted in Benjamin Hedin (Ed.), *Studio A: The Bob Dylan Reader* (New York: W. W. Norton, 2004)

Short, Don, interview with Bob Dylan, *Daily Mirror*, 9 August 1969

"Show Business Disease", The Garage, 3 June 2014: thegarage13.blogspot. co.uk/2014/06/show-business-disease.html

Siegel, Jules, "Bob Dylan: 'Well, What Have We Here?'" *Saturday Evening Post*, 30 July 1966

Silber, Irwin, "Open Letter to Bob Dylan", *Sing Out!*, November 1964

Simmons, Michael, essay for the box set *Michael Bloomfield: From His Head to His Heart to His Hands* (Columbia Records, 2014)

Skelly, Richard, "An Interview with Lonesome Dave Peverett", *Goldmine*, 1995: www.foghat.com/dave/goldmine.htm

Smart, Paul, "Bearsville's Baron", *Hudson Valley Times*, 24 February 2011

Smart, Paul, and T. P. Moynihan, *Rock and Woodstock* (Fleischmanns, NY: Purple Mountain Press, 1994)

Smith, Patti, "The Band: The Notch #3", *Circus*, September 1970

Sounes, Howard, *Down the Highway: The Life of Bob Dylan* (London: Doubleday, 2001)

Spencer, Ruth Albert, interviews with Levon Helm, Rick Danko, Robbie Robertson, Garth Hudson and Richard Manuel, *Woodstock Times*, March–April 1985

Spitz, Bob, *Dylan: A Biography* (New York: McGraw-Hill, 1989)

Stampfel, Peter, liner notes for Karen Dalton's *It's So Hard to Tell Who's Going to Love You the Best*, (Koch CD reissue, 1997)

Sullivan, Jim, interview with Rick Danko, *Boston Globe*, 9 October 1980

Sweet, Robert E., *Music Universe, Music Mind: Revisiting the Creative Music Studio, Woodstock, New York* (Ann Arbor, MI: Arborville, 1996)

Taplin, Jonathan, *Outlaw Blues: Adventures in the Counter-Culture Wars* (Los Angeles, CA: Annenberg, 2011, iBooks edition)

Thomson, Graeme, *George Harrison: Behind the Locked Door* (London: Omnibus, 2013)

———— "If Your Memory Serves You Well: The Band", *Uncut*, August 2013

Titus, Ezra, "A Miraculous Recovery", from Ezra Titus: 1966–2009, 23 April 2012: www.ezratitus.com/2012/04/23/a-miraculous-recovery

Traum, Happy, "A Recording Session with Bob Dylan", Happy Traum (blog), 30 July 2012: www.happytraum.com/_blog/Happy's_Blog/post/A_Recording_Session_with_Bob_Dylan

———— "My Recording Session with Peter Tosh (and the Stones)", Happy Traum (blog), 30 July 2012: www.happytraum.com/_blog/Happy's_Blog/post/My_Recording_Session_with_Peter_Tosh_(and_the_Stones)

———— "Van Morrison: In Conversation", *Rolling Stone*, July 1970

———— and John Cohen, "Conversations with Bob Dylan", *Sing Out!*, October/November 1968

Turner, Steve, "By the Time I Got to Woodstock", *Independent*, 4 August 1990

———— *Van Morrison: It's Too Late to Stop Now* (London: Bloomsbury, 1993)

Unterberger, Richie, "Karen Dalton: Artist Biography", AllMusic.com, n.d.: www.allmusic.com/artist/karen-dalton-mn0000299882/biography

———— liner notes for CD reissue of *Great Speckled Bird* (Collector's Choice Records, 2006)

Valentine, Penny, "Contemporary Songwriters: Robbie Robertson", *Sounds*, 27 November 1971

Van Trikt, Ludwig, "Karl Berger: Interview for *Cadence*", August 2007: www.karlberger.org/interview-for-cadence.html

Van Wagenen, Carl, letter to the *Daily Freeman* (Kingston, NY), 19 March 2013

Von Schmidt, Eric, and Jim Rooney, *Baby, Let Me Follow You Down: The Illustrated Story of the Cambridge Folk Years* (Amherst, MA: University of Massachusetts Press, 1994)

Wald, Elijah, *Dylan Goes Electric! Newport, Seeger, Dylan, and the Night That Split the Sixties* (New York, NY: Dey St., 2015)

Wale, Michael, *Voxpop: Profiles of the Pop Process* (London: Harrap, 1972)

Walker, Peter (Ed.), *Karen Dalton: Songs, Poems, Writings* (Woodstock, NY: Ark, 2012)

Warhol, Andy, and Pat Hackett, *POPism: The Warhol '60s* (New York, NY: Harcourt Brace Jovanovich, 1980)

Warner, Simon, *Text and Drugs and Rock 'n' Roll: The Beats and Rock, from Kerouac to Cobain* (New York, NY: Bloomsbury Academic, 2013)

Wash, Ryan Hamilton, "Astral Sojourn", *Boston Magazine*, April 2015

Weberman, A. J., phone conversation with Bob Dylan, *East Village Other*, 19 January 1971

Weller, Sheila, "Jimi Hendrix: I Don't Want to Be a Clown Anymore", *Rolling Stone*, 15 November 1969

Wenner, Jann, "Bob Dylan Talks", *Rolling Stone*, 29 November 1969

White, Timothy, *Rock Lives: Profiles and Interviews* (London: Omnibus, 1991)

"Who's Who in A&R at Bearsville", *Billboard*, March 1980

Wilentz, Sean, *Bob Dylan in America* (New York, NY: Doubleday, 2010)

Williams, Paul, *Bob Dylan: Performing Artist, 1960–1973* (London: Omnibus, 2004)

Williams, Richard, "Van Morrison: Gonna Rock Your Gypsy Soul", *Melody Maker*, 28 July 1973

Willis, Ellen, *Out of the Vinyl Deeps: Ellen Willis on Rock Music* (Minneapolis, MN: University of Minnesota Press, 2011)

Wirth, Jim, "Interview with Al Stewart", *Uncut*, February 2014

——— "Interview with Andy Partridge", *Uncut*, June 2014

Wise, Tad, "Jerry Wapner Hangs Up His Shingle", *Hudson Valley Times*, 21 November 2013

Woodstock: Can't Get There from Here, directed by David McDonald, 2005

Yarg, Irv, "Individually Yours . . . John Herald", *Woodstock Times*, October 1996

Zanes, Warren, *Revolutions in Sound: Warner Brothers, the First 50 Years* (San Francisco, CA: Chronicle Books, 2008)

NOTES

PROLOGUE: INTO THE MYSTIC

All quotes are from author interviews with Artie Traum, Simone Felice, David Boyle, Ed Sanders, Maria Muldaur, Elliott Landy, Jonathan Donahue, Karl Berger and Brian Hollander

Part One: A Place I'd Feel Loose

13 "Take advantage", Peter Walker (Ed.), *Songs, Poems and Writings*, by kind permission of Peter Walker

CHAPTER 1: THE UNEASY ALLIANCE

All quotes are from author interviews with Robbie Dupree, Keith Reid, Elliott Landy, Maria Muldaur, Ed Sanders, Bruce Dorfman, Norma Cross, Jonathan Donahue, Cindy Cashdollar and Brian Hollander, except as follows:

18 "Like Balboa, from his 'peak in Darien'", Evers, *Woodstock*, p. 414
22 "there are motives that bring opposites together", ibid., p. 476
22 "an uneasy alliance", ibid.
22 "If you come into Woodstock", Geertsema, "The Scene at Woodstock"
22 "You people think you've invented it all", Blelock and Blelock, *Roots of the 1969 Woodstock Festival*, p. 44
23 "the most cosmopolitan village in the world", Evers, *Woodstock*, p. 604
24 "you stoked your own wood stove", Meyer, *Night Studio*, p. 38

CHAPTER 2: FOLK SONGS OF THE CATSKILLS

All quotes are from author interviews with Mark McKenna, Richard Heppner, Dean Schambach, Billy Faier, Bruce Dorfman, Happy Traum, Maria Muldaur, Peter Yarrow and Milton Glaser, except as follows:

31 "I must have been in Woodstock", Griffin, *Million Dollar Bash*, p. 19
35 "For us it was an artists' community", Blelock and Blelock, *Roots of the 1969 Woodstock Festival*, p. 43

CHAPTER 3: INSIDE ALBERT GROSSMAN

All quotes from author interviews with Billy Faier, Paul Fishkin, Barry Goldberg, Michael Friedman, Peter Yarrow, Jim Rooney, David Boyle, Jane Traum, Dean Schambach, Arline Cunningham, John Byrne Cooke, Milton Glaser, Norma Cross, Peter Walker, Ronnie Lyons and Jonathan Taplin, except as follows:

37 "I got to Chicago", Jane Heil, "Dave Van Ronk"
38 "gross irregularities", Spitz, *Dylan*, p. 179
38 "He couldn't get a job very easily after that", ibid., pp. 564–5
38 "He was a very generous man", Goldberg, "Albert Grossman"
39 "If the audience wasn't attentive", O'Conner, "Albert Grossman's Ghost"
39 "Integrity bothered Albert", Spitz, *Dylan*, p. 178
43 "He would simply stare at you and say nothing", Hajdu, *Positively Fourth Street*, p. 56
44 "Albert was a most interesting man", Einarson, *Four Strong Winds*, p. 68
44 "He signed us as much for our looks", ibid., p. 67
45 "Not your usual shopkeeper", Dylan, *Chronicles,* p. 97
45 "a Cheshire cat in untouched acres", Shelton, *No Direction Home*, p. 106
45 "This was a real big deal", Hajdu, *Positively Fourth Street*, p. 96
46 "I thought he was a terrible singer", ibid., p. 106
46 "Albert wanted to get into music publishing", ibid.
46 "a general strangeness and mystique", *How Sweet the Sound*
47 "A lot of Albert did in fact turn up in Bob", Aronowitz, *Bob Dylan and the Beatles*, p. 250
47 "The mere mention of Grossman's name", Dylan, *Chronicles*, p. 290
48 "What you see today in the music business", O'Conner, "Albert Grossman's Ghost"

CHAPTER 4: "THE GREATEST PLACE"

All quotes from author interviews with Richard Heppner, Milton Glaser, Ronnie Lyons, Jonathan Taplin, Arline Cunningham, Peter Yarrow, Norma Cross, John Byrne Cooke, Jeremy Wilber, Paul Fishkin, Peter Walker, Daniel Kramer, John Hammond Jr, Fern Malkine, Billy Faier, D. A. Pennebaker, David Boyle, Al Kooper and Bruce Dorfman, except as follows:

50 "spied a house he liked", *Chronicles*, p. 116
51 "a little two-room hut", interview by Jim Delehant in *Hit Parader*, June 1968
51 "we stop the clouds, turn time back", Shelton, *No Direction Home*, p. 166
51 "Woodstock was a place", *Lost Songs*
52 "While we were watching *The Seventh Seal*", Blelock and Blelock, *Roots of the 1969 Woodstock Festival*, pp. 51–2

52 "I had real upward mobility", O'Conner, "Albert Grossman's Ghost"

53 "I believe in his genius", Rotolo, *A Freewheelin' Time*, location 2787

54 "I thought I was going to have a ball", Merrill, "Mason Hoffenberg Gets in a Few Licks"

54 "heart-stopping soprano voice", *How Sweet the Sound*

55 "I have rode alone", Rotolo, *A Freewheelin' Time*, location 2556

55 "He was so relaxed then", Israel, "Dylan Returns Home with Friends"

56 "We drove straight back", Spitz, *Dylan*, pp. 273–4

57 "He kind of moved in with us", Shelton, *No Direction Home*, p. 262

57 "Bob sure knew how to maul me", Rotolo, *A Freewheelin' Time*, location 2906

58 "We all thought he was God", Aronowitz, *Bob Dylan and the Beatles*, p. 265

58 "silent and creepy", Rotolo, *A Freewheelin' Time*, location 2864

59 "grew up together as kids in Minnesota", Short, *Daily Mirror*

60 "not going to sign with that fat pig", Hajdu, *Positively Fourth Street*, p. 209

CHAPTER 5: BOY IN THE BUBBLE

All quotes from author interviews with John Byrne Cooke, Al Kooper, Billy Faier, D. A. Pennebaker, Norma Cross, Daniel Kramer, Al Aronowitz, Peter Coyote and Paul Fishkin, except as follows:

61 "you had to brace yourself", *Chronicles*, p. 48

61 "I could never figure out", Aronowitz, *Bob Dylan and the Beatles*, p. 341

62 "an asshole who bent over for quarters", *Another Side of Bob Dylan*, p. 127

63 "Don't worry", Hajdu, *Positively Fourth Street*, p. 247

63 "He obviously fell for her", ibid, p. 249

63 "lovely blue nightgown", Heylin, *Bob Dylan*, p. 167

64 "a huge transparent bubble of ego", Baez, *Daybreak*, quoted in Scaduto, *Bob Dylan*, p. 202

64 "You travel with an entourage now", Silber, "Open Letter to Bob Dylan"

64 "I want to meet him", Aronowitz, "Eyewitness"

64 "very awkward, very demure", Miliard, "The Go-Between"

65 "Obviously Bob liked Elvis Presley", Helmore, unpublished interview with Sally Grossman

66 "[They] were a very special trio" *et seq.*, Rotolo, *A Freewheelin' Time*, locations 2972, 2865 and 2878

66 "I think the whole Albert thing", Scaduto, *Bob Dylan*, p. 205

68 "into a kind of piping whine", Siegel, "Bob Dylan: 'Well, What Have We Here?'"

68 "I came up with a nickname for Albert", Goodman, *The Mansion on the Hill*, p. 94

69 "going mad with it all", Hajdu, *Positively Fourth Street*, pp. 251–2
69 "I was just trying to deal with the madness", *How Sweet the Sound*

CHAPTER 6: SOMETHING IS HAPPENING

All quotes from author interviews with Al Kooper, Milton Glaser, Barry
Goldberg, Harvey Brooks, Michael Friedman, Bruce Dorfman, Ronnie
Lyons, Levon Helm, Rick Danko, D. A. Pennebaker, Al Aronowitz, Ed
Sanders and John Hammond Jr, except as follows:

70 "We had come up from New York", Crowe, essay for the Bob Dylan box
   set
71 "He was so excited", John Herald quote Miss Information, "Woodstock"
72 "cawing, derisive voice", Larkin, Review of *Highway 61 Revisited*
73 "They had gotten to the point", Goodman, *The Mansion on the Hill*, pp. 8–9
73 "This was the Birth of Rock", Boyd, *White Bicycles*, p. 107
75 "a rather persevering soul", Wenner, "Bob Dylan Talks"
76 "I used to remember Albert", Siegel, "Bob Dylan"
76 "something very dangerous", Ochs interview in *Broadside*, 15 October
   1965
77 "the circumstance of one man", DeLillo, *Great Jones Street*, p. 1
77 "Dylan represented a certain milieu", Bauldie (Ed.), *Wanted Man*, p. 76
78 "I got paranoid when I heard rumours", Warhol and Hackett, *POPism*,
   p. 108
79 "It broke my heart when Levon left", Gill, "The Band"
80 "knew [Dylan] was playing with heroin", Spitz, *Dylan: A Biography*, p. 344
80 "It was a source of his power", Hajdu, *Positively Fourth Street*, p. 282
81 "That onstage posturing and rock-star arrogance", Fowles, *A Concise
   History of Rock Music*, p. 42

Part Two: Going Up the Country

CHAPTER 1: HUNDRED-AND-FORTY-DOLLAR BASH

All quotes from author interviews with D. A. Pennebaker, Peter Coyote,
Danny Goldberg, Rick Danko, Al Aronowitz, Al Kooper, Happy Traum,
Bruce Dorfman, Jonathan Taplin, Artie Traum, John Simon, Jeremy Wilber,
Graham Blackburn, Al Kooper, Larry Campbell, Simone Felice, Garth
Hudson and Levon Helm, except as follows:

85 "the most commonly quoted crash site", Perry and Gilnert, *Fodor's Rock
   & Roll Traveler USA*, p. 57
86 "[This] was the time that he was most caressed", Holzman and Daws,
   Follow the Music, p. 341

86 "he seemed like he was very high on speed", Griffin, *Million Dollar Bash*, pp. 69–70
86 "comatose", Spitz, *Dylan*, pp. 366–7
86 "Something's gotta change", Fong-Torres, "Knockin' on Bob Dylan's Door"
87 "I was driving right into the sun", Sam Shepard, "A Short Life of Trouble", anthologised in Hedin (Ed.), *Studio A*, pp. 198–9
88 "It was away from his ordinary life", Sounes, *Down the Highway*, p. 263
88 "I just remember how bad", Shepard, "A Short Life of Trouble," p. 199
88 "This accident may have been a good thing", Pearl, "The Mystery of Folk Singer Bob Dylan"
89 "stared at the ceiling for a few months", Saal, "Dylan Is Back"
89 "We were all trying to live a 'normal life'", Batson, "The Original Woodstock 1960's Rock & Roll Band"
90 "I suppose they were close enough", Griffin, *Million Dollar Bash*, p. 64
91 "Robbie called me up one day", *Lost Songs*
93 "a typical basement, with pipes", ibid.
93 "We were dealing with men", Thomson, "If Your Memory Serves You Well"
94 "They were a kick to do", Wenner, "Bob Dylan Talks"
95 "It was the kind of music that made you feel", *Lost Songs*
95 "Bob would sit at the window", Fleming, "The Secrets of the Sessions"
95 "They seemed to be a million miles away", *Lost Songs*
96 "You kind of look for ideas", ibid.
96 "I didn't have nothin' to say about myself", ibid.
98 "It's always interesting when somebody", ibid.

CHAPTER 2: FRANKIE AND JUDAS

All quotes from author interviews with Jonathan Taplin, Ian Kimmet, Linda Wortman, Peter Yarrow, Bruce Dorfman, D. A. Pennebaker and Happy Traum, except as follows:

101 "is not seeing anybody" *et seq.*, Iachetta, "Scarred Bob Dylan Is Comin' Back"
101 "in my head like they always are", Bob Dylan quote from ibid.
102 "Bob did not know that he was giving away the rights", Maymudes and Maymudes, *Another Side of Bob Dylan*, p. 128
103 "I finally had to sue him", Shelton, *No Direction Home*, p. 379
103 "Did Grossman rip off Dylan?" Lefsetz, "Cowboys and Indies"
104 "There is the music from Bob's house", Aronowitz, "Friends and Neighbors Just Call Us the Band"
104 "the sound that Gordon Lightfoot was getting", Wenner, "Bob Dylan Talks"
104 "dealing with the devil in a fearful way", Cott, "Bob Dylan"
105 "wasn't all the way for Al Grossman", Weberman, phone conversation

105 "two *writers* were approaching", Goldstein, *Another Little Piece of My Heart*, p. 49

106 "My first hint of bad blood boiling", *Bob Dylan and the Beatles*, p. 257

106 "He calmed down", Scaduto, *Bob Dylan*, pp. 258–9

106 "far more friendly, far less distracted", Heylin, *Bob Dylan*, p. 291

106 "the ideal loving couple", Aronowitz, *Bob Dylan and the Beatles*, p. 263

107 "I don't know", Landy, *Dylan in Woodstock*, p. 96

107 "a primitive way of looking at things", Dylan, *Chronicles*, p. 283

108 "so changed, serene, smiling", Roxon, "The Woody Guthrie Concert"

CHAPTER 3: SOMETHING TO FEEL

All quotes from author interviews with Ken Mansfield, Rick Danko, Robbie Robertson, Al Kooper, Jim Weider, Elliott Landy, Artie Traum, Michael Friedman, Barbara O'Brien, Lucinda Hoyt, Jonathan Taplin, Happy Traum and Bruce Dorfman, except as follows:

109 "just as Bob was leaving", *This Wheel's on Fire*, p. 160

109 "I was there when Robbie realised", Helmore, unpublished interview with Sally Grossman

109 "transports him out of the longed-for American pastoral", Roth, *American Pastoral*, p. 86

111 "There was a Caravans song", Jan Haust, liner notes for Bob Dylan and The Band, *The Basement Tapes Complete*

111 "John Simon understood the recording console", Hoskyns, *Across the Great Divide*, p. 150

111 "[It] came as a bit of a shock in 1968", Houghton, *I've Always Kept a Unicorn*, p. 187

114 "*Music From Big Pink* is the kind of album", Aronowitz, "Friends and Neighbors Just Call Us the Band"

114 "Bob goes to bed every night by nine", interview by Toby Thompson, quoted in Cott, *Dylan*, p. 115

115 "He'd like to be somewhere comfortable", Scaduto, *Bob Dylan*, p. 209

115 "totally frustrating and painful", Love, "Bob Dylan"

115 "My old lady Joey", Spitz, *Dylan*, p. 389

115 "It was strange", White, *Rock Lives*, p. 170

117 "Bob was an odd person", Thomson, *George Harrison*, www.theartsdesk.com/new-music/extract-george-harrison-behind-locked-door

117 "Let's get all the boys over on that side", ibid.

CHAPTER 4: PAINT MY MAILBOX BLUE

All quotes from author interviews with Artie Traum, Danny Goldberg, Milton Glaser, Graham Blackburn, Cindy Cashdollar, Jon Gershen, Richard

Heppner, Robbie Dupree, Michael Lang, Keith Reid, Harvey Brooks, Jeremy Wilber, Dean Schambach, Fern Malkine, Lynne Naso, Mark McKenna, Daoud Shaw, David Boyle, Gary Klein, Warren Bernhardt and Larry Packer, except as follows:

119 "The visibility unnerved me", "Philip Roth Unleashed, Part One"
119 "a combination of social seclusion and physical pleasure" *et seq.*, Roth, *Shop Talk*, p. 132
119 "billboards, garages, diners, burger joints, junk shops" *et seq.*, Meyer, *Night Studio*, p. 174
122 "We like that name", Aronowitz, *Bob Dylan and the Beatles*, p. 277
122 "tilling the land in the Catskill Mountains", Goldstein, *Another Little Piece of My Heart*, p. 103
123 "a town but more a name", Evers, *Woodstock*, p. 668
123 "I can't say that Dylan" *et seq.*, unpublished transcript of video interview by Elliott Landy, 1996
123 "once in a while, after about his twelfth or fifteenth Irish coffee", Blelock and Blelock, *Roots of the 1969 Woodstock Festival*, p. 57
124 "The house is a beautiful country home", Atlas, "Interview with Tim Hardin"
129 "its sadness comes not from contemplation", Sheff, "Suite for Tim and Damion Hardin"

CHAPTER 5: EVERYBODY'S APPLE PIE

All quotes from author interviews with Happy Traum, Beverley Martyn, JoHanna Hall, Jeremy Wilber, Michael Friedman, Maria Muldaur, Bruce Dorfman, Dean Schambach, David Boyle, Robbie Dupree, Graham Blackburn, John Niven and Peter Yarrow, except as follows:

133 "He proceeded to fall apart", Wirth, "Interview with Al Stewart"
133 "The last time I saw him", Houghton, *I've Always Kept a Unicorn*, p. 55
135 "He didn't want me to be seen" *et seq.*, Martyn, *Sweet Honesty*
136 "In many ways [it] achieves the artistically impossible", Heylin, *Bob Dylan*, p. 302
136 "I wanted to set fire to these people", Dylan, *Chronicles*, p. 117
137 "went into the bucolic and mundane as far as possible", ibid., p. 123
137 "carrying this song around in my head for five years", Spitz, *Dylan*, p. 411

CHAPTER 6: COMBINATION OF THE TWO

All quotes from author interviews with Elliott Landy, Danny Goldberg, Paula Batson, Michael Friedman, Peter Coyote, Paul Fishkin, John Byrne Cooke, Jim Rooney, Linda Wortman, Norma Cross, Warren Bernhardt, Keith Reid,

Ronnie Lyons, John Simon, Ed Sanders, Dean Schambach, Ian Kimmet, Jonathan Taplin, Geoff Muldaur, Maria Muldaur, Al Aronowitz, Bill Graham, Robbie Dupree, Larry Campbell, Garth Hudson, Al Kooper, Levon Helm, Libby Titus, Jeremy Wilber and Rick Danko, except as follows:

140 "Only a fool would not smile back", Zanes, *Revolutions in Sound*, p. 38
141 "That man's got to be heard", article on Howard Alk, *Take One*, March 1978
144 "trying to snag Janis", Scully with Dalton, *Living with the Dead*, p. 103
144 "The most well-founded charge", Friedman, *Buried Alive*, p. 108
146 "They were wonderful players", Roeser, "Do What You Love"
147 "betrayed" *et seq.*, O'Conner, "Albert Grossman's Ghost"
147 "That put him in a whole other category", Jennings, *Before the Gold Rush*, p. 203
148 "burned out", O'Conner, "Albert Grossman's Ghost"
151 "Everything in rock was kind of going", Hoskyns, *Across the Great Divide*, p. 180
152 "It was a time of year when Woodstock", Baer, "The Band"
154 "One night, Rick and Levon", Merrill, "Mason Hoffenberg Gets in a Few Licks"
155 "They'd follow when [he] took me for rides", Titus, "A Miraculous Recovery"
155 "Though his relationship with Libby was tumultuous", Fagen, *Eminent Hipsters*, p. 127
156 "Some of the other guys in the Band", Roeser, "Do What You Love"

CHAPTER 7: BRAND NEW DAYS

All quotes from author interviews with Van Morrison, Jon Gershen, Ted Templeman, John Payne, Keith Reid, Bob Schwaid, John Platania, Graham Blackburn, Elliott Landy, Jeremy Wilber and Artie Traum, except as follows:

159 "a hateful little guy", Wash, "Astral Sojourn"
160 "He was . . . suspicious of us", Hoskyns, "The Eden Project"

CHAPTER 8: SOME WAY OUT OF HERE

All quotes from author interviews with Christopher Parker, Daoud Shaw, Jon Gershen, Martha Velez, Lynne Naso and Richard Heppner, except as follows:

167 "Dylan really turned me on", Lydon, *Flashbacks*, p. 70
168 "He came in with these Dylan tapes", McDermott and Kramer, *Hendrix*, p. 136
169 "Mike was taking a bunch of acid", Black, unpublished interview with Jim Marron

169 "He was telling me about how", Black, unpublished interview with Juma Sultan

170 "Nobody in Woodstock had a red Corvette", McDermott and Kramer, *Hendrix*, pp. 266–7

170 "puppies, daybreak, other innocentia" *et seq.*, Weller, "Jimi Hendrix"

172 "Mike Jeffery . . . did not like me", Black, "The Kidnapping of Jimi Hendrix"

173 "We tried to keep the groupies away", Hopkins, *Hit and Run*, sourced on Google Books

173 "[Jimi] could see the point of expanding", *Jimi Hendrix: The Road to Woodstock*

173 "drunk most of the time", Black, unpublished interview with Juma Sultan

173 "The band was grim", Obrecht, "Jimi Hendrix"

174 "If Jimi wanted to buy a car", Black, unpublished interview with Juma Sultan

174 "as a warning to teach Jimi", Dannemann, *The Inner World of Jimi Hendrix*, pp. 76–8

174 "Jimi told me that he was trying to end management", Black, unpublished interview with Claire Moriece

175 "It was less than a week before the festival", unpublished transcript of video interview by Elliott Landy, 1996

CHAPTER 9: BACK TO THE GARDEN

All quotes from author interviews with Stan Beinstein, Michael Lang, Keith Reid, Cindy Cashdollar, Ed Sanders, Elliott Landy, Jonathan Taplin, Mike Ephron, Steve Bernstein and Paula Batson, except as follows:

179 "There will be a village", Lang with George-Warren, *The Road to Woodstock*, p. 37

179 "joyous, healing feel", ibid., p. 39

179 "The spirit of the festival", Turner, "By the Time I Got to Woodstock"

180 "deloused and have their heads shaved", Kovach, "Woodstock's a Stage, but Many Don't Care for the Show"

181 "Now they call them hippies", *Ulster County*, 12 December 1968

181 "teeny boppers and overaged juveniles", Geertsema, "The Scene at Woodstock"

183 "romanticising" *et seq.*, Lang with George-Warren, *The Road to Woodstock*, p. 118

184 "[Michael] has a way of ingratiating", ibid., pp. 120–1

186 "been invited, so I know it'll be okay", Aronowitz, "Woodstock . . . Well, Dylan Likes the Name"

186 "but I can't remember anything about him", Aronowitz, *Bob Dylan and the Beatles*, p. 277

186 "last time we played here", Pareles, review of Bob Dylan at Bethel Woods

186 "You sit on the big stage", Anson, *Gone Crazy and Back Again*, p. 128

187 "I looked out there and it seemed", Lang and George-Warren, *The Road to Woodstock*, p. 233

187 "He said, '"Snow White Lady" in F'", ibid., p. 189

188 "We left by helicopter", McDermott and Kramer, *Hendrix*, p. 277

190 "some low-level Mafiosi" *et seq.*, Black, unpublished interview with Juma Sultan

191 "four or five mobsters", Black, unpublished interview with Jim Marron

191 "We had a lot of connections" *et seq.*, Black, unpublished interview with Jerry Velez

192 "Mike and his crew came in like gangbusters", Black, unpublished interview with Juma Sultan

192 "It was an eerie scene", Crowe, essay for the Bob Dylan box set

192 "I told Jimi I would be glad to introduce him", Richie Havens, *They Can't Hide Us Anymore*, cited in "Show Business Disease"

193 "He'd become an embarrassment to many in town", Smart and Moynihan, *Rock and Woodstock*, p. 76

193 "financial problems" *et seq.*, Moscoso-Gongora, "Woodstock Was"

193 "an odd memorial", Smart and Moynihan, *Rock and Woodstock*, p. 76

CHAPTER 10: HE'S NOT HERE

All quotes from author interviews with Richard Heppner, Martha Velez, Bruce Dorfman, Daoud Shaw, Cindy Cashdollar, Stan Beinstein, Maria Muldaur, Keith Reid, Bruce Dorfman, Larry Campbell, Jeremy Wilber, Ed Sanders, Michael Friedman, Al Kooper, Van Morrison, John Platania, Jon Gershen, Mary Martin, Graham Blackburn, Jim Rooney, Ted Templeman, Graham Parker, Warren Bernhardt and Ed Freeman, except as follows:

194 "You see them arrive at the village green", Kaufman, "Woodstock Up Tight as Hippies Drift In"

194 "We are not opposed to [them]", ibid.

195 "people living in trees outside my house", Cohen, "Don't Ask Me Nothin' About Nothin'"

197 "He was definitely into his kids", Scaduto, *Bob Dylan*, p. 263

197 "Woodstock had turned into a nightmare", Dylan, *Chronicles*, p. 118

197 "It became stale and disillusioning", Rosenbaum, "The Playboy Interview"

197 "the sum total of all [the] bullshit", Loder, "Bob Dylan"

198 "these really strange characters", Miss Information, "Woodstock"

198 "the Woodstock Nation had overtaken", Loder, "Bob Dylan"

199 "the stupidest thing" *et seq.*, Dylan, *Chronicles*, p. 137

200 "come to the conclusion that Dylan", *International Times* 106, June
    1971, quoted in Dallas, *Singers of an Empty Day*, p. 158
200 "and then Woodstock started *being* the scene", Richard Williams, 1973
201 "get too happy", Heylin, *Can You Feel the Silence?*, p. 232
202 "very human . . . there was no uptightness", Traum, "Van Morrison"
203 "the old ladies got involved", Rogan, *No Surrender*, p. 257
205 "The drinking thing was a fixture", Heylin, *Can You Feel the Silence?*, pp.
    220–1
206 "I've got a problem", sidebar interview with Doug Messenger, *Uncut*,
    May 2015
208 "I drove him to the closing", Wise, "Jerry Wapner Hangs Up His Shingle"

CHAPTER 11: OH LORD WON'T YOU BUY ME A MERCEDES BENZ

All quotes from author interviews with Barry Goldberg, Maria Muldaur,
Geoff Muldaur, Gabe Butterfield, Lynne Naso, Christopher Parker, Graham
Blackburn, Jim Weider, John Byrne Cooke, JoHanna Hall, Elliott Landy,
D. A. Pennebaker, Peter Coyote, Ian Kimmet, Michael Friedman, David
Dalton, Ed Sanders and Ronnie Lyons, except as follows:

210 "In the blink of an eye", Milward, *Crossroads*, p. 73
211 "That was the *dumbest* introduction", Sander, *Trips*, p. 60
211 "used to be a time when a farmer", Milward, *Crossroads*, p. 71
211 "It was thrilling, chilling", ibid., p. 113
213 "I would've plugged my guitar", Simmons, essay for the box set *Michael*
    Bloomfield: From His Head to His Heart to His Hands, p. 17
213 "The further Butter moved away", Houghton, *Becoming Elektra*, p. 175
214 "British rock and roll stars", Evers, *Woodstock*, p. 656
215 "Paul brought a lot of the great players", Hollander, "The Survivor"
216 "shaman mama", Lydon, *Rock Folk*, p. 91
216 "[she] was actually being merchandised", Friedman, *Buried Alive*, pp.
    148–9
217 "I love those guys", Lydon, *Rock Folk*, p. 102
217 "the elitist concept", Willis, *Out of the Vinyl Deeps*, p. 129
218 "We were all crushed", Roeser, "Do What You Love"
218 "[John] was very much a typical", ibid.
219 "there was only the chasm", Friedman, *Buried Alive*, p. 201
220 "women endowed the idea", Willis, *Out of the Vinyl Deeps*, p. 126
221 "I'll whip enough piss out of you", Hawkins with Godard, *Last of the*
    Good Ol' Boys, p. 198
221 "I knew that he really liked Janis", Roeser, "Do What You Love"
223 "We left our egos at the train station", *Festival Express*

Part Three: Dangerous Fun

CHAPTER 1: IF YOU BUILD IT

All quotes from author interviews with Michael Lang, John Simon, Paul Fishkin, John Storyk, Todd Rundgren, Paula Batson, Michael Friedman, John Holbrook, Jim Rooney, JoHanna Hall, Christopher Parker, Jonathan Taplin, Peter Walker, Jon Gershen, Maria Muldaur, Graham Blackburn, Daoud Shaw, Dean Schambach, Lucinda Hoyt, Robbie Dupree, Jonathan Donahue and Happy Traum, except as follows:

230 "everyone's talking about that now", Wenner, "Bob Dylan Talks"
232 "The original intent was just to be", Daley, "John Storyk"
232 "When Albert really started to live up here", "Who's Who in A&R at Bearsville"
233 "The accountants moved up", ibid.
234 "Ours were, as I recall", Hund, "Taj Mahal"
236 "doesn't have a hand in producing", Wenner, "Bob Dylan Talks"
237 "had rough edges but was also a soft", Smart, "Bearsville's Baron"
237 "a very private, very lonely", ibid.
238 "Paul and I hit it off right away", Rooney, *In It for the Long Run*, from excerpt sent by author
240 "The World's Foremost Rock Music Tsar", Moscoso-Gongora, "Woodstock Was"
240 "a small, terminally hip and incestuous universe", Goodman, *The Mansion on the Hill*, p. 107
241 "He gave Woodstock a new persona", Smart, "Bearsville's Baron"
241 "made [it] attractive for musicians", ibid.

CHAPTER 2: THE SHAPE THEY'RE IN

All quotes from author interviews with Libby Titus, Jonathan Taplin, Peter Coyote, Rick Danko, Richard Heppner, Paul Fishkin, Paul Mozian, Maria Muldaur, John Simon, Michael Friedman, Geoff Muldaur, Levon Helm, Bill Graham, Artie Traum, Jim Rooney, Steve Bernstein and Keith Reid, except as follows:

242 "The Band appeals to an intelligent segment", Bender, "The Band"
243 "Heroin was a problem", Hoskyns, *Across the Great Divide*, p. 232
244 "This wonderful, nymphomaniac group", Helm and Davis, *This Wheel's on Fire*, p. 184
245 "I thought, 'Let's have a little bit of a goof'" *et seq.*, Hoskyns, *Across the Great Divide*, p. 234
246 "pretty positive, looking at things", Smith, "The Band"
246 "It turned into a game", Wale, *Voxpop*, p. 70

247 "I did everything to get him to write", Hoskyns, *Across the Great Divide*, p. 236
247 "Some of the shows were real good", ibid., p. 235
247 "It was frustrating", Spencer, interview with Robbie Robertson, *Woodstock Times*, 4 April 1985
248 "When I heard that song" *et seq.*, Petersen, unpublished interview with Allen Toussaint
248 "The record poses the question", Hoskyns, *Across the Great Divide*, p. 254
249 "One day when I came in", Rooney, *In It for the Long Run*, from excerpt sent by author
249 "Everybody had been so easily satisfied", Baer, "The Band"
250 "There's this alignment", Helmore, unpublished interview with Sally Grossman
251 "There were no houses around", Petersen, unpublished interview with Allen Toussaint

CHAPTER 3: MUSIC AMONG FRIENDS

All quotes from author interviews with James Lasdun, Jim Rooney, Geoff Muldaur, Mark McKenna, Jim Colegrove, Happy Traum, Graham Blackburn, Maria Muldaur, John Simon, Stan Beinstein, Larry Campbell, Jeremy Wilber, Harvey Brooks, Peter Walker, Michael Lang and JoHanna Hall, except as follows:

252 "Two fiddles, a guitar" *et seq.*, Lasdun, "Oh Death"
255 "It was a peculiar marriage", Unterberger, liner notes
255 "We were the darlings of that tour", Einarson, *Four Strong Winds*, p. 232
256 "came crashing out of the woods", Frame, "Muldaur, Garrett, Keith 'n' Rooney"
259 "remember anyone with a steady old lady", ibid.
260 "Can you come into the city tomorrow", Traum, "A Recording Session with Bob Dylan"
264 "I still like the 'back-to-the-country' idea", Yarg, "Individually Yours"
264 "favourite singer in the place", Dylan, *Chronicles*, p. 12
265 "favourite female vocalist", Stampfel, liner notes
265 "She's disappeared now", "Fred Neil: Where's It All Going?"
265 "She wasn't Billie Holiday", Unterberger, "Karen Dalton"
265 "the only folk singer I ever met", Stampfel, liner notes
267 "Bob was one of those people" *et seq.*, Walker, *Karen Dalton*, p. 6

CHAPTER 4: THE BALLAD OF TODD AND ALBERT

All quotes from author interviews with Sally Grossman, Michael Friedman, Todd Rundgren, Lucinda Hoyt, Paul Fishkin, JoHanna Hall, Patti Smith, Jim

Rooney, Jim Colegrove, Bebe Buell, Paul Mozian, Danny Goldberg, John Holbrook, Mark McKenna, John Storyk and Barry Goldberg, except as follows:

270 "I think *Jesse Winchester* was a kind of run-through", Myers, *A Wizard, a True Star*, p. 36
273 "I was imitating Richard Manuel on that song", ibid., p. 47
274 "I think it's because somebody said", ibid., p. 59
275 "wanted four times the money he deserved", Leviton, "Badfinger at the Crossroads"
275 "rude and obnoxious", Myers, *A Wizard, a True Star*, p. 64
277 "Yeah, the guys really seem to like Cindy", Buell with Bockris, *Rebel Heart*, pp. 44–5
278 "Bearsville was a small company", Skelly, "An Interview with Lonesome Dave Peverett"
280 "He was an interesting man", Wise, "Jerry Wapner Hangs Up His Shingle"

CHAPTER 5: "CREATIVITY AND FERMENT"

All quotes from author interviews with Jonathan Donahue, Ed Sanders, Karl Berger, Steve Bernstein, John Simon, Lynne Naso, Warren Bernhardt and Mark McKenna, except as follows:

285 "People were more relaxed", Van Trikt, "Karl Berger"
286 "Some of the best people", Panken, "Karl Berger and Ingrid Sertso"
286 "The CMS became a woodsy outpost", Hermes, *Love Goes to Buildings on Fire*, p. 122
286 "Even before you get to CMS", Sweet, *Music Universe, Music Mind*, pp. 41–2
286 "a totally unique place in the world", Ratliff, "Creative Music Studio"
286 "It's not like you go to a music school", Panken, "Karl Berger and Ingrid Sertso"
288 "we really were running", Sweet, *Music Universe, Music Mind*, p. 90
289 "The kids of the nineties", Panken, "Karl Berger and Ingrid Sertso"
290 "kind of like a regal visitation", interview in *The Making of Jeff Buckley's "Grace"*

CHAPTER 6: IN A GOOD PLACE NOW

All quotes from author interviews with Jim Colegrove, Jonathan Donahue, Paula Batson, Jonathan Taplin, Robbie Dupree, Jim Rooney, Jeremy Wilber, Christopher Parker, Paul Fishkin, Barbara O'Brien, Maria Muldaur, Amos Garrett, Jim Weider, Lynne Naso, Graham Blackburn and Geoff Muldaur, except as follows:

292 "You learn to live with the underground", Bollinger, unpublished
      interview with Bobby Charles
292 "remote and near nowhere in particular", *Times-Herald Record*, June
      1974, quoted on www.jeffersonvilleny.com/jeffersonville_history_article.
      html
292 "One morning I was at the Laundromat", Bollinger, unpublished
      interview with Bobby Charles
292 "One afternoon, Colegrove and ND showed up", Rooney, *In It for the
      Long Run*, from excerpt sent by author
293 "It entered my heart and stayed forever", ibid.
293 "She's such a free spirit", Petersen, unpublished interview with Bobby
      Charles
293 "Albert said he would" *et seq.*, Bollinger, unpublished interview with
      Bobby Charles
295 "Someone brought Fred Neil along", Rooney, *In It for the Long Run*,
      from excerpt sent by author
297 "That was another song we did", Bollinger, unpublished interview with
      Bobby Charles
298 "The very first thing [Albert] did" *et seq.*, Rebennack with Rummel,
      Under a Hoodoo Moon, pp. 181–5
300 "knew that Butterfield was his ward", Goodman, *The Mansion on the
      Hill*, p. 107
302 "It was remote, cold and creepy", Ellis III, "Paul Butterfield"
303 "They were bitching and moaning", Goodman, *The Mansion on the Hill*,
      p. 106
304 "We're the only band around", cited in "AllMusic Review"
304 "It was definitely the furthest Paul ever got", Ellis III, "Paul Butterfield"
306 "He and I didn't get along at all", Escott, liner notes
306 "I've been to his house recently", Broven, *South to Louisiana*, p. 185

CHAPTER 7: "DOPE, MUSIC AND BEAUTY"

All quotes from author interviews with Happy Traum, Robbie Dupree,
Jeremy Wilber, Christopher Parker, Jim Weider, Michael Friedman, Jon
Gershen, Jim Colegrove, John Simon, JoHanna Hall, Bonnie Raitt, Stan
Beinstein, Amos Garrett, Jim Rooney, Libby Titus, Jane Manuel, Robbie
Robertson and Jonathan Taplin, except as follows:

307 "the Woodstock pop-music boom" *et seq.*, Moscoso-Gongora,
      "Woodstock Was"
307 "Everyone is plying his tapes", ibid.
311 "They were real good", Frame, "Muldaur, Garrett, Keith 'n' Rooney"
316 "My mom left New York in 1970" *et seq.*, LaBruce, "Terry Richardson"
317 "everything people ought to want" *et seq.*, Marcus, *Mystery Train*, pp. 63–4

318 "really fucked up", Merrill, "Mason Hoffenberg Gets in a Few Licks"
319 "You cocksucking little limey sonofabitch", Scully with Dalton, *Living with the Dead*, p. 271
319 "managerial ties", Salvo, "Playing in the Band"
320 "an emotionless trip", Crowe, essay for the Bob Dylan box set
320 "pulsing, cracking, shaking", Fong-Torres, "A Restful Farewell to Tour '74"
320 "The most significant thing", Hoskyns, *Across the Great Divide*, p. 293
320 "I found the show powerful", Alterman and Fong-Torres, "Bob Dylan's Star-Studded Homecoming"
321 "a branch of that old nastiness", Fong-Torres, "A Restful Farewell to Tour '74"
321 "The last time I went back", Frame, "Muldaur, Garrett, Keith 'n' Rooney"

CHAPTER 8: A HERMIT, A TRUE STAR

All quotes from author interviews with Todd Rundgren, Bebe Buell, Paul Fishkin, Michael Friedman, Sally Grossman, John Holbrook, Mark McKenna, Lucinda Hoyt, John Storyk, Linda Wortman, Kasim Sulton, Paul Mozian, D. A. Pennebaker, Ian Kimmet, Cindy Cashdollar, Danny Goldberg, Ed Sanders, Linda Sheldon, JoHanna Hall, Robbie Dupree, Jules Shear and Patti Smith, except as follows:

323 "Todd's willingness to self-sabotage", Grossweiner and Cohen, "Industry Profile"
323 "I don't think Albert kept that kind of distinction", Myers, *A Wizard, a True Star*, p. 41
325 "like Jean-Pierre Massiera backing", www.headheritage.co.uk/unsung/thebookofseth/labat-m-frog
328 "squirreling about in the backyard", Duncan, "Todd Rundgren"
328 "the scene" *et seq.*, ibid.
334 "tried desperately to keep the room", Traum, "My Recording Session with Peter Tosh (and the Stones)"
338 "being tied up in a bag", author interview with Mark McKenna
338 "It was a horrifying violation", Myers, *A Wizard, a True Star*, p. 208
339 "His people skills are like Hermann Goering's", Wirth, "Interview with Andy Partridge"

CHAPTER 9: TUESDAY NIGHT FEVER

All quotes from author interviews with Brian Hollander, Cindy Cashdollar, Michael Lang, Valma Offord, Jim Weider, Martha Velez, Ian Kimmet, Peter Walker, Christopher Parker, Harvey Brooks, Jane Traum, Kasim Sulton, "Disco" Linda Sheldon, Stan Beinstein and Eddy Offord, except as follows:

347 "Almost all the business owners", Frankel, "The Joyous Lake"
347 "it was where Woodstock met the jet set", *Woodstock: Can't Get There from Here*
349 "demented, brain-damaged boxers", Frankel, "The Joyous Lake"
350 "about to tear it down", *Woodstock: Can't Get There from Here*

CHAPTER 10: FORBIDDEN FRUIT

All quotes from author interviews with Levon Helm, Libby Titus, Peter Coyote, Ronnie Lyons, Peter Yarrow, Robbie Robertson, Robbie Dupree, Geoff Muldaur, Kasim Sulton, Valma Merians, Barry Goldberg, Lynne Naso, Jim Rooney, Gabe Butterfield, Danny Goldberg, Mark McKenna, Ian Kimmet, Paul Mozian, Liz Butterfield, John Simon, Al Aronowitz, Stan Beinstein, Jonathan Donahue, Michael Friedman, Jeremy Wilber and Aaron Hurwitz, except as follows:

352 "He had a face like a king", Petersen, unpublished interview with Bobby Charles
358 "hip tension", Meisel, "The Woodstock Myth"
359 "[Paul] looked me right in the eyes", Ellis III, "Paul Butterfield"
361 "It would have been nice to say", ibid.
362 "An unsuccessful alcoholic", Sullivan, "Interview with Rick Danko"
362 "Instead of coming up with new material", Gabites, "The Truth, the Whole Truth and Nothing but the Truth"
363 "There were some times", Jordan, "Backtalk with Levon Helm"
363 "has been defamed, humiliated", letter included in Aronowitz, *The Blacklisted Masterpieces of Al Aronowitz*
363 "Tom [Pacheco] came and sang", Aronowitz, "Tom Pacheco Honors Al Aronowitz with a Heartfelt Tribute"
364 "irked to the point of telling", Spencer, interview with Richard Manuel
365 "That's really what broke the Band up", Gill, "The Band"
365 "A lot of people worried about [Paul]", Ellis III, "Paul Butterfield"
365 "He looked terrible", ibid.
365 "I went to his funeral", ibid.

CHAPTER 11: BROKEN HEART

All quotes from author interviews with Al Aronowitz, Ian Kimmet, Kasim Sulton, Robbie Dupree, Cindy Cashdollar, Lucinda Hoyt, Mark McKenna, John Holbrook, David Boyle, Ronnie Lyons, Paul Mozian, Peter Yarrow, Dean Schambach, John Simon, Rick Danko, Ed Sanders, John Storyk, Michael Friedman and Barbara O'Brien, except as follows:

366 "creased old man", Morley, "Utopia in Woodstock"

369 "It was a Who's Who", Medenbach, "A Beacon in Bearsville"
371 "I guess we must", O'Conner, "Albert Grossman's Ghost"
372 "Albert's only comment", ibid.
372 "I'd loved Bearsville's output", Holsapple, "Anatomy of a Flop"
372 "After listening to me silently", ibid.
373 "rock and roll's Citizen Kane", O'Conner, "Albert Grossman's Ghost"
375 "I ran into Levon once", Helmore, unpublished interview with Sally Grossman
375 "He got what he deserved", author interview with Kasim Sulton
376 "He wasn't a very nice man", Spitz, *Dylan*, p. 176

EPILOGUE: "HOW DOES THAT OLD SONG GO?"

All quotes from author interviews with John Storyk, Mark McKenna, JoHanna Hall, Michael Lang, Peter Yarrow, Ian Kimmet, Ronnie Lyons, Marshall Crenshaw, Jules Shear, Paul Mozian, Jim Weider, Graham Parker, Rick Danko, Robbie Dupree, Jonathan Donahue, Grasshopper, Tony Fletcher, Simone Felice, John Holbrook, Karl Berger, Jim Rooney, Ed Sanders, Artie Traum, Richard Heppner, Milton Glaser, Geoff Muldaur, Bruce Dorfman and Brian Hollander, except as follows:

380 "it was a bit puzzling" *et seq.*, Griffin, "Rick Danko's Woodstock," parts 1–4
382 "Nobody really wants to charge their friends", Brown, *American Heartbeat*, p. 23
394 "I'm not from here, but people tell me", lyrics from "I'm Not from Here" used with kind permission of James McMurtry, with thanks to Jenni Finlay

CODA: DIDN'T HE RAMBLE

All quotes from author interviews with Levon Helm, Happy Traum, Ian Kimmet, Garth Hudson, Stan Beinstein, Grasshopper, Steve Bernstein, Barbara O'Brien, John Simon, Larry Campbell, Paul Fishkin, Marshall Crenshaw, Brian Hollander, Robbie Robertson, Jonathan Donahue and Rick Danko, except as follows:

401 "I sat with Levon for a good while", Robbie Robertson, post on Facebook, 18 April 2012
402 "The story is much more complex", Libby Titus-Fagen, email to the author, 25 April 2012
403 "I don't wish to denigrate", Van Wagenen, letter to the *Daily Freeman*

INDEX

All buildings, establishments and roads are in the Woodstock region unless otherwise specified. BD denotes Bob Dylan; AG denotes Albert Grossman; W denotes the town of Woodstock.

fee, 186; as BD's protector, 53–4, 68,
198; *Blonde on Blonde* recording, 79;
"Dear Landlord", 104–5, 105n, 106,
220n; dislikes *Nashville Skyline*, 136;
dispute with BD, 102–4, 105–6, 108,
115–16, 142, 198, 235–6; "feeds"
BD's paranoia, 53; first hears BD
play, 44; improved Columbia deal,
105–6; Kramer photo injunction,
74n; legal wrangles, 372; Neuwirth
as, 74; Peter, Paul and Mary connection, 47–8; pursues BD, 45; royalties,
70; schedules further 1966 shows,
86, 88; selects Pennebaker for BD
film, 66; signs BD, 46–7; tries to rid
BD of The Band, 76
CHARACTER: aggression, 67, 319n;
appearance, 43, 76, 140–1, 367–8,
374; arrogance, 37; Brown's loathing,
38–9; as "the Cloud", 68; in *Dont
Look Back*, 66–8, 140; generosity,
38, 366, 367; giganticism, 231; hipness, 141; on integrity, 39n; lone-
liness, 237, 368–9; Maymudes on,
62; Mimi Fariña on, 60; mythology
of, 140; as nay-sayer, 186, 258, 279;
posthumous assessments, 375–6;
post-Joplin's death, 236; radical politics, 141, 141n; sly and sneaky, 311,
369; vagueness, 367; Valma Merians
on, 344; vindictiveness, 281, 367;
Yarrow on, 43–4; as "yuppie", 52
PERSONAL LIFE: and Charles
drugs charge, 292, 293–4; death and
burial, 374–5, 392; drugs, use and
attitude, 42, 213, 218, 298, 318, 364;
Gramercy Park home, 74, 90; health,
368; horticulture, 144, 148, 150,
232, 328; at the Joyous Lake, 344,
348; Lee as mistress, 327, 368; love
of boxing, 366; love for Butterfield,
211, 212, 360–1; Morrison visit,
165–6; open marriage, 236–7, 327;
Spencer relationship, 42; Storyk
relationship, 231–2; "trio" with BD
and Neuwirth, 66, 68; unpredicta-
bility, 280; W as retreat, 120, 156;

W revolves around, 166, 215, 240–1,
379; will, 379; *see also* Fairfields;
Grossman, Sally
PROFESSIONAL LIFE: accountants,
372; acts leave, 147, 371; backstage at
Sound-Out, 126; The Band leave for
Geffen, 319–20; The Band's Capitol
deal, 109; BD's Kooper–Joplin plan,
199n; Bearsville vision and fiefdom, 9, 233, 235, 237–41, 279–80,
334, 363n; Big Brother's Columbia
deal, 143, 144; burnt out, 148; as
centre of W, 150–1, 179; Charles's
parting words, 306; commissions,
48; commitment to folk music, 39,
41; conflict with Helm, 3, 250, 396;
controls clients through drugs, 80;
copyrights basement tapes, 97–8; as
"country guy", 156; courts Sedgwick,
77; "creates" Better Days, 299, 300,
303; demands best quality, 41–2, 47,
241, 344; and Diamond, 357; estimation of The Band, 112; finances
Runt, 272; Fishkin leaves, 332–3; as
folk "Enemy", 47, 73, 212; Glotzer as
new partner, 143; Hafnelson rename,
276; Hawks record deal, 100; Jeffery
snatches Holy Moses, 309; Joplin
life insurance, 219, 224n; Joplin
relationship, 143, 146–7, 156, 217,
218–19, 221–2; and Joplin's death,
225; Lomax scuffle at Newport
(1965), 210–11, 212; management
style, 38; manages Butterfield, 211,
212, 215, 360; manages Electric Flag,
213; manages Kweskin band, 148–50;
manages Ochs, 76n; manages Yarrow,
40, 236; Moscoso-Gongora on, 307;
moves to New York, 39; musical
conservatism, 331; negotiating style,
43, 48, 140, 141, 238–9, 277–8;
office shake-up, 142–3; and others'
money, 233; out-best-dealed, 373;
Paul and Mary deal, 40; Rebennack
row, 298–9; as record label owner,
278; relationship with The Band,
156; respects Kimmet, 332; respects

sex: AG's private life, 42; AIDS, 259,
268, 362; at Big Pink, 93; Fairfields
orgy, 214; groupies at Traver Hollow
Road, 173; Joplin's addiction, 219–
20; Joyous Lake sex for cocaine, 347;
Maverick "orgies", 22; "orgy" during
Harrison visit, 117; Peter Pan Farm
teepee sauna, 125; promiscuity and
"cross-pollinations", 113, 153, 259,
277; Sea Horse affairs, 24–5; W vir-
gins, 93–4
Sha Wu, 254, 379
Shaar, Daoud Elias, *see* Shaw, Daoud
Elias
Shady, New York, 24, 30, 127, 253, 276
Shangri-La Studio, Zuma Beach, 355,
361n
Shaw, Daoud Elias, 127–8, 169, 195,
201, 202, 238
Shear, Jules, 380, 381–2, 382n: *The
Surreal Wives of Woodstock* (with
Sanders), 382; *Watch Dog*, 339
Shearston, Gary, 148
Sheff, Will, 129
Shehorn, Bobby Lynn, 291, 291n, 292
Sheldon, Linda "Disco", 334–5, 347–8,
349, 350
Shelton, Robert, 45, 51, 80
Shepard, Sam, 87, 88
Shivaree, 390
Shue, Otto, 238
Shultis, Nelson, 238
Shultis, Vernon, 253
Sickler Road, 282, 295
Sidewell, Denny, 267
Siebel, Paul, 256, 263; *Jack-Knife
Gypsy*, 263; "Louise", 263
Siegel, Jules, 68
Siemsen, Harry, 31
Sife, Buddy, 130
Siggins, Bob and Betsy, 195, 195n
Silber, Irwin: "Open Letter to Bob
Dylan", 64
Silver, Roy, 46
Simon, Carly, 86
Simon, John: advises AG on studio,
231; on AG and Fairfields, 150–1;

on "Band Is Back" tour, 362; on The
Band's fame, 151; on the Bauls of
Bengal's chillum, 93n; on Bearsville
Studios, 307; on bluegrass–jazz hook-
ups, 285; on Butterfield–Muldaur
pool game, 258; and Dalton, 265;
and Danko house, 85; on Helm and
O'Brien, 397; incomplete Charles
production, 296; on Joplin, 146;
on Lightfoot, 147; on Martyns
LP, 134; meal with AG, 141; and
non-AG artists, 315; plays on *Bobby
Charles*, 295; plays with Borderline,
315; produces *Big Brother & the
Holding Company*, 145–6; produces
Music from Big Pink, 110, 111, 145;
produces first Bearsville Studios
recording, 234; on promiscuity in
W, 153; plays the Ramble, 399; on
Robertson, 244, 247; on Robertson's
AG eulogy, 375; on "The Rumor",
246; Taj Mahal's rhythm section, 312;
on *You Are What You Eat*, 99; *John
Simon's Album*, 312n; *Journey*, 312n;
"Livin' in a Land o' Sunshine", 312n;
"The 'Real' Woodstock Rag", 312n
Simon, Paul, 133n
Simple Minds: *Once Upon a Time*, 371
Sinatra, Frank, 149, 201
Siral, Ismet, 286, 289
Sky, Patrick, 33
Sled Hill Café: Bang!'s cocaine, 308;
BD leaves fans, 198; closes, 341; Full
Moon, 300; Hardin, 130–1; as main
W hangout, 131; Manuel's drinking,
155–6; Morrison, 175; Morrison's
drinking, 164–5; Neil, 122–3; Paul
Butterfield Band, 215; Siebel, 263
Sly and the Family Stone, 28, 186,
220–1
Sly and Robbie, 289
Smart, N. D., II: Artist Road house,
291, 292, 383; in Great Speckled
Bird, 255, 256; in Hungry Chuck,
310; in Kangaroo, 312; moves to W,
256; plays on *Bobby Charles*, 295; on
Rundgren's gallows, 274